THE LATEST MORNINGSIDE PAPERS

THE LATEST MORNINGSIDE PAPERS

PETER GZOWSKI

McClelland & Stewart Inc.
The Canadian Publishers
481 University Avenue
Toronto, Ontario
M5G 2E9

Canadian Cataloguing in Publication Data

Gzowski, Peter
  The latest Morningside papers

Commentary on and correspondence to the CBC radio program Morningside.
ISBN 0-7710-3735-X

1. Morningside (Radio program).   I. Title.
II. Title: Morningside (Radio program).

PN1991.3.C3C94 1989   791.44′72   C89-094968-9

Printed and bound in Canada

CONTENTS

The Usual Note on Permissions

As with the two earlier volumes in this series, every effort has
been made to reach the authors of the various letters, essays and
poems that form the bulk of these *Papers*. But, once again, there
are a few people we can't track down. I beg their indulgence. I
know from experience that nearly everyone who writes to *Morningside* is pleased to see his or her work in print. (From more than
seven hundred requests for permission, we've had only one refusal
—and that because the writer didn't think her work worthy.) And,
as I've said before, I'd rather risk annoying them this way than by
leaving them out.

Dear Peter
Well I just receaved your lovely form letter so I just thaught that I'd
reply with a not so formal letter.
The truble with this dang lined papper isthat it is allways in the wrong
place.
I have'nt the slightest idea what your going to publish of mine as I
rarly keep a coppy of what I wrote as I'm usely to buisy to bother with
it and there are so many other stories I could have writen but just don't
have the time. I have a new home stead now I don't know if I menchuned
that to you or not but its a place that I'v been wonting for the last
twenty years. Its a beautyful place right along the Meleto creek and if you
don't mind the musquitoes it sure is a great place to unlaxe on the creek
bank eating saskatoons and wotching the beaver rebuilding there dam.
But I don't lay around to long as I have a million things to do with
this new homstead like clearing 320 ackers of land and building my log howse
and an old D-6 Cat that wonts to fall apart all the time but its all great
fun and my be some day I might even get to finish writing my book so
that its exsptable to them darn editors.
Well eny way I hear by authorize Peter Gzowski and McClelland and
Stewart to publish my letters(s) or poems(s) or story in the latest
Morning side papers,1989. First publication rights only. and I sure will
be upset with you if I don't get my free coppy of that book.
Yours truly Vic Daradick
            Box 60 High Level, Alberta.
            TOH 1Z0

And a Heartfelt Dedication

For Elly, my hero, and Krista, my friend.

INTRODUCTION

THIS IS THE THIRD anthology of material gathered from the CBC radio program *Morningside* during the seasons (seven of them now) that I have been its host. Like its predecessors, this collection has at its core the best of the extraordinary letters that came into the office during the time it represents, in this case the two broad-casting seasons that stretched from the autumn of 1987 to the spring of 1989. Some of those letters – the majority, I would guess – are in response to conversations or statements our correspond-ents have heard on the air, part of the continuing written dialogue that helps make *Morningside* what it is; as many as a hundred letters a day now come into our office. Some others were written by invitation. The collection of lists, for example, that makes up Chapter Eight, and all the letters in "Some Happy (and Some Sen-timental) Returns" and "Childhood Haunts" are the results of unabashed solicitation on my part, contests as we call them, from which we get much delightful radio. The letters from abroad that comprise Chapter Eleven are largely the result of our having asked specific people to write to us – though some of those, too, just come in the mail from people I haven't heard of before. Still other letters arrive for no apparent reason at all, except, perhaps, that their authors know that if they have something to get off their chests, *Morningside* – a kind of village bulletin board to the nation, as I once called it – is a good place to do that. The gripping account of what it's like to live with the disease ALS, for instance, which begins the chapter called "On Making the Best of Things," was simply waiting for me one morning in the mail that lies opened on my desk–and serves, I have to say, as an example of why, however weary I grow of the relentless routine of three hours of live radio every weekday, I still drive to work through the pre-dawn streets of Toronto with a sense of anticipation.

But also like its predecessors, *The Morningside Papers* and its sequel, the imaginatively titled *New Morningside Papers* (look, I didn't know there'd be more than one when we started), this collection contains departures from the theme of letters. Chapter Three, for example, begins with an account I commissioned from the producer Terry MacLeod of his adventures in trying to recycle some of the tons of paper that pass through our office. Later on, again commissioned, is Richard Osler's story of one day in his life as a member of our longest-running (and, in the years that followed the departure of our Tuesday klatch of Dalton Camp, Eric Kierans and Stephen Lewis, most popular) regular panel, the business column.

Chapter Six, called simply "Elly," is something we haven't put in either of the earlier *Papers*: the transcript of an interview. The conversation it records, first broadcast in November of 1988, made up, I am convinced, the single most powerful piece of radio *Morningside* has carried in the time I've been its host, and I wanted to preserve its essence. Because it gives some insights into how the program is made, because it gives me a chance to give credit to the people who made it possible, and, most of all, because it shows how much serendipity comes into play in the matter of what gets onto the radio we do, I also wanted to tell the story of how that interview came to be.

That story begins with a fact I've belaboured before: that in the late 1980s there isn't enough money in the CBC's shrinking budget to send the *Morningside* production unit out of Toronto. If we want to travel – and we continue to think it's important that we originate from as many places as we can–we have to find subsidies from other sources. Over the years, for example, I've accepted more speaking engagements than I'd like to admit just so a *Morn-*

ingside producer can ride along with me and do a program on the road. The series of interviews Terry MacLeod and I recorded in the spring of 1989 in Iqaluit and Pangnirtung were made possible because the Canada Council paid my way to the north so I could read in libraries during National Book Week; the most dramatic tour we've been able to take in all my seven seasons – the swing that took us up the coast of Vancouver Island to Tofino and back through the interior of British Columbia and the southern prairie – was largely due to the generosity of my hosts at speaking engage- ments in Victoria, Regina, and Pincher Creek, Alberta; with my expenses looked after, finding the money to send along support staff was just a matter of pinching other pennies.

In the autumn of 1988, a couple of opportunities lined them- selves up. For one, the Canadian Association for Community Liv- ing – the group that serves the cause of people with mental handicaps – wanted to present *Morningside* an award for a series of programs we'd done the year before, and invited us to their convention in Regina. At the same time, the Chamber of Com- merce in Moose Jaw, where I'd spent some time as a young news- paperman, was having its hundredth anniversary, and asked me to speak at dinner. Bingo. We began looking around for Saskatch- ewan stories to record on location (as well, of course, as lining up a panel I'd chair at the CACL, including the voices of some of the handicapped themselves).

This is where serendipity comes in – or, if you're so inclined, the hand of God. Just a few days before we were due to leave, my morning mail contained a letter from a man in Toronto who asked, among other things, if I knew that the events described in a book called *Don't: A Woman's Word* had taken place in my old stomping grounds of – you may have guessed this – Moose Jaw, and, fur- thermore, had taken place at a time I might have been there. Not only had I not known that, I hadn't even heard of the book, which turned out to be, when I looked around, a slim paperback pub- lished by Gynergy Press of Charlottetown (I hadn't heard of them, either), which had been among the dozens of unsolicited volumes that arrived at *Morningside* during my summer absence and which was sitting, unread, on an office shelf. My curiosity piqued, I dug into it. At first, I could see how it had been overlooked in the office. The prose was deceptively simple: short, vivid sentences distilled to near poetic purity. But, spurred by my correspondent's notes about Moose Jaw (the real location is not revealed in the book) and by the story that unfolded as I read, I was shaken – and gripped irrevocably.

Don't: A Woman's Word is a memoir of both unspeakable ugliness and radiant beauty. It is the autobiographical account of a woman named Elly Danica, prepubescent at the time of the offences it describes, whose father not only assaulted her sexually but invited his friends to witness and join in his acts, and took pornographic pictures of her for their amusement. The daughter grows up and lives, at first, a life of tragedy and confusion, hiding her sorrow in drugs and booze. But, later, reaching into herself and the writings of other women, she claws her way back, not only surviving the horror of her childhood but triumphing over it. As is evident to the reader of its haunting prose, the book itself – the writing – is part of the cure. Finishing it in the same session I had started reading, I knew I had to meet its author, and see if we could get her story on the radio. The next question was: was she still in Saskatchewan and, if so, near Moose Jaw?

Yes.

Nancy Watson, the producer who took up the case (as moved as I was when she read the book) tracked down both the publisher – Gynergy Press is an offshoot of Libby Oughton's remarkable Ragweed Press on Prince Edward Island – and the author of the letter that had sparked my interest, who had no phone at his Toronto address but responded to a telegram, and turned out to be a friend of Elly's who was able, at last, to put us in touch. Elly was living in a former church in a small town not far from Moose Jaw (though she has since moved away, I will keep my promise to her not to reveal exactly which town). Nancy called, liked her immediately, and reported that, though Elly was too shy and vulnerable to take a trip to a radio studio, if we would drive to her place on the prairie, she'd agree to an interview.

Scant days later, there we were, the two of us, on a lumpy old couch in the basement of her church, while a technician from Regina ran his tape recorder discreetly in the corner, and Carole Warren, the producer who had taken over from Nancy, and Hal Wake, our executive producer, waited outside on the church's wooden steps.

The interview that appears in these pages is the result. In introducing it – and I have kept the words I read on the air the day we played it – I have tried to set the scene, and I thought it best to include it here in the form it first appeared. The passages from the book that are interspersed through the questions and answers, by the way, are there because, for all her courage and even in the secure surroundings of her basement refuge, Elly was no more able to talk about some of the scenes she'd described in print than I was willing to ask about them. On the air, the passages were read for us by the actress Susan Hogan, who, before she accepted the assignment, read the book and talked to Elly on the phone to hear the cadence of her speech – and joined the list of people who, once touched by Elly's story and her quiet strength, were moved forever.

In the weeks and months that followed our broadcast, that list continued to grow. The next day, I began a promotional tour for a book of my own. My first stop was in Fredericton, and from there to the far west coast a week later, as *Morningside* listeners came into the bookstores where I sat, I met scores of people who had been shocked and enlightened by what they'd heard.

In fairness, I should also report that there were, as well, people who found they couldn't bear to listen, and had turned their radios off. But for every one of them, I felt, there was someone who had heard echoes of her own story in Elly's revelations and who had found inspiration in her honesty and courage. In Kingston, Ontario, to take just one example that sticks in my mind, a woman stayed in a crowded room above a theatre, which the owners of a local bookstore had rented, to hear me speak about my own book, then stood in the line of people wanting signed copies only to whisper to me, "Thanks for Elly."

By then–"You, too?" I asked the woman before she left the table where I was signing, and received a nod of affirmation–some idea of how common Elly's story was was sinking into my brain. Other women's experiences, and other men's, were different in detail, perhaps, but essentially the same. Statistics that had seemed far-fetched to me now had the undeniable resonance of Elly's truths. As a result, when *Morningside*'s producers pressed for further exploration of the sexual abuse of children on the program that season they found their host, sometimes reluctant to pursue subjects of earnest and depressing content, to be a willing if not eager supporter. We began with a conversation with Rix Rogers, the congenial former YMCA official whom Jake Epp, as minister of health and welfare, had asked to look into the situation for the government, and who, like me, had been snapped to awareness by the reality he'd discovered. In subsequent weeks we drummed away: with social workers, frustrated and enraged by what they knew and felt hopeless to cope with, with police officers, whose awareness and concern quickly gave the lie to stereotypes of cops, and, by opening our phones and, as always, reading on the air some of the mail we received (a few samples of which appear here, after Elly's interview), with some of the victims themselves. By spring, *Morningside*'s involvement in the cause had become so integral that, flatteringly, Rix Rogers invited me to give the key-note address to an important conference of the people behind his task force.

At one of the tables in that room, surrounded by deputy ministers, academics, politicians and social workers, was, to my pleasure, Elly Danica. She had put on a little healthy weight since we talked in her church basement–she lives in PEI now, and is writing on other subjects – and her eyes were shining. Her book is now selling around the world (she had a mock-up of the German edition with her) and it continues to make an impact on Canada, at least partly, I say recklessly, because of the exposure it had on *Morningside*. For reasons the transcript of the interview will make clear, I was still reluctant to hug her when we met again. But as I visited at her table, before I took to the podium to tell, among other things, her story once again, we held hands for a while, and I, for one, felt pretty good about things.

And, just for a moment, I thought again about how we came to Moose Jaw and the letter I had opened that day from the morning's mail.

YOU WILL HAVE NOTICED, I'm sure, the number of other people who appear in the history of just one *Morningside* interview: Nancy Watson who tracked Elly down; Carole Warren who produced the piece, which included editing the tape, finding, auditioning and directing Susan Hogan; Hal Wake who oversaw our excursion to Saskatchewan as he oversaw everything we did in the season of 1988-'89; the technician (his name is Mike Chipley) whose skills made a radio studio out of Elly's church basement. There could have been more: Gary Katz, our studio director in Toronto who put it on the air; Janet Russell, our script assistant who made sure it got on smoothly; John Johnston, our Toronto technician . . . and so on and so on. *Morningside* is a team effort. Though what goes out on the air can often – or so we try to make it – sound like one man making his casual way through life, calling up the people who made the previous day's news or who have thoughts or comments about the decade's issues, happily coming across the most interesting people in the land, the reality is quite a different picture: about a dozen and half people in Toronto supported by contributing producers and technicians all over the country scurrying incessantly to make things work. Behind every apparently casual encounter, as, indeed, behind every apparently fortuitous question, lie more planning, research, organization, and often sheer thankless dogwork than I can possibly describe. I've said this, in one form or another, in introducing each of these printed souvenirs of what goes on the radio, and I said it again in the journal of my own life I published last fall – the book I was flogging across the country when I first realized the impact Elly Danica had made. But since there are still some people who take these accounts of how *Morningside* works as *bragging* on my part, when in fact I am trying to do the opposite, I beg the forgiveness of jaundiced readers if I do it one more time, and, in the same breath, offer once again my heartfelt thanks to the friends and colleagues whose unsung labours make my performances possible. When *Morningside* works, it is because of other people; when it messes up, the fault is almost always mine. Producers, after all, don't ask dumb questions, forget titles, mispronounce the names of towns in British Columbia, stammer introductions or welcome listeners to hours by the wrong numbers.

OVER THE YEARS, the roster of the team that does the real work at *Morningside* has undergone steady and dramatic change. Of all the people in the unit when I moved into the chair vacated by Don Harron in 1982, in fact, only Janet Russell, whose cheerful professionalism is a foundation of everything we do, is still there. Hal Wake, "the Wayne Gretzky of producers" as I once described him (you didn't think I could get through a whole essay without a reference to Wayne, did you?), is the third person to have run the ship during my tenure. Susan Perly, who returned in the spring of 1989 briefly to manage what we call "the desk"–the draining position at the centre of our office where final decisions about each day's lineup are made–was, by my informal count, the fourteenth person to wrestle with the exhaustive and exhausting details there. Of the thirtyfive people whose names appear towards the end of *The New Morningside Papers* because they worked with me over the first five seasons, only five – Janet, Hal, Carole Warren, Gary Katz and Dave Amer, who came back to the CBC from a kind of semiretirement to pick our music shortly after I signed on – were still on board two years later.

This is not a happy situation, and it gives me pause to think there might be a connection between the turnover of our staff and the thanklessness of the tasks they perform. To put it in perspective, though, it may be worth noting that only one of the men who was premier of a province when I took over from Don is still in office, that the entire federal government in Ottawa has changed (along with most of the management at the CBC), and that Mario Lemieux has (alas) succeeded the player we used to call The Kid as the pre-eminent star of the National Hockey League. But, unhappy cirumstance or not, the ability to survive the revolving-door syndrome among its personnel is also, surely, a signal of the fact that *Morningside* has become a part of the Canadian fabric – a program with a life of its own, I would argue, more important than the individual people who work on it, including, of course, its hosts.

THE ANTHOLOGIES of which this is the third have not, of course, reached quite the same plateau, although the way we do them is also becoming a process that seems to transcend the sum of its parts.

In a capsule, their history is this. Some time after I returned to radio from the wilderness of television and free-lance writing, I realized that the quality of the writing in the mail I opened every day deserved a longer life than it got just by being read on the air. With the help of some other people, most notably Eve McBride, the first of the three indispensable assistants who have struggled to keep my life and my correspondence in order, I put together the first of them. (If I'd know then that there'd be more, as I've said, I'd have called it *The Morningside Papers I* and simplified the fig-uring out of later titles.) When Eve left to pursue her own writing career, Lynda Hanrahan, a bright young Queen's graduate, stepped into the breach. The daily mail continued to swell–partly, I am convinced, because of the success of the first *Papers* (some people were now writing with an eye to later publication, an ambi-tion I see through, by the way, and which almost always results in letters too contrived to fit into these books). But Lynda, as organized as I am scatter-brained, kept it under control, and, because we realized early on that there'd be another *Papers*, set aside letters we thought might be worth preserving. By the time I brought in Glen Allen, a producer who had a background in the world of print, and Edna Barker, an editor who'd worked with me on, among other things, the original *Papers*, we were as close as possible to being under control. *The New Morningside Papers* rolled off the presses and, once again – this may *be* bragging, but the hell with it – onto the best-seller lists.

Then Glen, a hummingbird, as he once described himself, with an almost spiritual need to sip from different orchards, went back to print.

And, shortly after, Lynda's husband won a scholarship in Australia. With tears in my eyes, I wrote a heartfelt letter of recommendation to an entire continent, and resigned myself to the realization that I'd never be able to cope with anything again.

But then, just when I was out promoting the *New Papers* (already convinced they'd be the last), Shelley Ambrose walked into my life. Shelley, like Lynda before her, is young enough to have me for a parent instead of a boss (she was, in fact, a classmate of my daughter's at Ryerson Polytechnical Institute in Toronto). She's also cheerful enough to light downtown Calgary, where she's from, as energetic as a bathtub full of Alka-Seltzer and, if anything, *better* organized than the incomparable Lynda. As well as looking after my travel, taxes, speaking gigs, golfing obligations (I couldn't run the tournaments I hold to raise money for literacy without her) and a thousand other petty but (to her) undaunting details, and answering the daily mail (*and* producing the segments Shelagh Rogers reads with me on the air every few days), Shelley began squirreling away the letters that might be the beginnings of a third volume of *Papers*.

We still couldn't have done it if Edna hadn't stepped forward. Edna Barker. "Among other things," which I said she has worked on with me, scarcely does justice to the role Edna has already played in the literary part of my life. Formally or informally, for I have been known to ask her to cast her exquisite eye over manuscripts other people have been paid to read, she has had a hand in every book I've published in the 1980s. Like a lot of other people in her craft, she is as self-effacing as a church-mouse. She lives with a couple of cats in a tiny house in the east end of Toronto, listens passionately to *Morningside*, gardens, rides her bicycle around town, works for the gay and lesbian community, and puts her pencil through prose that ranges from text-books to Harlequin romances. Like all fine editors, Edna, no matter how ruthless her cuts or amendments, has a commitment to preserving the voice of the original author, which has made her invaluable in trying to whip into shape documents that start, after all, as *letters*, and which come in forms that range from word-processor printouts to pencil and often barely legible scrawls. Edna is also, God bless her, totally unafraid of me, and, on the books of mine she's influenced, the only times I haven't taken the advice she's offered, no matter how painful it has been to hear, I've later wished I had, and the only paragraph to which I haven't let her suggest improvements is the one this sentence ends.

About halfway through the season of 1988-'89, with Glen and Lynda gone and Shelley and me swamped by the extra demands on my time that seem to increase every year I stay at *Morningside*, Edna asked what she could do to facilitate a third *Papers*. With some relief, I handed over to her the several cardboard cartons of accumulated possible inclusions, and for the next several weeks she worked diligently away, culling and sorting, making chapters, finding threads, making lists. She and Shelley became a team.

In the spring, an otherwise unhappy turn of events made it possible to increase the team's membership: CUPE – the Canadian Union of Public Employees, whose members at the CBC include a hodgepodge that runs from announcers to stagehands – went on strike. Quickly, I asked two CUPE members to give us a hand in their non-picketing hours: Alice Hopton, who had been working as a clerk at *Morningside*, and Shelagh Rogers, whose lilting and intelligent on-air readings of the mail had already made her a part of the family – and a letter of whose own, as it was to turn out much later, also appears in these pages.

As before, Gillian Howard, who shares my life in every way, was also drawn into the process, and the team that put this book together took shape. We met on afternoons and weekends, debated, argued, laughed, took files away and brought them back and, finally, wrestled together the manuscript of *The Latest* – I could do no better and only, in the end, barely overruled Edna who wanted to call them the *New New – Morningside Papers*. Debby Seed, who backs up Edna's editorial skills as Edna backs up mine, took on the painstaking task of imposing stylistic and spelling consistency on scores of different authors, and Lynne Reilly, working away at her farm, transposed everything into a computer. Once again, Laurie McGaw painted my scraggly visage for the cover (Alice and Shelley worked on the montage of real post-marks behind it) and Linda Gustafson designed the package.

The team of writers whose words we've worked to present has also changed, and among the nearly three hundred names of my fellow authors that appear in the index, the scholarly reader will note many new appearances – as, after seven years, I still find new and eloquent writers in every morning's mail. But there are familiar names, too, from Gail Mackay to Samm MacKay, from Dorothy Beavington in White Rock, British Columbia to Joan Baxter in the farthest reaches of Burkina Faso, and of course, from Chris Czajkowski in the Bella Coola Valley to Krista Munroe in Medicine Hat, Alberta. To them, and to all who've been in all these *Papers*, special thanks; they are, it hardly need be said, the backbone.

One of the functions these books have fulfilled, as I've noted in an earlier introduction, is to serve as a testing ground for more complete works to be published later on, and, once again, I can say with some pride that, just as "Elly" contains passages from an already-published book, each of the chapters "Did He Who Made the Rose Make Thee?" and "Chris's Year" is a preview of more extensive works to come. As well, the complete collection of Stuart McLean's reportage that was foreshadowed by a chapter in the *New Papers* will be on the shelves at the same time as this volume. Since Stuart has already talked me into writing a blurb for the jacket of that work – it's called *The Morningside World of Stuart McLean* – and since we're liable to be in competition for the same readers, I'll say here only that, as with all these works, it's heartening to see the *Papers* bear such fruit.

Stuart also has a piece in here, by the way, and maybe that, too, presages further publication.

ARE THE *Latest Papers* also the last?

Well, probably not. Throughout the final months of my seventh season, there were rumours afoot that I was running out of enthusiasm as host. Some of those rumours, I will admit now, were well founded. Seven years of rising before dawn – I seem to get up earlier every year in order to read the mail before I start to prepare for the broadcast itself – had taken their toll. The prospect of working yet again with untried producers who would, inevitably, step into the jobs in which yet another batch had been overworked to exhaustion, was, while in one way exhilarating – more fresh ideas! – daunting. There were still places to go and people to interview, but there were a lot of miles on my aging body and, by my figuring, some fourteen thousand interviews already logged. The continuing struggle against budget cuts was dispiriting. The comfortable success of my book of the previous fall had reminded me that I still thought of myself as a writer more than a broadcaster. I would be fifty-five in the summer. I thought deeply and at length of moving on.

But one night over dinner, as I agonized yet again about my indecision, Gill made a remark that, over the subsequent weeks, just wouldn't go away.

"If you leave," she said, "you won't be around to meet the next Elly Danica."

Or, I added to myself, to open the morning mail.

Peter Gzowski
June 1989

FIRST, THESE WORDS

Morningside – and its listeners – take words seriously.

The letters that begin and end this chapter (the last is as I received it, carefully typed by Peter Powning, a potter who listens by his wheel every morning) are in response to a specifically language-oriented item – in this case a campaign I tried to launch, just before Christmas, 1987, against the dreadful over-use of the adverb "basically," which, as I said in my opening salvo, had become the late-1980s equivalent of the meaningless "you know." Nearly all the rest, though, were triggered by words or phrases that just cropped up on the air (or elsewhere) over the seasons this book represents, from "eh?" to "well," with much in between. Since a love of language is at the heart of all *The Morningside Papers*, original, *New* and *Latest*, I thought this would be a pleasant way to begin this volume.

A couple of notes before we do. The expressions that mean the opposite of what they say were really compiled by G. Katz of Toronto (and, yes, that is Gary Katz, our studio director) as one of the lists that comprise Chapter Eight, but I thought they belonged here. And – totally unrelated – among the people who heard some of the musings on the lovely expression "storm-stayed," which was first used on *Morningside* by our Prince Edward Island columnist Daphne Dumont, was Nancy Howard, also of Toronto, who is both a student and an owner of thoroughbred racehorses. So the promising filly Stormstayed, named in 1988 and soon, perhaps, on her way to race-track glory, is, in her own way, a member of the *Morningside* team, too.

✉ Would it be too much to ask – or even to hope – that you could do something similar for (actually against) "hopefully," especially when it is employed in situations where realistic hope is far from being an absolute, as in "Hopefully, no guest on *Morningside* will ever use 'basically' again"?

Alan Dawe
Richmond, British Columbia

✉ One form of misuse I would dearly love to see banished before it becomes accepted practice is the use of the adverb "momentarily" to mean "*after* a moment." My *Webster's* still gives the meaning as "for a moment or instantly." Referring to time duration, the adverb properly modifies the event itself rather than actions following the event.

As an example of abuse, I cite television sports announcers who keep saying, "We'll be back momentarily" instead of "We will pause momentarily" or, more simply, "We'll be back after this commercial." Given this abuse of language, I wish they would reappear only momentarily.

Mervyn Norton
Regina

✉ I was pleased to hear confirmation of my understanding of the word "momentarily" as meaning "for a moment" rather than "in a moment."

My first introduction to the latter usage of the word occurred while seated on a plane on the runway prior to take-off. I was very alarmed to hear the announcement over the PA: "We shall be taking off momentarily."

I wanted to get off immediately and couldn't understand why no one else was alarmed at the prospect of such a brief flight! Whenever I hear the misuse of that word now, I remember my moment of panic all those years ago.

Another set of phrases I hear frequently over the airwaves that puzzles me mightily is as follows . . . "So, until next week at the same time, I'm Joe Blow," or, "So, for the CBC, I'm Jane Smith," etc. I wonder to myself, "Who is he after next week?" or, "Who is she for everybody else?" Do these announcers have a wonderful double life, slipping in and out of personae several times a day or week? I wish these phrases could be dropped before I'm hauled away yelling at the radio, "Oh yeah, and who are you to your husband then?"

Norianne Kirkpatrick
Armstrong, British Columbia

✉ Six Things that Mean the Opposite of What they Say
1. "Literally," as in "I literally died when I heard."
2. "I could care less," which means "I couldn't care less."
3. "Sleep with." No comment.
4. "Reverse discrimination," which means "discrimination."
5. "I'm not convinced that," which means "I am firmly convinced of the opposite."
6. "Went to the bathroom," as in "The dog went to the bathroom on the carpet."

G. Katz
Toronto

✉ My family was watching the news the other night and one of the stories prompted my twelve-year-old son to make a comment on the "near miss" between two aircraft near England.

He said, "What's a near miss? If they nearly missed each other then they must have hit. You either miss or hit, so which is it?"

Bob Miller
Brantford, Ontario

✉ On a cold and snowy New Brunswick morning, I was delighted to hear you and Professor Haines sorting out the advertisers on the use of "cheap prices."

Could you now, please, do the same thing for announcers who do weather reports and refer to "cold temperatures." Surely they are low or high, but never cold or hot.

Lloyd Crandall
Kings County, New Brunswick

✉ The other day, I heard a woman talking on the radio about the Crown ownership of Canadian lands and mineral rights. She uttered what I can only label a "tridundancy." She described this situation as being "very unique in the whole world." This must be a record of sorts.

Philip Slyfield
Ottawa

✉ It may be that in the Golden Horseshoe "eh" isn't used as extravagantly as in the rest of Canada, but here in Northern Ontario, we use it fluently. If I'm telling someone about an event, my listener will interject with "No, eh?" or "Yeah, eh?" But the one I like best occurred when I was showing a little girl of six some baby pigs. She stood looking down into the pen and said, "Ah, eh?"

John Keast
Bruce Mines, Ontario

✉ So you don't like the expression "Have a nice day."
Anglo-Saxon cultural imperialist! I say.
You let Brits and the Aussies take leave with "Good day,"
"I'll see you," "goodbye," and "so long" are okay,
But popular indigenous American – no way!
Rejected with a pompous parliamentary "Nay!"
  "Have a nice day" is insincere you decree.
Then a Gzowski "Goodbye" really means "God be with me"?
And when you ask "How are you?" I'll sincerely be flattered
For you ask after my health as if truly it mattered.
And a Gzowski "I'll see you right after the news"
Means face-to-face sharing of more of my views.

John Osterman
Vimont, Quebec

✉ Our dogs have cured my husband and me of the "well" word.
  Yes, that's right, our dogs! You see, every evening when the television or radio goes off and the knitting needles go back in their case, we take the dogs for a walk before bed. Once upon a time this activity was always prefaced by the question: "Well, dogs, do you want to go for a walk?" All hell would break loose for five minutes while we donned our boots and coats and got out the door. Anyone who has a dog will know that "walk" is not a word that can be used lightly; if you say it, you are obliged to *do* it. In the case of our dogs, because the words had been associated with each other, "well" became synonymous in their minds with

"walk," and produced the same results. Over the years we have learned to avoid it altogether.

Now the only time "well" becomes a problem is when we have guests. Heaven help the unsuspecting soul who utters that magic word in our house!

Kas Brobeck
Pouch Cove, Newfoundland

✉ We had just acquired yet another kitten. Inevitably, in a household including four children, it escaped from the house through a door left open and did not return. So my daughter wrote out twenty or more notes, beginning "Gone missing, small black kitten . . . " She and her sister set out to distribute them to our neighbours. They returned in tears. A kindly man living across the road had told them that, only that morning, he had buried a black kitten that a car had obviously hit.

I was still hugging and trying to comfort them when the phone rang. Thank God I answered it.

"Mr. Harrison?" asked a pompously precise voice.

"Yes," I replied.

"Would you tell your daughter that there is no such phrase as 'Gone missing.' What she should have written. . . ."

He had hung up before I really took it in that he had said what he had said. I still lie awake nights thinking up the right response. The insensitivity to language that permits one to correct the idiom of a grieving child is surely a far worse impropriety than "gone missing."

James Harrison
Guelph, Ontario

✉ How curiously our language changes! I had always thought that the term "sexy" referred to the attractiveness of one human

being to another, that it had something to do with fun and relationships. But in your business column this week I heard one of
your panel, with great enthusiasm, refer to the merger of two beer
companies as "sexy."

Is this the most recent sign of the aging of us boomers, that it is
now business enterprises, rather than people, that excite us and
arouse our passions? How dull for the human race when the mar-
ket-place replaces even the bedroom in our hearts.

The Reverend Alyson Barnett-Cowan
The Pas, Manitoba

✉ The other day, you made a passing reference to "a tinker's
cuss." In case you weren't being cute but serious, the reference as
it was fed to me in days past was the value of a "tinker's dam."
This, I was informed, referred to a small bit of earth used to dam
the solder flow – or whatever metal was used – as the tinker
repaired his pots and pans.

John Matheson
Yorkton, Saskatchewan

✉ The origin of the expression to "mind one's p's and q's," which
I've long held to be true, is an image of bygone days.

At Ye Olde Englishe Pub, our busy and very buxom barmaid is
accountable for every tankard of ale drawn for her boisterous
clientele. Her tab(ulation), hastily jotted between pinches and
advances (none sterling), is a mark under the "P" (pints) or "Q"
(quarts) column. With any luck, it should all tally with a day's
receipts at "time," lest she be admonished to "mind her p's and
q's," and bloody well collect from *all* us rowdy sots.

Murray B. Ripley
Halifax

✉ My understanding of the origin of the word "biffy" is that it denotes a sanitary facility for both number one and number two (bifunctional). It seems that in "missionary days" in "foreign lands," some of the communities separated these wastes, so as to be able to use excrement (night soil) as a fertilizer. If you had the comfort and luxury of a *real* residence, however, you didn't have to be concerned with the local custom, and the *indoor* facility was bifunctional (i.e., bi-fy). All this could be somewhat apocryphal, but it sounds plausible.

Arthur Reid
Toronto

✉ "The proof is in the pudding."

Why do people so often employ this meaningless phrase? One might just as well say: The proof is in the pancake or the *petit point* or the pansy-bed.

The original saying is, of course, the proof of the pudding is in the *eating*, and it comes from Miguel de Cervantes' *Don Quixote*. It means: don't judge by appearances alone.

Brenda Davies
Cherrywood, Ontario

✉ As a native islander of Prince Edward Island – one who was "born and bred" here (why don't we say that the other way around?) – I feel I must come to the rescue of the word "storm-stayed." It is a cherished word for a cherished activity.

"Storm-stayed" does not mean being closed in (by snow and high winds), or not being able to leave your place, which properly should be called "being stuck at home," a not uncommon experience in winter-time P.E.I. Instead "storm-stayed" means having to be put up for the night at someone else's house, because travelling conditions have deteriorated so much that "pushing on" is impossible. In another common case, it also means that it is impossible for your parents to retrieve you from wherever you are when the storm sets in.

Being "storm-stayed" is a rural P.E.I. word and represents something that, at least as children, we really looked forward to every year.

Even today my father, who is seventy-eight years old, still admonishes each of us, his eight children, to stop if the weather gets too bad when we're on the road and knock on someone's door to be looked after. (How sad today that people are too timorous to do so!)

Some of my fondest memories of childhood are of being "storm-stayed." On one occasion the whole family landed at the community grocer's less than a mile from our home. They had two older children, and everyone had such a wonderful time, sharing supper and conversation, playing board games together, and enjoying the sensation of sleeping in different beds – that is, different to us!

Arthur D. Reddin
New Dominion, P.E.I.

✉ Welcome to the Canadian winter! It's obvious you've never spent any time up in Grey and Bruce Counties during the winter. "Storm-stayed" some winters is about as common as "hello."

Valerie Wasserfall
Paisley, Ontario

✉ Storm-staid or -stayed is a nautical term, once applied to sea-going vessels forced into an intermediate port on their way home.

The word "stay" referred to a large strong rope used on sailing ships to support the mast. One of these went to the bow of the ship and was known as the forestay. That which connected with the stern was the aftstay. Supporting ropes that led to the vessel's sides were known as sidestays. Staysails and jibs were hoisted up and down along the stays.

In a more general way, a stay meant guy ropes used to hold parts together, contributing stiffness to the sail structure. "Staying," which is now more usually called tacking, used to be referred to as travelling "in stays" or "hoving in stays."

Stays prevented masts from falling; hence the word came to mean constrained from movement. Victorian women used the stay-lace to bind up corsets. Storm-stayed is meant in this last sense: prevented from leaving port, constrained because of possible damage to the staylines, masts and sails.

Rod and Anne Mackay
Sussex, New Brunswick

✉ "Storm-stayed" is a well-known expression in rural Saskatchewan. When I was a boy growing up on the Prairies, whenever we were unable to get somewhere due to a blizzard we were storm-stayed. I expect the term is still in use, although the days of getting storm-stayed are now few due to improved highways and fewer people living on remote farms.

I now live in northern Saskatchewan, where flying is a way of life. Now I use the terms "weathered in" and "weathered out" employed by pilots. If I can't get home due to weather, I'm "weathered out." If I can't leave home due to weather, I'm "weathered in."

Ross Moxley
La Ronge, Saskatchewan

✉ So you're not familiar with the term "storm-stayed"? It is obvious you live in Toronto rather than on a farm on the Prairies. The school *requires*, even in 1988, that every farm family have a place in town where the children can be billeted in case of a storm. Even at their young ages (Dora is eight, Shelley-Jo is six), they have been forced to stay at home, or storm-stayed, from some important events because the snow was blowing so thickly you couldn't see fifty feet across the yard or down the road. Last year they missed their Christmas party; the year before their skating carnival.

One winter we had a five-day blizzard that blocked our vision beyond a few yards. At times we couldn't see the hydro pole on our lawn thirty feet from the window. Wally's cattle were across the road and had to be fed twice a day. I insisted on going with him, for if he had an accident no one would know where to find him. The wind was so strong it sucked the air right out of my lungs. It took conscious effort to breathe. We would aim at known, though unseen, landmarks and strike out. After a moment a shadow would loom up from the swirling snow–first a hedge, then a fence, then a snow-fence. The final "dash" was the longest and most dangerous. The shed, cattle and trees lay somewhere before us but if we missed them, at least there was a fence around the little pasture, and if exhaustion didn't overtake us, we could follow it back to the starting point. Fortunately, that never happened.

When the wind finally let up a strange, new world was revealed. The cattle were thick with snow – they looked like big sheep. Huge, tree-top-high drifts of snow surrounded the feed stacks behind the house. The garage, gas tank and outhouse (not in use!) were covered over. A ten-foot bank had to be removed from the yard before the car or truck could be taken out of the garage.

Later that spring, you could see where the driven snow had polished the old wood off the fence posts, leaving them light brown on one side, except where banks of old snow had protected the base from the snow blast and kept them grey. You could see the height of the snowbanks by the grey-yellow colour on the south-east sides of the posts. One farmer said the whiskers were blown off the chins of his range horses, but I didn't see them and I am a bit sceptical. As to the rest, I have pictures!

Wendy Caldwell
Ceylon, Saskatchewan

33

✉ "Doesn't Ed Broadbent believe in Santa Claus?"

This troubled utterance came from my seven-year-old son, Xan (Alexander, for long), apparently in response to something overheard on *Morningside*! It was December 23, only two days before the great, jolly fellow in red – Santa, not Ed – was to make his much anticipated visit.

Seeing the look of lip-quivering concern on Xan's face, I tuned out of buttering toast, trying to keep straight who wanted jam and who wanted honey and who had to have margarine, Daddy, because of lactose intolerance or did you forget, and tuned into the discussion on the airwaves – with some trepidation.

It was the weekly triumvirate of political correspondents from Ottawa discussing the ramifications, federally speaking, of the passing of Bill 101.

"There. D'ju hear that?"

It all came together. It was not Santa Claus the leader of the NDP had trouble with, but that other claus, *the notwithstanding clause*. I breathed a sigh of relief. Ed Broadbent's name could still be spoken with all due respect in our household of "ordinary people."

Tim Wynne-Jones
Perth, Ontario

✉ Several weeks ago I listened with interest to your financial analysts discuss the announcement that Brazil would no longer pay out the interest charges on that country's loans.

The "new" term "braziling" was mentioned, as in he brazils, she brazils; they, we, it brazils. That is to say, we take out a loan to pay off the interest charges on an existing loan.

Shame on you, Peter! The word for that is *not* new! How out of touch can you get? We call it *farming*, as in he farms, she farms; we farm . . .

For example, when we go to Bank of X to renew our annual operating loan, the bank manager politely explains that *his* bank does not feel it is worthwhile to waste time and money on farm financing. They have much more *interest* (ha!) in Third World and foreign investments.

We did get our loan renewed, but spent the money to buy supplies from our local feed co-operative, fertilizer from our local grain elevator and fuel and propane from our local dealers. Our five hundred lambs and tonne of wool will be marketed in Canada.

If the day ever comes that we cannot pay back the operating loan, we will still know that the bank's money was spent *within* Canada and supported farm-related industries and businesses.

"Braziling" or "farming"? I guess it's just a matter of perspective.

Debbie Koppel
Dawson Creek, British Columbia

✉ Well, er, ah, hum, like basically, between you and I, you literally have hit the nail on the head with this can of language worms, which I think is about time, eh!

Well, being like an English teacher, you can, er, imply that this controversial (kän tra vur′ se′ al) and very unique problem is faced squarely by me in many cases continuously like it is by you, so in this instance, I, uh, wanna say, you know, thanks Peter, for helping we English teachers orientate the people of society towards the direction of good language.

David Sims
Little Britain, Ontario

✉ You might consider going a bit easier on your criticism of the word "basically," especially on its use by your guests.

I have heard you encourage people – the famous and the not so famous – to summarize their lives in time slots considerably shorter than twenty minutes. I have heard your regular columnists capsulize mergers, failures, successes and disasters in far less time. I have heard you ask for answers to a complex question before you break for the Dominion Time Signal. If this is not asking for the fundamentals, the essentials, the *basics* of a story, what is?

Seven years ago a colleague drew my attention to my own use of the word "basically." I then became very aware of just how often I *did* use the word. However, I was just then working as an interpreter for the Canadian Wildlife Service. My job was to explain the entire Canadian prairies, from climate to crested wheat-grass, in ten minutes flat. I was also supposed to include a brief orientation to the Prairie Wildlife Interpretation Centre (where I worked). My audience wanted the basics, and I was giving them just that – *basically.*

I would suggest that your problem with the word "basically" has more to do with modern life than with careless usage. Every night we see the problems of the entire world squeezed into a predetermined time period between commercial announcements for sanitary napkins and processed cheese. And, in those inter-vening moments, Barbara Frum does not ask her informants to present a monograph on biochemistry. She asks them why three people died from eating poisoned mussels.

Although I agree that our language is fairly full of fudge-words, you will, I think, hear fewer repetitions of the word "basically" when you begin to phrase questions like this: "Well, we've got three hours to kill this morning – damn the Dominion Time Signal and the regional news – so tell me about what happened to you yesterday afternoon."

Jim Gibson
Nanton, Alberta

February 11,1988

Dear Peter,

Basically, basically,basically, basically, basically, basically, basically, basically, basically, basically, basically, basically, basically, basically, basically, basically, basically, basically, basically, basically, basically,

HAVE A NICE DAY.

Peter Powning
RR#5
Sussex, NB

SOME HAPPY
(AND SOME
SENTIMENTAL)
RETURNS

The trip to Moose Jaw that produced my conversation with Elly Danica – described in some detail in the introduction to this book – was also, though in a very different way, the catalyst for the letters that appear both here and in Chapter Seven.

As the introduction says, one of the reasons I was invited to Moose Jaw was that I had been a young newspaperman there. That was in 1957, when I was twenty-two, and the experience had a seminal affect on me. It introduced me, among other things, to a politics I hadn't seen before, and taught me new ways of looking at the landscape. I wrote about some of those impressions in the book I published in 1988, and when I went back that autumn I read some of the relevant passages at the dinner I had been asked to address – not quite what the local Chamber of Commerce had expected, perhaps, but something I wanted to do.

To my chagrin, I realized that evening – I couldn't *help* realizing it, since there were murmurs in the audience – that I had made a couple of factual errors in my account. I had changed a vowel in the name of the hotel where I had once drunk a lot of draft beer (the Harwood, as I ought to have remembered) and moved the location of a town, Belle Plain, that I had driven through dozens of times on my way to court the woman I later married. Time, I learned as I read my words aloud, had blurred the details of a place I once knew well.

The *essence* of Moose Jaw, however, remained as I had written it: the wide streets, the politics that mattered, the early evening light. The faulty details in my memory aside, I knew it well. I felt at home there, and when the evening's events were over, I had to stop myself from rushing back to the office to write them up for the next day's *Times-Herald*. I was glad I had gone back, and moved by the experience.

Later, on *Morningside*, I wondered if listeners had made similar journeys, and asked them, if they had, to write to me about them. Our mailbag bulged with the results. As always, my correspondents expanded my ideas, and used my questions about places they had revisited as a springboard for other stories.

Here is the first of two collections of their responses in these *Papers*. The one that appears later on is about going back to places the writers knew as children. This first sampling is about . . . well, read on.

✉ There are few things in this life so inclined to concentrate one's mind as the knowledge that your bodily soul indeed may be immortal, but from now on the fleshier parts are on their own.

It doesn't come about through some blinding revelation so much as through an accumulation of petty irritants and slight failures. Instead of swinging out of bed in the morning, you lower yourself over the side. The stairs are taken one step at a time – going down as well as up. Despite new trifocals, the TV listings still look fuzzy. The bran flakes bowl becomes your security blanket; that digital watch you were given by a grandchild last Christmas is still on daylight saving because only he knows how to adjust it, and he's not yet back from the day-care centre.

You have now entered what the gerontologists have chosen to describe as the Young/Older Period – young enough to fill out a pension application unaided, but not yet old enough for the waiting list at Sunny Acres Housing Co-Op. These are the so-called "golden years"–no mortgages, an empty nest and, at this moment, knee-deep in travel brochures filled with luxury liners, swaying palms on sandy beaches covered with bronzed young bodies and not one upper plate amongst the lot of them.

A ringing telephone rudely interrupts this tropical reverie. It's long distance. The caller says it's a bonnie wee girl this time and everyone's fine and when are you coming home? She knows I swore years ago that I'd never go back there, but she still calls it home – a rocky outcrop in the middle of the Canadian Shield and about as far away from a coral reef as it's possible to get.

The reverie is fast fading; sun-bronzed bodies give way to hunched-up parka-clad figures plugging in their heating coils. In her part of the world, sand isn't for sprawling about under a hot sun; it's for spreading over snow-slicked roads and under spinning tires – front-wheel drives included. The trees don't sway; they just split right down the middle from all that freezing and thawing. To merely recall chills the blood, which is somewhat thinner since fleeing to this West Coast island paradise. (Through the window I watch some multi-hued Windsurfers scud over wave tops that glisten in the December sun. On the vacant lot behind the ice-cream palace, a shirt-sleeved fellow is selling Christmas trees. Business seems brisk in both places.)

She knows that it could be a difficult journey. Booking the flight and boarding out the cat would be easy enough. The tough part would be lugging around all the emotional baggage left over from the last time, the kind that the airlines never seem able to lose no matter where it's stowed. Anyway, they say that absence makes the heart grow fonder, so mine should be a real gusher by now. And it *is* the first granddaughter, and she *has* been a long time in coming, and the bygones can take care of themselves.

So now it's up, up and away aboard the Red Eye Brownbag Seniors Discount Special; departure at 5:00 A.M. Pacific Standard Time.

From twenty thousand feet the Rockies are truly awesome. A sibilant hiss from the jets hung under the wings does little to disturb the reverential silence. Eyelids droop as the mind drifts back to childhood in a distant place whose name no longer exists, where a Sleeping Giant still snores like thunder in the hills behind the bay.

Images emerge, crystal clear and fresh coloured. Faces recognized, names instantly recalled from more than sixty years ago (alas, a skill no longer present); neighbourhood roots nourished, up one side of the street and down the other; school-yard tensions and ethnic scuffles; the joy of victory and agony of defeat played out on sheets of ice contained by frozen earth embankments on every vacant lot; and the secrets between friends, which were kept from parents – parents who, in those days, knew everything about anything, if you had only been able to ask.

And the smells now remembered: the pulp mill's sulphur, and acrid smoke from forest fires so thick it blotted out the light.

The sounds return: river ice cracking and grinding in early spring, and being double-dared to scamper in a zigzag across the floes without falling in. The drawn-out moan of a whistle mounted atop one of those great steam-driven, piston-engined locomotives with their eighty-four-inch driving wheels snorting upgrade into town. We'd stand beside the track counting cars and reading off the names: Great Northern, Canadian Pacific, Grand Trunk, Canadian National; then we'd wait for the caboose to pass so we could retrieve still hot-to-handle pennies lying flattened on the rails.

And winter's relentless grip: the morning when the school thermometer registered thirty-five below and the classroom fish tank froze and burst. Chunks of ice with fish enclosed were lowered into the only vessel with flowing water available; by recess the bowl was empty.

The seat-belt sign comes on and we're under the clouds in a wide sweep over the Kamiskotia, the river named by those to whom this land once belonged, in a tongue now seldom heard: Kakabeka, the waterfalls higher than Niagara, located in the park called Chippewa where a proud people first traded with the white man two hundred years ago.

The pilot takes aim at a snow-cleared runway, and then the great bird gently settles as tires grab at the tarmac underneath.

She is waiting by the Arrivés/Arrivals gate. The wee bairn is snug in the sling on her mother's back.

We embrace as if it was only yesterday.

"Good flight?" she asks, "you arrived right on time."

"Fastest ever," I say. "I covered sixty years in seven hours and all in living colour."

"You always were a kidder," she says. "Welcome home."

Deryck Thomson
Sidney, British Columbia

✉ I have lived all but two of my thirty-five years in the cosy and familiar surroundings of Chilliwack, British Columbia, but my grandfather and several of his siblings homesteaded near Cabri, Saskatchewan, in the early part of this century. My grandparents were forced to leave in 1936 because of my grandfather's ill health, but Cabri is still the focus of my father's family. They always refer to Cabri as "home."

The first time I visited there was in 1958, when I was five. I accompanied my recently widowed grandmother on what was meant to be a two-week vacation. It turned into a month-long sojourn, as my grandmother broke her ankle the morning we were to return. The flat, dusty, golden prairie was very different from my home in the verdant Fraser Valley. I didn't feel homesick, though, because I was among *my own*. Everyone seemed to know my name, whose child I was and that Bertha and I were staying at Hannah and Edwin's.

Those memories stayed with me for twenty-five years, until I returned to Cabri with my mother, some aunts and uncles and several cousins to lay my grandmother to rest next to her husband in August 1983. When I got to Cabri, the memories came flooding back. I was "home" again.

After the ceremony, the family gathered at my second-cousin Beryl's home. As we sat on the front lawn, my eyes travelled around the circle of friends and relatives. Here was a profile so much like my father's and brother's (both dead now for seven years); there a hands-on-hip stance shared by my grandfather and my youngest brother. I saw familiar features and flickerings of expressions on every face.

I went in the house. As I switched on the bathroom light I glanced over my right shoulder and there, looking back at me from the mirror, was another face just like the ones I had seen outside. I had never viewed myself in quite *this* way before, and it was a comfort to know that here, back "home" in Cabri, existed a part of me that I had not consciously known before.

It isn't always necessary to have left in the first place to find oneself "coming home."

Diane Gummeson Hamel
Chilliwack, British Columbia

✉ This morning, as I took my lollopy young retriever for our morning constitutional, I was thinking about sentimental journeys. I've lived most of my life in one place, so I don't have memories of returning home. But as I stumbled over the rocky beach, I looked up to see that the slanting sun was pinpointing my favourite island lighthouse. This little island is often bathed in sunlight with the dark firs of Denman Island as backdrop. As I stopped to gaze, I realized that the island was my sentimental journey – that stalwart little island with its crown of buildings, topped by the beacon. We have recently retired to this lovely part of Vancouver Island, having spent our working years in the Fraser Valley, and part of the reason we chose this area was that lighthouse!

When I was born early in the Depression, my dad was not working – surely it was a worrisome time. But when I was three months old, Dad got a steady job as steam engineer at the Deep Bay cannery. My first three years were lived in an atmosphere of love, happiness and growing confidence in the future. I lived on the beach, I am told, with a faithful and long-suffering cat as my constant companion. The lighthouse beam was also constant. My mother tells me I loved to sit on Dad's knee waiting to greet each blink of the light with a delighted crow. Sometimes we'd listen to the foghorn with that small fillip of fear to add fascination.

The years went by and I left the sea behind, although on holidays we seemed to gravitate towards water in one form or another. Some years we brought our children to Deep Bay to enjoy the fishing. I introduced them to "my" lighthouse and hoped they sensed some of the serenity I felt. Some time ago we found this little beach cabin, impulsively (we *never* do anything impulsively!) bought it and have retreated to it over the years for many precious breaks from the growing frenzy of mainland living.

The peace of this place heals my soul; the persevering sea keeps me going. My lighthouse beam seems to point a way through all the confusions of life. A great blue heron stands in the shallows for hours waiting for breakfast. Bald eagles nest here and soar endlessly overhead. Seagulls scream and swoop for tidbits. Ducks "duck" into the pounding surf and pop up, smug and safe, on the far side. Seals and sea-lions observe us between waves. I have learned so much about patience, faith and joy looking out from this haven.

There is a mystery about this little islet with its red-roofed white buildings and lofty light, standing aloof and inviolate, bathed still in the beam of sunshine. My idea of God is personified in that beacon. It says: I am faithful, I am giving. I am a certain safeguard from danger. I will always be here. And even when you cannot see that I am here, if you listen I will speak to you through the fogs of despair or disenchantment.

It is good to have a lighthouse in my life once more. Once every few seconds it winks at me. I smile back, content.

Jennifer E. Lord
Nanoose Bay, British Columbia

✉ I grew up on my father's hill farm. Our house is in the middle of a square mile of land that sits on a ninety-foot plateau overlooking the Medicine River Valley. Looking west across the valley, you can see the land sloping gradually upwards to the foothills and the Rocky Mountains on the horizon one hundred and twenty miles away. Twenty miles to the north lie the Medicine Lodge Hills, and to the south you can see the edge of the Red Deer River Valley. Grandfather's farm was there.

As kids my brother and I went there for visits. It was a quite different place from our own high, exposed and windy hill: flat black soil with a well-treed creek bisected the land. The place was heavy with the scent of the spruce shelter belts my grandfather had planted in the 1920s.

When my grandfather died, he passed the land on to my brother and me. It was there my mate and I moved after university. We delighted in the wildlife and flora that graced the creek valley and in the productive black soil of the fields. Just to the south of the place, less than a mile and a half away, is the spectacular Red Deer River Valley.

How can I describe that parkland valley? That point, just south of us, was a favourite camping spot for the native people who lived in the area. The river meandered there. It had cut itself deeply into the shale and gravel and formed a cliff about one hundred feet high; this sheltered an area of about eighty or so acres from the cold north winds. The result was a unique micro-climate. The forest was a mixture of spruce and aspen trees; this on the very southern edge of where spruce grow naturally in central Alberta. Seepage from the north cliff provided the source for a small creek and many springs; there were ferns, moss, orchids and lichens as one would find in a moist B.C. forest; not at all like Alberta. When the July sun made the air dry enough to burn your nose, you could walk down that one hundred feet into a moist and humid world, all quite different and refreshing on a hot summer's afternoon when summer fallowing could wait for a cooler evening. The river channel itself was braided with gravel bars, and one of these channels was a favourite swimming hole for the "locals"—after all, only we knew about it! The river water was just warmed enough by the sun to be safe for small kids.

I'd love to go "home" again, but the Alberta government decided to build a dam on the Red Deer River, right on that spot in 1978. All that parkland valley is gone now, even the sides of the river valley; all replaced by a crude earth-fill dam, thrown without elegance across the river valley. When I first heard of the dam proposal, I envisioned one of those graceful high-arch concrete dams of which we see so many pictures. It wouldn't be a real improvement, I rationalized, but at least in its own way it would be an expression of technological prowess and intellectual elegance: an assertion of human intelligence putting its mathematical stamp on the earth, if you will. Alas, not even such a thin saving grace was to be. The Dickson Dam is a crude piling of dirt across the flow of the river, a bruising demonstration of power and hardly a worthy addition to even the footnotes of human achievement.

Ken Larsen
Benalto, Alberta

✉ Like many Canadians, I grew up on the go, while my father pursued his career. Early in life, the need to feel that I belonged somewhere – anywhere – grew close to an obsession.

We lived in England, Uganda and four Canadian provinces, and I attended eight schools in twelve years. The experience was devastating. I grew socially inept, hampered by a crazy-quilt accent and an equally jumbled set of teeth. Each school had bullies, cliques and impatient teachers who were unwilling and unprepared to accommodate a shy, unhappy and perversely independent-minded child.

After a move, it would take about three months for the school records to catch up with me; in the meantime the principals cursed the anomalies in provincial grade requirements and were seldom sure they'd placed me in the right class. Ah well, they'd be rid of me in June and next year I'd be someone else's problem.

My parents lived private and busy lives, and I was expected to work out my own social life–within a limiting set of rules designed to protect me from new and unfamiliar neighbourhoods. The scenario was not encouraging.

As I provided an inviting target to my peers, I took to fleeing from them, running from school to the safety of my house. The first two or three years I regularly became lost on these mad dashes, alternately dazed and enchanted by the variety of houses, streets and vacant lots. By the time we got to Banff, I had figured out that each new setting offered delightful territory just waiting to be explored and, for a few months, at least, I made it my own. In Banff it was Tunnel Mountain, acres of pine and meadow. In Vancouver several years later, I found haven in an abandoned field with chicken coops, trees and a rope. Each evening I swung into the heavy mists that seemed to perpetually shroud the UBC campus. I could escape from the day's small miseries.

For years, when people asked me where I was from, I'd shrug and answer, "Hard to say." They wanted a simple reply, the name of a city or a province that would define my background in terms they could understand. I began to think of myself as an international citizen.

In Toronto, busy playing the world traveller, I was courted by an American. I think the attraction was my studied *savoir faire* and my newly straightened teeth. I smiled a lot.

He didn't mind doing business or visiting for a week or two in Canada, but he preferred his home in L.A. During the information exchange that accompanies romance, he listened sympathetically to my tales of a lost childhood and pointed out in his practical way that Los Angeles was at the same end of the continent as several places I'd lived–only warmer.

Months after he left, I was flattered to receive a letter with airline tickets enclosed, inviting me to visit him for part of the summer. "If you come," he promised, "I'll drive you back through Vancouver and across Canada with my trailer, and we'll have a look at the places you've called home."

How could I resist?

For four sunny weeks I was immersed in American landscapes, department stores and restaurants. I found the number of people and the limitless consumer goods wearing, and although I tried to be appreciative, he noticed my discomfort. A week later we departed for Canada, both slightly miffed.

The drive through Washington State took longer than expected. High winds rocked his trailer, and he became morose as we fought the heavy rain into British Columbia. We drove round and round the UBC campus in a fog until I overcame my pride enough to admit that I couldn't recall the street where we had lived; he overcame his long enough to stop the car so I could ask directions.

It was all gone, torn down a long time ago. Of course it was, I should have known. Who would keep chicken coops on prime property? It hurt, and my friend's scowl didn't help. I felt less of a piece, and he felt taken for a ride. But we'd have better luck in Banff, my companion said, and then I'd see.

It snowed in Roger's Pass, and we saw a semi jackknifed in the ditch. We ran out of gas, then drove all night to make up time and missed our turn into Banff. We had to go back. He insisted.

This time we started from a known landmark, the Confederation Buildings. We drove past the brick school and along the blocks to the hill, but . . . No log home, no pines. Just suburban boxes and tricycles, and a confusing number of new streets.

He broke the silence, as we drove across the prairie, to complain that the sky stole everything away. I couldn't respond. For me, the sky arched from place to place. It was large enough to encompass all my homes.

When we finally got to Ottawa, my prince brightened and declared it a quaint little town. Canada wasn't really bigger than the United States, he explained–just backward, and more bloody-minded.

I declined his offer of rescue and marriage. He shook his head and said that I was ungrateful and foolish beyond his understanding. Who would choose, for heaven's sakes, to stay in such a god-forsaken country?

Perhaps he was right. But I had just discovered, travelling that long stretch of highway once again, that I did belong in Canada, and I intended to stay here and enjoy it.

Anne E. Tener
Merrickville, Ontario

✉ I was born in Pouce Coupé, British Columbia, and lived next door in Dawson Creek until I was ten, when I was forced to move to Vancouver.

I waited eagerly for the summers when I could return to stay with my grandmother in her little house. I would fly "student standby" to Fort St. John, always terrified that I would get bumped in Prince George. It never happened, and I now realize that CP Air would probably not bump a young girl; but then, listening to the stewardess read the names of the passengers who would have to disembark added spice to my travels. After the flight landed in Fort St. John, there would be the mad scramble for my suitcase, then the endless wait for the airport limousine to take me the hour and a half drive to Dawson Creek, past stinky Taylor where the oil refinery is, over the Peace River on an orange bridge with a deck that hummed, past miles and miles of green fields and skinny trees, and finally into the outskirts of town, past Texaco and Rotary Lake, the Slumber Lodge and Kentucky Fried Chicken, before turning and pulling up beside the Windsor Hotel. During all this, I sat perched on the edge of my seat in joy and anticipation, talking a mile a minute to my seat-mate. When the limousine stopped, I would grab my suitcase and run through the warm dusk the three blocks to my grandmother's house, wanting to shout, "I'm home! I'm finally home!" to anyone who would listen. I contained myself until I got through the alley behind Aspol Motors, ran down the slope of the lawn, through the shed –really a lean-to at the back of the house–and burst through the kitchen door to all the sights and sounds and smells I had been longing for.

The summers passed quickly. They are now blended into an unsortable tangle of snapshot memories: playing endless games of Scrabble and Chinese checkers with my patient grandmother, sleeping over next door with Darla at her grandmother's house, walking miles and miles in the bright prairie sunshine, and drinking hot chocolate in the coffee shop of the Windsor Hotel the August day the temperature dropped from thirty degrees to minus three and it snowed.

The fall fair would mark the beginning of the end for me. I knew it was almost time to go back to Vancouver, and my spirits would sink lower and lower. I would try to get Gram to ask me to stay all year, but she never did.

When it was time to go, a friend would drive us back past the now golden fields to Fort St. John, and I would cry. One year the flight was full, and I cried all the way back, too, so happy to have another night in the creaky twin bed, covered with the slippery green comforter, listening to my grandmother's ferocious snores and smelling the heart-filling scents of baking, late-blooming flowers and prairie dust.

Gradually my visits got shorter and shorter and finally deteriorated into a last duty visit during a Victoria Day long weekend: I sat around reading, barely acknowledging my grandmother's presence.

The house is empty now. I was passing through Dawson Creek a couple of years ago with my husband and baby daughter, and we stopped at the old place. Drunks had taken over the shed and the lawn was unkempt. The rose bush I planted on one visit was flourishing, though, and just for a moment, when I was walking up the path, my heart gave that familiar flip, and I thought–home!

Susan DeSandoli
100 Mile House, British Columbia

✉   My parents were always on the move when I was a child. We moved almost every year. The last house we moved into as a family was when I was in Grade 11, and so I call that house my home.

Deep within me, where fantasy mingles with reality, I think of my real home as a little bedroom in the basement of that last house. That's where I dreamed my happy family times and plotted and planned for the future. It was my retreat, a place to be alone – away from all I didn't care to hear or see. Its four walls seemed to enfold me, giving me comfort with their closeness.

One of my favourite things to do, in the few short years we lived in that house, was to read in bed on Saturday nights. I'd wash the sheets and remake the bed so that each blanket and sheet was firmly tucked in. I'd scurry about cleaning the room so that everything was perfectly in place. Then I'd dash over to Woolco and buy myself some Smarties. Home again, I'd take a bath, then crawl into my deliciously fresh-smelling bed linens and crack open a library book, the Smarties at my side. My parents would usually be out, and my kid brother would be rattling about the house, making a noise here and there to keep me company.

I still like to go to bed early on a Saturday night in fond memory of those nights in my little room. But time slips by so much faster now. If I do find time to read in bed, my husband is usually reading alongside me, and it just isn't the same. His breathing, wiggling, flipping of pages and occasional chuckle impose on my solitude. Furthermore, he disapproves of my passion for Smarties, so I must sneak them out from under my pillow. I long for time alone in that little room I called my own.

It's been four years since I saw that room. There is a distance between me and my home, but not the kind of distance you can measure by metres or miles, for the house is only a few blocks away. My parents and I, however, have been estranged for four years. During this time, they moved again. My anguish took me by surprise. Maybe time would heal the wounded family, but my room was gone forever. I could never return.

I walk by that house often, with my four kids. When I get there, a profound sadness almost overwhelms me. I think of how much more I've lost than just a bedroom. I search the house, hoping there were better memories of life in that house than just time spent in a tiny cold room in the basement.

Kathryn Adria
Edmonton

✉ I was born and raised in Grey County, Ontario, in a place called Vail Point. My grandfather was Scottish by birth. He took his bride to the point, where he had cleared eleven acres of forest and built a log house. He was an inspector for the government. When he died in his early fifties, my father brought his bride to the same log house. I was born there, along with six brothers and sisters.

Our house was atop a bluff overlooking Georgian Bay. The point, heavily covered with pine and evergreen trees, jutted into the bay, forming a calm cove where we played on our own handmade rafts.

Today I am eighty-three and legally blind, but all I have to do is shut my eyes and in my memory I sit on the shore and listen to the waves washing on the beach and the sea gulls screaming and circling overhead. The fish tugs had come into the harbour, so the food was plentiful. The setting sun cast a shimmering golden road for miles, from shore to shore.

I married and went to the city to live, but I would take my family back to the point for vacations, and they loved it as I had.

Then came the war. The government took the land from the residents of Sydenham in St. Vincent Township to make the Meaford Tank Range. The people were given a pittance for their homes. My dad received five hundred dollars for thousands of dollars of property. This was a prosperous farming and apple-growing district. Many people had built beautiful new homes. They were given an ultimatum – get out or be forcibly removed. One neighbour, a prosperous man, went mental over this. Who could blame him?

Many years after the war, I wanted to go home. My brother also had this wish, so in 1960 we drove as far as the blockades would allow, then started across the fields on foot. The weeds were shoulder-high. My brother put my one-year-old grandson on his shoulders. Then we came to where our home had been. I say "had been" because the house had been shelled by the tanks. The orchard was wild, the roads overgrown. With sinking hearts we retraced our steps, wishing we had not come.

J. Lumley
Windsor, Ontario

✉ The Columbia River begins in the glaciers atop the Purcell Mountains of the East Kootenays. It starts as a stream, grows into a creek and has become a river by the time it flows northward past the town of Golden. It swings in a wide arc to the north and west, stops briefly at the Mica Dam, curves to the south, pauses impatiently at the Revelstoke Canyon Dam and flows southward, carving a valley between the Monashee and Selkirk mountains past the town of Revelstoke. Thirty-five miles to the south, the river widens out and becomes Upper Arrow Lake, a long finger of water that constricts at the southern end as though someone had tied a tourniquet around one of the knuckles, then widens again into Lower Arrow Lake, from whence it narrows into a river again and flows past Trail into Washington and on to the Pacific. Where the Columbia becomes Upper Arrow Lake, it scoops out a bay from the forested shoreline. That place is called Galena Bay, for the lead ore mined in the nearby mountains, and it was home to my husband, Bill, and me.

We had come there in 1972 as part of a back-to-the-land commune from south-eastern Pennsylvania. How we found Galena Bay is another story. Suffice it to say that the commune broke apart shortly after we arrived in British Columbia, and that Bill and I ended up with twenty acres of forest about half a mile inland from the bay.

There is no town at Galena Bay. Were it not for the fact that the ferry, which carries travellers across the lake from the Revelstoke side to the Nakusp side, lands there, it surely would not merit inclusion on any map. There is no electricity, no grocery store, no gas station, no hotel – just the ferry landing, a lot of trees and about six residents. It was the isolation, the wildness, the beauty, the ruggedness of the place that drew us and held us.

What was Galena Bay? Trees. Snow. Mosquitoes. Black bears. Black flies. Skunks. Coyotes. Martens. Thrushes. Owls. Stellar's jays. No-see-ums. Thimbleberries. False Solomon's seal. Wild blueberries, huckleberries, strawberries. Queen Anne's cup. Indian paintbrush. Ospreys. Bracken and fiddleheads. Three glacier-clad mountains across the lake, as majestic and forbidding as their names: Odin, Thor and Freya.

Bill and I lived in Galena Bay for the better part of eight years. Those eight years were full and good, an extended honeymoon, an education in natural living. Yet in 1980 we moved away, to Vancouver. And when, in 1985, we came back, it was to pack everything up and take it away for good.

In Galena Bay Bill and I learned many things, and what we learned, put together, became a way of life. We learned to identify trees, plants, birds, bird calls and animal tracks in the sand and the snow. We learned crude carpentry and cruder plumbing. We learned post and beam, A-frame, gambrel-roof and regular stud construction. We learned how to start a fire in a wood-stove and how to put out a chimney fire. We learned how *not* to select a site for a garden, by walking over the land in a spaced-out daze and choosing the spot where the sun played the most prettily on the thimbleberry leaves, without ever thinking to dig up an exploratory spadeful of soil. (This lovely spot turned out to be an old creek bed, full of rocks ranging from egg-sized stones to boulders, which required two months' digging in the cold fall rain to remove.) We learned how to plant a garden by the phases of the moon; how to plant companionable species side by side; how to transplant, mulch, make manure tea, prune and weed. We learned how to keep bees, to identify the queen and to recapture a swarm. We learned how to make cedar shakes. We learned not to roof a sauna with cedar shakes (after our first sauna burned down). We learned that chickens are not cute, fluffy, benign creatures of the barn yard. We learned that bantam hens are smarter than leghorns but not smarter than skunks or owls. We learned the slow, suspicious ways of country neighbours. We learned to be patient and quiet around them, to trust and to earn their trust.

Bill and I grew up together in Galena Bay. Our romance became a partnership. We argued, loved, dreamed, planned, got to really know each other. On a few occasions we saved each other's lives. Our relationship survived the pulling apart of two maturing, inde-pendent-minded individuals. We conceived our first child.

And yet, and yet. By the sixth or seventh year I was beginning to be unhappy there. It wasn't the place or the life-style. It was the lack of neighbours, the lack of a community, the lack of some-thing to be part of. I wanted to live among people with values like mine, people to talk to about books, art, politics, philosophy, peo-ple to swap baby-sitting with, people who wanted to change the world and believed that by the way they lived they could help make it happen. The half-dozen people who lived in Galena Bay were fine people, but they did not fulfill those needs. Bill did, but he alone and my love for the place were not enough. I wanted to leave.

An excuse presented itself in the form of a one-year job for Bill in Vancouver. One year, we said. Can't hurt to try. Time for a change. One year turned into two, three, four. I went back to school. Our second child was born. Bill started a small business. It has now been eight years. This summer we bought a house.

The same year we moved to Vancouver, we bought another piece of land in the West Kootenays, an eight-acre farm in a rural community, near some of our close friends and other members of the back-to-the-land generation. (Kindred spirits, as one of them would say.) But we didn't sell Galena Bay right away. We couldn't, emotionally. We kept the two properties, visiting both of them at Christmas and summer. Every time we drove up the driveway, Galena Bay felt like home: the ferry's foghorn, the view of Mount Odin from a certain spot on the back road, the cluster of birches at the side of the driveway, the feel of the four cabin walls around us. I didn't want it to feel like home. "I love this place, but–" I began, trailing off, unable to articulate the push or the pull, unable to resolve them.

Meanwhile, neglect was changing the face of home. The gardens grew up to nettles and quack grass and burdock. The bird feeder fell down. The raspberry canes were broken by snow and bears. Bracken and pine seedlings moved in from the edges of the clearings, reclaiming their former territory. The A-frame storage shed tilted ever more dangerously towards the bush. In a last ignominious gesture, the outhouse fell over, toppled by a falling cedar bough. Each home-coming became more painful as we witnessed the deterioration of the homestead, more frustrating as we frantically tried to make up six months' worth of work in a week, more discouraging as we realized that we couldn't do it.

In 1984 the man who had sold us our land asked if he could buy it back. We debated. We agonized. We said yes. In 1985 we made our final trip home, to clear eight years of living out of our homestead and move it away.

"We must be ruthless," we told each other, and indeed we burned and threw out a great deal of stuff. But we lingered over many more things, reminiscing, unable to part with them, finally tossing them into boxes to be moved to our other piece of land. I found (and kept) Bill's old tartan-plaid boxer shorts, one half of which had served to make curtains for our hens' laying boxes. We saved our firebox ash cleaner, made from a flattened tin can and a coat hanger. We hauled two cords of cedar shakes in wheelbarrow loads from the bush where we'd stored them ten years before; the wood was still rosy-orange and redolent. "Toss it or save it?" was our cry as we went from building to building, from the cabin to the tool shed to the chicken coop to the sauna (the second one), to the storage shed to the wood-shed to the root cellar. The accumulation of our growing-up decade passed through our hands; every item brought a memory, a regret, a smile.

So long as we were busy sorting, packing, burning and hauling, I didn't succumb to emotion. But there came a day when the buildings were empty, the moving van was packed and there was nothing left to do but leave. Arms around each other, Bill and I walked over the homestead. We didn't talk. We said a silent goodbye to each building, each favourite place. As we circled back to the cabin, I pushed my face into Bill's shoulder and wept. For what? For dreams unfulfilled, our innocence, our work, our mistakes, our idealism? I don't know. Then we climbed into the truck and drove away. We haven't been back since.

Ellen Schwartz
Burnaby, British Columbia

✉ After years of living in Canada I was going home to Jamaica. I had stayed away during all those years when the media told us that political problems made visiting unsafe, or, at the least, uncomfortable, particularly for expatriates.

Now, as we approached Montego Bay and those unbelievable ocean colours slid below the plane, my heart lifted. Then came the wonderful moment when that warm air hit me as I stepped from the plane. No northern summer air is quite the same.

To my great joy I was to find that the entire North Coast seashore is *not* obscured by high-rise hotels, that people still smile and wave as you drive by, that donkeys still graze by the roadside, that mangoes, ackees, avocados are still to be had for the bargaining and that a "hextra" is usually added.

Two days later we were back at Montego Bay airport – no, not to leave. We had come to watch another Air Canada plane land. My heart lifted again and tears welled up, for as the wheels touched down I knew that my first grandchild, a Canadian, aged three, had come to share the land I still think of as home – to run barefoot on beaches, to see a baby goat, eye-to-agate-eye, to pat a warm furry donkey and to sit in the sea eating a fresh juicy mango.

The circle was completed.

Dorothy M. Prosser
Scarborough, Ontario

✉ My mother died when I was fifteen, just as we were in the midst of our mother-daughter turmoil. I had no chance to get to know her as a person, but she had told me stories about growing up in Lethbridge, in a family with eight boys and two girls. To me, an only child, the thought of such a big family was enchanting. A few years after she died, when I was a university student, I arranged a trip to Lethbridge. I called a family friend and asked her to show me where my mother had lived.

My mother had arrived in Lethbridge in 1905, a frightened five-year-old fleeing the pogroms in Russia. My grandfather had come two years earlier. He was followed by his eldest son, who wore the only winter coat available to him – his mother's, with its leg-of-mutton sleeves. Somehow they found work, saved money and sent for the rest of the growing family.

I liked the big old house immediately. It had a solid, rounded shape and was painted an airy cream colour. I knocked on the door. The lady who answered was a bit taken aback but agreed to show me around. The rooms were pleasant but struck no chord until we came to the summer kitchen. That room, looking out to the garden, seemed to resonate with my mother's stories about her mischievous brothers–how they sold the same pair of homing pigeons four times before my grandfather squelched their entrepreneurial spirit; how they could make up most of their own baseball team and lick all challengers; how they would swoop down on my grandfather's fruit store and devour his profits.

I could see my mother as a young girl of thirteen. Her own mother had died during the 1918 influenza epidemic; she had put her long red-gold hair into a braid, quit school and learned to keep house after her dreamy, beautiful older sister had escaped into marriage.

This was where my mother had struggled to cook, where she had chased the boys while trying to keep them in check, where she shouted at my grandfather to sell the stocks he had just bought, not knowing that years later the company would strike oil in Turner Valley. She could have been rich.

Business sense did not run in my mother's family. My grandfather, a pious man, collected empty bottles to sell when he wasn't at the fruit store. A local man was starting a brewery, and he offered my grandfather a partnership in return for his bottle-collecting. My grandfather refused. The man went on to found Sick's Brewery, a great success in the West. I used to see his big sign blinking on and off near my home in Edmonton.

My grandfather's income covered only the basics plus one thing – violin lessons for my handsome, blond Uncle Sam. With his good looks and romantic music, Uncle Sam wooed and won nearly every woman around. In fact, he had so many sweethearts that even his wedding day he spent part of with another woman. Or so my mother's story went.

As they grew up, the brothers headed south one by one. My mother stayed and cared for my grandfather until he died.

I stood in their house, so filled with their presence. I could almost hear their laughter, their jokes, their financial schemes, their music, my mother singing, the arguing and scolding that went on as my grandfather tried to read. My mother had been a girl surrounded by laughing, quarrelling brothers. Later, she married a quiet, passive man, had only one child and was locked in loneliness for the rest of her life.

When I left the house, my friend pointed across the street. "There's an old lady there who will remember the family," she said. And so she did. The white-haired woman told me another tale. There were so many brothers and they had such forceful personalities that they could set the fashions. When their socks had holes, the brothers flaunted them, saying it was a new style. Soon other boys were wearing socks with holes in them.

Best of all, the old woman remembered my mother, "that slim little girl with such long, thick hair . . . the girl whose mother died so young. She looked after her father, you know." My mother – so like myself.

Claire Goldman
Westmount, Quebec

✉ The trip home begins at least a week in advance. By the time we reach Toronto we will have crossed five provincial borders and leaped from the nineteenth-century life as a trapper in the Yukon bush to the twentieth-century hustle and bustle of a major city.

With excitement and queasiness we prepare ourselves for the transition. Each stage of the journey brings us closer to the future. In the beginning our little settlement must be closed down, windows shuttered against bears, the hand pump drained, the floors swept and the food put into the high cache or root cellar to keep the mice out. And then all the dogs are hooked up, Bruce mushing the first dog team, and Sylvie and I coming behind with a smaller load and a smaller team. In four days we will travel more than a hundred miles on the river to reach the small town of Mayo, in the heart of the Yukon. For us Mayo means roads, stores and civilization.

Leg two of our journey begins. The dogs are safely parked at a friend's yard in town, and we hop into our aging pickup truck and drive down the highway to Whitehorse, the big city. Even though I was born and raised in Toronto, the transition from our wilderness home, which has no roads, plumbing or electricity, to Whitehorse is a quantum leap. The crowds of people, the constant traffic – even flush toilets – feel like a novelty at first.

We park our truck with yet another friend and fly in a jet to Toronto. The anticipation becomes so great on this last leg of our homeward journey. Who will meet us at the airport? If it's Mom, we'll take the slow circuitous route home through quiet streets. If it's Dad, who is not afraid of the 401, we will reach home in fifteen minutes.

Homeward bound. First comes Avenue Road off the 401. I see more new stores and the McDonald's restaurant where I had my first summer job. We then turn into our quiet neighbourhood with its sturdy brick houses still unchanged and maple trees lining the street. More and more young families of ample means are moving in because of the proximity to the school. We drive past houses where I baby-sat; the house of my piano teacher still has its venetian blinds closed just as they were fifteen years ago when I was a student.

This is my territory. These are the streets I've walked down hundreds of times. A few more corners to turn and then I see my old home. Where once a huge ash tree grew, the little cherry blossom tree is beginning to have more of a presence. Up the steps, onto the walkway, up three more steps and through the yellow door, and then we're home. It's no longer a house full of rambunctious kids, but the quiet space of a grandmother, filled with dark hardwood panelling – a house built in the twenties that has changed very little in sixty years.

The macramé hanging I made years ago is still hanging on the living-room wall. Family photo albums of children and grandchildren sit on top of the pile of magazines on the table. And the beaver pelt we sent from the Yukon has begun to rot in the more humid climate of Ontario and become a home for moths.

I left home ten years ago. It all feels so familiar, yet the newer additions of a VCR and a microwave and a fancy bathtub remind me of how long I've been gone. I left when microwaves were still a novelty and VCRs unheard of. My ineptitude with both technologies pleases me rather than embarrasses me. I see them as more luxury I can happily live without. In the bush I enjoy my time spent cooking on the wood stove and any leisure time I can scrounge up after the day's chores are done, I spend knitting or reading by propane light.

I feel as if I've come a long way, and I guess I have – from the nineteenth century to the twentieth. From the quiet unpopulated wilderness where silence hangs so heavily you can imagine orchestras playing, to downtown residential Toronto and the constant drone of the city. From simplicity and hard physical work, to a highly complex technological world. The transition can be overwhelming.

Beth Hunt
Mayo, Yukon

✉ The year 1978 marked the end of an era for me. It was the year my Volkswagen Beetle was impounded three times. In disgust I finally gave it to a friend for the price of the fine. And 1978 was the year my long-standing – and therefore long-suffering – girlfriend abandoned me for a 1957 Chevy (and its owner). It was also the year I completed my Bachelor of Applied Arts degree at Ryerson.

I blamed all my problems on Toronto, but I knew something had to be done. I packed up what few belongings I had and set out for the Maritimes with a friend. We drove her car.

Despite the fact that I was born in Toronto and had lived there most of my life, it was with great relief that I hit the road that spring. The suffocating effect of the Toronto ethos quickly dissipated in the clear blue skies that followed us up the north shore of the St. Lawrence and all the way down to the rocky shores of Halifax.

I had no plans and fewer expectations, but I did have my new Ryerson degree and three brothers who lived – conveniently for me – in Halifax. They had all arrived – or should I say "escaped" – at different times and for reasons of their own.

I remained in Halifax for four years; the proximity of the ocean and the picture-postcard villages of coast and valley were a balm to my poor Toronto-battered soul. I did some research for a film that never was produced; I wrote advertising copy and eventually produced some promotional films.

Then, one dank and dreary day in 1982, I found myself stepping off a plane in Sydney, Cape Breton. I had come for a job interview at the local college (now the University College of Cape Breton).

In fact, it was so dank and dreary that day that I rather hoped they wouldn't hire me. But they did.

I returned in late December – this time driving a rental van full of my newly acquired East Coast belongings. The fresh snow was three feet deep and drifting, but the sky was blue, and the view of the Bras d'Or as I skidded over Kelly's Mountain was thrilling. I didn't know it at the time, but I was coming home.

I should explain that both my parents are New Brunswickers, and like all good Maritimers they used to return every summer to the beach at Shediac. I had spent all my summer vacations swimming in the "warmest waters north of Cape Hatteras," as the ads used to say, and eating sweet, plentiful lobster. It was cheap, too. This was thirty-five years ago before lobsters were flown first-class to Paris for Christmas dinner.

For me the Maritimes have always been associated with the taste of those savoury New Brunswick crustaceans, the endless summer days and *real* water, the salt kind in which you can float unaided for hours across a placid, green bay. A magical place, the Maritimes, where grandmas always have hot blueberry cake and muffins waiting for a young boy just down from Toronto. And where – no matter I was born in Ontario – relatives would always ask innocently, "How long you *home* for?"

Well, I've been "home" now for ten years. The summers are no longer endless, although winters are; lobster is too expensive even if bought right off the boat; and I can no longer float more than five minutes without developing an arthritic hand from the chilly ocean water. But I am home. I've married a lovely Sydney girl and we now have a fine son.

I like living here. It seems to suit. There's a sense of community in Cape Breton. People here still talk to you in grocery store line-ups, and they never seem to wear the lost look of subway riders waiting, like Godot, for their train to arrive. Governments keep trying to drag the Island into the twentieth century, but it never quite works. The attitude seems to be that prosperity would be nice but let's not take it too seriously. And it's pretty hard not to like a place that votes solidly Liberal during a Tory sweep. As one fellow said on a post-election phone-in radio show, "We may be Cape Bretoners but at least we still have our pride."

Tim Belliveau
Sydney, Nova Scotia

✉ I returned to Calgary in March 1985. I had grown up here, and after five years in the fleshpots of Vancouver and Ottawa, three years in New York City, war-weary and battle-fatigued from divorce wars, I was coming back.

I flew from La Guardia to Malton and then took a compartment on the train from Union Station to Calgary. Travelling the wilds of northern Ontario in early March, just after a snowfall, on a sparkling day, helped restore my spirits.

A four-hour stop in Winnipeg to visit my cousin, have a nip and chips at the Salisbury House and stretch my legs in Assiniboine Park Zoo didn't hurt, either. More salve to soothe the soul!

Back on the train again, with a chilled bottle of wine and a picnic basket full of goodies, I settled in for my last night on the train. Normally, I sleep like a log, but not that night. By 4:00 A.M., I was up, dressed, packed and firmly ensconced in the dome car, waiting for Calgary to appear.

No finer sight have I ever seen than the view that morning. The sun was kissing the horizon and spotlighting the Calgary Tower as it rose above the plains. The mountains looked almost surreal, suffused in an orange glow.

I spent a couple of weeks getting settled and waiting for my belongings to arrive, but the first weekend I had my skis, I high-tailed it up on the ski bus to Sunshine Village. I had learned to ski there ten years before and was anxious to get up to the mountains, *my mountains*, again. Going up on the gondola, I could barely restrain the tears. This was my *home*. The ride up the triple chair to my favourite place in this universe, off the top to the left, was just as I had remembered it – incredibly spectacular. It was a flaw-less day, the snow-shrouded horn of Mount Assiniboine rising triumphantly in the distance. I could have stood there all day, tears freezing as they slid down my cheeks.

Linda M. Cunningham
Calgary

✉ My experience of going home began with two days' notice to start a new job (which I hadn't applied for) in my home town. After living with the frightening pace and plastic glamour of Montreal for three years, the transition to the slow motion and the "come as you are" of St. John's was like letting the batteries wear down in a wind-up toy. I discovered that living away from my home town brought me closer to the heart of it.

Montreal gave me the anonymity I had dreamed of as a young adult. But I learned that anonymity has limits. Strangers are viewed as strange – hence the fear of friendliness. If not for my room-mates, I would have gone days without talking. In Newfoundland if you don't chat, people assume you've just had your tonsils out. They want to talk and be friendly. When you're at the vegetable section in the Dominion and you get the urge to ask the person next to you if he's tried a Sprung cucumber, he'll tell you he wouldn't spring out of bed for one. Or imagine you're waiting for a prescription at the pharmacy: the druggist will roll his eyes and dryly comment on the increased sales of sleeping pills since the advent of double daylight saving time.

In St. John's, everyone calmly drives on congestion-free roads. I chose instead to do a lot of walking and had access to pleasant, crowd-free sidewalks.

All the pavement, brick and concrete of Montreal were replaced by wooden houses and thick maple trees. My eyes, slit and weary from looking at pillars of grey, were abruptly opened to the vast greenness of the parks, yards and valleys in St. John's, and by the bright multicoloured housing in the residential downtown. I saw again the liberated blue of the Atlantic crashing around the fog-worn barrens of the south side hills. I had forgotten what the colour blue looked like.

I could also smell freshness in the clean salt air. I'm sure the memory of clean air had been savagely snatched from me when I moved to Montreal.

Have you ever managed to work up a lather with soap and water in Montreal? If so, where did you import the water from? Newfoundland? In the city, I tried in vain to produce lather by rubbing soap and water together. I'd usually give up in frustration and watch a tar-coloured, slippery film swirl down the drain. Having a bath in Newfoundland is like white-water rafting, without the raft. Your instantly clean body squeaks around in the porcelain and is quickly engulfed with rapidly reproducing bubbles, bubbles that gleam in purple, red and yellow silk. After three years I was finally clean.

I didn't appreciate any of this until I lived far away in a mainland city. Because of high unemployment and few job opportunities, many Newfoundlanders (John Crosbie included) have traditionally been forced to leave the island to find work or to further careers. My return to Newfoundland is a paradox – I came home because I was offered a job. Not many Newfoundlanders get the opportunity to come home to work. I was given a chance to become closer to the people, countryside and values of the land that is home in my heart.

Margot French
Ottawa

CLEANING UP

Terry MacLeod, who wrote the story that opens this chapter, is a chunky, hard-headed, outspoken Prince Edward Islander who joined the *Morningside* staff in the season of 1987–88, after a career that had taken him, among other places, to Arctic Quebec and northern Ontario. Partly because of the number of places he'd lived, I think, Terry had developed a fierce commitment to environmental causes long before they became fashionable, and when we began to focus our attention on this transcendent issue of the 1980s, he was the logical quarterback.

Our coverage of the environment took us in a number of directions. We convened panels of experts, talked with activists, dug into organic gardening, called people in their homes and asked them what they had under their sinks or in their bathrooms and tried to publicize as many alternatives to pollutants as we could find. In these *Papers*, I've tried to show some of the results and list a few of the alternatives we discovered (including Greenpeace's list of acceptable materials to use around the home). But first, as they say, here's Terry, with his story of *Morningside*'s own not-always-triumphant battle to practise what we preach.

In the Beginning Was a Fly

✉ On Labour Day, 1988, Peter dedicated the next season of *Morningside* to the earth, the air and the water around us. The dedication came at the end of a story about his efforts to kill a house-fly. He had been sitting at breakfast with some friends at his cottage, and a late summer fly had flown in circles overhead, pestering people with its buzzing. Without thinking, Peter had reached for a can of bug spray. As he was about to zap the fly, he heard someone say: "I think he's kidding."

Peter felt foolish to be caught reaching so blithely for the bug spray. He had given no thought to the damage he would do to the ozone layer with his quick and chemical dispatch of that house-fly. (He found out later, in a conversation on *Morningside* with an aerosol manufacturer, that his guilt was misplaced. Without much fanfare, the aerosol industry removed ozone-destroying CFCs from bug sprays two years ago.) The incident reminded Peter "how much all of us are going to have to change the way we behave, personally, socially and politically, if we are going to turn this thing around."

With that thinking in mind, Hal Wake, the program's executive producer, and I decided to start a recycling project in the *Morningside* office. We didn't know exactly what we were going to recycle, we didn't know how to do it and we still don't know how it's going to turn out, but we decided to do it anyway and trace the course of it on the radio. I was no expert in recycling when I started this, so I've learned what I know by the seat of my pants. Setting up this project has been more difficult and more interesting than I expected.

Deciding Where to Start

Before I started the *Morningside* recycling project, I had never given much thought to our office garbage. I knew my waste-paper basket was full at the end of the day and empty in the morning. I didn't know if anything in there could be recycled. To find out I called some people I figured would know a lot about garbage, the people at Metro Toronto Works. They run Toronto's dump and the garbage collection system. Metro Works directed me to one of their garbage specialists, Mary Stewart, whose position, according to her card, is Assistant Recycling Co-ordinator – Industrial Waste Reduction, Refuse Disposal Division of the Metropolitan Works Department.

I told Mary about my recycling project, and she said she'd be glad to help. The way to start, she said, was to take a good look at the contents of our waste baskets. She called this examination a "waste audit." A waste audit is similar to an accountant's audit, but it balances garbage cans, not books. Mary wanted to account for everything we throw out, to determine if there was anything of value in what we think of as garbage.

What's in the Waste-paper Basket?

Before Mary's visit to the *Morningside* office, I carefully saved my garbage for a few days by hiding it from the cleaning lady. I wanted Mary to have something worthwhile to examine. As soon as she arrived I picked up my dented office-issue waste basket and we plugged our noses and headed down the hall to Studio R.

We poured the soiled record of my last three days on the studio table. We found: three glossy magazines, a Styrofoam lunch tray, four newspapers, a white plastic sandwich tray with a clear plastic lid, two plastic knives and forks, two glass juice bottles, three pop cans, three apple cores, some orange peelings, a disposable pen, a handful of audio tape, a pile of carbon paper, a cardboard milk container, a dozen press releases, four large manila envelopes and ten sheets of fax paper.

Mary picked through my garbage with the care of an archaeologist. After a few minutes she offered a brief synopsis. "Most of the weight of your garbage is paper, both high-grade and low-grade. You have some pure plastics and some mixed plastics. You have a small amount of organic matter, some glass and a little steel and aluminum." Most of the stuff was recyclable, she said, but some of it was more practical to recycle than the rest. After another quick assessment, Mary announced: "Much of your garbage is good-quality paper, and the average office worker throws out half a pound of paper a day. Your garbage looks pretty average. You should start a high-grade paper recycling program."

By high-grade paper, Mary meant photocopy paper, computer printout, letterhead, bond and manila. There's a ready market for this stuff, she said, and it's easy to handle and easy to store. She added: "Waste-paper contractors will haul this paper away for you and pay you up to $150 a tonne for the right to do that." This sounded good to me – someone who will buy our garbage!

Mary said that magazine paper, which we had a lot of, is considered by paper contractors to be a low-grade paper – it's hard to recycle because of its clay coating, which makes it glossy. (The clay contaminates the paper.) Magazine paper is sometimes used to make cereal boxes, but demand for it is low. Fax paper and carbon paper are not recyclable at all – they are chemically coated. As well, Mary said, there is a glut of recycled newsprint on the market; it was unlikely we would find a paper contractor who would buy ours.

We decided glass was not suitable for our recycling project: it's heavy and hard to store, and it fetches a low price. Plastics are a problem – they must be classified by type to be recycled, and recycling companies have trouble getting enough of a single type. What about the orange peels, apple cores and lunch leftovers? Mary said we didn't produce enough organic garbage to bother with it.

Hey, Mister, Want to Buy Some Great Garbage?

On Mary's advice, I looked in the Yellow Pages and called two waste-paper contractors at random to get quotes. I chose YV Recycling of Toronto and ISC Recycling of Don Mills. Both companies had a few routine questions. "What kind and quantity of paper are you throwing out now?" (I didn't know the exact quantity, but I knew we threw out lots, both high and low grade.) "How many employees would be taking part in the program?" (Sixteen in the *Morningside* office to start. Three hundred in the whole building.) "How much support do you have from the management of the building?" (I didn't know. I said it was a *Morningside* project at the moment.) "Do you have a central place to store the paper?" (This is an old, crowded building. We probably have very little storage space.) "Who will move the paper from the individual offices to the central storage site?" (I didn't know, but I hoped the cleaning staff could do it.) "Do you have elevators?" (No.) "Could you assure us that our pickup vehicles can get close to where the paper is stored?" (We have no loading bays. If the paper can't be stored inside, perhaps it could be stored in some sort of shed the trucks could drive up to.) I realized this project was going to be a little more complicated than I had expected.

I had a few questions for the paper contractors. "What kind of equipment will we need to collect the paper?" (Both firms offered to supply collection barrels. As many as we need. Free. They're three feet high and eighteen inches in diameter, with reusable bags inside that hold the paper. Small desk-top collection containers are supplied free to each employee by Ontario's Ministry of the Environment.) "Will there be any cost to us?" (You may need to buy a shed for storing paper outside. There also may be some staff costs to organize the project.) "What is your minimum pickup and how often will you collect?" (One firm had a minimum of a thousand pounds, the other three hundred. Both companies said frequency of pickup would depend on how long it took us to accumulate the minimum.) "Much of our garbage is magazines and newspaper. Will you take those two grades of paper as well as the high-grade paper?" (One company said no, the other said yes.) "Does the paper have to be separated into its various grades before you take it?" (Yes, and we also have to make sure no contaminants get thrown in. Contaminants include any garbage that is not high-grade paper, such as apple cores, Styrofoam cups, pop cans or low-grade paper.) "How can we tell recyclable paper from non-recyclable paper?" (Both companies promised to give us a simple list.) "How much will you pay us for the paper you take?" (One firm offered one hundred and fifty dollars a tonne for high-grade paper only. The other said it would pay less for the high-grade paper to subsidize taking the low-grade stuff. They promised a firm price quote within a few weeks.) "What would you do with the paper you'd buy from us?" (Both companies sell it to paper mills in Ontario and Quebec. There is a shortage of high-grade recycled paper in Canada, and much high-grade paper is imported from the United States.)

After considering both offers, I selected the recycling company that would take our magazines and newsprint as well as our high-grade paper. We'd make a bit less money, but we wanted to recycle as much of our waste paper as possible. It was only a week since Mary Stewart had analysed my garbage. I was pleased with our progress.

Getting Started

It was time to figure out how to collect the paper. I needed the support of CBC management to make the project succeed. I started by calling the head of building services, George MacMillan, who oversees the cleaning and garbage collection staff, and I arranged to meet with him in two weeks. I also called the Ontario Ministry of the Environment, to take them up on their offer of free equipment. Their "paper growers" are cardboard tubes the size of a two-litre ice-cream tub. They sent over a case. I also asked our recycling company, YV Recycling, if they could provide some large collection barrels. They sent over three big cardboard barrels.

On November 22 I talked to George MacMillan. He wasn't optimistic – he pointed out a number of staff and building problems. For example, there was no storage space available in the building. Since the paper would be a fire risk, it would have to be stored outside in a fireproof building. And there wasn't much room outside for a storage building. He also said his janitorial staff would not empty the paper-collection barrels or move the paper to the storage building. But he said he would talk to his superiors. Despite George's hesitations, I decided to press on, and set November 23 as the date *Morningside* would begin collecting paper in the office.

How Do You Like My Tutu?

If I wanted recycling to succeed in the office, I had to convince everyone to take part. We had to recycle as much paper as possible, but we also had to guarantee it was not contaminated with low-grade paper or anything else that didn't belong. Our recycling company warned us that if we sent them contaminated paper they wouldn't pay us for it; if it happened consistently they would stop accepting our paper altogether. Everyone in the office had to know exactly what could and could not go into our collection bins. On November 23, I called a meeting to launch the project. To mark the momentousness of the occasion, I dressed in my recycling cheerleader's costume – a newspaper tutu and newspaper pompons. I began with a hastily improvised theme song, to the tune of "Mickey Mouse": R-E-C/C-Y-C/C-Y-C-L-E! Once I had everyone's attention, I explained the desk-top recycling bins, the paper growers. On the side of each was a list of what paper was recyclable, and what paper was not. Recyclable paper goes into the paper growers; all other paper and garbage should go in the waste basket. Desk-top bins were to be emptied into one of the two central collection barrels in the office.

I explained that we couldn't recycle fax paper, carbon paper, phone books, envelopes with windows or sticky rubberized glue on their labels, file folders and envelopes with plasticized coatings. Nor could we recycle our newspapers and magazines, since we had nowhere to store them.

A lot of little questions followed. "What do we do about paper clips or staples?" (I asked our recycling company; they said paper clips and staples didn't have to be removed.) "What about the

sticky part of our memo pads? That glue seems to be rubberized."
(Perhaps you could tear off the sticky part before tossing the paper
in the recycling bin.) "I get a lot of mail. Do I have to sort through
all of it and separate everything?" (No, just do what you can.
Recycling shouldn't be a burden.) "What are we going to do with
the money we make on this?" (I don't know. It won't be a huge
amount – around fifty dollars a tonne for the paper. Maybe it will
go back to the CBC, or perhaps we could give it to charity.) "When
is our first pickup?" (As soon as we collect three hundred pounds.)

My newspaper tutu fell apart, but otherwise the launch went
well. Everyone took a paper grower, and by the end of the day I
could see paper in almost every one.

Running the Bureaucratic Gauntlet

In the next few weeks, I continued my efforts to get CBC's management to back the recycling plan. Meanwhile, word of our
efforts began to spread through the building. People came around
to ask when they could start to recycle. I told them the project
would include the whole building once we'd worked out the problems of storage and movement of paper. We were diverting so
much paper from our waste baskets to the recycling barrels that
our cleaning lady noticed the difference. She asked, "Why is there
so much less garbage in your waste baskets? Is someone else doing
my job when I'm not here?"

In mid-December I was invited to attend a meeting of the executive producers of all the current affairs programs produced in our
building. They were curious about what we were doing, and they
wanted to take part. They voted unanimously to support the
enlargement of the project to the whole building. Also in mid-
December I met with the CBC's director of network resources,
Walter Unger. He's George MacMillan's boss.

I told him I thought we should recycle on moral grounds – CBC
should be doing more than talking about environmental responsibility; we should be demonstrating it by our actions. I argued, too,

that recycling was good business. It costs CBC about eighty dollars to send a tonne of garbage to a landfill site. The waste-paper contractor would pay us fifty dollars a tonne for our high-grade paper. So for every tonne we don't throw in the garbage we save one hundred and thirty dollars. I also hoped the janitorial staff could move the recycled paper within the building. Before recycling, the cleaning staff handled all the garbage in the building. After recycling they could still handle it, since the weight of the garbage would not change – it would simply be sorted into two bags.

Walter Unger wasn't convinced. He thought it sounded like more work for the cleaners. He was also worried about where we'd store the paper. He knew we had no room inside the building. I suggested an outdoor storage shed. Mr. Unger said he didn't think there was room for it, but he would agree if the director of engineering, Dave Currie, also agreed.

I called Dave Currie. He told me he thought a storage shed outside the building might create traffic problems or become a fire risk. He said I should talk with Kel Lack, the manager of radio technical operations.

Just before Christmas, an official quote arrived from YV Recycling. They promised to pay us ten dollars a tonne for newsprint and magazines and fifty dollars a tonne for high-grade paper.

On January 6, 1989, YV Recycling picked up our first load of paper – about two hundred and fifty pounds. (The sixteen people at *Morningside* had collected the two hundred and fifty pounds in six weeks. Mary Stewart's estimate of half a pound a day was right on the money.) Our paper earned us the grand sum of $6.25.

On January 18, I met with Kel Lack, the manager of radio operations. (Kel was the fifth level of bureaucracy to whom I had made my pitch. I was beginning to feel like a salesman.) Kel didn't want the recycling project to cost CBC any money or increase the workload of an already bare-bones cleaning staff. He said he would give it his blessing, providing I could work out details with George MacMillan, the head of property services.

The Buck Stops

On February 22, 1989, I had come full circle. George was the first person I had talked to in the bureaucracy; here I was meeting him again three months later. This time George had the authority to give us the green light. Under what conditions would he approve a recycling program in the radio building?

George said a recycling program had been tried in the radio building in the early 1980s. It was set up by a fellow named Stan Fryer, who had a lot of enthusiasm for recycling. Stan had convinced most of the people in the building to save their newspaper for recycling. Lots of paper was collected, but before long Stan ran into the problem we were encountering – there was no storage space for the paper. It began to pile up in the hallways and closets.

The fire marshall intervened and insisted the paper be stored more safely. It was piled outside the building. Vandals set it afire three times. Recycling had become a headache for the property manager, but the rest of the staff were still enthusiastic. A lot of paper was being recycled, and money was being raised. The recyclers celebrated their success by planting a tree they bought with the money they raised selling the paper.

As George described it, almost immediately after the tree-planting celebration, the project began to falter. The price paid for newsprint fell, and the paper contractor no longer wanted CBC's paper. The staff continued to collect paper, and the paper began to pile up. Exits were jammed with it. Broom closets were piled to the ceiling with it. Stan Fryer lost interest, and George MacMillan was left with tonnes of paper no one wanted. I began to understand why CBC management was hesitant about my project.

In answer to my question about the conditions under which he would permit a recycling project, George said:

1. Do not add to the work-load of existing staff. The contents of office garbage cans are collected in huge bags at the top of the stairwells and carried down by the cleaning staff. George told

me his staff was willing to haul our bags of recycled paper down the stairs if we would muster our bags at the top of the stairs.

2. The paper must be stored neatly outside the building in a fireproof, locked storage shed. George said he would provide a place for the shed.

3. The paper contractor must pick up the paper regularly. George also wanted their assurance that the pickup would not be affected by fluctuating paper prices.

4. People involved in the recycling project must sustain the program. George looked at me and said, "What is going to happen to this project when you leave *Morningside*? I'll still be here as director of property services. You could be at another program or in another city. Who'll run the project when you're gone?"

I have yet to be able to answer all those questions adequately, but I think the most troubling one is the last. Where does the commitment come from, so an institution can change? I know our staff at *Morningside* is still diligently tearing sticky tops off their memos before tossing the memos in the recycling bin. Recycling has become a habit in our office, and every day or so I hear someone gently remind a co-worker that envelopes with Scotch tape on them can't be recycled.

George's questions crystallized for me the problems facing people who want to start a recycling project in the work-place. Employee goodwill and energy are there to be tapped, but employees alone can't carry the full weight of and responsibility for maintaining such projects. How do we get our employers to re-evaluate and change their waste-management practices, especially when those practices seem on the surface to be working well? How do we get them to start up and pay for a new environmental ethic? As Peter reminded us, "We have to change the way we behave, personally, socially and politically, if we are going to turn this thing around."

Terry MacLeod
Toronto

Five basic ingredients serve as the building blocks for most home cleaning needs:

Baking Soda: Cleans and deodorizes. Softens water to increase sudsing and cleaning power of soap. Good scouring powder.

Borax: Cleans and deodorizes. Excellent disinfectant. Softens water. Available in laundry section of grocery store.

Soap: Biodegrades safely and completely and is non-toxic. Available in grocery stores and health food stores. Sold as liquid, flakes, powder, or in bars. Bars can be grated to dissolve more easily in hot water. Insist on soap without synthetic scents, colours, or other additives. Synthetic detergents cause more poisonings than any other household product. Even phosphate-free, biodegradable laundry detergent contributes to water pollution.

Washing Soda: Cuts grease and removes stains. Disinfects. Softens water. Available in laundry section of grocery store or in pure form from chemical supply houses as "sodium carbonate."

White Vinegar: Cuts grease and freshens.

Use the simplest, mildest formula that will get the job done. First try warm water mixed with soap (or vinegar if the surface will show spots), adding vinegar, borax, washing soda, or baking soda if needed.

Commercial air fresheners work by masking smells, coating nasal passages, and deadening nerves to diminish sense of smell. Instead:

- find sources of odours and eliminate them;
- keep house and closets clean and well-ventilated;
- grow lots of houseplants;
- to absorb odours, place two to four tablespoons baking soda or vinegar in small bowls in refrigerator and around house, and pour half a cup of baking soda in bottom of trash can;
- for natural fragrance, boil sweet herbs and spices.

All-purpose Cleaner: Mix two teaspoons borax and one teaspoon soap in a quart of water for a cleaner you can store in a spray bottle.

Ammonia: Use ammonia only when other cleansers won't do the trick. Ammonia cuts heavy grease and grime, but can be dangerous. Fumes irritate eyes and lungs and can be harmful to people with respiratory problems. Always provide good ventilation. Never mix ammonia with bleach or commercial cleansers – deadly fumes may form.

Disinfectant: For a hospital-quality disinfectant, use a quarter cup of borax dissolved in half a gallon of hot water. Keeping surfaces clean and dry reduces the need for disinfectants.

Scouring Powder: If available, buy a powder without chlorine, colours, detergents, or talc; or scrub with a sponge or firm-bristled brush, soap, and one of the following: borax, baking soda, or table salt.

Carpets: Remove stains promptly by scraping up solids and blotting liquids; follow by dabbing with a solution of water and vinegar. Sponge with clean water and blot dry. For getting rid of odours and greasy soil, mix two parts corn meal with one part borax, sprinkle liberally, leave one hour, and vacuum. Using doormats or removing shoes at the door will lessen the need for cleaning. (Again, as a last resort, a solution of water and ammonia can be used; if used, neutralize spot with weak vinegar solution.)

Dishes: Use liquid soap or powdered soap. For tougher jobs, add two or three teaspoons vinegar. In automatic dishwashers, use equal parts borax and washing soda, increasing the proportion of soda if your water is hard. Standard "dishwashing liquids" are detergents designed to create unnecessary suds.

Drains: Again, prevention is top priority. Some rules-of-thumb: never pour grease down a drain, always use a drain sieve or hair trap, and clean metal screen or stopper mechanism regularly. If necessary, remove hair with a piece of a coat hanger. Once a week, as routine maintenance, plug overflow drain with wet rag, pour a quarter cup of baking soda down drain, follow with half a cup of vinegar and close drain tightly until fizzing stops. Flush with a gallon of boiling water. If flow slows or stops, plug overflow drain, dissolve a pound of washing soda in three gallons of boiling water, pour down drain and use a plunger with petroleum jelly on its rim for a good seal. If clog persists, flush drain with same formula and use a plumber's snake instead of a plunger.

Ovens: Prevention is top priority. Avoid over-filling pans, scrape up spills as soon as food is cool enough to handle, and put a cookie sheet or a piece of foil on bottom rack when baking pies. When clean-up is needed, use steel wool and washing soda with a small amount of water. (As a last resort for particularly bad grime, use half a cup of ammonia dissolved in a gallon of hot water for scrubbing; provide plenty of ventilation.)

Tub, Tile and Toilet: Scrub with sponge or firm-bristled brush, using powdered soap and a scouring powder of baking soda, borax or table salt. Use undiluted vinegar to loosen lime deposits.

Windows and Mirrors: For routine cleaning, use three tablespoons vinegar with a quart of warm water. If glass is particularly dirty, first wash with warm soapy water.

When making the initial switch from a detergent to a soap laundry cleaner, wash items once with washing soda only. This will eliminate detergent residues which might otherwise react with soap to cause a yellowing of fabrics.

Bleach: Substitute half a cup of borax per wash-load to whiten whites and brighten colours. If needed, occasionally use powdered, non-chlorine bleach.

Detergent: Add a third of a cup of washing soda to water before placing clothes in machine and substitute soap flakes or powder for detergent. Add half a cup of borax for additional cleaning power. If you have "hard" water, use a phosphate-free detergent.

Dry-Cleaning: Buy items you can wash or clean on your own. Most dry-cleaning solvents, such as perchloroethylene, are toxic. If you must dry-clean, air clothing out thoroughly before bringing indoors. Many garments whose labels specify "dry-clean only" can be safely handwashed using milk soap or vinegar.

Fabric Softener: Add a cup of vinegar or a quarter cup of baking soda during final rinse. To reduce static cling in tumble dried synthetics, dampen hands when folding or line dry instead.

Presoak: Soak heavily soiled items in warm water with half a cup of washing soda for thirty minutes. Rub soiled areas with liquid soap.

Spray Starch: Dissolve two tablespoons cornstarch in a pint of cold water in spray bottle. Shake before each use. For delicate fabrics, dissolve one package unflavored gelatine; or add two tablespoons granulated sugar to two cups hot water. Dip corner of fabric into solution to test; if fabric becomes sticky when dry, add more water.

Stain Remover: Take immediate action! Soak spot in cool water at once and sponge away as much of stain as possible. Treat remaining stain as outlined below, observing these additional rules: test remedy on hidden area to make sure fabric isn't harmed; repeat remedy if necessary; air dry fabric, since dryer heat can "set" some stains permanently.

    Blood: Soak in cold water thirty minutes, rub with soap, rinse in cold water. If stain persists, put a few drops of ammonia on stain, rub with soap, rinse. If necessary, wash with borax.

    Chocolate and Coffee: Soak in cold water, rub with soap and a mild borax solution, rinse. Wash in water as hot as fabric can tolerate.

    Fruit and Wine: Soak in cold water thirty minutes, rub soap into remaining stain and wash in water as hot as fabric will stand. Bleach with lemon juice and sunlight if needed.

    Grass: Rub with glycerine (available in drug stores), let stand one hour, wash.

    Grease: Pour boiling water on white cottons, rub with solution of washing soda in water. For other materials, blot with towel, dampen stain, rub with soap and baking soda. Wash in water as hot as possible, using extra soap.

    Ink: For ballpoint stains, sponge with rubbing alcohol, rub with soap, rinse, wash. For felt-tip stains, rub with soap, rinse, wash.

Lipstick: Rub with cold cream or shortening to dissolve colour, rinse area with solution of washing soda in warm water to remove grease. Wash in soapy water as hot as fabric will stand.

Mildew: Wash with soap and water. Rinse well and dry in sun. If spot remains, apply lemon juice, rub with salt, dry in sun, wash.

Perspiration: Rub with solution of vinegar or lemon juice in water.

Rust: Saturate with lemon juice, rub with salt. Place in direct sunlight until dry, then wash.

Soiled Diapers: Presoak in three tablespoons baking soda dissolved in warm water.

Urine: Rub with solution of baking soda in water, rinse in warm water, and wash.

Bath and Hand Soap: Use soaps without artificial scents or colours.

Deodorant and Antiperspirant: To minimize body odours, apply coconut oil, baking soda, or baking soda mixed with corn starch.

Hair Conditioner: For normal hair, saturate hair with olive, sesame, or corn oil, wrap head in very hot, damp towels for twenty minutes, and shampoo. For dry hair, mix a quarter cup of honey and a cup of olive oil, and warm. Apply two tablespoons to scalp and massage. Cover head with very hot damp towel for ten minutes, then shampoo. For treating split ends, massage hair and ends with warm olive or avocado oil and wrap head in towel for eight to twelve hours. Wash with shampoo to which one egg yolk has been added, and rinse with diluted vinegar.

Hair Shampoo: (a) one cup liquid castile soap with a quarter cup olive, avocado, or almond oil and half a cup distilled water; or (b) liquid castile soap diluted in an equal amount of water.

Hair Spray: Use hair styles that don't require sprays; or chop a lemon and boil in two cups of water until volume is reduced to half. Cool and strain. Refrigerate in a spray bottle.

Insect Repellent: Apply very small amounts of citronella oil.

Medications: Follow your doctor's advice for *all* medications. But for diseases and toxic pollutants alike, "An ounce of prevention is worth a pound of cure." The formula is familiar and it works – clean, whole foods, fresh air, exercise, laughter, rest, etc. Many people find folk medicine and herbal cures at least as effective for some diseases as complex drugs.

Mouthwash: Dissolve a teaspoon of baking soda in a glass of water, or a teaspoon of salt in a glass of warm water; or use sage, birch, or mint tea.

Nail Polish: Powdered, dried henna (the leaf of an Asian tree) is available in several colours. Combine colours to produce desired shade. Mix a quarter of a teaspoon with water to make a paste. Rub into nails, allow to dry, then buff.

Perfume: Buy "natural" rather than "synthetic" or "artificial" oils. Use very small amounts. Essential oils can be substituted.

Shaving Cream: Use a thin lather of plain soap.

Suntan Lotion: Sesame oil acts as moisturizer and sunscreen. Also try cocoa butter, or a mixture of olive oil and cider vinegar.

Toothpaste: Use plain baking soda or baking soda mixed with peppermint extract or your favourite essential oil or extract.

Baby and Body Powder: Substitute corn starch.

Baby Oil: Substitute vegetable oil.

Diapers: Use cotton diapers rather than disposables. Diaper services usually cost no more than disposable diapers.

Greenpeace
Toronto

✉ I never thought I'd see the day when I wanted other people to know about the goings-on in my bathroom. I am, however, concerned that many of us are unknowingly contributing to the contamination of our drinking water by what we pour down our toilets and sinks, and so I thought I'd tell you about a recent success of mine.

Last Saturday, as I descended upon the bathroom, scrub-brush and sponge in hand, I had with me a bucket half full of a baking soda, water and vinegar mixture. I'm happy to say that the tub, sink and toilet came through it all looking spiffy as ever. The baking soda was not only abrasive enough, it lasted longer on the sponge! At a time when we seem to have accepted that lakes and rivers unfit for swimming and drinking are the price we have to pay for super-clean bathrooms, I came away feeling satisfied, knowing that I had done the job just as effectively without having resorted to the toxic stuff.

Alain Cloutier
Ottawa

✉ I've been cleaning with vinegar and water and newspapers for years. However, my husband, being the terrific guy he is, has been cleaning the windows for the past few years. He prefers Glass Plus. I must tell you this stuff leaves a kind of greasy film on the glass if you look at the window with the sun shining full on it. Vinegar and water does not do this.

However, if Frank wants to clean the windows with this stuff—fine. I'm lazy enough that I let him. Do I complain about the streaks? No, I just say how much I appreciate him. Aren't I lucky?

Jean Greenough
Edmonton

✉ Not you, too! This week, you're looking in somebody's refrigerator, next week you're going to poke under the sinks? Well, if our house is any example, you'll find:

• a catch-bag of burnables with which we start the wood heater each chilly day
• a small box in the pantry for clean glass to go to the recycling depot

- a bright red compost catcher with a red lid situated proudly beside the front door
- one big yellow plastic garbage bag slouching in a corner of the utility room to collect the worst garbage of all: unsolicited and unburnable junk mail, plus a few bent nails and about twenty tin cans per year.

Many weekdays, our mail brings, unasked and unwanted, as much as five hundred grams of bulk, junk and unsolicited mail. Environment ministries talk (defensively) about each member of the public "generating" tremendous quantities of garbage. Generate, hell no; it's dumped on us, and we must collect and haul it away somewhere. Blanket mailings are encouraged by the post office. To my mind there's a social crime involved here: destroying trees to create unwanted multicoloured toxic unburnable advertising, which the public is forced to collect and, in my case, haul in my car some thirty miles to the nearest authorized public dump. There is no dump on Pender Island.

As well, two of life's simple joys are in jeopardy if I am sincere in trying to stop commercial production of true garbage:

- a gift of money to a charitable cause initiates a deluge of mail about related causes, until it seems as if my gift has simply generated garbage instead of aid;
- from out of any newspaper or periodical I subscribe to drops a wad of multicoloured toxic ads about things I don't want. Periodicals sell their subscription lists, so I am swamped with unrelated toxic glossy unburnable and uncompostable trash.

The worst garbage and pollution is commercially based and government-approved, usually over the protests of the public.

Mary Mackie
Pender Island, British Columbia

✉ Your recent discussion about organic gardening brought to mind my first attempt at organic pest control.

About seven years ago I decided that ladybugs were the solution to my garden's aphid problem. I found a store that sold such things. I went down and bought two sacks of ladybugs and some organic rose dust. As a bonus, the clerk included a praying-mantis nest. He retrieved this walnut-sized, greyish brown ball from a freezer in the back and told me to hang it in a tree. What he didn't tell me was that this was to be done immediately.

I arrived home that evening to find a plague of baby praying mantis all over my bedroom walls. The heat of the upstairs room where I had left my purchases earlier in the day had thawed the nest and the eggs had hatched. What followed was not pretty. Off came my sandal. The slaughter lasted twenty minutes, the clean-up considerably longer.

Since then I have enjoyed varying degrees of success using organic gardening techniques, although the grim memory of that murderous episode will no doubt haunt me forever.

Mary Nicol
Edmonton

✉ Recycling is much more than changing the identity of old newspapers, tin cans and pop bottles. It is not something new under the sun. For years, recycling was the accepted practice in most families.

I was raised on recycled spuds, onions, turnips and ground roast beef. On a Saturday night warmed-up leftovers appeared on our table as "shepherd's pie." My mother called variations on this theme "casserole."

Granny was an expert at recycling Robin Hood flour sacks. With a few snips of her scissors and with needle and thread, the sacks blossomed into sturdy blouses, bloomers, aprons and dish towels.

Granny also unravelled well-worn sweaters and reknit them into scarves, socks and mittens. Odds and ends became patchwork quilts. I still trip over Granny's hooked rugs recycled from rags, remnants and hand-me-downs.

In our culture, recycling is a fact of life. Political parties are reborn with new labels, platforms and leaders. Ministers of the Gospel resuscitate old sermons. TV is plugged up with reruns. Year after year teachers recycle their favourite jokes.

Chunks of my own writing are often born again, thanks to fresh coats of adjectives, sanded-down phrases, gingerbread titles. (Academics call this process "poetic licence.")

Sometimes it is easier to recycle old ideas than to explore new ones. Fuddy-duddies, stodges and old fogies like to stick to the tried and true, not venture out on a high wire.

But wait! Hold everything!

Do I not know many old-timers who have minds and hearts fresh and pristine as daisies or seniors who are as lively as young trout jumping in mountain streams?

Of course I do.

I have sat around our fireplace for hours listening to old folk recycle their memoirs. Grim hardships and heart-break are dismissed with a smile. Blizzards and snowstorms of the past become everyday adventures. Forgotten love affairs blossom like a rose garden.

And best of all, seasoned truths, time-worn from another age, rekindle, come alive. Virtues like endurance, trust and good deeds burn once again with a secret flame.

Sam Roddan
Surrey, British Columbia

THE DUMB AND THE NOT-SO-DUMB

Are cows stupid?
I asked that question on *Morningside* once – I've long forgotten the context – and someone in the CBC's promotion department used a tape clip of it in a television commercial. Now, wherever I go (see Rose Robart's letter in this chapter), people, some of whom don't even know the radio program, fling it back at me.

I don't know how we first got into the cow business. Stuart McLean, my Monday partner, once presented a poignant portrait of the Jersey, and that's what inspired at least the first few letters in this chapter. Others came in response to those letters, and, as usual, later writers broadened the subject to include their thoughts on all kinds of animals.

So: Are cows stupid?

Who knows? Some of them are blue, of course. But that's another chapter.

✉ Some of my early years were spent on my grandparents' farm. I attended the rural school where it was compulsory to study agriculture instead of the domestic science I had taken in my city school. I guess the rural school system thought farm girls learned all their household science at home. I enjoyed agriculture and at one time could reel off the names of most of the breeds of farm animals and identify them by sight. I knew the Jersey cow was "la crème de la crème" of milk cows. While driving through the country, I can still remember exclaiming when we saw a herd of Jersey cows in a pasture, "They must belong to a rich farmer!"

So, when my husband and I moved to the country at one point during the Great Depression, and had to rely on our green thumbs and my slight knowledge of farm life to help us get by, I yearned for a Jersey cow. One day my husband attended a sale, and to my joy, he came home with Goldie. She was the prettiest, most gentle little tawny-coloured animal you ever did see. She was a bit smaller than the average Jersey cow – maybe that is why my husband could afford to buy her. She turned out to be worth her weight in gold – in golden butter, and of course gallons of rich creamy milk she produced to make the butter. I knew how to make butter, because one of my Saturday jobs on the farm had been to help churn the butter, and then I would watch, fascinated, as my grandmother processed the golden lumps when the butter had reached the set stage.

We expected Goldie to supply us with lots of milk, cream and butter with perhaps a little left over to exchange for groceries. To our astonishment and deep appreciation, Goldie outdid herself. I could not believe that one dainty little Jersey could be the source of so much butter. Soon, I had regular town customers for my surplus butter, and we had lots of rich milk, cream and buttermilk – we even had skim milk to feed to a pair of little pigs we were raising. That little Jersey cow really did her part in helping us to beat the Depression. We later sold Goldie to an eager farmer when we decided to try city life again.

Jeanne Cuthbert Miller
Revelstoke, British Columbia

✉ Since I was brought up in Ayrshire, the only cow I knew as a kid was the big splotchy, brown and white Ayrshire cow, so when we came out here six years ago with the intention of farming, that's what I had in mind. My wife, however, had other thoughts, and we ended up with Jerseys. What a blessing they have been. All of our creatures have been given St. Trinian's type names – Eunice, Millicent, Josephine and the like – but the star of them all has been Stella, our remaining milk cow.

She has been with us for almost five years now. She knows her name and will come bouncing up to you when you call her. Once a farmer wanted to borrow her for a while and came to pick her up when she was standing in the barnyard among half a dozen other animals. I opened the door and called her. She raised her head, acknowledged me and then trotted into the barn. You should have seen the farmer's face as he confessed that he couldn't get his dog to do that.

We have been having some trouble getting her bred by AI lately, so I walked her down to the neighbour's and had his bull have a go at her. It didn't take so the next time she was in heat she hopped over the fence and trotted down the road herself. We didn't actually see her but the neighbour did and he said you would have sworn she was on a leash. To bring her back, all I had to do was put my hand on her collar and walk beside her. The fence by the way is electric but you don't really need to have the current on. Jerseys know their place.

There is a downside to Jerseys, too: what do you do with them when, for whatever reason, they no longer do their thing? After all, you wouldn't send Rover to the abattoir just because he was no longer any good as a gun dog. How can you do that to a creature who comes over to see what you are doing when you go into her pasture and is just as likely to stick her neck out for you to scratch at the same time? What the world really needs is a good retirement home for Jersey cows.

Max Wolfe
Jemseg, New Brunswick

✉ I am surprised that you didn't hear what the people of this country were trying to tell you about Jersey cows. Jersey cows are akin to motherhood. I dare say that there isn't a farm family in the world who could not regale the wonders of the Jersey cow, or one of her cousins. For instance, there are stories about families who survived the Depression only with the aid of the dear old family cow who nourished the children with her rich milk. The cream that was skimmed from the milk was sold or bartered, as was the butter and cheese. When I was a boy we had many cows at our farm, but our favourite was a mongrel black Jersey who was our pet. She would adopt any orphaned calf that Dad would bring home from the auction barn or wherever, or that the big Holstein had rejected (she would kick any calf that was not hers).

When I grew up and left home, Mother sold all the cows. She could not part with the black Jersey, however, even after the fences had fallen down and the old black cow had wandered down the road to visit with the neighbours' cows. But she was always at the barn to be milked at six o'clock, and she always watched for the traffic on the road and would never dash out in front of an oncoming car. Soon she was the envy of every farmer in the country.

Later I met one old-timer who was aghast that a mink rancher should even suggest that he sell his faithful old cow for mink feed. The poor old cow was next to death's doorstep: she was crippled with rheumatism and had bad feet and only half of her teeth, but she still had a calf every spring and gave all the milk that her poor old body could produce. The distraught elderly rancher told me – his eyes full of tears – that I could no sooner sell that cow than I could sell my own mother because the cow had fed my children and kept me when I had had nothing else. The old cow seemed to know we were talking about her, for she came up to the rancher to have her ears scratched and be petted. "See," said the old-timer, "she gives so much and all she asks for is a little love."

When the black Jersey dies I will bury her on a nearby hill, and she will have a gravestone to tell the world of her many virtues.

Did you ever hear the expression "bum as a cow"? Have you ever had a cow (and I mean a thousand-pound cow!) standing on your foot, nonchalantly chewing on a straw, oblivious to all your yelling and screaming as you try to dislodge her? Do you believe she does not know she is causing you excruciating pain? Not on your life!

When I was a young boy I milked so many cows I had wrists and forearms like Popeye, and I could write a book on the experiences I've had with bovines in general. Every cow has her own personality; some are downright vicious, and others are so gentle it makes you wonder if they belong to the same family. When I was eleven or twelve, we had one big Holstein that would give eighty pounds of milk a day, and when she freshened we sometimes had to milk her three times a day, because she would stand at the barn door and bawl her head off as the milk streamed from her overburdened udder. Her udder was so tender she would kick you at a mere touch, and no amount of coaxing could gentle her. This cow was almost twice the size of a Jersey, and she could kick like a mule. The only way we (my mother and father and I) could milk her was to tie her head and feet. My father finally sold her for a very good dollar, as she was such a champion milker, but the poor man who bought her did not find out she was also a champion kicker until he got her home.

Vic Daradick
High Level, Alberta

An ancient legend in Jersey says that the Jersey cow was once a form of fairy deer brought to the island by the ancient Celts.

Jersey cows are by law the only breed allowed on the island today, although there is much pressure to allow other breeds in. Unfortunately, as the island has become more and more of a tax haven and centre of finance, fewer farmers can afford to keep the beautiful animals.

I don't see many Jerseys in Saskatchewan. But even though I've lived in Canada for twenty years, the sight of one still makes me homesick.

Antoinette Hérivel-Sweetman
Qu'Appelle, Saskatchewan

✉ We were living in Wembley at the outbreak of the Second World War. We had to move out into the country, and a friend of my father's offered us a small brick building in the field next to his home. My father had to do a little work to make it habitable. Also sharing the field was a ramshackle old shed and a pretty pale brown cow. The brick building had been intended as a grand new cow shed, but as we were desperate it was decided that Jennifer the Jersey could make do for the duration of the war with her old abode. So, with minimum alterations, such as a few windows and partitions, we moved in and, in honour of the ousted cow, named it Jennifer Cottage.

We were told we could make ourselves a garden in the field, and Dad duly fenced us off from the cow with a good strong barbed-wire fence and set about planting vegetables and so on. Jennifer was very curious and spent her time leaning over the wire watching us and trying to eat the grass on our side. She had the most gorgeous liquid-brown eyes and long, long eyelashes, and she loved to have her nose stroked. I used to watch her being milked and eventually learned how to do it, too, though I could never get the smooth, steady rhythm of her owner. But, oh, the joy of that warm milk straight out of the pail and the thick yellow cream that we ladled over cereals and fruit! Time went by and gradually Dad added embellishments to Jennifer Cottage, such as a covered walk-way between the house and the barbed wire so that my mother had a place to hang her washing without getting mud all over her feet. There were no such niceties as tumble dryers in those days.

One day she went to bring the washing back in and found the line broken and several garments missing. Certainly, it was wartime and clothes were hard to come by, but it seemed incredible that anyone would actually steal our bits and pieces. Then Jennifer became ill and listless. Her milk yield dropped away and she lay looking pathetic. The vet was called. Sad to say, Jennifer died. As it was all so sudden, the vet decided on a post-mortem. There, inside the cow, was the answer to the missing washing. Even with her several stomachs, Jennifer had not been able to digest Dad's pyjamas, several buttons, assorted clothes pegs and a length of washing line. Jennifer had finally found something more interesting than grass on our side of the fence.

Sarita Berges
Oakville, Ontario

✉ Back in the forties, we had to leave the farm for family health reasons. Dad, however, used to buy the odd cow here and there and take it to his brother-in-law's to raise on a shared basis. In 1948 we were able to return to farming and so brought these cattle and some of their offspring home.

One of these cows was the "old Jersey" as we called her. She was small and past the age of being pretty and didn't give a lot of milk, but like all of her breed the milk was very rich. I don't know how many pounds of butter we made to sell besides what we – a family of six – used plus the milk we drank and the cream we used on puddings and pies.

Before we got her she had been beaten, more than once I imagine, and so she was very nervous and timid.

One fall day in 1953 or 1954 Dad said, "I guess the old Jersey's had it. I don't know if she'll have any more calves or not." We children asked him if he was going to ship her away. "No," he said, "she can just stay around here till she dies. She's been such a good old pet I wouldn't have the heart to send her away." As near as we knew she was about seventeen years old then. Well, she did have a calf the next spring but she never seemed to really recover after that.

One Sunday morning we did the chores and put the cows out

to the pasture and went to church. When we came home she was standing by the gate wanting to come home. "Something's wrong," my father said. "Maybe she's coming to the barn to die." We let her through the gate and followed her home. We drove into the yard and left her walking up the lane to the barn. Then we quickly changed our clothes and ran out to the barn. The cow was standing at the corral gate. Dad opened the gate but she just stood there a minute and then lay down. A minute or so later she rolled over on her side and then died. There was no thrashing around or anything: she just shut her eyes and let out a big sigh. I don't remember that we were particularly sad or upset. We just thought how good it was that she had died so peacefully at home. I guess she'd been happy.

Mavis Johnston
Hanna, Alberta

✉ A few years ago, I watched a Jersey bullock, whose head came up to my chest, being loaded onto a truck at the Ontario Veterinary College. Five men with sour expressions stood around the usual deer-faced, tawny-coated, slender-legged beauty. The bull lay stubbornly on the floor. I made the same sort of drooling, sentimental remarks your letters have been making, and the sour faces turned to me. I was given to understand that among dairy bulls, which are not known for their docility, Jerseys are the worst: nasty, cross, tricky, temperamental, unpredictable and just plain mean.

It took the five men two hours to load the little bull onto the truck. His eyes never held anything but a melting, soulful expression, but none of the men escaped being kicked, butted or trodden on.

Sarah Mainguy
Morristown, Ontario

✉ During one vacation our family travelled through dairy country. My four children had never tasted that wonderfully creamy, pale yellow treat called Jersey milk, and I promised to try to get some for them. We stopped in a small town and went into an equally small grocery store, where I asked the lady if she had any Jersey milk, or knew where I could buy some. She disappeared behind a curtain that separated the store from the living quarters, and had a discussion with several people there. When she returned to the counter, she told me with innocent sincerity, "No, we don't have any Jersey milk. I just have Jersey Nut." She then handed me a chocolate bar! I stifled my laughter, paid for the bar and went out to face a puzzled family, waiting in the car.

Diane Armstrong
South Porcupine, Ontario

✉ the greatest insult
offered me
before i married down
was young swain stuttering
you are like a . . .
like a jersey cow

having lived farm years
encountered many a cow
i would know i was
blue ribbon class
if called a jersey now

Eileen Burnett
Milner Ridge, Manitoba

✉ You may think me rather bovine but I firmly believe our Holsteins are as smart as any Jerseys. It is too much a reflection on

96

my family, having raised this herd for sixty years, to admit otherwise. In the past years our cows have gone to Spain, Venezuela and the United States to represent this country. From their milk we enjoy butter and whipped cream aplenty.

I've seen my cows open gates by unhooking the inside latch with the tips of their tongue. They know when it is Sunday, our day off, that it's time to break the fence. With a mere glance from the corner of an eye they can be deadly accurate at putting their tail in one's face.

Although they are not smart in human terms, I'll match my cows to Jerseys any day.

Bob and Susan Halliday
Sarnia, Ontario

✉ There was a certain Guernsey cow we owned when I was a small child many years ago. This beast had as much curiosity as the proverbial cat, though the results were not quite as disastrous. It was in this wise:

The weather had been excessively hot and Mother had taken to doing the family wash out on the porch, which was on the shady side of the house. This was the old tub and scrub-board method, before electricity came to the farms. Having finished for the day, Mother went into the kitchen to prepare the noon meal, leaving the heavy tubs for my father to empty when he came home for dinner.

Now it chanced that the cows came ambling along the lane on their way back from the creek where they had gone for a drink of water, and this most curious of cows just had to have a closer look at the arrangement of tubs on the porch. It was at this point that Mother happened to look out the window, and there was the Guernsey cow, nearly up on the porch and dripping clouds of soap bubbles from her mouth. She had tongued down the bar of Sunlight soap left on the ledge of the scrub board! Mother didn't know that and thought our best cow was having some kind of fit. When it dawned on her what had really happened, she was both furious and worried. What would that much soap do to the poor cow's insides? Dad made the obvious remark, but he watched her closely for a few days. She was not hard to track, I can tell you!

She seemed, after all, to suffer no permanent damage, but her milk was no good for several days, having a distinctly soapy flavour. And I wouldn't be surprised if, as she lay ruminating after the manner of all cows, she didn't think to herself, "Gee, I wish I hadn't eaten that."

A few months later, Mother had a failure with a batch of bread. The yeast, being stale, did not work, and Mother, in disgust at the waste, dumped the glutinous mass out in the henyard for the chickens to pick at. You guessed it. Along came that same Guernsey and proceeded to lap up this interesting-looking treat. My young brother was nearly hysterical with laughter as he recounted how heroically the cow tried to get the spongy, jelly-like substance into her mouth. Great swags of dough hung from her lips and her tongue worked furiously trying to manage what must have resembled a monstrous wad of bubble gum. Mother and Dad were not so amused, fearing the effects of such an eruptive substance, but the cow's stomach proved equal to the task, and no harm was done.

Had I more time I could tell you about the pig that ate the lace curtains, but I will spare you that!

Colleen Ray
Sault Ste. Marie, Ontario

✉ I came from a long line of singers. Not the kind that make records but the kind that don't. My mother sang at the clothesline, my grandmother sang over the washboard, I sing on my bicycle or while washing dishes or just walking along the road.

A few years ago I left Montreal for farm life in northern Alberta. One of the numerous thrills was milking old Rosie (no relation) the cow. Every day I'd haul two buckets into the barn: one for milkin', one for sittin' on. Naturally, I'd sing my heart out. And you know what? The old dear loved it. She'd sway this way and that to the rhythm, her eyes half closed while she chewed her cud. It was the one time of the day when I was at perfect peace, with myself, with Rosie, and with the world.

But that all changed the day I started yodelling. I yodelled all the yodelling songs I knew, and I wasn't half bad, either. At least *I* thought so. But Rosie had other notions. Had I been more experienced I would have seen it coming, but being fresh from the city . . .

Just as I got underway with the milking and the yodelling, Rosie started mooing. Then I noticed her calf–I knew it was hers–lurking outside the barn and mooing back. There was definitely some communication going on between the two but I'll be darned if I could make it out. The cow would moo, then the calf, then the cow, a real sense of urgency in their voices. All the while, the calf was dashing back and forth outside the door, looking in at her mother.

Suddenly, the calf darted into the barn, knocked me head over keister on the straw, and finished milking Rosie the way nature intended. It happened so fast I could only watch in horror as the milk for the day got sucked up by the calf.

When I gained some semblance of composure I burst out laughing. Of course, my pride was bruised more than my hide, but I can't help but take my hat off to the two animals that outfoxed me that morning.

And you ask if *cows* are stupid. Tell me about it.

Rose Robart
Montreal

✉ This is a letter about fowl. Not chickens and eggs, but my one and only rooster, an extremely handsome fellow who went on a walkabout the night of the general election. Ordinarily, he and the hens move from one hen house by night to a large enclosed pen by day – enclosed because of the racoons, who have been known to wipe out an entire flock in one night. (The mink will do this, too.) But the ground in their pen was mud puddly, because of the rain, and always before, when I've taken a chance and let them out, they come hurrying home as soon as dusk falls. So – I let them out and they hung around the yard, eating grass and bugs and the leaves off the beets that remained in the vegetable garden. I could hear them cluck-clucking as I wrote and hear Placido (the rooster) crowing from time to time as is his wont. (I think he celebrates each dawn around the world.)

I went up to vote at the North End Community Hall at 8:00 A.M. I was determined to be the first voter – North Galiano had a ninety-per-cent turnout by the way – and let them out shortly after. At 5:00 P.M. I figured they'd want to go back to their house and so they did – all except the rooster. He refused to budge from the garden and gave me a sound peck when I tried to pick him up. I had to shut the hens up but every hour on the hour I put on my gumboots (eventually gumboots and nightgown and rain jacket) and tried to entice him to bed. It was pouring, I pointed out. Inside the hen house it was dry, with clean straw/hay just changed the day before. No dice. So I told him I was sorry, I hoped he'd find a place to hide for the night and I shut the garden gate. (Not that this would help much. A determined racoon can easily climb a wire fence.) At this point he suddenly flew over the fence – he has never bothered to fly before – and disappeared into the woods.

He didn't come back the next day – or the next – or the next. I put a notice down at the store (notice enclosed), drawing around a cookie cutter to add some graphic design. A picture, as we know, is worth a thousand words. The storekeeper said he had seen him but couldn't get him to come near. But that was on Tuesday. By now, he'd been gone six days. Perhaps, I thought, even with the NDP victory in British Columbia, he felt, given the overall Tory victory, that there was nothing more to crow about. The hens drooped and I was barnacled with guilt, one of those bleeding hearts who manages to kill with kindness. He was by this time probably the Thanksgiving (U.S.) dinner of an immigrant racoon.

! MISSING !

Lost / STRAYED
grey & white Rooster
with HANDSOME TAIL
PROBABLY RACOONED
by now but who KNOWS?
The hens say "please
COME HOME, ALL IS
FORGIVEN."
phone: 9-3177 (AUDREY)
(REWARD)

Now I have a friend who believes in creative visualization. I don't, but lying in bed on Sunday night I decided to try it. I visualized Placido back in the yard, unmutilated, greeting one of his several dawns. I concentrated with all my might. It was a bit like that old prayer: "Lord, I believe, help Thou my disbelief." Only I didn't believe; I thought creative visualization was just new wine in old bottles – "You can do anything you set your mind to" – which, with rare exceptions, is only true for certain sections of the population.

On Monday morning, I heard a rooster crowing in the garden. I was rushing to the door with a saucepan of grain when the phone rang. My neighbour Dorothy, who likes my hens and rooster, had heard him too. And there he was – bedraggled, thin, minus some feathers but all in one piece.

Now what do you make of that? How I should like to know where he had been, what marvels he had seen, what dangers he had overcome.

I have not decided what to visualize next – my novel, maybe, all done and neatly piled on my desk? A washing machine? 20/20 vision? Peace on Earth?

It isn't only the cat who comes back.

Audrey Thomas
Galiano, British Columbia

✉ It's been a rough year on the animals in the family. Sometimes it makes me wonder if the pain of owning pets is worth having them at all. But I have a hard time envisioning my home life without furry creatures and feathered creatures so I have a feeling that pets will prevail. But like I say, it's been a rough year on the animals in my life.

The first disaster struck when my eight-year-old daughter's hamster, Nibbles, died rather noisily in the middle of a cold dark night. The tragedy stung us all and my wife and I responded in traditional fashion: we bought Sunyata another hamster. Nibbles 2 was only the size of a thumb-nail but the pet-shop owner assured us he'd grow. Since he could squeeze through the finest mesh of bars, he had to stay in a fishbowl until he was large enough for a standard cage. Over the year, Nibbles 2 managed to escape his several homes in Houdini-like fashion, throwing the household into panic and chaos. Once he went AWOL for an entire night, and it wasn't until the morning that a new search revealed him curled up behind the toaster oven in the kitchen, totally unconcerned over the traumas he had caused. There were a few other near disasters, but somehow he managed to survive 1988 unscathed.

I wish I could say the same about my pigeons. The pigeons were bought when the rabbits died of old age. I had raised pigeons as a kid and loved the sight of them careening around in the sky. Our first two new birds were fancy showpieces called trumpeters. They were named Rosa and Gandhi. When I let them out, Gandhi kept getting lost. I had to drive around for hours until I found him, baffled and bedraggled, in a neighbour's yard. Then I'd have to chase him with a fishing net and return him to his roost. Finally, however, Gandhi got himself good and lost, never to return.

My daughter pointed out that Rosa was lonely and near suicidal. There was nothing to do but get another bird. Chez was one of the slowest homers in the loft of a racing enthusiast in West Chezzetcook. Despite the fact that he was from good Belgian racing stock, Chez tended to dawdle on his flights home from various parts of the province. He could fly from Truro to Chezzetcook in less than forty-five minutes (it takes an hour and a half to drive the distance) but by industry standards, this still made him a laggard.

Chez and Rosa, as nature would have it, hit it off. A pair of eggs appeared and were dutifully watched over but a cold winter prevented them from hatching. Rosa and Chez tried again in more favourable weather and soon Gandhi 2 came into the world. Shortly after Gandhi 2 could fly, he was kicked out of the nest and two more eggs appeared. Like clockwork, they too cracked open and out came Flutter and Rosette. (Credit for the names goes to my daughter.) After that I started taking the eggs away from Chez and Rosa. The look they gave me upon my theft still lingers like an icy spear in my heart.

Rosa and Chez tried to trick me by laying eggs outside, under the eaves and on windowsills, but I'd always find them out. Then Rosa started laying eggs on the roof. No sooner would one appear than it would roll down the sloping asphalt and smash on the ground or strike some unwary visitor. August was the month it rained pigeon eggs, and it didn't stop until fall cooled pigeon passions. Back home in the loft, Papa Chez was harassing the young ones. He wanted them out of the house and on their own. I was forced to subdivide the tiny loft into two apartments lest I find blood and feathers every morning from the family squabbles.

There were other dangers for the pigeons: hawks, weasels, free-ranging Irish setters, eagles and hunters. But I refused to keep them shut up. The joy of pigeons for me was sitting on my roof watching my birds circle the house, against a backdrop of an electric blue sky. Each time my spirit soared.

The bird life at my house was not limited to the outdoor type. Last summer, my brother-in-law was driving up from the States. He stopped on the Trans-Canada to tie down a loose tarp on the roof when a budgie landed on his shoulder. It was middle of nowhere so he brought us a new houseguest. We named him Petey after the brother-in-law. Petey lived long enough for us all to become irretrievably attached to him, but then he grew ill from what was diagnosed as cancer and died. So Petey was superseded by Trixie, who unfortunately came home already equipped with a terminal disease.

But we didn't give up. Sunyata saved up twenty dollars and bought a new baby budgie. She called him Prince, but the new bird had ideas of its own. Hours of futile, absurd repetition failed to get him to say his assigned name; eventually he did simply insist, "I'm Chewy" over and over, until we stopped calling him anything else. He's been Chewy ever since, and a day doesn't go by without his insistence on who he is.

Over the years I've had goats and chickens and ducks and a raven but nothing has been quite as special to me as my dog. Jemima was fourteen years old this year. Part lab and part beagle, she adopted us during my first summer in Nova Scotia. At first she lived with Terry and me in a 1963 Volkswagen van during the summer that Terry and I were married by a justice of the peace in Halifax. The van broke down on the way to the wedding ceremony and we had to hitch-hike, taking Jemima with us. We waited outside the courthouse door while some other people were getting divorced. Jemima peed on the floor. Then our time came before the judge. We asked if our puppy could be involved and he thought it was a wonderful idea. A class of Dalhousie Law School students watched on as the three of us got married.

Fourteen years is a long time to have a dog. She was getting old. On Good Friday of this year, the neighbour's Irish setter got nasty and ripped a big gash in Jemima's face. I rushed her to the vet who stitched her back together. Jemima healed like nothing had happened.

This was also the year I published a book on nuclear disarmament and the need to remove nuclear weapons from Halifax Harbour, just twelve miles from my back door. The day the books arrived from the printer, a new bird also arrived. A pure white pigeon, small and dove-like, flew down from the sky and joined my flock of birds. I knew that pigeons sometimes forsake one owner for another, but I was certain this living metaphor was more spirit than pigeon. That evening he allowed me to pick him up. I kept him in the greenhouse, fearful that the territorial battles of my own birds might cause him harm. He was a quiet guest; he ate out of my hand and hopped on my shoulder to be let out in the morning. He stayed around for three weeks, then, just as mysteriously as he had arrived, he disappeared.

One night after going to see a movie, we returned home to find Jemima seriously sick. The vet confirmed that my good old dog was dying. On her final, painful night on earth, I slept on the floor alongside her and suffered her pain as much as any human could share. In the morning, after she had died, I sat with her alone in my lap in a dreamy pool of sunlight. People who have lived with a dog for a long time will know I'm not lying when I say it was one of the saddest moments of my life. After a long while I got up the courage to walk outside. I stood outside the back door just looking up into the sky and suddenly I saw something land on the roof. It walked to the edge and looked down at me. The white bird had returned. I laughed in the midst of crying. Later, when he allowed me to pick him up and return him to the greenhouse, I vowed that I would have to take very good care of this pigeon that was more than a pigeon.

Almost within days of Jemima's death, Chewy got very sick. Soon he couldn't stand up in his cage. I cursed the unfairness of mortality and hauled him off to the bird specialist in Halifax. Dr. Beal told me that Chewy had chewed once too often on something he shouldn't have. He had lead poisoning, probably from the ceiling paint of my old farmhouse. She said she'd give him potassium injections, but warned that small birds hardly ever survive lead poisoning. Those were bleak times around the kitchen table.

Soon after that, my wife phoned me at work to say that something had fallen down our chimney. She could hear scratching but didn't know what it was. I told her to turn off the oil stove and hang tough until I got home. Before I got there my daughter figured out it was the mystical white bird, which she had named Snowflake, that had fallen down the chimney to his potential demise. Sunyata had taken control of the situation. She lifted off the iron clean-out door at the base of the brick chimney and stuck her head inside. Sure enough, there was Snowflake, clinging to a ledge a few feet away. Sunyata lured him to the ground and hauled the sooty bird to safety.

I had phoned a dozen times about Chewy and the reports were pretty grim, but then suddenly it seemed the potassium shots had begun to work. Aside from a rather lame foot, Chewy was dramatically improving. He returned home with the pluck and courage of ten tropical birds and hasn't stopped chattering since.

Despite my attempts to turn Snowflake into one of the human family, I could tell he preferred the company of pigeons, so he began staying in the subdivided pigeon pen. Then we returned home early one evening to discover a racoon in the pigeon cage. Two of the pigeons, Gandhi 2 and Rosette, were dead. Flutter and Snowflake had somehow escaped. They hovered nearby on the roof. My attempts to catch the racoon have so far failed.

It's been a year of death and miracles at this old house on the eastern shore of Nova Scotia.

Lesley Choyce
Porters Lake, Nova Scotia

⊠   A short while ago my dog Jennie died. That is, I decided to let the veterinarian put her to death because it was clear that Jennie was suffering, and there really was nothing more we could do for her.

So I lifted Jennie up on the table, and while the doctor gave her the lethal injection, I talked quietly to my old companion, remembering the many adventures we'd had together over the years. And I stroked her head and scratched her behind the ears and tried not to notice my reflection in her large, brown eyes. I knew I was doing the right thing, but all the same I was not feeling particularly good about myself. As Jennie slipped quietly into sleep, the last thing she heard was my voice telling her that I loved her, and thanking her for the years of lively companionship she had given me.

Sixteen years ago I had walked into the local humane society with the intention of buying a dog that could be trained to guard the small farm I had just rented. I went to school in the city during the day, and I wanted a dog I could trust to look after the farm and the chickens while I was away–a German shepherd was what I had in mind, or a large Collie cross of some kind. What I came away with was about two pounds of black powder-puff with the largest, dampest brown eyes I had ever seen, eyes that had stared up at me with such a big question mark in them that I knew there was no point in looking any further. The German shepherds, the Bouviers, Great Danes and Dobermans would have to fend for themselves. I had found my watch-dog.

And Jennie took to country life as a person born to it–a person, mind, not a dog: she slept in my bed, ate my leftovers, spilled my milk, chased the chickens and tracked mud all over the house in complete ignorance of what life for a rural guard dog is supposed to be like. When strangers came to the door, she would greet them like long-lost relatives and show them in; when I left for school in the morning, the last thing I would see in my rear-view mirror was my watch-dog, trotting off in the direction of a neighbouring farm. She chased the neighbour's dairy cattle until the poor animals nearly dried up from exhaustion. But her favourite pastime was to hunt mice up and down the drainage ditches that bordered the fields until the fertilizer runoff had bleached the black fur on her belly and legs a rust-coloured red.

Jennie loved life. She had a complete disregard for authority and discipline, but she showered her affection on me and my friends with uninhibited generosity. And she was patient. Of all the dogs and people I have known over the years, Jennie was surely one of the most faithful and patient I encountered. She would come with me on canoe trips, and sit absolutely still in the bottom of the canoe, watching the water and the shore with intense but silent curiosity. She would travel with me in my car, spending hours with her head hanging out the window and her tongue flapping joyfully in the wind like a flag. On one such trip, I fell ill, and while I spent three days in a motel room, alternatively shivering in bed and dashing to the bathroom, she lay quietly on the mat by the door. There was never so much as a peep out of her. And, for the first time ever, she made no attempt to hop up into my bed.

Yes, it's true that Jennie had weaknesses – she was only human, after all. She loved bananas and ice cream, and she would hop up into a vacant chair and inhale the butter before you could say "geddown!" And on rare occasions, there would be traces of egg yolk in her whiskers, with a corresponding decline in the daily egg count in the chicken coop.

But Jennie's greatest weakness was her promiscuity. My dog was given to sudden disappearances, which lasted for two or three days, and which would end with her coming slinking home under the cover of darkness, stinking to high heaven from having rolled in something unspeakable in a field somewhere, trying to creep silently back in under the dining-room table to pretend that she had really been there all along, her matted fur and lumps of bur-dock attesting to the disreputable sort of company she kept. No amount of scolding or lecturing could change her mind about her infrequent but Bacchanalian bouts of merry-making, and eventu-ally I came to accept this as just another side to her many-faceted personality.

For me, this stubby-legged, fertilizer-bleached, cow-chasing grinning little imp of a mutt was a one-in-a-million dog who saw me through moves, death, marriage, divorce, success and failure with the same even-tempered, good-natured attitude. She tried hard to tell me not to take life so seriously, and that if I would just chase a few cows or come trotting up the drainage ditches with her, I would see how much fun the world could be.

Well, she's gone now. A few years ago she started to limp and her eyes began to cloud over. She still smiled at me with that familiar expression of someone about to tell you a really good dirty joke, but it took her longer to get up to greet me, and she even stopped going out on her full-moon excursions. The black hair around her muzzle became whiter and whiter as time went on, and finally it was clear that any movement at all was almost too painful for her. Her life was over. All that remained was for me to pay back all those years of fun and love and trust and patience by allowing her a comfortable and graceful exit.

She died quietly a few days ago, free of pain, and in the company of a friend. I hope as much will be allowed to me when my time comes.

O.A. Rosenkrantz
London, Ontario

✉ When I was a boy we had a dog who was part collie and part German shepherd and maybe a few other breeds we couldn't determine. I called him Rover, and he was a very clever dog and helped me immensely whenever the cows decided to test my stamina. When the young heifer got into the garden I set Rover onto her. Rover took after her with a vengeance, slashing her thighs with his sharp teeth. The poor heifer was crying for mercy, and I was wishing I had never put Rover onto her. But the lesson was not forgotten; after that, all I had to do was whisper Rover's name whenever a cow was out of place, and immediately that cow froze with fear and was good as gold.

Now Rover really wasn't that vicious; he simply did as he was instructed. If you asked him in a gentle tone to fetch the cows for milking a little early, Rover would nonchalantly wander out to the pasture, stopping near a tree here and inspecting a rabbit hole there until you figured he'd never get the cows. But presently the cows would be coming in unhurriedly, with Rover in the rear.

My dog Rover could do anything, and many is the time he did the work of ten men. He could herd anything from chickens to pigs and cattle, and he was always there at the most crucial moment, without even being called. One day my father sold a two-year-old Jersey bull who was getting a little too snorty for his liking. When the butcher's truck came to get him, he must have known his demise was very near, and he promptly lay down and refused to move. Not even the electric prod would move him. All this time Rover had been trying to get into the act, but the butcher, who had a dim view of dogs, kept scolding him, and kept him away. Finally my father said this is enough, and told the butcher to stand back – he would show him how to load that bull onto the truck.

The butcher was worn out, and was only too glad to let Dad have a try. My father said, "Okay, Rover, put that bull into the truck." Rover was happy to oblige, and promptly barked right into the ear of that prostrate bull, who immediately jumped to his feet and ran up the ramp into the truck.

That happened nearly forty years ago, but I've never forgotten the day Rover did what four grown men could not do.

Vic Daradick
High Level, Alberta

✉ I am a forty-too-much spinster teacher-librarian, and I fork over fifty dollars a month on pet food.

I did buy a house for the dog. Really. While looking, my instructions to the agent were, "A fenced yard and a fireplace." My father said it sounded like a provincial park.

The dog is a mongrel. It's supposed to be part Spitz, according to the pet store. In my dictionary spitz is a word for an Eskimo sled dog. It weighs eighty-five pounds and sleeps on the couch. Would you argue with an eighty-five-pound dog that is cute and has a curly tail and large paws?

The cats are standard garden-variety domestic shorthair. They are standard if you believe in rising at 4:38 A.M. Did you know that cats can set themselves like alarm clocks? I've learned to do a lot early in the morning, after I've fed the cats. Sometimes I even go back to bed.

The rabbits and the guinea pig are my school sidekicks. Both rabbits – a mini-lop and a Siamese Dutch dwarf – and G.P., the guinea pig, are part of my school library's Rent a Rabbit program. Kids borrow them, with their parents' permission, for the weekend. One lop lives in my house permanently because she is an attack rabbit. Remember what happened to Jimmy Carter? The animal must have been a relative of my Flopsi. She's house-broken and runs free when I'm at home, peaceably living with dog and cats, but she bites me when I pick her up. I have to wear gloves then, but I can pat her anytime or anyplace.

I'm not sure if I own my animals or if they own me, but most of the time I love them. I must investigate day care – or a timer food dish for cats.

Fran Geitzler
Calgary

"DID HE WHO MADE THE ROSE MAKE THEE?"

Before we leave the menagerie (not to mention the barnyard), here is a brief sampling of poetry – a quartet – neither commissioned by *Morningside* nor submitted to it in the mail, but first unveiled to the world there in the season of 1987–'88.

The author, the bard of Canadian swine, is by day an expert on pigs who works in Ottawa for the Department of Agriculture. By night – and on weekends, I guess – he rewrites the classics of English poetry to salute his favourite animal.

His name is David Fraser. He is in person as delightful as his parodies – a kind of Paul Hiebert of the civil service – and it is my pleasure in presenting this tantalizing mini-collection to tell you that a more complete anthology called *The Loveliest of Pigs* will be published soon by Deneau.

Porkyr! Porkyr!

Porkyr! Porkyr! sound asleep
On the farm's manure heap,
What immortal code of dress
Condoned thy rank untidiness?

From what nostril, from what lung,
Breathed thy love of filth and dung?
By what finger wert thou bidden
To thy place upon the midden?

In what perfume vat in hell
Steeped the essence of thy smell?
Did He, one step from cleanliness,
Still thy filthy pelage bless?

When thy stench at last arose
And all heaven held its nose,
Did He choke, His work to see?
Did He who made the Rose make thee?

Porkyr! Porkyr! sound asleep
On the farm's manure heap,
What immortal code of dress
Could stand thy rank untidiness?

Snuffle, Snuffle

Snuffle, snuffle, toil for truffle,
Snorter dig and trotter scuffle –
Underneath the moss and grasses
Lies the meal that none surpasses;
Under roots and rotting board,
Locust's grub and mouse's hoard,
Under centipede and slug,
Corpse of mole and skin of bug,
There within the musky earth
Dwells the prize of highest worth,
Choicest gift the gods have flung us:
Scrumptious subterranean fungus!
For the treat that's worth the trouble,
For the feast that fills us double,
Snuffle, snuffle, toil for truffle,
Snorter dig and trotter scuffle.

Sow-Fever

I must go down to the sows again, to the lonely sow
    in the sty,
And all I ask is a plump gilt and an hour to mate her by,
And the gate's creak and the straw's crunch
    and the black mud splashing,
And the fast grunt and the white froth
    and the bright tusks flashing.
  I must go down to the sows again, to the free
    philandering life,
To the bull's way and the ram's way, where love
    and libido are rife,
And all I ask is a quiet stall with the sows left unattended,
And a long sleep and a full trough when the
    day's work's ended.

Simple Sigmund

Simple Sigmund met a pigman
Going to the shrink.
Said Simple Sigmund to the pigman,
"What do piggies think?"
The pigman answered not a word,
But made a funny look.
Said Sigmund wisely, "So I thought."
And ran to write a book.

ELLY

This is the interview whose origins I describe in detail in the introduction to this book. In presenting it on the radio the first time – it has since been replayed more than once and, I am proud to say, been used in some seminars and training sessions in the growing movement to fight the kind of abuse it describes – I said:

It will be hard for you to realize, as you read passages from Elly's book, that you're reading a victory story, even though I think you'll like the person you're meeting as much as I liked her when I met her. Her name is Elly Danica. She lives in a clapboard church in a small town on the Saskatchewan prairie. She is poor. She supports herself financially with the art she produces in the main room of the church – her studio – paintings and weavings, which she not only sells but often barters for shoes, for books – books are viscerally important to her – or for food. She may have bartered for the lunch she served us when we visited her. We pulled up outside the church with the wind singing through the unruly brown grasses in the yard and the brass knocker set in the old wooden door. Elly is not quite forty, slight, pert, still vulnerable. If you want to hug her you should warn her first.

Her victory has been in dealing with the horror of her

childhood. She had to come to understand that the pain she had felt all her life was a result of the sexual abuse she had suffered as a child, abuse perpetrated by her father. She's written a book about what happened to her. The book is called simply *Don't – A Woman's Word*. It's beautifully crafted yet very difficult to read. It was painful to write, but it was also part of what Elly calls "the process of healing myself." So, too, is talking in public at last about what happened to her.

In the interview are passages from the book. The story, victory and all, is very, very disturbing. This is Elly and her story as she told it in the basement of the church last month.

PETER   How much has this place, where we sit, got to do with putting yourself back together? How much is the setting important in the healing?

ELLY   Oh, it's really important. I bought this place because I needed some sort of refuge. I can see that in retrospect. At the time I didn't understand that quite the way I do now. I walked around this empty building. There were no windows in it, and I knew in my gut that there I could heal. I had no money. I didn't know how I would do it, but somehow or other I got this building, and it is vital to my healing.

PETER   It's a church. What do we make of that?

ELLY   At first I didn't even make anything of it. With some friends I toured the neighbourhood I grew up in. Half a block or less from the house I grew up in there was a church very much like the one I live in. And I was shocked. I thought, My God, how could I have missed that connection? Then I thought, Ah, so that's what you're doing. You've done exactly the same thing you did when you were about fifteen years old. You've come to a place you perceive to be safe.

PETER But the church wasn't a refuge in the bad times; you weren't able to go to the church and say, Help me, church.

ELLY No, not even the people who ran the church, the nuns and priest, were there for me in a significant way. But I think I must have seen the church as a refuge I could build for myself. This building, when I got it, wasn't a refuge, either. I moved in in January. It was freezing God-awful cold. I had to rip wood from the basement ceiling to put into a Quebec heater to stay warm; and I had plastic on the windows. In the prairie wind, it would flap and snap, and it sounded like guns going off all night. It was not a refuge. I had to build that refuge around me. I spent nine years living in the basement before I could go into the studio upstairs, which is a really beautiful room.

I think I had to discover the connection between my pain and the basement, and that took most of those nine years. I didn't understand that there was a problem about a basement; and I remember thinking about the house I grew up in. I knew every room. I knew details about things like the kitchen sink or the bathroom or the room where we used to eat or my parents' bedroom. All those things I remembered quite graphically. But I didn't remember anything about the basement. Once I remembered that there was a basement, and that there was some danger, or something there, then the process began. I started to look at what had happened there, at what I was hanging on to so tight.

This is the one I most want to forget. This is the time it all came apart. This was the night of my death. Eleven. Beautiful girl-child. A bright and charming elf. She wants to be an archaeologist. She dreams of a life of her own. She wants to be a writer.

Saturday supper. Bread and soup for the kids. Roast chicken for daddy. Watch him eat. Don't get caught watching. You know you can't have any chicken. Don't even dream about it. Clean up. Be quick. Company for daddy tonight. Be quiet. Do the stove and the counters again. Company tonight, everything must be spotless. He wants to check the work. Don't let him find anything undone or done badly. Be quick. He is impatient.

Bath time. First the little ones. Be quick. Be quiet. Get those kids to bed goddamn it. Hurry up I said. The older kids bath themselves. I bath last. No fresh bath water tonight. A clean nightdress. No you can't stay up. Go to bed. I'll come for you when he wants you. But Mom, I won't be able to sleep. Try, she says.

I do sleep. She wakes me. Come, she says. He wants you now. Barefoot. Cold. Walking behind my mother. Into the basement. Laughter. Are they having a party? Be quiet. Do what he says. Don't talk unless he tells you to. Do exactly what he says.

PETER I want to hear as much of your story as we can put together, but I don't know where to start. I'm very tempted to say, "Describe the person who crawled into this basement."

ELLY A woman who was twenty-seven years old, who was filled with self-hate, who couldn't function on any level in the real world. I couldn't hold a job. I couldn't handle a relationship. I couldn't handle anything. I was totally broken. I needed a place to burrow down into, and that's what this building represented to me.

PETER   Did you know why?

ELLY No, I didn't know why. I thought I was just one of society's basket cases. I knew I hated my father. At the time, the only thing that was safe for me to remember was that he had beaten me, so I hated him for that.

PETER Would you remember, for example, that he would eat chicken while the rest of the family had lesser food?

ELLY Yeah, I remembered that.

PETER   And you remembered being beaten?

ELLY Yes. My whole attitude around food is still very difficult. It's been a long process to heal my relationship with food and to learn to nourish myself emotionally, physically, in every way. I hated him for things like that, things that seemed to be safe because they didn't uncover things I couldn't cope with.

I came to this building and I read for ten years. That's all I did. I curled up in a chair with a blanket around me and just read. I was looking for a story similar to mine, anything so I could find my way into my own story. Any hint.

PETER So you knew there was something to find?

ELLY Yes. Maybe not at the beginning, but halfway into that ten years I started to recognize that I was looking for something. That what I called my compulsion to read was not how normal people handled their lives. So I started to look at the fact that there maybe was a problem. But I thought the problem was me. I didn't see the problem as something that had been done to me or something in my past that was abnormal or painful. It was just me. I couldn't cope. I couldn't deal with real life. It was all my problem, whatever it was.

PETER And now we know it wasn't.

ELLY Now we know it wasn't.

My mother opens the door of the studio. Three men. Strangers. And my father. They watch every move I make. Why are they so interested? I notice they all have drinks. They laugh when I rub the sleep from my eyes. I am dazed. I don't understand why I am here. I stand near the door. My mother sits on a chair in the corner, behind the camera. He is preparing the camera and joking with the men. He switches on the photo lamps. Sit on the bench he says. Face the camera. The men behind the camera snicker. One man chews a cigar. They lift their drinks. I try to make eye contact with my mother. Laughter. Move your head and shoulders so you face the door. Now turn your head back. Wet your lips. Again. Smile. Click. Tilt your head. Click. Open your mouth a little. Click. Wet your lips again. Hold it right there. Click. Smile. Smile I said. Click. The glasses are refilled. I am awake now. Click.

ELLY The sexual incidents with my father began when I was four. The incident I remembered was with my father and several other men, and it's very difficult to talk about. I can't even read it. When I had to do the final look at this material before the book went to publication, I could check the rest of the book, and I sent the manuscript back and I said I can't do it. I just couldn't do it. It's still the most difficult part of the book. I can't imagine ever reading it in public – I'm still afraid I'll fall apart.

Take your panties off. Slowly. Like I showed you. No. Do I make myself clear? Take your panties off. No. No. Mom? No answer. Mom? She looks at me finally. Do what he says. I do nothing. My mother has a whispered conference with him. I hear her say she will make coffee for later. He gives his permission. She leaves. Now take them off. Stupid kid. She can't do it with her mother watching. They're so stupid about their mothers. You know what will happen if you don't do what you're told? You remember what we talked about this afternoon? You remember your promise? Promise. I never promised you anything. Don't say that. If you say what you're thinking he'll hurt you. Slowly, so slowly, the panties come off. He doesn't notice that my skin comes off with them. I peel myself out of my own skin. I am no longer myself. I am someone else. Someone I don't want to be. Someone I don't want ever to remember having been. Someone I used to know sits on a white brocaded bench, under photo lamps, in front of a camera. A body sits here naked. The body tries to cover itself. Its hands move automatically. It clenches its thighs. It stares at the heat duct on the ceiling. It focuses on the little t-bar which controls the opening and closing of it. It hears the furnace. Now it can watch the dust blow out of the duct. It hears nothing else.

PETER How did your understanding of what it was begin to come through?

121

ELLY Well, I'd been trying for a number of years to listen to what was inside me, although I was afraid of it at the same time. I was trying to pay attention to things that were coming up in my mind and not dismiss them because I was afraid. That was a very long process because, as I got closer and closer to finding out what was going on, it was going to take courage to find out.

About three years ago, in late winter, I started to get an image in my mind of light under a door. It was very odd, because the door was much too high off the ground. There is usually about an inch or an inch and a half of clearance between a door and the floor. But this was eight, ten, twelve inches, something like that. The image stayed in my mind, and I couldn't make anything out of it. Then, several days later, the image had changed a little bit, and I noticed that my perception of the light in relation to the door was odd. The only way I could have seen light like that is if I had been on my back.

The body is no longer capable of response. The voice was peeled away with the skin. Give her a good stiff drink. She needs a drink. The body sees a drink being poured by one of the men. He gives it the drink. It sniffs the drink and makes a face. Take it all in one gulp somebody says. It drinks and chokes. Coughing brings tears. Here, wipe your face on this. Let's give her a couple of minutes. The drink should loosen her up. How much did you give her anyway? Three fingers of CC. That ought to do it. Laughter. They refill their own drinks. The body, naked and shivering, sits on the bench. The body searches for escape. One of the men sits in front of the door. He tilts his chair and rocks on it. No escape. The alcohol begins to work. Nausea.

Daddy, I don't feel good. Never mind about that, it's the whiskey he says. You'll start to feel good pretty quick. Then we'll have a little fun. He turns to the men. Are you ready for a little fun, your honour? You bet I'm ready. Say when, says the man in the brown suit. He removes his jacket. He wears a vest with a large gold watch chain. The body wonders if he would let it look at the watch. The chain is pretty. The body looks at the chain. It can't make itself look at the man. He has been smoking a fat cigar. Now he chews it, moving it from side to side in his mouth. He rubs his hands together. Say when.

ELLY   I remember being on the floor, and then I got a sensation of cold on my back and I remembered the floor was concrete. Then I remembered where in my past there was that relationship – concrete floor, a door a long way off, off the normal clearance, and that kind of light. It was in what my father called a studio in his basement. Then, very rapidly over the next two or three days, the incidents that had happened to me in that space started to come out. It was like opening the floodgates. It was very, very emotional and very painful.

Then, when that process was done, I phoned a friend and she congratulated me on finally having brought this to the surface. She asked me how I was and gave me lots of warmth and support. Then she said, at the end of the conversation, But there's probably more. I said, No, no, that's plenty, that's enough. There is no more. And she said, I don't mean to take away your victory, but there's probably more. And she was right.

He holds the body down. Hand on its right shoulder. Thumb pressing at the base of its throat. Its hands held above the head. The body stretched out. She won't give you any trouble this time your honour. Hand like a vise at the throat. Bring your knees up. Trapped wrists. Can't move. The body tries to move the torso out of the way. He spreads its legs. The man is between the body's legs. He tries to put something into it. It feels his fingernails and it screams. He's hurting me, he's hurting me. The body moves its head from side to side, crying, screaming. No. No. No! Shut up a voice snarls. No. No. No! He slaps its face, hard. The head feels like it will roll away from the body with the force. He slaps it again. Now shut up. If you make a fuss it will take longer. Shut up. No. No. No. It tries to get away. It can't move. The hand at the throat. It chokes. They don't stop. The man in the blue suit crouches near the father. He holds the body's wrists. Puts his other hand over its mouth. The man between its legs is breathing funny. Suddenly he stops, he collapses on top of the body. It is over. At last it is over.

The body's hands are released and the hand over the mouth is removed. The father still holds the body by the shoulders. The men talk over the body. It looks at the faces above it. They are negotiating something. The man in the blue suit will now have his turn. The body thinks he has a nice face. It hopes he won't hurt it. He removes his jacket and hangs it on the back of a chair. He kneels at the body's feet. He leans over and kisses it on the mouth. Kisses the chest. The body's legs are clenched. Pull your knees up he says, that's a good girl. I want to have a look he says. He spreads its legs apart. Again. It's going to happen again. He's going to do the same thing as the other man. What is this? Why do they want to hurt me? Why can't they leave me alone?

It hurts. I cry. It hurts. It hurts. It hurts so much. Please daddy don't let them hurt me any more. Shut up. He's not hurting you. Shut up and lie still. Hand over the body's mouth again. This man hurts more than the other one did. He pushes into the body. Harder and harder he pushes into it. It feels like something is ripping. The body thinks it will die. It hurts so much. The hand over its mouth barely muffles its screams. It chokes. It bites. It bites as hard as it can. He takes his hand away. The body throws up. He hits again. Somebody gives him a magazine to throw over the puke.

It's over. He gets up. The father lets go of the body, my body. I don't move. I can't move. I want to die. I hear them talking. They are trying to talk the other man into taking his turn. He doesn't seem to want to. They discuss who will hold me down. They come back to me. It's not over. The other man and my father will have a turn. So it's fair I hear them say. Fair.

ELLY   This happened in Moose Jaw. One of the things I thought about while I was writing this book is that people have an idea these are isolated incidents, that the perpetrators are monsters, that if you saw them on the street you'd recognize them for the

124

monsters they are. That's not so. These were people who had status in the community, people who went to church every Sunday. It's amazingly hard to get some people who know these men to accept that's what they did. People say, Well, how could they? They're so nice, they're so charming. That's what's bizarre. That's what makes you crazy.

In some ways, making this public is part of the process of healing myself. One of the things that is most exciting to me is the number of copies of this book there are. To me that translates into people who know about this. It's no longer a secret. It's no longer a burden I have to carry forever. I'm no longer haunted. But that doesn't mean I have a really good, strong sense of where this is in my life. The healing process is lifelong, you know. That's why I find it so ludicrous, the sentence that is handed out to men who assault children. You get a higher sentence for traffic violations in some cases than you do for assaulting a child. The man gets three months to serve on weekends, and a woman gets life. And it has to do, primarily, I think, with power, with how certain men abuse the power they have, or which society feels is theirs. If you don't see a child as a human being, there's no problem. That's the real issue here.

PETER   If you and I went into Moose Jaw now – and you go there from time to time – you could see on the street men who bought pornographic pictures of you from your father when you were nine years old. Does that happen?

ELLY   Well, there are certain men in Moose Jaw who know who I am. They don't know my name, but they recognize my face. The first time I twigged to that, I was shocked. I didn't know if I'd be able to go into that town again. Then I realized I'm not the one who did anything wrong. I have every right to be there. Those men should be skulking around, not me. I look them right in the eye and I don't make any bones about what I think about that kind of scum.

PETER   Do they look back at you?

ELLY   No, they don't. I think that tells me all I need to know. But I don't have any legal redress. None–even if I could get my hands on those pictures now. Because it's just my word and my memories against all those upstanding citizens.

PETER   Your story's been corroborated in a way. We know you're not making all this up. Your story's been witnessed by others in the family; you know it's true beyond your own knowledge of its truth.

ELLY   Well, I know it's true in a couple of peripheral ways. I had many sisters. I was in the house when it happened to the youngest of my sisters. I carry an enormous load of guilt because I should have known, but I was in so much pain at the time that acknowl-edging her pain would have meant acknowledging my own, and I couldn't do it. I saw myself in this eleven-year-old who was totally shattered. She broke like glass in front of me. It's the most horrific memory. In some ways it's more horrific than my own experience, because I should have been able to help this baby sister, and I couldn't do it.

PETER   What about your mother?

ELLY   I yearn for a relationship with my mother, but it's not pos-sible, and she's dying. She can't let herself see her daughters, because she does know. The family dynamic and the politics are pretty horrific; the denial is phenomenal. It's going to kill most of those people.

PETER   Do you understand how you overcame the denial?

ELLY   When I was nine years old I made a commitment to write this book. I didn't know what book it was yet.
    I remember talking to my little Hummel statue of the Virgin Mary that was on a shelf in my room and making a promise to write this book. I forgot what book it was, but once the book was written, that memory came back, and it was a great gift. Then I went for a reality check to a counselling centre in Regina, at the women's centre. The woman I saw helped me come to terms with

this whole body of memories, and once that was done I decided I didn't have to do anything more. I'd gone for some counselling, I'd got some help, I'd sorted out my life, I knew everything was going to get better and I was going to have control over things. That lasted for about three months, and I was working on another man-uscript. Then the manuscript just died on me. I couldn't under-stand why. I hadn't run out of ideas; it just stopped. Then the content of this book came to the surface and demanded that I sit down and do it. I didn't have a choice.

PETER   How long did it take you to write?

ELLY   Less than six weeks, but I was so sick the whole time I wrote. Physically sick. Because I felt that I'd put it behind me by going for counselling and talking it out and dealing with it. I didn't want to have to deal with it again. But I had to go back inside this material, and I had to go back to it as a child. I couldn't do it as an adult. I wanted to write that little girl's story because I needed to comfort her in some way, and the only comfort she would accept was that I write her story.

PETER   So you had to walk out into that room again.

ELLY   Yeah. And I had to deal with those men. I'd had a body memory I carried for a long, long time about somebody's hands around my throat. I thought that was most bizarre, and every time it came to the surface I'd push it back. I've read since that one of the most common responses as an adult is to have problems breathing, to feel pressure on your chest. It's a memory of your child body, of the weight of an adult on your body. You remember it as pressure. It's very, very creepy. And I can remember, even as I talk to you I can remember one of the men and what his hands felt like on my body. It's like it was yesterday and not thirty years ago. It makes my stomach knot.

PETER   If a man touches you now, do you cringe?

ELLY   I do. When anybody touches me I freeze because I think I'm going to be beaten or hurt. If my friends want to give me a hug, they have to announce themselves. They say, Elly I'd like to give you a hug now. And then I can. I don't put on a protective posture.

In the last several years I haven't had any relationships. I'm leery of getting involved because I'm afraid, still, that I will play a victim role. Until I get that straight in my heart and in my life, I keep people at a distance. Before, the only way I could have any relationships with anyone, sexual or otherwise, was to be drunk. That was the only way I could cope emotionally with having any kind of relationship with an adult.

PETER   There was a period of drugs and booze?

ELLY   Oh, you just try everything to get rid of the pain, and you don't understand what pain you're trying to soothe, and you're crazy. It's awful.

PETER   This is a triumphant book. This book is about so many things beyond the simple facts it deals with. It's distilled. This is essence of Elly, this book.

ELLY   I can show you the two thousand pages I wrote to get to it.

PETER   I suspected there was a lot, because it's one sentence here, one word there. But it's your triumph. You weren't picked up by other people or helped by other people, except by women who'd written and women you could talk with.

ELLY   Which was very late in the process.

PETER   Are you mad that you had to do it all by yourself, that there isn't some system where you could have flung yourself onto the stretcher and said, I'm Elly, they did this to me, they should get me out of it? You came in and holed up in this building and worked your way through it and came out the other end.

ELLY   I think the process is different for different people. There aren't enough support services for women and for children. If we need anything in this country it's more support services for abused women and children. I don't think they would have helped me, because the denial would have been in the way of me asking for

128

help. I did not trust the "helping professions," and I knew the kind of crazy I was was going to get me institutionalized or drugged out of my mind, which I didn't need. I needed time and I needed a space to work my way through to my own healing. I think it's much easier to have help; I'm not sure I could have accepted it, though.

PETER   People say your paintings and pictures and weaving are happier, because you're happier now. There's more light. Is that right?

ELLY   Oh yeah. The show I just did, I danced through most of the painting of it. That's what I do. I put on loud and raucous rock music from the sixties and put my air-brush compressor on, and I dance and I paint. There's a lot of joy in my life. I'm no longer haunted. There's pain there, still, and there probably always will be, but I'm not haunted any more. I'm not running any more. It's wonderful. Five years ago I wouldn't have believed it was possible for me to be happy. But I am.

PETER   You are, aren't you?

ELLY   I am. One of the things I wanted to do with this book was to say yes, it's survivable. No matter how horrible the hell you are in as a kid, at some point you can deal with it. You can survive. Once you come to terms with it, life is good. It's possible to have joy in your life. That's probably the most important thing I want to say with this book, and with talking about it, as well.

Light. A crack in the wall of darkness. A single moonbeam of understanding. Waxing. New. Brilliant. White gold promise.

No rescuer. No mother wisdom. Fingernails. Teeth. Determination. Process. Crawl through the mire forever. Toward the mirror. Reflection of scars. Multiplied. Each scar holds a book. Reversed. Read it in the mirror. It is done.

Beginning. Always. From the secret place. Soul dwelling: found. Self: found. Heart: found. Life: found. Wisdom: found. Hope, once lost: found. Process: never lost.

Wandering. Maybe. The path.

Rope ladder. Words in the mirror. Moon. Climb. Count the stars. Count the words. See the Goddess. In the eyes of a lover.

Woman. Dreaming. The mind. Free. Freedom. Bestowed from within. Self. This night. No longer dark. Star messages. Silver and gold. Blessings. I dream. I love. I am.

WOMEN ON THE
VERGE OF
SILENCE

E lly Danica's honesty and strength, as I've said, had a profound impact on *Morningside*'s listeners. Here is a small sample of what we heard after the interview was first broadcast – from people who'd had similar experiences (some of whom, for obvious reasons, wanted to remain anonymous), but also from people who, as this first letter shows, just . . . understood.

✉ Yesterday morning I did my illustrating work through a glaze of tears, and more than once I had to catch a tear from landing on my water-colour painting. Ms. Danica's story echoed through my head all day, and it continues to haunt me today. She and I are about the same age, and we grew up in the same small-town world of the fifties in Western Canada. I don't know her story from the inside, having had an enviably happy childhood, but I witnessed the social dynamics of a small town, and I can imagine the context in which she grew up.

This is what bothers me: in my town, there were half a dozen or so families that were considered by the rest to be "crumb bums," with "the morals of alley cats," to use phrases I heard as a kid. These were poor families – not just poor financially, but poor in every sense – including education, manners, proper dress, religion and all those things that characterized the upstanding citizens. They were large families; the children were a ragtag lot; and all of them, right down to the babies, were considered to be something less than full-fledged human beings.

When I was nine or ten, I remember finding a toddler from one of these families wandering around in the snowbanks with no clothes on. I went to my aunt's house, which was nearby, and I told her about the boy. She gave me a blanket to wrap him up in, and I took him home. His mother didn't care one way or the other, which surprised me. Later, when I talked about the incident with my mom, she regretted that she had to make clear our inability to interfere with their lives. Young friends shrugged and said, "He's just a Smith. Don't worry about it." They were faithfully reflecting the town opinion that if this one suffered in any way or even if that one died, there would always be more of the brats born in the future, for they "live and breed like rabbits."

I remember a lot of joking about the parentage of some of these kids. The red-haired one must be Red Whosit's little bastard, and the blonde curly-headed one was Curly Somebody-Else's, of course. When a teenage daughter got pregnant, there was talk about whether the baby was the father's or the brother's.

And there was the pretty, gentle, and simple young woman of one of these incompetent families, who would never advance beyond the five- to six-year-old level, who was the sexual target of a number of unscrupulous but publicly respected men in town.

These are hazy memories for me. I never knew any of these poor kids as playmates – in part because, by chance, there were none in my age group, and in part because those who failed several grades and ended up in our group for a short time before they dropped out of school weren't like us in too many ways. They and their families scared me. I would never go into their homes, and none of us, except some boys on a dare, would even call at their doors to trick or treat at Hallowe'en.

When Ms. Danica said she came from a large family, with lots of sisters for exploiting, I thought, Uh-huh, I know just how the town felt about them. I know how the lascivious men looked at them, and I know how the prim and proper wives talked about them. I know how the most respectable citizens were politely silent about their lot, or shook their heads in condemning sympathy, but never made a move to change anyone's attitude and stop the abuse. I can see the whole social stage, set for action, characters in place. I can hear the tut-tutting and the snickers; I can feel the same sickening gut response I experienced at the unfairness of it all, although when I was a child I never said a word or shed a tear. Some of the tears came out yesterday; some of the words beg to be said now.

When I think of the beautiful, soft-spoken, simple girl in my town, who bore someone or other's baby without understanding how it happened to her, I'm outraged and profoundly sad that she never had a chance. She could barely write her name; she could never tell her story. When I heard Ms. Danica's story, I cried for learning some truths that were even more shocking than what I would have guessed for all my small-town experiences, and I rejoiced that one of these "ragtag" kids found her voice and had the intelligence, skill and just plain guts to tell her tale. Through such unbelievably painful processes, there comes great relief and joy in knowing that maybe, just maybe, the whole social conspiracy that led to her suffering is being exposed and maybe, just maybe, in the future, none of us will let children like her – born innocent and equal – pay for the sins of the father, not to mention all the town fathers.

Brenda Guild Gillespie
Dartmouth, Nova Scotia

✉ Happily, for me, my brother died. I was so glad. It meant that I no longer had to face him across the dinner table – pretending, always pretending, that nothing was the matter in front of the rest of the family. I hated him so much.

He first sexually molested me when I was seven years old. He was eighteen. It happened many times.

I am forty now, and I feel that I have finally come to terms with what took place. For the most part, I am a happy person. I realize a seven-year-old child is very vulnerable. Usually, I can overcome my self-imposed feelings of guilt, and shrug away the troubling thoughts. But sometimes the memories explode into existence, without warning, leaving me gasping and extremely afraid.

Maybe I'll be fixing supper, or brushing my teeth, or just relaxing. Suddenly, I'm back in that room, upstairs in the old farmhouse, on that ancient, sagging bed. I feel torn apart, because I am both afraid and hoping, at the same time, that someone will come through the door. I know that what I am doing is wrong, but he said "the game" would be fun. I like "dancing" for him–*that* is fun! Taking my clothes off, like he wants me to, just makes the dancing easier. I can twirl, and twirl, and twirl–it feels so lovely and free. But I don't like it when he pulls me close to him and won't let me go . . . or when he rubs against me. His pock-marked face is ugly . . . and the *smell*, the *smell* is so terrible.

After the first time, there is no escape. You're little, he's big and he'll tell on you. You know you'll be in bad trouble if he does.

I lived this fear, day in and day out, for an eternity. Finally, one time, I managed to summon up the courage to say, "No, no, *I* will tell on *you!*" The answering fear in his eyes freed me from his power, but not from a lifetime of mental anguish.

People do not always realize how a child's mind works, how ordinary things can instantly remind them of a horrible experience. For years afterwards, the very sight of a "long garlic sausage" would make me want to vomit–to me, it looked like his hard, ugly penis. Winding stairs were terrifying; anyone with acne was an appalling monster.

I was terribly confused. My brother was an epileptic, who suffered *grand mal* seizures. Somehow, the sight of him twisting and writhing on the floor during a seizure became mixed up, in my young mind, with the sexual encounter. His seizures were brought on by stress, and because he was usually stressed when he approached me, he would often have a seizure when I tried to deny him. To this day, I can still see my parents, standing there, desperate to help him, and yelling at me, "See what you have done to him. You're bad – go to your room!" They didn't realize. Nevertheless, these episodes compounded my guilt and confusion. I also remember seeing my brother try to sexually abuse another child. When her parents and mine questioned me, I lied on my brother's behalf. Again, I knew it was wrong, but I was dreadfully afraid of him.

Eventually, I came to understand everything. I realized how very young I was at the time – that it was not my fault, and that it did not have anything to do with the epilepsy. After my brother was gone, I decided there was no point in hurting my elderly parents by telling them any of this, and that is the reason that I wish to remain anonymous.

Yet I know how important it is to make people aware of what is happening, so children can be taught they have the right to say no. I did not realize how prevalent child abuse was until I started to talk about my own experience. Several of my close friends admitted that they, too, were victims. Compared to them, I feel lucky – their *fathers* abused them! One woman described to me how her preacher father would routinely molest her and her twin sister in the same bed every Saturday night, before delivering his sermon the next morning!

I do not want to see mass hysteria create a situation where adults may be falsely accused – but I do know that child abuse is taking place in communities, large and small, across the country. It is happening down the street from you, next door and even, perhaps, in your own home.

The child's faculties are not yet fully developed, and she does not stand a chance against a persuasive, determined adult. But even as I write this, I have to remind myself of that fact, over and over again. It is difficult, for the shame and anger are so overwhelming, at the moment, that I can hardly breathe.

Anonymous

135

✉ I believe I've heard that half of all women suffer from some form of sexual assault before they reach the age of eighteen.

I am, unfortunately, one of those women. I was, at home, a victim of incest, and at the age of twelve I was brutally raped and almost killed. In my early adulthood, I chose not to deal with what had happened, and when I did start to examine it, I was able to blame it on my background: an alcoholic father, a mother working full-time, evenings and night shifts, to put food on the table for eight kids, et cetera. But, I told myself, I had survived. I was married, living in a different country, it was over and best forgotten.

The one thing I have learned out of these experiences is just how circular the effects of these events are. The fear, the guilt, the pain . . . no matter how hard I try to push them away, they always come back.

You are probably thinking I should go for "help." I have. It is hard to comprehend, in light of how prevalent the experience is, just how inadequately we deal with its aftermaths. Without even thinking hard, I know of at least six other women in our small community who have similar backgrounds.

The experience of sexual abuse shapes its victims, just as all other experiences in our lives do. Our legacy is one of guilt (maybe if I'd said or done something differently it wouldn't have happened, or would have stopped), of shame (how could someone in my own family, so close to me, have done this?) and of pain. Is it really so hard to understand that we cannot stand, exposed to the world, to fight it?

Our screams are silent.

Pam Brown
New Sarepta, Alberta

✉ When I was eleven years old my father began sexually abusing me. He came in to my bedroom at night and touched me, fondled me, rubbed his penis against me and tried to put it in my mouth. My response was to pretend I was asleep. In this way I tried to protect myself not so much from his touch as from the threat of losing him. How could I keep him my father and have a sexual relationship with him? As a child, I couldn't figure this out. I lived in constant terror of what I didn't even know.

I don't remember how often he came to my room. I remember lying in bed and waiting, wondering. I mostly remember days and days when all I did was wait and wonder how I could go on living, how would I find myself and my life in all the confusion. It felt like my life was fading away just like my voice. My stuttering became worse and worse until I hardly risked talking at all.

Three years later I began menstruation. I don't remember exactly when I began enjoying his night visits. The mixture of feelings is like a bouquet of summer flowers brought in from the garden with love and left unattended, some blooms still bursting with raucous colour, others beginning to rot. I just remember my masturbation activities became central in my life, challenging my devotion to the spiritual experiences I savoured and sought so desperately by attending daily mass. My burgeoning sexuality was not allowed into the arena of my social relationships. If I let myself feel those feelings for a mere boy, surely I would lose my father as father, protector, God and lover, forever.

I wanted to find some way out of this living nightmare of confusion. I wanted to be me. I felt I was losing myself. I tried to get help.

I finally found the courage to tell a priest in the confessional. I had to wait until there was a visiting priest, because my priest knew me and my father. The priest told me the next time my father came into my room at night, I should scream and wake up everyone in the house. I never did.

At fifteen, I did try to take my life back. One night as both my father and I were dressing to go out for the evening and my stepmother was in the kitchen giving instructions about bedtimes for my younger sisters and brothers to the baby-sitter, I went into his bedroom where he stood by the dresser tying his tie. "Daddy, I need to tell you something. I haven't been asleep at night."

My father fell on the floor and started to cry. I helped him to the chair and held his head to my breast, rocking him. "It's okay, Daddy, I still love you. But why, Daddy, why? Is it because my mother died? Why?"

I never got an answer. My father never came into my room again. I felt I had lost him and myself. I tried to get help through the system. I got caught stealing at school and was sent to a psychiatrist. After I told him my story, he called my parents in and told them I was having sexual fantasies about my father. My father never mentioned it. My stepmother assured me that all girls did, and it was "normal."

At college I would go from getting As to Fs and back to As. I was told to take a year off. I was terrified to go home. Being in my father's house was worse now. No more nightly visits. No more father. No more protector. No more God. No more lover. No more me. I told the Mother Superior but she responded just as the Mistress General of my high school had – with silence.

I convinced my father to let me live with my maternal grandparents and go to the university my mother had attended. I took the radio, TV and film program in the school of speech, to follow in my father's footsteps. He was manager of New York City's top radio station in the 1950s and 1960s. It was hard because I couldn't talk without my terrible stuttering.

And I never stopped trying to get help. I told the priest at the Newman Centre after I got pregnant. I told my all-American football player hero; I don't remember his response. The priest married us. During football training camp, I told the priest at our church in Toronto. I told the priest who baptized our second child.

I told the seventy-year-old *Monseigneur* who baptized our third child after we moved to Montreal. I told the priest marriage-counsellor who advised me to leave my husband and go back to my father's house. I did leave, but I didn't go back. When I sold my first radio documentary to the CBC, I went to tell *Monseigneur*, who I was closer to than anyone. After all, I saw him every morning at mass. I had my two sons with me, one on each hand. The *Monseigneur* took the opportunity to put his hands on my breasts.

I told the psychiatrist I had agreed to see at the request of my married lover, who wanted to find a way out of his marriage that wouldn't hurt anyone. The psychiatrist couldn't help my lover, and what he offered me was a real good "fuck" when I got over idealizing my love affair. I didn't take him up on his offer. It took me a long time to get over my lover even after the affair was over.

I stopped telling people.

The system didn't work for me. The system did not want to know. The system did not want to change.

At the age of twenty-six I was separated with three children, no lover, no father and no God, and I began researching "alternative therapies" for a radio documentary for the CBC. That's when I first heard about "psychosynthesis," a holistic approach to healing and growth. It took me another four years to go see a psychosynthesist for therapy. That was nineteen years ago.

As a therapist myself now, I know that the way "the system" responds to someone who has been abused plays a big part in the healing process. If the wound of the abuse is acknowledged immediately, the healing is able to begin. If the wound is denied, infection sets in and sometimes results in death.

By the time my healing process began my wound was twenty years old and very infected. It took me fifteen years to clean out the infection. And now the healing is well under way.

Rosemary Sullivan
St. Armand, Quebec

✉ Elly Resurrect

You are an Easter person:
you lived for years
on the cross
derided, abused, alone.

You lived there
until you buried you
your body your grave

139

in which you hid
in unrecognized death
until you could
perceive the chink of light
roll your death away
and emerge into the arabesque
of air-blown art danced
onto canvas in light shed
by your discarded you.

Joanna M. Weston
Duncan, British Columbia

✉ **On the Verge**

On the verge of silence, she lives inside,
Afraid of umbrellas, afraid of stairs,
Searching in vain for a place to hide.

Knives are companions, and sharp shards of glass,
But paper is suspect. Shredded, unread,
Small pieces of letters are strewn on the grass.

Though daily she writes, with invisible pen,
Only the cat comprehends her thick thoughts.
"When it's over," she says, "you will understand then."

She plants tiny seeds in the living-room rug
Which she waters each day with her tears.
When they come with the jacket to take her away,
She'll deny all her fears.

She's looking for fire or water to boil
To erase the unspeakable.
"The weakness of woman is silence," she quotes,
When I get her to open the door.

Only her father knows the truth,
But he missed detection with timely death.
"He loved me, he loved me," she chants,
While smashing the dishes he sent for her wedding.
I can't figure out what she wants.

"I'm rereading Shakespeare," she says,
"I see he says he sees reason in madness."

The weakness of woman is silence.
The weakness of woman is
The weakness of woman.

Barbara Florio Graham
Gatineau, Quebec

THE
MORNINGSIDE
BOOK OF LISTS

As with most of the contests we run on the radio, this one, in which listeners were asked simply to make a list in the style that made such a best seller out of the original *Book of Lists*, started with a composition of my own, in this case (though I tried some others later on) a compilation of what I blithely called "the ten best things in the world." I reproduced that list – home-made strawberry ice cream, Sable Island, Roger Angell writing on baseball, gas barbecues, hand-knit socks, September, shirtwaist dresses, Evelyn Hart, newly talcumed babies and Judy Garland singing "Somewhere Over the Rainbow" – in the journal I published in 1988, and one astute critic, Mark Abley of the Montreal *Gazette*, who once wrote a profile of me and knows me well, chastised me in an otherwise friendly review for being, shall we say, hypocritical. For home-made ice cream, he suggested as an example, I might more honestly have substituted single-malt Scotch; for newly talcumed babies . . . well, never mind.

Though I bridled a bit at Mark's review – wrote him a shirty letter, in fact – the truth is he had me; if I don't appreciate Scotch whisky, single-malt or otherwise, more than I like ice cream, you'd never know it from my record of consumption.

But, what the heck. The point of my opening salvoes is really just to get the listeners going anyway, and this time, once again, it worked. With much more wit and imagination than I'd been able to show, they sent me lists of everything from jobs they'd liked to have had to reasons they were still married. They sent in lists they'd found around the house, used for other occasions (the wonderful and self-explanatory "Forty Lines," for example, was written by Carole and Martin Gerson for a birthday) or written for our contest. As well, as with this first offering, they just sent in letters *about* lists.

⊠ Consider these items: telephone poles, flag-poles, street lamps, deserted totem poles, strung-up Christmas trees, TV towers, tents, drunks, sailboats and leaky freighters. Do you see the connection? Well, then consider these: creative *Morningside* listeners, successful real estate agents, generally absent-minded people and most folks who have one leg shorter than the other. Have you got it yet? Yes, of course, they all list.

It's endemic. It's uncanny really. Why, when I open my eyes every morning, my whole world is on its side. (Well, very nearly. I have a small pillow.)

"Straighten up," I say to myself, rubbing my eyes and rising from my cot. "Straighten up and fly right."

And I do. (Most days.) I try not to list.

Karen Alton
Oakville, Ontario

⊠ I have always been amazed by my neighbour Lois Hayes, who starts each morning off by composing her "list for the day."

143

Lois has her entire day laid out for her on a list. Each morning, at exactly 9:10 A.M. Lois calls me and tells me all the things on her list of "Things to tell Dianne" so we will not waste the entire day yacking on the telephone. But I'm not as well organized as Lois, since all my lists are in my head.

One morning, however, Lois called me in a panic because she had lost her list for the weekend. Friday mornings she plans a big list that will get them through to Monday. She wondered if I'd seen it at our exercise class the night before, or perhaps in my car. We went back and checked the exercise room and then we went over to the video store where we had stopped on the way home. We tried to describe this pile of crumpled paper to the man who had given us the video. The only success we had was amusing a group of onlookers.

I still don't know if Lois ever found that list, but that question would be on my list of "things to ask Lois" if I had one.

Dianne Wood
Newmarket, Ontario

✉ Last winter my fifteen-year-old son and I were watching television when one of those "the-sale-you've-been-waiting-for" commercials came on the air. Now, at last, we were being offered the rattan the movies made famous. Rattan furniture? The rattan the movies made famous? What movies?

And then it came to us. *Rattan Wars! Dr. Rattan!* How could we have forgotten? The list goes on, of course, and we pinned it to our bulletin board so we'd never again forget. It's our favourite list, and we wanted to share it with you.

The Good, the Bad and the Rattan
Three Rattans for Sister Sarah
Return of the Magnificent Rattan
The Rattan Strikes Back
Rattan Goes to Hollywood

Bedtime for Rattan
The Rattan Always Rings Twice
The Big Rattan
The Search for Rattan
The Wrath of Rattan
Evil Under the Rattan

Karey Perks
Victoria

✉ This past summer (or was it one hundred years ago?) when I was lounging on a beach and intermittently gazing at the sunset, I read this amazing little book by J.P. de Coussade called *Abandonment to Divine Providence* (published in 1792) in which he advises us to "Embrace the present moment as an ever-flowing source of holiness." The gist of it is that every event of every instant is a gift from God, to the end of His glorification and my sanctification. Wonderful, edifying stuff (especially while watching the rose turn violet turn blue turn black that evening sunset).

Well, now I'm home, mucking along in the old sanctifying day-to-day routine with three little kids, and you have invited us to send you a list. Here's mine:

A Partial List of What I Needed to Embrace at 4:32 P.M. Last Night:

1. The whole white wash has been stained again by an errant runny blue sock.
2. Mariko's furious because her new shirt is ruined.
3. We forgot her optometrist appointment.
4. Someone spilled a glass of juice and now I've walked in it.
5. Toshi just grabbed Erin's doll and she's screaming.
6. We're late for music lessons.
7. The meat for the stew is smoking.
8. I sliced my finger in with the onions.

9. The telephone is ringing off the wall . . .
   Enough! I'm embracing! I'm embracing!

Eileen O'Donnell
Victoria

✉   I am sitting beside Sarah on the piano bench (this is the fourth Sarah I've taught in three years) when she turns to me with an eager smile and says, "I learned a piece from my friend." I know what is coming, but smile encouragingly and reply, "Would you like to play it for me?" Of course, it is "Chopsticks," with which she has been regaling (tormenting) her family all week. "Well," I say in my brightest voice when she has finished, "that was very nice. But you know that's what people who don't really know how to play can sometimes play." Will this put an end to the torture? Sometimes. Actually, the piece could also be "Heart and Soul" (the top or bottom of this charmless duet): it's second on my list of least beloved music.

We turn our attention to her beginners' book. The next piece is called "Indian Dance," or "Indian Song," or "Indian War Dance," or "Indians" or "Tom Toms," depending on which book we are using. I would like to skip over this piece with its incessant left-hand fifths. I have taught some version of it several times a year for the past fifteen years. But the attractive picture on the page has caught Sarah's eye, and she would really like to learn this piece. It has no musical merit as far as I can see, but maybe it reinforces some of the concepts she has been learning, so of course we do it. Why does every beginners' book have to have an "Indian Song"? It certainly has nothing to do with Native culture.

Most beginners' books also have versions of the following pieces: "Good King Wenceslas" (which no seven-year-old has yet pronounced), "Twinkle Twinkle Little Star," "How Much Is that Doggie in the Window," and "Oh When the Saints Go Marching In." Please put these high on my list.

As students progress, the main clichés are Beethoven's "Für

146

Elise" (usually attempted about two years before the student can play the middle bit, and often with extra twiddles in the main theme), and the first movement of the "Moonlight Sonata." I never teach these pieces unless a student asks for them, but sometimes, surprisingly, the person's enthusiasm makes up for lack of technical skill.

I should say that there are some wonderful teaching books available that do avoid the clichés. And I remember my own experiences of learning to play. Every piece seemed extraordinarily important. I would have felt terribly cheated to have missed my turn at the "Indian Dance," although I was probably the fourth child in our family to pound it out.

But as a teacher, I have taken one sacred vow. In memory of my father, who sat through four kids' worth of student recitals over many years, and endured many renditions of his least favourite piece, no student from my studio will ever perform the "Variations on Three Blind Mice." Please, Sarah, don't ever ask for it.

Ruth Kazdan
Toronto

📧 Things I Miss

The way the air used to smell first thing on a spring or summer morning – a smell, I was told, that was from ozone, but which I suspect came from some form of pollution – a smell I clearly associate with a special freshness.

Ten-cent comic books.

The ads for X-ray glasses, sea monkeys, growing crystal gardens and body-building schemes, to be found only on the inside and back covers of those comics.

Paperback "Pocket Books" that sold for thirty-five cents.

The horse-drawn Brown's Bread wagon that used to come down our street, with its smells of bread wrapped in waxed paper.

The smell of one of my uncle Moe's freshly lit cigarettes, but it had to be lit with the electric cigar lighter in the car. Only that first caramel-sweet puff counted.

The ditch that ran in front of all our houses. It carried rain water and the foamy grey waste that the sump pump would rhythmically spew out the red clay pipe sticking out from the front shoulder of our lawns. This ditch, our mothers swore, was the source of polio and every other hideous disease known to humankind, but it was so much fun to dam up or to race paper or stick boats in. We would watch them enter the culvert tunnels under the driveways and then speed to the other end to see which would emerge first.

The sump pump.

The ice truck, smelling of damp canvas and rich sawdust, wafting a cool breeze over the tail-gate even on the hottest summer day. It was the only source of crystal-clear cold and sweet chunks of winter when most needed.

Findlay Dairy Bar, which was not close, but not too far away, where a single scoop of ice cream cost six cents, a double ten and a triple fifteen – they wouldn't pile up more than five. We would order Swiss mocha for me, maple walnut for my mom and orange pineapple for Mom's friend Rose.

Fountain pens, with a little lever on the side to pump them full of ink with, even though the levers slid painfully under my thumbnail more times than I like to remember.

My grandmother's music box that played Brahm's waltz in A flat.

Fall bonfires where the leathery smell of damp leaves blended with the smell of burning. At night bright leaves of flame would leap into the air, blue-jean fronts would be hot as ironing boards and steam would rise from smiles and from potatoes baked under the leaves.

Hardware stores with floors, shelves, barrels and bins all made of wood smelling of metal and oil and fresh putty; stores with all the nuts and bolts and washers and nails exposed so that you can run your fingers through them and feel their weight and quality.

Real chips (not foppish french fries) made from potatoes that have never heard of a freezer, never felt hot oil twice and were served in paper cones, drenched with salt and malt vinegar, and eaten with a toothpick.

The elegant vase shapes of elm trees.

The smell of paste floor wax and lemon oil.

The sound of a push mower, and the smell of new-mown grass uncontaminated with exhaust fumes.

The smell of DDT.

The sound of metal-wheeled roller skates on the sidewalk.

The knife-grinder's bell, the uneven sound of his foot-pedalled grindstone and the burned flint smell of the shower of sparks that spin bursting from its edge.

The heavy slippery shininess of the dollop of mercury acquired from the dentist's office.

Bob Lackie
Toronto

✉ Ten Jobs I'd Have Trained for If When I Was Eighteen I'd Known They Were Going to Exist

1. Oyster farmer
2. Genetic engineer
3. Consulting sinologist
4. Ethicist
5. Consulting philosopher to an artificial-intelligence project
6. Cryptobiologist
7. Arbitrageur
8. Patent lawyer specializing in living organisms
9. Lyricist-songwriter-singer-arranger-synthesizer musician
10. International treaty negotiator.

Gail Bell
Burnaby, British Columbia

✉ How to Behave When You Are in My Room

1. No kicking
2. No pushing
3. No jumping on the bed
4. No hitting
5. No swearing
6. No acting like a maniac
7. No slapping
8. No fighting
9. No calling names
10. No stealing
11. No picking your nose

Kari Annell
St. Anne, Manitoba

✉ Questions Parents Ask in the Month of August

1. When does school start?
2. Why do children fight over who sits in the front *every time* they go out in the car?
3. When does school start?
4. Why does my child's energy level increase in direct proportion to the decrease in my own energy level?
5. Why does the kid selling Dickie Dee frozen treats park right outside my door for half an hour at a time?
6. When does school start?
7. Why does water that is sloshing around in a swimming pool or lake elicit so much unrestrained joy when the same water contained in a bathtub can cause near-panic?
8. How come I'm ready for bed each night long before the kids are?
9. How come the children are ready to wake up each morning long before I am?
10. Why does my young daughter preface at least half her statements each day with the words "no fair!"?

11. How does the common house-fly know that it takes the average four-year-old two and a half minutes to close the screen door?

12. Where do children get all that energy? What happens to it at the merest whisper of household chores?

13. When does school start?

14. Why do children spend all of May and June waiting for summer holidays, but as soon as they begin, complain that there's nothing to do?

15. What's it like to have nothing to do?

16. Where are my pens, writing paper and scissors?

17. Why am I overcome with glee whenever I see teachers I know with two or three of their own children in tow?

18. Why are summer holidays so long when you're a parent, but so short when you're a kid?

19. Why do all those scrapes and bruises magically heal when I "kiss it better"?

20. Am I the only parent who feels thankful for children to remind me of the boundless joy and sense of freedom with which I, too, once greeted each warm and sun-filled day?

21. When does school start?

Linda Moffatt
Aylmer, Ontario

✉ Things New Mothers Don't Need to Hear

1. Don't pick the baby up – you'll spoil him.

2. You've got too many clothes on him/her.

3. You haven't got enough clothes on her.

4. Your milk probably isn't good enough – or you haven't got enough milk.

5. How come you're not nursing?

6. How do you put in your time?

7. What have you done all day?

8. You've just got to let the baby cry.

9. You're not feeding solids *yet?*

10. We thought *you* could have the party, since you're home all day.

11. When are you going back to work?

12. You're not going to leave your child and go back to work?

Alice Thompson
Willowdale, Ontario

✉ Some things mothers should tell their city daughters who are about to leave home to marry farmers

1. Just because a pregnant cow is panting in the hot sun, it doesn't always mean she is about to give birth.

2. When giving your pigs a drink at the dug-out in winter, make sure you dig two holes in the ice. (In case any fall in, they will at least have an exit.)

3. During spring seeding, never make right-hand turns when pulling a discer behind your tractor. (It will make crunching grinding noises and turn into a different shape. It will turn your farmer all red as well.)

4. Never phone your mother to complain. (She'll tell you, "I told you so.")

Myrna Kendall
Stoughton, Saskatchewan

✉ Things I Hate About Computers

Item 1. Just when I need the computer most, something is bound to go wrong.

Item 2. When things are going right, see item 1.

David F. Fayram
Bellingham, Washington

✉ Cross-Country Culinary Catastrophes and Their Victims

1. Oshawa, Ontario. Set back of my sweater on fire (I was wearing it) while poaching eggs. Hot fudge sauce hardened and it took a week to get spoon out. Victims – my family (parents and siblings), the Proutys.
2. Val d'Or, Quebec. Tomato aspic melted over edge of dish, and I should never have tried to thicken the cake's icing with flour. Victim – John Kennedy.
3. Wolfe Island, Ontario. Chocolate cake turned to rubber due to substitution of sugar-cube-style saccharin for white sugar. Victims – the Mullins.
4. Wolfe Island, Ontario. After church, crossed from Kingston on ferry to home, no electricity – so had to warm elegant meal on Coleman stove. Victims – the Hinckeys.
5. Lower Sackville, Nova Scotia. Guests seated at table. Opened hot oven to remove centre-piece of meal – vegetarian roast. No roast – still uncooked in fridge. Victims – the David Bartiliers.

Eating at our house is often an adventure – at least it gives guests something to talk about when they eat in safer venues!

Janet Brock
Thunder Bay, Ontario

✉ The Four Most Useful Things I Have Learned in Recent Years

1. You *can* get rid of "fairy ring" in your lawn, and it costs nothing. Pull the little mushrooms up carefully, then rub fireplace ash into the spaces that are left. You may have to do this several times in a summer, but the following year the problem is gone.
2. If you have a leg cramp, lift your foot off the floor and stretch it hard, heel first.
3. An old spray bottle filled with clean water takes the pain out of ironing. Just "spritz" as needed to dampen wrinkled areas.

4. If you can't read a number in the phone book *upstairs* and your glasses are *downstairs*, hold the book up to your magnifying make-up mirror. (Okay, so it's backwards, but it's easier to figure that out than walk down and up again.)

Joan Cope
Calgary

✉ Here are a few of the incorrect predictions I've made over a fairly long lifetime:

1. In 1933 I predicted that the only threat to peace in Europe was Mussolini, and that Adolph Hitler was a clown who would never amount to much.
2. While I was doing research on explosives during the war, I was aware that many scientists were quietly disappearing from their usual haunts to labour in what was cheerfully known as the "Bubble-Gum Factory" in Los Alamos. I predicted that an atomic bomb could not be made. Actually, I feel in good company here as Ernest Rutherford, the father of nuclear energy, thought so, too.
3. I was in England in 1963 when the Beatles returned from a tour of Germany. The headlines screamed "The Beatles are going to America." Yes, you're right – I predicted they'd flop.

Ken Cheetham
Willowdale, Ontario

✉ Fatal Misses (Too Depressing to Contemplate)

1. Offered a half share in London's *first* McDonald's restaurant – turned it down as I didn't think it would take off as we had several A&W fast-food outlets.
2. Turned down *free* double lot at Blue Mountain, Colling-

wood, and help – *free* – to build a chalet if we would just come. Didn't bother as who would go there and I would be all alone and it would never get off the ground.

3. Offered a two-storey colonial-century home in Niagara-on-the-Lake for $20,000 – turned it down as how would we get our money back when we would have to spend so much to fix it up?

4. Turned down Chrysler stock at $3.50 a share. I wasn't a fool – it had no hope.

Helen Nisbet
London, Ontario

✉ Why We Are Still Married

1. Who else would have either one of us?
2. We are still waiting for the "for better" part.
3. We are still waiting for the "for richer" part.
4. We are staying together for the sake of our parents.
5. Two can live cheaper than one (one what?).
6. Neither one of us really wants the cat.
7. Both of us want the computer.
8. We only have one TV set.
9. He won't take the kids, and neither will I.
10. We promised to stay together, in front of witnesses!

Cath Field Povaschuk
Edmonton

✉ Here are ten observations I have made on life and the world in general on the occasion of my turning forty.

1. I will never, ever, get used to or like going to the dentist.

2. The disposable diaper is the greatest invention of the twen-tieth century.

3. Whenever I take my children to a park, there will always be a puddle at the bottom of the slide.

4. The flip side of not accepting personal responsibility for myself is feeling powerless to change myself.

5. My mother was right when she nagged me about wearing a hat when I'm out in the sun.

6. I will probably never vote for any one of the three major political parties in Canada, even when I'm grown up.

7. Speaking out is about all I can do to change the world.

8. As a mother it is not my job to be continually appeasing the great god of boredom.

9. Even though I don't have a $340 graphite tennis racquet and a pair of $89.95 designer tennis shoes, I have somehow managed to get the ball over the net for more than two decades.

10. Brussels sprouts, spinach and liver taste exactly the way they did when I was ten. But, then, so does a hot-fudge sundae.

Annabelle Cooper
Toronto

✉ A Few Nice Things About Being Over Fifty

1. Accepting the fact that, no matter how hard I try, I'll never have thicker hair or thinner thighs.

2. Changing priorities, from filing recipes I've clipped but know I'll never use, to learning new tricks on my computer.

3. Being able to laugh at the latest fashions, as I gloat over things I've saved that have come back into style (rhinestone jewellery, crinolines, sweater sets, pearls, gloves).

4. Holding onto some old-fashioned clocks, to back up the digitals that go crazy at the most momentary power interruption.

5. Telling people who telephone before 9:00 A.M. and ask if they woke me up (they always do, and I always used to lie and say no) that I'm still in bed and will call them back later.

6. Using my bad knee as an excuse to get out of anything I don't feel like doing.

Barbara Florio Graham
Gatineau, Quebec

✉ Forty Lines

40 days and
40 nights
40 winks
40 years in the desert
40 thieves
40 toes – in your family and mine
and also 40 fingers.
40 immortals in the Académie Française
42nd Street
The Forty-Second Parallel
and also the forty-ninth
and the miner, forty-niner,
and the forty-two-line Bible.
40 is not in the *Shorter Bartlett's Familiar Quotations* index,
nor is 40 in *Canadian Quotations and Phrases*;
but there is Eugene Forsey.
There must be 40 of something in 10 4-H Club kids.
We all know about 40-oz. bottles,
and "tea for two and two *for tea*."
Forty Fort is near Scranton, Pennsylvania
and in the Yukon there is an abandoned settlement named Forty
    Mile.
That exhausts the *Canadian Encyclopedia*; however, there are
    32 entries beginning with fort, eh?
plus a full page on forti-fication.
Forty-spot is the Tasmanian name for the bird *pardalotus quad-
    ragintus* (OED);

"forthy" was once a word (for this reason, therefore) and also
  "forby."
Forty Years for Labrador (1933) was written by Sir Wilfred
  Grenfell,
Mozart composed 41 symphonies, of which No. 40 is many peo-
  ple's favourite;
Ronald Reagan is the 40th U.S. president.
A quarantine lasts for 40 days,
and somebody in this room must wear size 40 somewhere.
Article 40 of the Canadian constitution deals with amendments
  relating to educational or cultural matters;
Article 40 of *Roberts' Rules of Order* refers to "Dilatory, Absurd,
  or Frivolous Motions";
Stephen Forty lives in Coquitlam
South Dakota was the 40th state to enter the Union
Bach's 40th prelude and fugue is in D Minor
and his 40th Cantata was written for Christmas Monday, 1723.
The Forty-Foot Drain is a canal connecting Old Nene to Old
  Bedford in Cambridgeshire.
Concocting lists isn't everyone's forté
But we have managed 40 lines of 40.

Carole and Martin Gerson
Vancouver

✉ Things I Swear I'll Never Do Again Every Time I Do Them

  1. Plant too many zucchini.
  2. Wear panty hose.
  3. Give the baby an Arrowroot cookie in my car.
  4. Raise chickens.
  5. Shop at Canadian Tire.
  6. Work full-time.
  7. Buy a magazine subscription that must be paid by cheque
  or money order in U.S. funds.

8. Drink more than three cups of coffee.

9. Lose my Swiss army knife.

10. Drive Highway 401 through Toronto on a Friday or Sunday night.

Deb Chatreau
Thomasburg, Ontario

✉ Why I Like an Outhouse

1. There is no toilet to scrub or back up.
2. There are two seats, so the little girls can go together.
3. It is far enough from the house so that the phone can't be heard.
4. Most important, it gets you outside first thing in the morning.

On A Visit Home

The fat, red-apple pincushion sits
on the window sill of my mother's kitchen
where it has always sat. It holds:
Straight pins,
    like the ones I bent, pushing prints, posters, and (I thought)
        personality into the unyielding plaster of parental walls;
Safety pins
    many-sized, to keep one safe: no-nonsense, steel giants to fasten
        hems and hanging jacket pockets, book bags, and other bro-
        ken business;
      apologetic, tiny brass ones to fasten ribbon ties under Peter
        Pan collars, and sometimes name-tags for political meetings;
      self-effacing, medium ones for everything, from mittens on my
        snowsuit cuffs to yellow roses on my wedding dress;
Hat pins –
    There used to be three, one black. Now just two, pearl-tipped,
      bear witness to the changing times: my mother hasn't worn
      a hat for thirty years.

All sorts of points to this . . .
Perhaps the main one is
how fastened to this house I am.
My dreams, my failures, and my several wins,
though seeming free,
and moving in and out with me,
are tethered here,
attached with pins.

Muriel Sibley
Victoria

✉   Three Pleasant Meetings of Opposites

1. Drinking cold milk from a warm cup.
2. Skiing hard enough that you almost sweat.
3. In a cold land . . . a warm people.

Bill Barr
Vegreville, Alberta

CHRISTMAS, PAST AND PRESENT

It's years now since *Morningside* solicited letters about Christmas, but still they come: stories, memories, emotional recollections – so much so that reading them on the air as the season approaches, and sometimes on the magic day itself, has become the program's own Christmas tradition.

Not all these stories, I should warn you, are happy ones. But somehow, as with the collection that appeared in the *New Papers* a couple of years ago, they convey the richness and the power of this enduring occasion in our lives.

✉ *I wrote this letter for my mother for Christmas. In our family we always give a present and "something else." This was my mother's else. She is seventy-seven years old.*

I remember you when you were twenty-four, because I remember being four and standing in the garden on Grantham Avenue with pink peonies taller than I was waving around me. I remember the smell of them and the satiny feel of the petals on my cheek. I remember that garden, and it seems that everything was in bloom at the same time – the peonies, the irises, the lilac, the plum trees, the cherry tree and the funny bush with the pink flowers that we were never sure of the name – flowering quince, japonica? I remember when the cherry tree was taller than I could reach, and when a blanket hung over the forks of the branches made a tent. I also remember the shine of the bark and the way it felt to swing on the big branch and hang upside down from the forks.

Summer was hollyhock dolls and rhubarb eaten raw with a handful of sugar, and eating peas out of the pods and sticking bean leaves on our noses and faces. The bridge of your nose was the place to stick maple keys in the spring. I remember baskets and baskets of cherries, and pies, and what a surprise it was when I was much older to realize that there were cherries that were black and sweet and not bright red and tart.

I remember the currant bushes and the plum tree that only produced one plum a season; the plum was usually waspy when we found it. I remember cocoa and cinnamon toast. If anything can bring back winter, they can. Walking home from Brownies or the Red Shield, up Wellington Street hill, stopping to slide down the hill, bouncing and bumping on pieces of cardboard, getting caked with snow (remember how it stuck to those melton cloth ski pants?), getting cold and running home and being brushed off with the broom and then eating cinnamon toast and cocoa. If I want a sense of warmth and home and comfort, I make cinnamon toast.

There are small bright pictures still in my mind – so clear and real I can feel, smell and touch the things I see. The water in the creek in the park – brown and dark and smooth and cool – and you swimming with me, you lying on your back, me with my arms around your neck. Sitting in the water in the "baby part" and watching the clear water rush over the pebbles and the crabs scuttling around. Walking home from a ball game wearing Dad's sweater, eating double-dip cones from Stokely's, side-by-side cones they were and a whole six cents each. Baseball and Dad playing first base. And Dad taking Fred with him to hockey games at night and me watching the lights of the car disappear from the dining-room window and being mad because I couldn't go because I was a girl and they were going to have pie. Still sulking after fifty years? Probably.

I can still feel and smell the cool black of your sealskin coat and how I used to love to stand with my face buried in it after you'd been out in the cold. And how you liked high-heeled shoes, and what great legs you had. Buying you stockings from Parson's, with seams, and having the lady put her hand in the stocking to show the shade.

And the Sewing Circle. We would lie on our stomachs in the hall, listening to the laughter and the talk, eyeing the sandwiches and hoping they wouldn't eat all the salmon or the egg salad. We would watch you through the grate wrapping Christmas presents in red and green tissue, and freeze on the linoleum in an attempt to see the presents. Then we would run downstairs to stand over the grate to get dressed – those damned vests with the garters for the brown stockings I was always destroying by ripping out the knees. And the bloomers. And how I hated that brown teddy-bear coat I had in kindergarten. I tried to destroy it by putting snowballs in the pockets but I don't think it worked. I wanted a Red River coat with a woollen sash.

Hallowe'en – running for the nuns, trying to get fudge, then choking on a piece of candy and Dad holding me upside down and shaking me to get it loose. I remember the exact colour of his hair, too – it was reddy brown – and combing it and making funny parts while he tried to read the paper. He could bounce an orange up his arm by flexing his muscles. We would lie on the floor laughing while he read the newspaper Fred and I had written – it must have been great stuff or his delivery was good, because I can still remember how hard we laughed. And I remember you reading to us by candle-light and always being there no matter what we did – me playing "Silent Night" on a harmonica at a Christmas concert. Oh, those Christmas concerts and the Sunday-school picnics!

I remember peanut-butter cookies that never got a chance to cool and chocolate cake from the baker and cream buns and blocks of ice and red and green Jell-O. And Bailey's when Minerva was young and Grandpa got blocks of chewing tobacco and gave me the metal bits that were pressed in the centre.

I remember standing in the sink while you washed me, and how a flyswatter feels when applied to the backs of the legs. And listening to the radio–Amos and Andy, Charley McCarthy and the hockey games. And the way you cooked sausages, and meat pie, and lemon pie.

And Christmas and Easter and the taste of grass in summer.

And how I could tell when I opened the door if you were home or not. I'm glad I can still do that. I love you.

Joan Williamson
Guelph, Ontario

✉ It's my first Christmas in retirement. For thirty years I've had a congregation to care for through all the hectic days of preparation: the decorating of the church by the faithful ladies of the Altar Guild; helping the Sunday-school superintendent select the readers for the children's pageant and the Christmas Eve family service; consulting with the organist on the music, which had to be co-ordinated with all the liturgical necessities, including the traditional midnight Eucharist. I would also arrange Communion for the shut-ins who were at home, in hospitals or at the local nursing home and help my faithful wife plan not only the family Christmas with grown children and our beautiful grandchildren, but also that tradition we began on the first Christmas in our first parish so many years ago – open house for any and all in the rectory after the midnight service.

In between mad shopping trips, my wife would prepare her famous seafood chowder, tortière, glazed baked ham, Christmas cake, assorted sweets and a huge punch bowl. We never retired before three or four in the morning, only to be roused at the crack of dawn for the family Christmas-tree opening of gifts.

I always admired my wife's concentrated dedication to this part of our ministry. Even approaching age seventy, on our last Christmas in our last parish, she did not omit one thing: she helped the Altar Guild and the choir, both of which she was active in, and did not forget anything for the kids and grandchildren, including a huge fresh turkey for the festive board along with her wonderful fruit-cake and plum pudding made from an ancient recipe passed down through the generations of her English family. Needless to say, she was much loved by all and sundry in the two parish churches we had served together over the last thirty years. She'll be greatly missed by all who knew her.

Now I'm in Toronto, after thirty-eight years away, with no busy church to be concerned about. I reflect on what it all meant. Through it all, that eternal verity trying to burst through the din of the frantic search of human hearts in the commercialized reality of a great modern city, I sat in the sanctuary of a church so huge that my small-town parish church would have fitted nicely into the transept with room to spare. I stole a glance at the nave, full with more than twenty-five hundred faithful worshippers. They sat quietly as the rector spoke words of wonderful hope and comfort for anyone who might be lonely or in despair, or seeking absolution and strength to go on, and for those who simply had hearts full of faith and happiness to share with their fellows at the crib of the blessed Child of Christmas.

He is, to me, a very wise young priest. Not only did he need help to administer the Sacrament to so large a gathering, he also knew that the old clergy who were no longer active in the ministry needed likewise to serve, to be part of God's great act of grace in receiving our poor pleadings and returning to us the wonder of His own self-giving to uphold and upbuild us in our journey through life.

At the time of Communion, it was my great privilege to offer again the blessed Cup and murmur the sacred words: "The blood of our Lord Jesus Christ, shed for thee, preserve thy body and soul unto everlasting life, drink this in remembrance that Christ's blood was shed for thee, and be thankful." And once again it all came together – all the long years of looking into the expectant eyes of the kneeling communicants as they looked up and gently received the Cup, tipping the Cup to let the wine touch their lips. Such faces, especially tonight–in a polyglot congregation–there are old faces like mine, the young faces of children and teens and couples with sleeping babes in arms, black faces, East Indian faces, Oriental faces, plain faces and beautiful faces, but faces mysteriously alike with a kind of special radiance.

It's the stuff of heaven, and in that vaulted splendour, the smell of candle wax and the muted voices of the choir, it has the ring of truth. All else can be ordinary or beautifully created from the best human endeavour, but this lifts the faithful hearts of our common humanity to the uttermost realms of glory. All becomes possible and there is hope and peace for the rest of the long way home.

The Reverend William Ashby
Toronto

✉ It happened twelve years ago, just a few days before the first Christmas in the first and only house my wife and I ever had, a little house on lots of land.

Though there were plenty of white pines of Christmas-tree height on the property, we had decided that cutting down trees didn't fit with our recently adopted ecological stance. The night before a close friend was to visit, we hauled out the bag of artificial tree parts.

After assembling its credibly flat needles in its carefully studied asymmetry, and after stringing on the twinkling minilights (all twinkling now, thanks to an hour of fiddling), my wife and I sat down and stared at the tree. Neither of us said anything. Then she caught my eye.

"Are you thinking what I'm thinking?"

"Yes. This is ridiculous! Here we are surrounded by acres of trees and we put up this musty-smelling hunk of plastic. Maybe we could find a group that could stand some thinning out . . . "

"Let's go."

By this time, though, it was after ten o'clock. It was dark and cold. But we had to get the tree up that night. Our friend was coming the next day.

I grabbed the saw (I couldn't find the axe) and the flashlight with the batteries I had been going to replace more than two months before.

Choosing a Christmas tree is never easy. But try choosing one in pitch dark with a flashlight that can't muster anything more than a six-inch spot of medium brown light.

"See that tree over there?"

"Where?"

"Where I'm shining the light."

"Could you give me a clue?"

I wiggled the light.

"Oh! Over there. Okay."

"Now watch carefully. I'm going to flash the light back and forth across the tree. I'll do it from top to bottom. Try to remember what you see. Ready?"

"Ready."

I painted the tree with the spot of light. "What do you think?"

"Send me another transmission."

I did it again.

"I'm having trouble remembering the top. Start from the bottom this time."

For the next half hour we wandered all over the property, painting every tree in light that got increasingly more brown. Finally, numb with cold and with visions of disembodied branches dancing in our heads, one of us said, "Let's take that one." We sawed it down and carried it home.

It smelled good. Unfortunately, we couldn't say the same about the way it looked. It was rather gangly. But no one could say it wasn't symmetrical: every gap on one side was balanced by one on the other. But it was our tree.

We decorated it, turned out all the room lights and admired it in its own twinkling light. But as the tree warmed up, its branches began to droop. Our perky little white pine was turning into a weeping willow as we watched. Nevertheless, we still liked it:

our first tree in our first house. And at least it was real.

And so was the fit our friend took as soon as she saw it the next day.

"Oh . . . it's . . . it's so . . . "

She seemed to be puffing up.

"It's so . . . it's . . . " She became totally incoherent.

In the middle of it all I thought I heard her say something about Charlie Brown. But by then my wife and I were gone, too. Between gasps and guffaws we managed to tell her the highlights of the selection process of the night before. We laughed ourselves as limp as our tree.

Since then I've had bigger and bushier trees. But I've never liked one better than our little Charlie Brown tree. No other tree made us feel so good.

Norm Esdon
Kingston, Ontario

✉ Christmas is a problem for me. As a Baha'i, I'm trying to make our Baha'i holy holidays special for my family. It's a young religion, so there are no traditions of carols, holly and ivy, or even special foods to augment the holiness of the days themselves. I look at the materialism and big business of Christmas and am quite happy about the opportunity to leave that behind. On the other hand, there's so much about my memories of Christmas that enrich the fabric of life and family. I'm looking for, and finding, ways to bring those magical qualities into our new traditions.

Although I've been a Baha'i for many years, my departure from Christmas coincided with our departure from Canada. We were in the final stages of packing for our move from St. Anthony, Newfoundland, to the Fiji islands. It was Christmas Day and the boys had been asking about their grandparents, because their friends had been talking about spending Christmas with relatives. I explained that Nanna and Grampa were far away in Toronto, but that we could go and visit some other grandparents.

We spent the afternoon making shortbread cookies and decorating a tin. I phoned the seniors' home to see if we could come and visit.

All the folks who were still there had no families to go to, so they were alone. We went into a sitting room where a few women were gathered, and Geoffrey, then three years old, took the cookie tin around to each person. While I chatted with each of them, Blair – he was one and a half – did his exuberant skip-hop around the room, to the delight of the old ladies.

The one everybody called Aunt Bertha slowly shuffled out of the room. We made our way down the hall and met three gentlemen. Geoff again passed out shortbread, while I chatted. One of the men pulled out his wallet and gave the boys each a dollar. I tried to decline, but he insisted. Tears filled his eyes, and he said, "Please, I have no one to give presents to." The kids pushed their fortunes into their pockets and Geoff told the man what he was saving up for. His benefactor smiled broadly.

We continued to visit everyone in the home before returning to the sitting room. Aunt Bertha was waiting to give us a tin of Danish butter cookies. She was ninety-six years old, and had been given four such tins by distant relatives. Geoff was fascinated by her lack of teeth. Before we left, he went around and shook hands with everyone, wishing them a Merry Christmas, while Blair put silk flowers into the fake wishing well. Two elderly ladies watched, giggling with tears in their eyes.

Why does this mark my departure from Christmas? I guess because through this experience with my young children and elderly folks – strangers who became friends – I discovered that the cliché is true.

The things about Christmas that are precious to me can happen anywhere, anytime, not just in December. But when I use Aunt Bertha's cookie tin here in tropical Fiji, I can't resist whistling "I'm Dreaming of a White Christmas."

Pat Cameron
Fiji

✉ We lived, when I was small, at the top of Capilano Road. We were just about the last house before the watershed, and our winters were marked by animal migration and snow.

Our small house was rented, and its cedar siding was painted a deep factory green, but my parents were young and made the house a place of joy. The house even had a name painted on a sign and tacked to the siding. It was called Smilin' Through.

If you walked down our road and along the gravel street to your right, you would come to Taunton House. Taunton House was a private school for girls. Wendy and I wished we could join in the noisy midday play, but we were too little then to go to school.

One evening in winter, on a day too cold to play outside, Mother hurried us through an early dinner. "Where are we going?" we asked her. She answered, "To Taunton House. Tonight is the night of their Christmas concert." We knew that that meant we could stay out late.

She dressed us in our Christmas party dresses and helped us tie our blue-and-white Scandinavian bonnets. Through the sleeves of our coats she threaded our matching mittens with our names, Wendy and Gail, knitted into the design. Booted and coated we tramped through the snow.

Taunton House was alive. The lights from the windows were laminated to the snow outside. Music burst from the door with each opening and closing.

Excitedly, we rang the large brass key in the centre of the door. Brrng . . . brrng . . . Big girls in braids and white blouses answered the door and helped us undo the buttons on our coats and the laces on our warm fur boots. They walked us down the oiled-floor schoolroom and lifted us onto wide wooden chairs.

The neighbourhood fell silent.

The headmistress sat at an aging piano, and the choir began to sing. The first songs were familiar. Mother and Daddy were both good singers and had taught us lots of Christmas carols. But then the choir began to sing "God Rest Ye Merry Gentlemen." Captivated, I forgot about Mother, about sitting still, about being good. I slipped from my chair and stood in the centre of the aisle. Mother's hand attempted to restrain me, but an elderly neighbour whispered, "It's okay, Minnie, let her go." Entranced, I walked closer and closer to the singing girls, until I stood in front of the stage. "Oh, tidings of comfort and joy," the choir finished.

I knew I was standing up there all alone, and that was why the neighbours both laughed and clapped. I loved that concert, that night.

The world was a silent white nest when it was time to head for home. We even had to walk in Daddy's footsteps because the snow was so deep.

The parking lot of the Cleveland Dam has replaced Taunton House, and Smilin' Through is gone, but my eyes see and my ears hear now what they heard then, that Christmas when I was four years old.

Gail Mackay
North Vancouver

✉ Josephine Littledeer, a big, gentle woman with greying hair held back in an elastic, lived on the streets. Her father was in the old folks' home. She was the only one left and had no friendly place to go. Her eyes saw something beyond the borders of herself: her arms called to me. She held me and it seemed like we could both touch the earth. She whispered like a rabbit.

Josephine rarely spoke out loud. She'd move her lips and motion, then shake her head and cry. She'd hug me and whisper something I couldn't understand.

When she got her welfare cheque, she'd go to Pete's café and get food to go. She'd carry her lunch around the streets and let people bum from her. I took her out for lunch once, to a cafeteria in a hotel, but she wouldn't eat anything. She sat and watched the people around her, shook her head and whispered. I saw all that fear spilling out of her eyes. She wrapped up her lunch in serviettes – a chicken-salad sandwich and a Danish – and took it out on the streets and walked around with it.

Josephine took two kinds of pills every day and she left them with me to look after for her. My desk phone rang.

"Josephine's here for her pills."

She hugged me and whispered, "Can I have fifty cents?"

"I can't give out money, Josephine. Too many people ask me."

"Just fifty cents. This is my own father. I want to go to the old folks' home to visit him." Her voice was as fragile as glass.

She was a big apple doll of a woman who liked to decorate herself with a ribbon or a rhinestone pin, or a flower that grew wilted in her buttonhole. She bought lottery tickets. If she won, she'd take me on a trip to Chicago. We'd go in a taxi. Chicago, the windy city. She had an uncle there. We'd all go out for dinner to a five-star restaurant. I said, "Josephine, how could we go for dinner to a five-star restaurant? With all those courses? You'd want to take yours out on the streets and walk around with it."

She sat and watched things. Watched and listened. I think she was listening for the drum; to hear it beating inside her. I saw Josephine dance, big and soft and quiet. The drum called. Josephine moved like wind in the stars.

She always buttoned whatever she was wearing right up to the top button. She sat on a concrete step outside the friendship centre and watched the feet going by. She watched and listened to the autumn, listened to the papery rattle of the autumn grass, and the voices shivering there. All those voices moving towards her. The sun, falling into the flowers.

Josephine, who'd been silent all this time, sang the week before she died. It was mid-December. The cold arms of winter offered no comfort. Her eyes had a look of shocked disbelief: the tin walls inside her reverberated. She wept. She walked around the streets, singing carols from *War Cry*. It was a bright winter day. She came into the centre, singing in a thread-like voice, "It came upon a midnight clear . . . "

Josephine was wailing and trying to sing, but people didn't want her there. They booed her and told her to get out.

A little while later, she came back, singing the same carol.

"Cut it out, Josephine," someone shouted. "You can't make all that noise in here."

The world pulled away and left her in its shadow. She walked out to the empty street. She had her *War Cry* and a couple of pieces of bannock stuffed in the front of her brown coat with the big fur collar. She wore a scarf of robin's-egg blue.

The town Christmas tree stood at the intersection, a tree made perfect by boring holes and adding branches. The lights were like sugarplums, mocking her.

She walked blindly through the cold town. One thought, like a Ferris wheel, kept turning inside her. Home . . . home . . . home . . . She wanted to see her mother, the place where her mother once had been. Had her mother ever held her like a tree holds sunshine in its branches?

She came to the highway east. The sky was dizzy with falling snow.

Josephine walked a long way down the highway. Snow covered her clothes and made a lacy pattern in her hair. The wind came up and drove the snow at her. Home . . . she was returning to the gift of home.

She began to feel very heavy. The road was empty. She thought she was moving, but nothing seemed real. There was nothing to mark her distance; nothing to prove that she was real. She felt so heavy. She tried to keep moving. Seemed to be climbing a huge rolling hill, a hill soft with the fresh snow of Christmas. There was light, a beautiful warm Christmas light. She was walking into her mother's arms.

"Mother."

At last, there was someone to hold her. The sky began to open. There was light all around.

Josephine lay like a question mark beside the road. Snow fell on the meadow of her face. Her crumpled body was covered with mounds of lacy snow.

Sandi Johnson
Ganges, British Columbia

✉ It was my last year of university, and I was on my way home for Christmas. But I wasn't feeling very "Christmasy." My father had died the Christmas before. Just a few weeks ago, the house had been sold. I was heading to my mother's new place. I was excited about seeing it for the first time, but I longed to see the old place again. It wasn't occupied yet. I was going to arrive a bit early at Mother's anyway, so I decided to make a little detour.

I wasn't quite five when I first saw the place. Dad took us all out to see it while it was still under construction. Two planks were propped up to the door where, I was told, the front step would be. When we walked along them, their flexing almost catapulted me into the sea of mud where, I was told, the front lawn would be. Inside was a rickety ladder where the stairs to the second floor would be, and a yawning black hole in the floor where the basement steps would be. And the window, in what would be the living room, was a huge opening with no cross-pieces – an opening which, I was told, was called a "picture window."

By moving day, solid stairs had replaced the flexing planks and rickety ladders. And grass seed had worked a miracle on the mud.

We were in a new subdivision, only a few minutes' walk from the woods. We dug up four little spruce trees and planted them around the house. None of them was taller than I was.

For the first five years, there was little sign of growth. Every spring I checked. Every summer I watered them. Every fall I untangled the dead grasses and weeds from their needles. Every winter I shook the wet snow from their branches.

One particularly harsh winter killed two of them, but the sixth spring brought new growth in the other two. Each year after that they grew by a foot or more. I remember the first year they bore cones, the first spring the robins nested in their branches.

By the time I went to university, one of them had grown almost to the peak of the roof and the other wasn't far behind. I looked out the picture window through a tracery of spruce branches. It was like being in the woods.

Every time I came home, I would relax as soon as I saw those two trees sheltering the house from the road. Even this year, despite the sad memories of the previous Christmas, I was buoyed a little by good memories and looked forward to seeing the trees.

I rounded the last corner. The house was completely exposed to the road. Both my trees were gone.

It was almost dark when I arrived at my mother's. She explained that the new owner thought the trees obscured too much of the house, so he got City Works to cut them down. She said I could still see them, and told me where I could find them. "Go ahead," she said. "Dinner can wait."

I got back in the car and drove to City Hall. There they were, one on either side of the main entrance, both ablaze with Christmas lights. There were my private trees, cut down, gussied up. I liked them better when they were decorated with snow or with robins' nests.

In the middle of a crowd of passing strangers, I stared at my trees for a long time. They embodied all that was home to me; our roots were in the same place. We had grown up together. Now my father was gone, the house was sold, and my trees had been cut down. We both were severed from our roots. I couldn't share the pleasure of the passing crowd.

But as I got in the car, the image of the trees moved into the rear-view mirror, and it stayed there as I drove away.

That was more than twenty years ago. But today those trees still go with me wherever I go.

Norm Esdon
Kingston, Ontario

✉ The Christmas concert has always been a fertile training ground for future politicians. Many public figures got their first start on the stage as shepherds, wise men and Virgin Marys in the pageants put on in school auditoriums and church basements.

Although no politician, my earliest claim to fame was as a shepherd in the *Star of Bethlehem* – written, directed and produced by Miss Snelgrove, my Grade 3 teacher at Laura Secord Elementary on the outskirts of a little town named Neverville.

For the occasion I was dressed in my sister's blue bathrobe with a Turkish towel draped over my head. I wore an itchy beard of cotton wool and excelsior. On my feet, I had my dad's black bedroom slippers and carried a shepherd's crook fashioned from my granny's rubber-tipped cane.

My only line in the pageant was "Behold in the Heavens, the Star of Bethlehem," which I was to shout out when I got the signal from Miss Snelgrove, who was prompting from behind the manger. Wise Man Two was then to plug in the electric cord in order to light up the star supported by a coat hanger near the ceiling.

On the night of the concert, Wise Man One forgot where he had put his frankincense and myrrh, a special mixture of rosewater and brilliantine. Shepherd Four lost his whiskers. And, before I could let go with "Behold," my shepherd's crook got tangled with the extension cord to the Christmas tree standing in the corner of the stage.

Instead of the star of Bethlehem brightening the heavens, a burst of sparks showered down from the fuse box, which brought on utter darkness, crackling sounds and frantic shouts from parents in the front row to their loved ones on stage.

Miss Snelgrove cried out not to be "sore afraid" and ordered everyone, including the angels, to join hands and sing the first and last verses of "Silent Night." Mr. McGregor, the school janitor, came forward at once to check out the fuse box.

And, oh, how we sang! We rounded our lips, shaped our vowels, let our voices soar past the ventilators in the ceiling and held our notes firm and steady until at last Mr. McGregor found a new fuse and our sixty-watt star of Bethlehem shone again in lonely splendour.

Then I got the high sign from Miss Snelgrove and raised my voice in a mighty shout: "Behold in the Heavens, the Star of Bethlehem." A great cheer went up from the parents, and the pageant unfolded as it was supposed to. When the curtain finally came down, Miss Snelgrove was in tears of joy on yet another successful Christmas concert.

Today I sometimes wonder whatever happened to the Josephs and Marys, the shepherds, angels and wise men who took part in our pageants of old.

I do know that two Josephs ended up as senior aldermen on the town council of Neverville and that one became a judge. Three of the wise men eventually were on the police commission; another landed a job as chairman of the school board; and two shepherds made it to the Agriculture Land Office. Berty Bunt, who tumbled out of the manger one year and cracked open his head, is now a school superintendent somewhere in Northern Ontario. Patsy McBride, the best Virgin Mary we ever had, became a beauty queen and took all the prizes three years in a row at the Superior North-West Farm Implements Fair.

Ah, yes, the beautiful angels with their cheesecloth wings and haloes of tinsel and wire. What happened to them? Well, it takes all kinds to run this world, and as time passed the angels became mothers, members of the local PTA and the Temperance Union. One even chaired the Commission on Divorce Reform for years.

Before we bid farewell to the Christmas concert for yet another year, we must praise Miss Snelgrove, who for so long kept alive its customs and traditions. After thirty-seven years of faithful service at Laura Secord, Miss Snelgrove was promoted to glory on June 30, 1938, with highest honours. Her like has not passed my way again.

Sam Roddan
Surrey, British Columbia

The coast was lashed with storm after storm. At night our house shook in the gale, and our old spruce trees left twigs and branches buried like knives in the grass. Bird watching was kept to a minimum, yet after each storm I walked the forests and mead-ows looking for wind-blown waifs. The Christmas bird count date was approaching.

The weather calmed, we had a few days of quiet. Our friend Peter arrived from Toronto to count birds with us. We drove our small dune buggy thirteen miles to Rose Spit, which pointed the way to the mainland and was washed by seas both north and south. Early dawn saw us crouched behind an eight-foot drift log, out of the wind and rain.

The bird numbers were outrageous. We counted wave after wave of long-tailed ducks as they flew by in the storm. The gulls by the shore, screaming and holding into the wind, were joined by scoters, seals and pounding surf. After counting more than twenty thousand birds, our hands were so cold we could hardly take notes. We began to shiver and saw no point in dying on the wind-blasted beaches of the world. We hiked back to our vehicle and headed for the shelter of the trees. In a pond by the tree-line we found three water pipits, and three more species to add to our count.

We did three more days of counting in neighbouring communities. None were as dramatic as Rose Spit, yet they had touches of gold. Our friends across the inlet heard four saw-whet owls, which kept us from being too despondent after a high tide at the Yakoun estuary had forced the birds to hug the far shore all day, making counting difficult.

The brant at Sandspit, feeding daintily in the shallows, looked like elegant ladies, their black garments trimmed with lace. They allowed us a view at close range and talked softly to one another in the stillness of a high-tide afternoon.

An uncommon mountain bluebird reminded us of how a blue summer sky would look. It had taken on its colours, with traces of grey for the season, and had given them to us for Christmas.

The golden-crowned sparrow at the feeder, the joy of good companionship, the tally and the hot rum at the end of the day made the bird count an undeniable part of Christmas and left us with traces of laughter that carried over long after our friends had left.

Christmas Eve, I put on my scarlet velvet doublet, looked "noble" and went visiting – first to David's with roast turkey and Jenny's for Christmas carols, then to Pat's with mountains of food and good friendship. Then came the church service and eggnog in the light of the Christmas tree.

Christmas day had a slow start and a quiet breakfast. We dressed the turkey, stoked up the wood stove and visited friends.

A stroll on the beach before dinner reminded us of the importance of living on the edges of the world where energies flow and change with the tides. There was a calm sea today and a quiet gentle rain falling. Friends were here also, sharing bird sightings and shells.

Back home to dinner, laughter and music. Noni Nora, now eighty-five years old, digs out the accordion and plays an old-time waltz. At midnight we shared delicious, large, rich and beautiful clams – our Christmas gifts from the sea.

Margo Hearne
Masset, British Columbia

✉ I look at the old black-and-white photo. Our parents, Christmas 1944, caught forever by a Calgary street photographer. Daddy's last Christmas. I gaze at them. My father, tall and thin, his fedora set at a rakish angle, dark suit, long grey overcoat. He should look sombre, but he looks so gay. There is a child's happy grin on his face; in fact, he looks like an overgrown kid dressed up in his father's clothes, fooling everyone into thinking he's a grown-up. He's holding four large boxed packages, and another small one pokes mysteriously out of the pocket of his great grey coat. Where his hands clasp there is a paper sack out of which rises the wooden handles of a broom and mop. My Christmas gift! How disgusted I was, that pompous five-year-old girl, when I opened that gift Christmas morning. Even then I scorned housework! Daddy took one look at my face and lifted me high in the air. Then he raced around the house with the broom and mop, using them as swords, as part of his comic routines, as magic wands, until I giggled so hard that I wet my pants. Did you see a future feminist in my face, Daddy? Did you see the woman I was to become? The woman you would never know?

Beside Daddy in the photo, slightly behind him and to the left, is Mom. She's wearing her second-hand black coat with a dead fox draped over her shoulders. How we used to stare into those beady eyes, my sister and me, when we could sneak into Mom's closet. We would stroke the glossy reddish-gold fur and chant endlessly, "Poor fox, poor wee fox!" Mom's hair rises like black wings above her widow's peak. Her stylish black felt hat sweeps away from her face. On the top of the hat nestles a dead bird. All the women in the family seemed to have dead birds perched on their hats. Mom's was not as grand or as large or as gaily plumed as the one Aunt Doll had. Mom's bird was small and sad-looking, its feathers faded. When we stroked it, small feathers floated languidly to the rug.

Mom holds a large parcel and clutches a satchel full of smaller gifts. The fine line of her shapely legs, the ones all three daughters were lucky enough to inherit, are glimpsed below the dark hem of her coat and above her feminine black pumps. She looks – there is no other word for it – adoringly up at Daddy. It is a look of such love, such happiness, that even now, forty-three years later, I weep as I look at them. Twelve years married and still in love. My parents, Bessie and Kit. My mom and dad.

Then I remember. It had never occurred to me before. There is a third unseen person in the photo, Chrissie, to be born in July. Not the son Daddy wanted, but Chrissie. I pick up the photo and look at Mom's face more closely. Did you know you were pregnant, Mom? Is that radiance partly from hormones and knowledge of the baby growing inside you? Probably not. It was just Daddy, wasn't it? He made life seem such fun, he made it seem like child's play. For me, that last Christmas, he transformed a dumb old mop into a magic wand. Oh, Daddy, my funny, carefree Daddy, you hung like an albatross around my neck for so many years, until finally I forgave you for dying.

Dorothy Beavington
White Rock, British Columbia

The Content
of Tables

I—or anyone else, for that matter—can't say *anything* about food on *Morning-side* without eliciting a response. This is the first of three chapters that will show you something of what I mean. The others deal with specific events or conversations on the program. This one comes from all over the lot (or the kitchen). It ends with a salute to a cookie to take upstairs to bed with you and begins, of course, in the morning.

✉ Your opening story this morning about the odd things that people eat for breakfast reminded me of my now-departed father's gastronomic adventures with his breakfast meal. Not that he did these every morning, but he did them often enough. . . .

Sometimes when he was late for work, he would put a couple of pieces of bread into the toaster and then finish dressing. When he would return to the kitchen, the toast would be up and waiting for him to "decorate" with butter, to melt into the toast, and with a fairly generous sprinkling of instant coffee and a teaspoon of sugar. This way Dad could have his toast and coffee on his way to work.

The second peculiarity my father enjoyed was perhaps more unusual. You see, my sister used to make the most scrumptious chocolate cake, one that would remain very moist for several days. Her icing was (and still is) second to none. Unlike the rest of the family, my father would save his piece until the next morning. If there was any leftover gravy from the roast, Dad would extract it from our old Kelvinator fridge and spread the gelatinous mass on his piece of cake. The look of obvious ecstasy on Dad's face always made me want to taste this concoction myself, but even now, all these years later, I can't bring myself to try it.

Gordon Pickup
Spruce Grove, Alberta

✉ Those breakfast descriptions took me back to a sunny spring morning in the early 1950s. My mother was lying on the chaise out on the porch, nursing a particularly gruesome hangover. My brother, aged nine and a half, and I, aged six, were endeavouring to entertain her. My brother was being reasonably successful. I remember much happy giggling in the middle of which I asked, "What's for breakfast?"

"Bruce, you may have anything you like," my mother replied. My eyes lit up. "You mean I can have chocolate cake?"

"If that's what you want, go right ahead."

Precedent set, I ate chocolate cake, mousse and milk shakes for breakfast for the next eight years. My mother rationalized that there were milk and eggs and flour and butter in such things. I was the envy of many friends and equally the horror of several mothers. My brother staunchly ate cereal, eggs and toast.

Life in the land of chocolate for breakfast continued peacefully until the age of fourteen when I was dispatched to boarding school. The first morning I dutifully took my place in the dining hall under the watchful eye of a stern, imposing and thoroughly intimidating headmistress. "You will have some prunes, Bruce." Decidedly a statement of fact, not a question. Gag. Prunes, which I cannot eat to this day, were followed by fried eggs and toast. Perhaps this was what they called character-building.

Released to the real world at age eighteen, I resorted to my pancreatic-arresting breakfast habits. Somewhere in my mid-twenties, I finally started to eat "real" breakfasts and to recognize how important they are to the rest of the day. But to this day, I have been known to sneak a chocolate with my first cup of tea in the morning. It jump-starts my heart and makes me smile in recollection.

Bruce Blakemore
Cape Negro, Nova Scotia

✉ I want to share my recipe for a crazy sandwich with you.

Spread two pieces of whole-wheat or light-rye bread with mayonnaise. Now slice up some red pepper and cover one slice liberally with the pepper. Here's the crazy part: put a good layer of potato chips over the red pepper and then sprinkle on some black pepper and garlic powder. Crush down the other slice of bread, mayonnaise side down.

Cut the sandwich in two. You can eat one half and I'll eat the other. Great!

George Foster
Way's Mills, Quebec

✉ When I met my husband, Brian, he had very definite ideas about foods he liked (the list was short) and disliked (the list was long). But he considered himself a connoisseur of condiments and sauces. Ketchup had to be made by Heinz; raspberry jam had to be made by Kraft.

It so happens that food is one of the focal points of my life. The more unusual or creative the dish, the more I enjoy it. (It is only because of Brian's many fine qualities that our relationship in fact survived the differences in our taste for food.) I was convinced that Brian had not even tasted many of the foods he was passing up. I believed that with the right presentation he could be won over to the delights of so many of the world's gastronomical experiences.

We honeymooned on the East Coast (chosen selfishly, I admit, because of my love for seafood). I feasted on all the treasures the sea produces for the table while Brian alternated between steak and scallops.

When we settled into our little apartment together, I started a silent and gentle campaign to get him to try foods that I believed he had dismissed without tasting. It was easier than I thought. I would introduce a test item each time we had company, and I made sure that the rest of the meal consisted of many of his favourite dishes. Brian was a most willing subject. We sailed through broccoli, asparagus, Caesar salad (now he makes a lovely one himself), assorted fish, salmon and lobster. The evening he ordered escargots in a restaurant I had to fight back the urge to stand up and cheer.

It was then that I figured we were ready for rabbit. I'd been waiting for this because I really wanted Brian to like rabbit. I order it every time I see it on a menu, which isn't often. Although I could accept the fact that Brian would never like mushrooms (another favourite of mine), I didn't want to go through life cooking rabbit dinners for one.

I brought the little three-pounder home from the local market and chose a recipe, from my volumes of cookbooks, called "Rabbit with Apricots." I chose the apricot version over some of the other recipes because I hoped the apricots would camouflage the taste and shape of the rabbit. It was to be left on the bones, and I was hoping Brian would think it was chicken – at least long enough to give it a good try.

I served the meat on our china plates and lit the candles.

"What are these?" he asked, eyeing the apricots.

"Apricots. They're soaked in wine."

He was preoccupied with turning the apricots over and moving a candle a little closer to his plate. He then leaned over to inspect my plate while I tried to stick-handle an apricot into place over an exposed rabbit leg.

By this time conversation was impossible. I was afraid he would realize what was on his plate before he gave it a fair try. I decided to just lower my head and dig in, hoping that he would do the same. After a moment or two of silence I became aware of a low hum that gradually grew louder. I dropped my fork.

Even I could not eat rabbit while being serenaded with "Here Comes Peter Cottontail"!

Gloria Currie
Burlington, Ontario

✉ Imagine my chagrin when I heard you utter the opinion that the only thing worse about dieting than having to eat carrot sticks is having to eat celery. You give celery short shrift. It's crunchy and it tastes good cooked or raw, which is more than you can say for broccoli or cauliflower (but that's another story . . .).

Just think of the contribution celery has made to the tables of the world, from the humble to the sublime: from the prosaic potato salad or tuna-fish sandwich to the ultra-French *céleris braisés* or *céleris en vinaigrette*. The French say the secret to gourmet cooking is never to cook anything in plain water, and you can't make a *bouquet garni* without a rib of celery. Celery can be filled with anything, from peanut butter and raisins (what kids call "ants on a log"; it is, I'll admit, a little bizarre) to smoked salmon and cream cheese, which is heavenly. Just think of what Chinese food would be like without celery, or stuffing for a turkey, or turkey soup. For soup, of course, you also need the leaves. And what are the three indispensable aromatics with which every Creole dish begins? Exactly: onion, green pepper and celery. What would the platter of raw vegetables surrounding *aioli*, that wonderful dip from Provence (garlic-scented paradise!) be without celery? And, finally, what do you put in your Bloody Mary to stir it with? A green onion? Of course not. A strip of green pepper? Sacrilege!

I hope you are able to reconsider your obviously untenable position before the more radical celery-eating faction of the country, who are less reasonable than myself and less content with writing letters, throw down the pale green gauntlet and demand satisfaction.

Sandy Waddell
Ottawa

✉ I listened with mounting disgust to your mushroom love-in. I could have guessed that British Columbians would eat so many mushrooms. I grew up in Vancouver, and I've been plagued by their fungiphilia for most of my twenty-five otherwise uncareworn years.

As with so many childhood things, my first gustatory explorations were timid and brief. Most vegetables lived in distant realms, the seas around them guarded on the nutritional charts by unappetizing monsters. Through rigorous disciplines, time and inscrutable changes in my biochemistry, I've since come to know the pleasures of the herbivore. Cabbages, kin to the already beloved salad greens, hold terrors no more, and I can foresee next conquering either the steaming muck of the squashes or the hog fodder of the parsnip and allied root crops.

However, in my otherwise insatiable hunger to expand the boundaries of my palate – in my *Drang nach Essen*, as it were – I shall ever retreat from the mushroom.

Mushrooms are primitive, as though they reached their evolutionary zenith during those first few minutes on land, when the last drops from the primordial soup dried on their puffy skin. They even retain gills, the guts of an aquatic oxygen eater, through which, instead, they perversely propagate, casting their spores upon the ground. I don't deny that this has been reproductively successful; fecundity is a trait they have in common with other early evolvers, like sharks and cockroaches. Presumably mushrooms also share with those atavists the propensity for surviving a nuclear holocaust. Where civilized creatures are to envy the dead, mushrooms thrive. What shape is an atomic cloud?

Who could be attracted to something both bloated and chewy? What is there to admire in so base and parasitic a vegetable? When will people stop larding my dinner with them? Where do they grow, but in dank, unwashed nooks, the athlete's foot of dead trees? Finally, why must you encourage the rest of the country to emulate yet another decadent tendency of the West Coast?

I think you owe me an apology.

Richard Poutt
Vancouver

✉ I think things were going better before we started the healthy eating. If I was serving a slab of chocolate cake or apple pie, I could tell everybody what they should be doing, and no one seemed to mind. But over soya macaroni and miso soup, it's more dangerous.

Things seemed to fall apart the day I was thawing the cow's tongue in the back of the closet so the kids wouldn't know what was going to be in the meat loaf. I really hadn't wanted to get the tongue at all. It was the furthest thing from my mind. But I picked up the cookbook the day I went to use the phone in the health store and there it was: six ways to serve tongue. And in large print at the bottom of the page was this warning: "WHAT YOUR FAMILY EATS IS UP TO YOU. DON'T FEED THEM DISEASE AND DESPAIR."

Not another thing I was responsible for. I groaned. Last week it was Barbara's lazy eye that I hadn't noticed soon enough, and this week I'd apparently been stirring up Peter's latent hostility.

I bought the book and huddled over it at home. It was full of sneaky ways to slip ground brains into the lasagne, apricot pits into the salad and the one I decided on, tongue-burgers. The book became incoherent with excitement when it told me all the things that tongue was going to do to my family once I got it inside them.

As the yellow bus drove away, taking the kids to school, I hauled my tongue out of the closet and we surveyed each other. I refused to think about how it had been pulled out with roots still attached, and I would not let the grey colour or the taste-buds chill my fervour. No way.

I made a sling out of a tea-towel and managed to hoist the tongue into the pot of water. I left it licking around the edge of the pot and went to the other room and turned on the TV.

The soaps were on, and everyone was fighting and crying as usual. A skinny woman was slinking across the screen saying, "Don't blame me for the trouble in your marriage." And then I smelt something burning.

When I got through the smoke I could see my tongue was ruined. Prying it from the bottom of the pot, I dropped it with relief into the garbage where it lay with the tip stuck out at me from under the white lid.

I worried the rest of the day about the disease my family would get without that tongue. However, I know already the kids won't eat anything without their father eating it first, and his taste-buds are set way up for hot-fudge sundaes and pork chops. So now I give a lot of food to my dog who is very healthy, and I haven't seen him look despairing in days.

Hazel Jardine
Fort Qu'Appelle, Saskatchewan

✉ In the days immediately preceding Christmas, along with the usual blend of political, economic, sociological and cultural topics that enrich my mornings if I am at home, you included at least two interviews concerning the preparation of Christmas dinner. One was with a Canadian home economist while the second was with a "Turkey Hotline" lady. In her tips for cooking a turkey, one of these experts included this suggestion: to place the stuffing inside a knotted section of panty hose in the turkey cavity. The practicality of the idea appealed to me, and Christmas afternoon found the ingredients for mushroom-almond stuffing neatly enclosed in a popular brand of "off-black" panty hose, inside the roasting turkey.

The delicious aroma of turkey wafted throughout the house for hours, whetting everyone's appetite for the feast to come. Thanks to the modern invention of pre-basted poultry, the turkey remained essentially undisturbed in the oven until almost dinnertime. At 6:45 P.M. the dining-room table gleamed with crystal and silver, the wine was chilled, the vegetables ready. All that remained was to remove the turkey from the oven, transfer it to a place of honour on Great-grandmother's Limoges platter and prepare the gravy.

The golden-brown turkey was a delight to the eye, and the transfer, sometimes a bit nerve-wracking if the turkey sticks to the roasting pan, went smoothly. Having gathered a whisk and thickening ingredients, I turned my attention to the drippings in the roasting pan. At first I thought it must be a trick of the light against the dark enamel, or perhaps the before-dinner sherry had been a mistake on an empty stomach. I looked again and realized with mounting panic that what I saw was no illusion – dark, greenish-black streaks marbled the rich brown of the drippings. In a flash I turned to the turkey and whipped out the panty hose-enclosed stuffing, which as promised I was able to remove easily and completely from the cavity. Wherever the panty hose had been in contact with the turkey, the meat and bones were stained an evil greenish black; the stuffing defied description!

I stood frozen to the spot for a few seconds and then walked slowly into the family room. "It's a good thing I am a mature woman," I said through clenched teeth, "or I would *scream*." Following me back to the kitchen, my husband surveyed the disaster. Obviously there could be no stuffing or gravy, but the big question was whether we dared eat any of the turkey. We decided to risk eating a little of the meat that had not been resting in the pan drippings. Carving the turkey included examining the meat for any sign of discolouration and removing every trace of succulent golden skin.

While the problem may simply have been one of appearance, it is also possible that harmful chemicals were transferred to the food. Only laboratory tests could provide the definite answer. If a lighter shade of panty hose were used, perhaps chemicals would be transferred without any noticeable colour to alert the cook of the possible danger. I am disappointed that one of your turkey experts obviously recommended a cooking method that had not been thoroughly tested. I believe your listeners should be made aware of my unfortunate experience and warned *not* to use panty hose in the preparation of food!

Beverley Colpitts
Kanata, Ontario

✉ Use a bag made from nylon net instead of panty hose (ugh!). Just give the bag a good rinse in hot water, then stuff it in the cavity of the fowl and lightly fill it with the stuffing. When all is ready for serving, just ease the bag out and gently turn it inside out over a bowl and presto out dumps the dressing . . . pardon, the stuffing. If your stuffing is the wet kind, it may make a mess of the bag, which will not be worth rinsing for reuse. In any case a bag is very cheap to make – I sew at least a half a dozen each year for friends. Nylon net can be purchased at fabric shops.

I have another trick. Before stuffing the mixture in the net bag, stir in a teaspoon of ground ginger. You won't taste it, but it is supposed to prevent indigestion in anybody over forty. Maybe that is why folks I know like it – they never get indigestion!

Here's another tip. When the turkey is cooked, wrap it in lots of tin foil, put it on a heated plate and then swaddle the whole bird in towels or blankets or anything to keep it hot for at least an hour – the longer the better. I was really sceptical about this but have been doing it for years now. It does not go on cooking but is so tender and, yes, juicy. It will also stay steaming hot if you wrap it with lots of things to keep it hot. I take the stuffing out after resting, but if you want, take it out before.

Bon appétit! Now I must go and shovel the snow.

Valerie Clarbrough
Thunder Bay, Ontario

✉ For future reference and for all the people who find the thought of feasting on turkey à la panty hose a little hard to digest, there is good news! You can actually buy – el cheapo – a cheese-cloth type of bag just for stuffing a turkey. No more succulent dye-streaked breast to worry about, and no more "gross out" comments brought on by the sight of a reinforced toe sticking out of the turkey!

What will they think of next?

Sylvia Lee
Omemee, Ontario

✉ I am the laughing-stock of my family. Your show about Christmas cake started the urge that would result in my ignominy. I dug out an old recipe from a Christmas magazine and began an odyssey. I copied the list of ingredients, grabbed my knapsack and headed off to the market with my wife-to-be, Linda.

We arrived at the market full of excitement to buy a massive amount of nuts and candy. But something was wrong. Our purchases were costing much more than we expected. We will never be able to afford the stuff at this price, we said, so we left the store to discuss our options. While we were walking around the market we came across a stall that sold all the ingredients at less than half the cost of the first store.

We carried our purchases to our apartment. In our drive to economize, we had purchased unblanched whole almonds. Have you ever tried to blanch and halve endless cups of almonds? Oh joy, oh bliss.

Well, the final fiasco occurred after we had baked the cakes – four loaves. As I had forgotten the cheesecloth, I left the four cakes on the table near an open window and a squirrel had helped itself to about a third of one of the loaves. I cried. I telephoned home to seek sympathy from my mother, and she could not stop laughing at my story. Now my entire home town knows. Thank God I didn't make chili sauce.

If you are ever in London, beware of drunken squirrels.

Gerard van den Wildenberg
London, Ontario

✉ In her talk with you this morning about the joys of making Christmas cake, someone mentioned one very hard-to-get ingredient – the brown paper to line the baking pan. She's quite right. But I have found that if you are lucky, you can get sheets of heavy brown paper, at Christmastime only, at the places where you buy your gift wrap. I guess they figure people are going to be mailing Christmas parcels.

But there is another ingredient that I find hard to get: cheesecloth. A few years ago it was a staple in the smallest supermarket. Now it's hard to find even in big city stores. Don't people put a *bouquet garni* in little cheesecloth bags any more? And what happened to jelly-making? Do you remember the big cheesecloth bags hung from the backs of two chairs into which you poured the stewed fruit so that the liquid could drip through overnight into a bowl underneath?

Alice Sinclair
Kleinburg, Ontario

192

✉ Here is my husband's recipe for getting heavy paper bags:

1. Go to the liquor store.
2. Buy six bottles of booze.
3. Save the paper bag they give you.

These directions must be adhered to exactly. If you buy fewer than six bottles, you will receive a small lightweight bag. If you buy more, you will receive a cardboard box.

Elisabeth Plain
Scarborough, Ontario

✉ You must be aware that the north-western Ontario raven is the most voracious, rapacious and downright greedy of all God's creatures. The ravens in Dryden sit in the back of the half-tons in Safeway's parking lot and eat fresh-bought groceries right out from under the purchasers' noses. The ones in the country clean up a cow carcass in less than half a day. Road-killed skunks are a treat.

My wife, Wanda, is of Polish descent.

My sons attend high school.

Do the paragraphs above have any relation? A common thread? A reason? You're bloody right they do!

What Wanda did, given her implicit faith in you, was to duplicate in every detail your recipe for potato pancakes–latkes. It was to be a seasonal treat, a contribution to multiculturalism, a sort of celebration.

The second son, Patrick, the diplomat, suggested that, though they were horrible, it wasn't the cook's fault. It was just not right to do that to perfectly good potatoes.

The first-born, Ted, who is very blunt, pronounced them inedible.

The dog, Smokey, who got their rejects, took a bite, ran downstairs to drink out of the toilet and asked to be let out.

Meanwhile, Wanda, who is a determined woman and a good

cook, continued to work away at the first half of her first pancake. She finally threw in the towel.

Assuming that everyone else was wrong (I do that by nature) I sat down to a feed of Gzowski-recommended pancakes. I finished one.

It was then that we cooked up the rest of the batch, which in the raw was rapidly turning bright pink and somehow in the cooking process took on a decidedly bluish hue. The finished product was taken unceremoniously out to the bird feeder.

The red squirrel has sat sedately on the pile, tail curled, paws folded reverently into his chest, for two days now. Chickadees, grossbeaks and juncos have all ignored the new treat and ninety-two per cent of the ravens of north-western Ontario have said *no* to Gzowski's latkes.

Bob Mitchell
Dryden, Ontario

✉ I grow a garden every year that includes a variety of vegetables, especially beans.

I heard one of your guests talking about cooking beans, and I couldn't figure out why someone who has been involved with beans for some time didn't know how to get rid of bean gas. This would have been known in her grandmother's time.

Here is my recipe, which can be doubled. I prefer using lima beans.

> 1 cup beans
> ½ teaspoon baking soda
> Salt and pepper to taste
> 1 tablespoon onion, chopped
> 1 clove minced garlic
> 1 teaspoon margarine or bacon grease (optional)

Wash and soak the beans in warm water overnight. In the morning drain the water and add enough warm water to cover the beans. Bring them to a boil, then add the baking soda, which will make the mixture fizz. Drain and rinse the beans and add the salt and pepper and onion. Bring to a boil, then simmer and cook in a covered pot for 2 to 3 hours – slow cooking counts. If the water should run out, add a little. About a half an hour before the beans are cooked, add the garlic.

If you like your beans mushy, you can mash them before serving. The beans will be quite soft – there's no need to stir them while they are cooking. You may also want to add margarine a half-hour before serving.

I use this recipe for one of the twelve meatless dishes for Christmas Eve supper.

Fran Hnatiuk
Saskatoon, Saskatchewan

✉ No, it's not throwing out the soaking water that takes the "wind" out of beans. Or putting baking soda in the water, or vinegar, or anything else. It all has to do with digestibility, and that has to do with the amino-acid balance. The problem is that people eat a whole lot of beans without the other foods necessary to complete the protein.

I prefer overnight soaking, which requires no energy or attention. Pinto beans don't seem to require soaking. Salt and fat should be added before cooking, otherwise the beans tend to be tasteless inside. The fat should be from beef or pork, or butterfat may be used. Vegetable oils are not suitable. Molasses or brown sugar (not both) can be used with the white beans, along with a touch of mustard and a lighter touch of garlic. Nearly all bean dishes use tomato – I simply add tomato juice while the beans are simmering. Garlic and fresh green, yellow or red peppers are basic to any bean dish south of the fiftieth parallel.

Now about completing that protein: beans should make up no more than thirty-five per cent of the protein part of the meal. The other sixty-five per cent should be rice, corn, wheat or some combination thereof, plus cheese. Real cheese, not the processed stuff. And there you are. Very nutritious and very filling; don't overdo it. Have some salad before, sip a little beer during and nibble some bittersweet chocolate after. Pure enjoyment with no regrets.

Tom Anderson
Summerland, British Columbia

✉ My Nan's greatest culinary achievements (at least to my young taste-buds) were her baked beans. They were light golden in colour, like the August tans of many years ago, and they would swim in a thick, creamy sauce. They were not made with salt pork or molasses; instead these beans were slow-cooked in the wood stove all day with nothing but salt, white sugar and butter. As simple as it sounds, I've never tasted them outside of Nan's farm in Victoria County, Nova Scotia, nor have I ever been able to duplicate them – though I have come close.

After your bean show I got the old bean crock down from the cupboard and began soaking the beans for the next day's dinner.

They were some good!

Betty Goodfellow
Burlington, Ontario

✉ The discussion of baked beans brought back memories of a meal we had at home in London about forty years ago. An ice storm had swept across south-western Ontario, and the whole area was without electricity for several days. Luckily our house was heated by an old-fashioned hand-stoked coal furnace, and Dad had some oil lamps, so we had heat and light, and it was all very exciting for my brother, sister and me. One of the meals Mother prepared was a pot of beans, which was left overnight on the ledge just inside the furnace door. The next evening, as we sat around the dining-room table, the bean pot was brought in. I can still smell

196

the rich aroma when the lid was removed. Delicious, the best beans I have ever had. I know I couldn't repeat that with my modern high-efficiency gas furnace.

Jack Armstrong
Ottawa

✉ One of the greatest inventions since the VCR is the hot-air popcorn maker. In about five minutes, this wonderful device pops the popcorn, melts the butter and tosses the popcorn into a bowl. All that is left for me to do is sprinkle on the butter and decide whether tonight it will be the traditional flavour, or whether I'll opt for garlic salt, onion powder or cayenne pepper. There is nothing to wash except the little tray the butter melted in and the bowl I eat from.

I see no reason to get more *involved* with the process, as one of your guests suggested, and will never go back to the oil-and-pot method. It's far more fun to get involved with eating the popcorn and watching a good movie.

Mark Stevens
Toronto

✉ I was astonished to hear you messing about with corn poppers, microwaves, pots and stoves. Are you all too young or possibly too urban, to know the only true, original primitive way to make popcorn?

You put a thin layer of corn in a covered wire-mesh basket with a long handle and pop it over an open wood fire. Never mind that some of the kernels don't pop and some get burned. The rest of it, with just a faint taste of wood smoke, is pure heaven. I admit that a demonstration would be difficult to mount in your radio studio, but you might at least have mentioned this method, if only for the purists among us.

Alice Sinclair
Kleinburg, Ontario

✉ I lived in India for some time, and one day I went into the kitchen of my host to discover his wife and three children squatting on the floor around the typical Indian stove, a camp stove. Looking to see what was cooking, I saw a large, shallow pan about fifteen inches across filled with silver-grey sand. The stove was roaring away, and everyone was watching this sand being heated up and stirred with a large, flat spatula. Naturally, I was rather amazed at this and asked what was going on. For an answer I received large grins from everyone, but not a word of explanation. I tried again and got even larger grins. Obviously no answer would be forthcoming. I was quite confused and had no idea of what was happening, but squatted down and waited. After all, something this odd must have some purpose. Besides, we were in the kitchen so it was probably something to eat. A sandwich, perhaps? (Sorry.)

After a few minutes of perplexity on my part, plus enjoyment at my perplexity by everyone else, the sand was apparently cooked to satisfaction. The whole pan was lifted from the stove, dumped into a sieve and shaken. As I watched the level of sand go down, there slowly appeared larger white objects caught in the sieve. Suddenly, I realized that I was witness to another method of making popcorn! The sand was clean and dry, and it all fell through the sieve. Hot white popcorn was left behind. I dug in and ate with as much enthusiasm as the children. The only part of the operation that I had missed was removing the popcorn from the cob and putting it in the sand.

Walter Eisenbeis
Toronto

✉ An Oreo for Peter

My mother never bought Oreos
She would shiver at even the hint
of such a request.
"Make a dog sick!" were her words
as she steered our grocery cart
towards the Peek Freans,
and I with helpless wonder
left my eyes to feast on those
chocolate delights,
praying she would buckle under
the pressure of my unspoken desire,
trying hard to put to rest
the memory of the cereal aisle
which, too, denied me the sugar-coated
bed snacks of my peers.

Now at thirty
I still feel my mother's disapproval
and limit my wanton feasts
to a single row.

Lenora Jean Steele
St. Marys, Ontario

HOW ARE
THINGS IN
OUAGADOUGOU?

O r, for that matter, Suva, or Rio Negro, or Opononi?

Morningside is a current affairs program, and a Canadian current affairs program at that. But every day our mail-bag contains letters from people all over the world—Canadians—who write to us not so much about the news where they are as just the ways things are going, and we supplement our more topical coverage with their informal reports. Our correspondents range from published authors (Isabel Huggan, whose letter from Kenya appears here, is one example, and so, of course, is the incomparable Margaret Visser, who spent part of the seasons of this book in Europe and wrote to us from there) to former newspaper reporters to just people with itchy feet and observant eyes. This is an album of some of their communiqués, letters from all over the world that seemed to me, and to Shelley Ambrose, who co-ordinates all our foreign correspondence, to be worth preserving.

Christiansted, St. Croix, Virgin Islands

✉ We returned to Winnipeg in October 1986. I was seven months pregnant and decided I wanted to give birth somewhere with modern medical facilities. I also wanted to be surrounded by family and friends. Katie Marley Reynolds was born on December 18, 1986. She is, of course, a perfect child.

I spent a year trying to learn to be a mother, a task I imagine I'll still be working on long after Katie has left home. I did some free-lance writing, mostly for my old newspaper, and revelled in the excesses of North America. I spent a lot of time at grocery stores, looking with amazement at the products available. I'm still stymied by pasta salads in a bag.

By midsummer, however, my husband had itchy feet again and strong memories of Winnipeg's winters. A friend offered him a job in St. Croix, an island we'd never visited and knew very little about. After a few weeks of tears and arguments, the decision was made. Once again we'd sell everything we owned (an easy job this time) and move. The hardest part was telling our parents we planned to take their granddaughter.

Our friend Ray rented us a duplex in a small village. We arrived on St. Croix exhausted after two days of travel. Katie was sick with a cold and nearly hysterical from all the changes. I wasn't in much better shape. My first view of my new home came at dark. We drove through the village slowly, dogs howling at the truck, a few radios and TVs sending off faint noise from behind louvred windows. Ray drove up a mud road and swung his headlights on a darkened house. I wanted to weep. Inside, three rooms. The last tenants had left just one light bulb. It was enough to illustrate the dirt, the lack of furniture, the cockroaches skittering across the floor. There was a new bed Ray had bought us, two chairs and several boxes of belongings we had mailed down in advance. No hot water, a stove that didn't work, no telephone. When the men left to buy some basic groceries I did weep. I held my daughter in my arms – she was wailing with fright and lack of sleep – and we wept together.

I'd like to say it all looked better in the light of day. It didn't. It was a small, squalid house with no furniture. There were chickens in the yard. The neighbours stared, but none seemed willing to approach us. We wept a lot the first weeks, my Katie and I. We had no car and the nearest store and laundry is about a mile away. Every morning around seven, before the sun got too hot, I'd bundle Katie up in the stroller, bump her down the mud road and walk to the store. Still no sign of welcome from the neighbours. We are the only white family in the village. I was naïve enough to think it wouldn't matter.

We've been here two months. We celebrated Christmas in this house and Katie's first birthday so it has claimed a special place in our memories. There's furniture now, scrounged from friends of friends and liberated on its way to the dump. I have a telephone and a car. I'm learning to like the chickens, especially the one who lays an egg every day on our porch. I have found work with the *Daily News*, a paper serving the three U.S. Virgin Islands. Katie begins spending half days with a sitter this week. We're building a life, one that can't replace the one we left behind, but one that is teaching our family new skills and values. I still long for Winnipeg, for the company of family and lifelong friends. But I don't spend most of every day in desperation over the choice we've made.

I have no idea where we'll be a year from now. In one sense, that's a liberating thought. In another sense, it's very frightening. I turn thirty this year, still young I realize, but old enough to wonder if it isn't time to settle down, buy a house, have a steady job. The questions increase when I look at my daughter and wonder if we're providing for her in the best possible way. I have few answers.

✉ The plates on my car claim St. Croix is America's paradise. Having lived here for several months, I now consider this an oxymoron.

The American part is all too real. Junk-food chains abound. Mothers feed their vacant-eyed babies Cheetos and grape soda for breakfast. Children are named for soap-opera characters, reflecting what sadly will be their heritage.

I work three days a week, and Katie, now sixteen months old, stays with a woman in our village. Pat is young and still childless, itself an unusual situation in the West Indies. She lives in a two-room shack with concrete floors that she keeps immaculate, despite her lack of running water and indoor plumbing. The dominant piece of furniture in the house is her huge colour TV, complete with cable. It blares most of the day, promising Pat cleaner wash, happier children and more boyfriends if only she will buy, buy, buy.

And she does, as do so many Cruzans. Kentucky Fried Chicken has replaced home cooking. Of the hundred or so families living in our village, only a handful plant vegetable gardens. Lean Cuisine is readily available. Our insistence that Katie not be fed candy or Kool-Aid, not be taken to a restaurant for burgers and fries is regarded as odd behaviour for parents who claim to love their child. She earned a gold star from me when one of her first words was "apple." If she can also say "Big Mac," I don't want to know.

The American Dream is constantly reinforced by the thousands of tourists who pour off the planes and the cruise ships. They have money, big money, and they spend like mad. I work one day a week in a gift shop at one of the most expensive hotels on the island. We sell toiletries, cards and non-essentials like liquor and chips. Most of my customers don't blink when I charge them $2.75 for a stateside paper, $8.25 for six beers (it's $2 at the grocery store) or $10 for a roll of film.

The paradise is still here, though it shrinks visibly every year. They are, quite literally, paving it. Hotel chains are snapping up land, the best beaches are at resorts whose entrances have guards and most Cruzans can have access only if they wear a waiter's uniform.

It's a beautiful island, and it tears at my heart to watch it lose its sense of identity, to slowly become swallowed up by vast money-making machines. I look out my door and see the flame-red flowers on my flamboyant tree starting to bloom. The nut trees my husband planted last month are blowing gently in the breeze. The neighbourhood kids are just coming home from school, their pink and grey uniforms untucked as they race down the dirt roads. Later, they'll fly their home-made kites in the churchyard next to us, and at least one will be shouted at for teasing the chickens.

I have learned so much in the time we've spent here. I've learned that money and jobs and the frantic search for success really should take a back seat to more human values. I've learned, from spending countless humid hours at the neighbourhood laundry, of the strength of women to endure burdens most North American women can't begin to imagine. I've learned which leaves from which trees will cure a cold, will drop a child's fever, will help me sleep. I've learned that years of university didn't make me smart. Or even educated. I'll be leaving with mixed feelings.

We return to Winnipeg in a few weeks. I have no concrete idea what I'll do there. The cultural adjustments will be difficult, for us and for Katie, who really has never known a world other than the Caribbean. I'm sad, because I really wanted to raise her here. I can only hope our family can hold on to the good we've gained, lose the negative and somehow get a toehold in North America.

Lindor Reynolds

Addis Ababa, Ethiopia

✉ Ethiopian coffee is the best in the world. The slightly acidic topsoil of Kaffa province yields a superb Arabica, valued on world markets both for its taste and for its excellent seedlings. The ornamental ceremony with which the Ethiopians serve their coffee is an invitation with honour. "Come for coffee" does not mean a teaspoon of the instant kind in a mug of boiling water. Instead it means, "Please let me prepare coffee for you; we'll have a good visit."

Mama spreads a carpet of long fresh green grass about the straw-thatched gazebo. In a corner, she gathers a tray, sugar, *siennies*, water, a basin, and then stocks a squat tin burner, fanning the flame with an old piece of cardboard. When the charcoal chunks are red-hot, she pours precious dried green coffee beans onto a flat hammered metal tray, moving them back and forth across the heat with a broken twig. As the beans heat they start to smoke and turn black, and when they are roasted they crackle and pop. Mama brings the smoking tray past the circle of guests, who fan the smoke towards them as an "appetizer." Sitting again on her cowhide stool, she makes a spout with her hands and carefully transfers each roasted bean into a carved wooden mortar whose pestle may be wooden, or it may be a heavy pipe with sealed ends. Talk flows around the circle of guests, or they sit quietly, savouring the preparation ritual. Mama settles the narrow-necked round-bottomed coffee-pot or *jebena* onto the glowing coals, and soon steam puffs out its sharp nose and out around the corn cob stuffed into the top of its neck. Then she methodically and rhythmically pounds the coffee beans with her right hand, while guarding the top of the mortar with her left. Not a granule of the precious coffee must escape. Mama spends up to one-sixth of her wages on coffee each week.

The powdered beans are tipped carefully into the two-litre *jebena*, then gently swirled with its boiling water. Sometimes she adds a special touch of spice: cinnamon bark or whole cloves. A *jebena* is said to be shaped like Ethiopia. Made of black or red clay, its pour spout sits like a sharp nose on the side of its fat pot belly, and a Grecian handle lazily joins its long graceful neck to the belly. One live coal is placed in a shallow cone on a stand and a large pinch of straw-like incense thrown on it. Immediately the coffee aroma is twinned with incense in an age-old custom. An Ethiopian's earliest memories are of the smell of incense swirling through the house, signalling the call to coffee.

After setting out a place of chewy *kollo* snack, Mama grasps the handle, looks up and catches my eye. *Awol jebba*, she says with a twinkle. "Make the gift of a blessing." I enter the drama: "May

God keep you." She bows her head graciously and quietly says, "Amen" (pronounced A-mane), her hands outstretched to signify "keep coming." "May you have good health." Amen, she responds again, still moving her fingers for me to say more. Then she awaits the third blessing like an excited child: "May you return with me to Canada." She bursts out laughing. "Amen," she says. I have my right arm out straight and am hissing, an Ethiopian prayer sound. Dutifully and laughingly she takes my hand in both of hers and kisses it in thanks. The drama is completed.

A generous spoon of sugar goes into each handleless, saucerless demitasse, or *siennie*, and is topped by a long stream of coffee poured cup by cup. The coffee-pot rests on a doughnut of multi-coloured hemp, or a threaded ring of pop-bottle caps, or a squat tin can with both its lids cut out. She lifts the tray and passes to each guest. We take our coffee leisurely, then pass the *siennie* back. When all are returned, Mama dips water from a bent tin basin and rinses the cups. The ritual is repeated.

After an hour, I am relaxed, and I feel well visited. I feel tied in to the customs of the ages.

So why shouldn't Ethiopian coffee be the best? After all, Kaffa province gave its name to what is now known world-wide as "coffee."

Carol Wallace

Suva, Fiji Islands

✉ We came here almost two years ago when my husband, Brian, was fresh from training as a surgical resident after a one-year stint in St. Anthony, Newfoundland. He was going to work as a tutor in surgery at the Fiji School of Medicine. Ten months and two coups later, he was catapulted into the position of acting head of the school, and he has been acting head ever since. This is a story in itself, but for now I want to tell you about a trip to Bau.

Bau is Fiji's royal island, where the *vunivalu*, or high chief, lives. We were invited to visit by a *bauan*, Dr. Tabua, who has relatives there. This is something like having the Queen's cousin invite you to tea at Buckingham Palace. Bau Island is important to Fijians, but it's also a living place, and since those who live there don't want it to become a forty-acre museum, very few visits are permitted.

The fifteen-minute boat ride under grey skies and drizzle brought us to the tiny island. In the last century Tui Seru Cakobau consolidated his political and military ascendancy from this tiny island, using trickery and enormous war canoes. His conversion to Christianity and the ceding of the former Cannibal Isles to Queen Victoria were engineered from here.

We were received by our host's relatives and walked around the island to his sister's house, where tea would be served. We were shown through Soso and Bau, the traditional fishing villages, which provide the island masters with fish for meals and for feasts and ceremonial events. We came to the third village, Lasikau, where the defenders reside. Lasikau looks out to sea and is right beside the great Cakobau residence, where Ratu Sir George Kada Vulevu, a Cakobau, the current *vunivalu* and the grandson of the notorious Ratu Seru, lives. Immense sea walls fortify the island.

My husband and I presented a large bundle of *yaqona* to Ratu Esekeli, the chief of Soso village who was to be our guide. (*Yaqona* is the root of a pepper plant, which is pounded to a fine powder and mixed with water to make a muddy-coloured drink.) After a welcome ceremony and a reverential address to the *yaqona*, we began the more relaxed taking of tea. We were all seated on the floor, made soft by pandanus mats, and the household was presented to us. Then the *yaqona* was pounded and Dr. Tabua explained the importance of the *yaqona* ceremony and why it precedes any important function.

The ceremony starts with everyone seated on the floor, at the same level. This is meant to keep everyone humble. Those too used to sitting on chairs become uncomfortable and leave shortly. (That's all right, Dr. Tabua explained, because such people are usually trouble-makers.) Then the revered *yaqona* is brought to the *tanoa* – a large wooden vessel – with the help of ceremonial words. It's passed around one cup at a time to guests, who clap once upon receiving it, drink it all in one go, then clap three times. Several rounds of *yaqona* will pass before any serious business takes place. The *yaqona* has a sedative effect, and it makes people relaxed and conciliatory.

When the ceremony was over, we followed Ratu Esekeli in single file to the *vunivalu*'s ceremonial residence. It's a traditional structure elevated on a platform of rocks about two metres high. The roof soars to a peak of about ten metres, and over the metal roofing it is thatched in the traditional way. To my amazement, we were invited to go into the building.

We found stateliness and grandeur inside. The walls are decorated with ornamental bamboo and the ceiling is lined with decorative matting. The massive support beams are covered with *magimagi*, a dyed and braided coconut fibre woven into geometric designs. The fine wood floors are covered with mats and a magnificent tapa cloth, a mulberry-bark fabric printed with black and brown traditional designs, decorates a room divider. This room has seen much history and held people of undeniable dignity.

We were led up a hill to a ceremonial burial ground where Tui Cakobau and his family are buried. There's a commanding view of the mainland island to the west, and smaller islands to the east – islands which Tui Cakobau conquered to become "king" of Fiji. It seems fitting that he should still preside over his lands from this strategic spot.

We descended the hill to the seat of the real power in this country – and the source of Tui Cakobau's legitimacy in the previous century – the Methodist Church. The cream-coloured wood and cement building is easily the largest structure on the island. The baptismal font stands in silent testimony of a people capable of radical change.

Our next stop was the political meeting house. It's elevated on a double tier of rocks. The walls of bamboo and leaves have three doors on each side, and a door at both ends, representing its accessibility from all directions. This is where important political decisions are made by the chiefs and elders of all villages on the island. The building has no furniture – only mats cover the floor. The ornamented walls, together with mat-lined ceiling and support beams decorated with *magimagi*, lend the dignity of ancient craft to the elaborate political structures that continue to thrive in the Fijian culture today – a culture that is reasserting itself and demanding ascendancy in its own land.

When our tour was over, we returned to Dr. Tabua's sister's home where a fabulous banquet of fish, *dalo*, cassava and *palusami* was served. Dessert was tapioca and papaya pudding. On our walk to the punt that would take us back to the mainland, we were accompanied by countless children who materialized from behind doorways and back rooms where they had been shyly hiding. Our visit to the small Bau Island will remain a revered highlight of our time in Fiji.

Pat Cameron

Nairobi, Kenya

✉ Last week, my husband and daughter and I and two friends from Canada drove to the home village of Mary, our housekeeper. We were going to visit Mary's mother.

A parade of children met our car at the gate to the village. There were fifty or sixty children, all of them wearing hats they'd made themselves out of school paper, fringed to look like feathers, all of them dancing and singing songs of welcome in Kikuyu and Kiswahili. They'd learned our names and put them into the songs to make us feel special, and they took our hands and led us into the village compound. The procession went by the hut where maize is stored, a small wooden building raised on poles off the ground, then past the cow pen, where two cows kept up a steady mooing during the singing.

The first time I saw the village, a year ago, I had been struck by what seemed like poverty: chickens and goats roaming about, barefoot children, mud walls and tin roofs. But a year later, after I knew more about Africa, the village seemed to be a lively, rural community. My terms of reference are changing.

In the centre of the village is an open square surrounded by buildings that had been decorated with paper streamers and balloons. The children led us to couches set outside Mary's mother's house, where we sat watching in admiration as they performed for more than half an hour. It was a hot day: perspiration flew off their faces like rain, the red dirt beneath their feet blew up in clouds of dust and they barely stopped for breath between dances.

Translated from Kikuyu, one of the songs went like this: show us your teeth if you're glad to be here. Well, I had no trouble with that since I've got a great big smile, and they could see I was ready to get up and dance when they invited us to join them. I failed to imitate their incredibly agile hip-shaking; I suspect I looked pretty funny because there was a lot of laughter.

After these opening dances, we were led into Mary's mother's parlour, which had been specially decorated with floral wrapping paper for the occasion. We were given a celebratory cup of *uji*, a thick potion made of milk, water and slightly fermented millet; it was extremely filling and tasted slightly of strawberries. Sitting with us in the small room was Mary's older brother, Laurence, who had driven up from Nairobi where he works as a statistician in a medical research centre. He told us that *uji* is recognized as one of the best antidotes for dehydration during childhood diarrhoea – a traditional food has turned out to have modern merit. With Laurence we also chatted about computers – in a setting where it might have seemed that Western civilization has no influence – except for the country-and-western music playing in another room.

This is what my time in Kenya is like – unexpected contrasts and juxtapositions. I am learning never to make generalizations! In this village, for example, made up mainly of Mary's brothers' wives and their children, there are people who have college degrees who have travelled and seen the world, and there are also people who speak little English, who have seldom gone far from home.

After a while we went looking for Mary and found her in the small mud-walled kitchen, stirring a pan of mixed vegetables she was cooking on a charcoal *jiko*. She was wearing a stylish pale green dress and had done her hair in a sophisticated fashion. Her sisters wore scarves tied round their heads in the usual Kikuyu way, and their clothes ranged from blouses and tartan skirts and bright dresses of shiny fabric to cotton kangas tied around their waists, in colour combinations like the colours of Kenya itself: iridescent blues and greens, yellows and oranges and reds.

In the corner of the dark and smoky kitchen lay the woolly skin of the sheep that had been killed that morning by Mary's uncle. He and some of her brothers and male cousins did the barbecuing of the meat for the feast, and the women prepared the vegetables on *jikos* and over an open fire in the kitchen. They made traditional Kikuyu food for us – dishes such as *ilio*, a tasty concoction of peas, beans and maize, and another one called *miji*, I think, made from mashed black-eyed peas and potatoes. Mary made coleslaw for us as a gesture towards *mzungu* cuisine – *mzungu* means white people.

The five of us sat to eat on the couches outside, and the children sat in rows across from us and stared! Mary explained they were interested to see *mzungus* using knives and forks; but, in an attempt to look as if we belonged, we'd been trying to eat more traditionally with our fingers, much to their disappointment. I noticed that Mary's mother, a very dignified woman in her late sixties, was looking very stern during the meal and asked Mary if anything was wrong. She said no, explaining that her mother was so worried that we be treated perfectly; someone had forgotten the napkins, which had really upset her. On the other hand, we made the mistake of not washing our hands in the customary way before we ate, which was really bad manners on our part.

In typical African fashion, the men sat together inside to eat and were given the best portions of meat first; the women sat together outside with the children and were served meat later.

After the meal, the women danced for us, performing as many old dances as they could remember. They were assisted in their collective memory by a very old woman, who was at least ninety and dressed in a bright purple hat and cardigan. She was wizened and tiny, with bright eyes that looked as if they held great wisdom and experience. This old lady and some of the other older women there were widowed by the British during the Mau Mau emergency about three decades ago.

At the end of the afternoon came the formal section of the festivities, the giving and receiving of gifts. We'd brought several items for Mary's mother: a paraffin lamp, teacups and tea-towels, scissors, and candy for the children. We all made speeches, which were translated by Mary to much applause and laughter.

I lead a privileged life out here, but the biggest privilege of all so far has been this unusual chance to cross the barriers and to share Mary's life a little, to be made so welcome and to be given such a day to remember by her family.

Escorted to the car by singing children, we were hugged good-bye and told we must come back again. Believe me, we will.

Isabel Huggan

Ouagadougou, Burkina Faso

✉ By now everyone has probably heard, then forgotten, the name Burkina Faso. It means "Land of Dignity" and it's a country of about eight million people in West Africa. It's a long way from the international stock exchanges.

On October 15, 1988, this obscure little country hit the world's headlines for a few hours. The reason was another coup d'état, the fourth in seven years. Coups and famines are so routine in Africa it's easy to lose track of them.

But this coup was different from any other I've seen. It was not a case of replacing one despot with another. In the most dramatic sense of the word, this one was a tragedy.

I first passed through this country, then called Upper Volta, in 1982. At that time it was a desperately poor, disorganized, corrupt, disease-ridden land of illiteracy, broken machinery and broken dreams. I came back to live here in 1985, two years after the "revolution" began. The country had taken on the name Burkina Faso, and it was still desperately poor by our definition; still ninety-per-cent illiterate and still plagued by disease.

But there was something in the air besides dust. It was hope. You felt it everywhere. People believed they were on the right path. And the most hopeful of all was the then thirty-six-year-old president, Captain Thomas Sankara. His "revolution" had worked small miracles in a country with almost no natural resources on the southern doorstep of the Sahara. There was order, and things *worked*. There were mass health programs, public anti-corruption trials, mandatory fitness sessions, family planning and small development projects. And it all worked.

Journalists flocked in to tell the world about Thomas Sankara and this "Land of Dignity." Sankara, charismatic and immensely witty, became known as the *enfant terrible* of Africa, a head of state who shunned Mercedes, sloth, alcohol, tobacco and imported luxury. He earned the reputation, along with Jerry Rawlings of Ghana, of being the most sincere, honest and hard-working president on this troubled continent.

There were problems, of course. Sankara was dogmatic, naïve, idealistic and radical. He angered Western diplomats with his revolutionary rhetoric and angered his own people by forcing them to start at the beginning, with picks and shovels and wheelbarrows to build a new country. The people were simultaneously proud of and tired of their revolution and their unrelenting president. Progress was painfully slow, but there was progress.

Then, on a Thursday afternoon, at 4:15, dressed in a red track suit in preparation for the mass sport event at 5:00, Sankara and twelve other men were gunned down at the headquarters of the ruling Revolutionary Council. Sankara's body lies in a dismal mass grave on the dusty, decrepit outskirts of the capital, Ouagadougou. People are still filing past, to stare in disbelief at the mound of earth that covers their former president. Many have placed scraps of paper on the grave, weighted down with small stones. These bear poignant messages: "For us you are still alive,

Thomas," and "We will never forget you and what you did for our country."

What went wrong, they ask. The new president of the Popular Front, which assumed power, is Captain Blaise Compaoré, a best friend of Sankara's for ten years, and the man who helped bring him to power in 1983. He now says Sankara had become an auto-crat, that Sankara had been plotting against him, that problems could no longer be resolved with words. In the end it was Comp-aoré's security forces, not he, who decided Sankara had to go, and so they killed him.

Blaise Compaoré is a tall, subdued and soft-spoken man – the antithesis of his predecessor. He says he never liked politics and admits he is not a natural president. But his own men put him there and now there's no turning back. He will be president, but it is a blood-stained regime. The country, meanwhile, falls back into old ways. Compaoré hardly dares leave his office. There is no more Sankara riding through town on his bicycle or taking up his guitar at outdoor concerts.

The people are left with little option but to follow and accept their fate. Thus is born the fatalism that helps Africa survive, but that prevents any great changes on this continent.

In Burkina Faso, the biggest loss of all is the people's confidence in themselves and in their leaders. Life will go on here – the Bur-kinabe are quite used to fending for themselves. But it will be a long, long time before they allow themselves to hope that one day life will get better.

✉ I have a black-and-white photograph in front of me, one I took recently of a ten-year-old boy, smiling at my camera. Quite una-ware, he wears a mask of dust that turns his black face grey. His cotton T-shirt is ragged, and one sleeve has been torn off com-pletely, revealing bony shoulders and upper arms. Behind him the thatch huts and the barren, rocky plains are over-exposed, bleached almost white. Already I've lost the feeling I had when I took the picture. Away from the site it is difficult to imagine and recapture it, but I'll try.

It was almost midday, about forty-five degrees Celsius. The heat and wind were whipping up miniature tornadoes of sand that caused spasms of coughing and made eyes run and mouths dry. The boy in the picture covered his head protectively with his arms, afraid of the malevolent souls that turn themselves into wind funnels to bring ill will to those who get in their way.

The whole setting was strangely quiet. Voices were muted, just murmurs. People were using all their energy other ways – digging, heaving, sifting and pounding. That is what I remember most clearly about the place, the sound of the stones being pounded, thump . . . thump . . . thump . . . the hollow sound of hope that one of those lumps of laterite would produce a nugget of gold.

The boy in the photograph came with his family two months ago to the gold-fields of Yako, in the north of Burkina Faso – a Sahelian country plagued by Sahelian problems – drought, malnutrition, thirst, disease and locusts. The Yako gold-field, that faded background in the photograph, looks like something from some century long past, or the opening set of some futuristic doomsday film – blowing sand, gaping craters carved out of the earth by hand, squalid huts and people, ragged, unwashed and squatting, pounding away with stone tools.

In the past six months about twenty thousand people have migrated to Yako, which is only the latest, not the largest gold-field to be opened up in Burkina Faso. Twenty thousand people who have left their mud huts empty and their villages empty, their fields unsown, their real selves behind; twenty thousand people who have forsaken everything in the desperate, irrational hope for sudden wealth. This phenomenon is not new, of course; it is well known by the name gold-fever. But in Burkina Faso the gold-rush seems particularly pathetic. It is desperation that draws the gold seekers to these sites. They are not greedy. Most are simple peasant farmers who have finally given up trying to eke out a survival with millet fields that either wither with drought, or are devoured by storming locusts. Gold-fever is nothing else but one last, desperate hope.

The boy came two months ago with his grandfather, Boukary Sawadogo, who is seventy-two years old. The boy's older brothers work the family claim, a hole that looks like a dry well, ten metres deep. They take turns manning the shovel at the bottom of the pit, removing tonnes of soil, bucketful by bucketful, which they haul up with a rope. The man at the bottom of the pit is barely visible in the darkness – just a black naked torso gleaming with sweat. The women and girls pound the soil into fine powder, and the grandfather and the boy do the fine washing of the soil. Water, firewood and food are such precious commodities on the site that most families eat perhaps once a day and drink the same water they've used to pan the gold. Disease and crime are rampant, and people die by the hundreds, but no one is counting those figures.

The government – ah, the government in the capital, Ouagadougou, which has a monopoly on all gold dealing in the country – has so far not had to provide any kind of facilities on the site, or to disclose how much it makes each year from gold revenues. The presidency has other preoccupations, such as its order this month for twenty brand-new Mercedes sedans. In Yako, government officials vie with unscrupulous gold merchants from neighbouring countries who buy the gold illegally, but neither the official nor the illegal buyers pay more than half what the gold is worth. And the point is, few people find enough gold to pay for their daily bread. One security official describes the gold-field as a lottery in which no one wins but the organizers.

I took the photograph of the smiling boy shortly after his grandfather proudly showed me what gold he had found in his two months of labour. Neither he nor the boy was complaining. Both seemed pleased at my interest in them. Village people in this part of the world learn at infancy that complaining will get them nowhere, and it apparently never occurs to them that their lot in life is, by almost any standards, too miserable to contemplate. No, they were not interested in arousing sympathy–they both smiled, creating wrinkles in their dehydrated dust-covered faces, and asked me if I didn't want to take a picture of their new-found wealth. I agreed, expecting to be shown a shining nugget. But all I could see were a few microscopic grains of gold dust in Boukary's ancient weathered hand. "Is it enough to pay for all your labour or even today's meal?" I asked. "No," said the old man, "but we will find something bigger soon. Anyway, it's the only thing we *can* do. Life in the village is no good any more."

Joan Baxter

Rio Marauá, Rio Negro, Brazil

✉ At the moment someone is combing through my hair with their fingers looking for ticks and lice. This practice is common among Indians in the Amazon. It's an act of caring and friendship, as well as being necessary and healthy grooming. So far, no bugs have been found in *my* hair.

Since I arrived here in the *maloca* (communal village) of this group of Yanomamo, I too have picked through the straight, black hair of several children when we sit together listening to someone speaking or when yet another curious person investigates all my possessions. They ask me what a compass is, what a fountain-pen is, what a razor-blade is.

Three days have passed since we reached the big granite boulder where the path from the *maloca* comes to the river. Now I am a guest in the house of the chief.

To speak of a house perhaps gives the wrong impression. Each Yanomamo family lives in a small shelter, usually open on three sides, with a hard earth floor and a roof of palm leaves supported on poles. Each shelter faces a large circle of bare, hard ground, like a school playground. There are fifty-eight people in eleven families in this community, and each shelter stands separately around the circle. However, traditionally, the house of the Yanomamo adjoin one another with one continuous roof, so that from above the whole structure of the *maloca* looks something like a huge straw-coloured doughnut.

Each household has a fire on the ground towards one end of the shelter, beside which the husband and wife sleep. The children and guests sleep a little farther away. Everyone has his or her own hammock. None of the households has any furniture. There's a mat woven of palm leaves for the baby to play on and several little blocks of wood that serve as stools. Possessions such as a comb, mirror, needle and thread, a shirt, fish-hooks and line are kept in well-made baskets hanging from the rafters to keep out children, dogs and chickens. Farinha and tapioca, both foods made from manioc roots, are kept in tins and boxes in one corner, along with salt and coffee, sugar, rice and other supplies a visitor might infrequently provide.

We are eight people in the chief's house: six males, including a baby, and his wife and their daughter. She is ten years old and already betrothed to a twenty-year-old man who lives with the family and who works as one of its members. He goes out at dawn to fish and hunt and gives whatever he catches to his mother-in-law. Soon after the daughter has her first period, and is "formed," as they say here, they will become married. Until then, the man must work for his father-in-law, providing food and working in the plantation to grow manioc and bananas. I, too, have planted manioc cuttings, and this has helped ease people's agitation that an outsider is among them.

So far there's been only one ugly moment, when the chief accused people of taking goods from me without paying. Pacing up and down in the circle just in front of his house, raving and shaking his fist, he warned everyone that I am as his own son and that anyone interfering or threatening me must answer to him. People in turn shouted back with great anger that they had paid for whatever they had taken, which was true.

This business of trading began as soon as I arrived, when many people came to see what I had that they wanted. The chief suggested I give three arm's lengths of very strong cord to an old and important man in the *maloca*, which I did, and an hour later he returned with two clusters of small parrot feathers in exchange. This was the price he was suggesting. I readily agreed. Since then I've rarely sat in my hammock without people coming to see what there is, or just to sit and watch me writing letters or in my journal, or playing the tenor recorder. They also come to look through my strange possessions.

Machetes – knives about two feet long – are especially prized, and at a price of one bow and two arrows, four machetes have already been exchanged. One man told me he obtained his machete for a hammock and a metal cooking pot. My prices are regarded as low, for which I'm happy.

Yesterday, five women brought their babies to me to be treated. Each child has a fungal infection around the neck, armpits and legs – a very common infection in the humidity here and almost impossible to cure because treatment takes weeks and reinfection from other children is almost immediate. Surprisingly, the Yanomanis use no medicinal plants from the forest. All illnesses have supernatural causes and therefore supernatural remedies. I've used iodine to clean sores, and the purple-coloured liquid is now sought after by the men, who want it to decorate their bodies. So far I've refused to give them any.

Two other objects are highly prized for decoration. One is a short length of steel wire, a leader, designed for catching piranhas without them biting and breaking the line. The other is a little brass swivel, which stops the fishing line from becoming twisted. Both the leaders and the swivels are desired only as necklaces and earrings, and my supply was exhausted when word of an exciting novelty spread around the *maloca*. Fortunately, I have orange, yellow, red, blue and black plastic combs for people much disappointed that the other items are finished. Two men have told me vehemently not to exchange goods with anyone without giving them an opportunity to buy.

Though everyone is friendly at the moment, I'm aware how quickly moods change here, how suddenly people become enraged and violent. A couple of times the chief has warned me of hostility despite the smiles, and that if I were not his guest, in his house, I would already have been robbed and probably killed. I'm coming to believe these stories more – not because of sudden treachery but because most of the people in the other families do not know anything about me. Few people trust me, and they rightly view all white men with great suspicion. There are items they want in my baggage; I am not Yanomamo and therefore inferior; and it's their option to take what they want. However, I'm a guest of the chief so that there's nothing to fear.

After the excitement of my arrival, life is returning to its own very slow pace. People are relaxing. Most women are bare-breasted again, and one old woman is completely without clothes in her open house. A couple of the men, too, have put aside their clothes when they dance and chant to the spirits, which they do every afternoon. I believe it is a very important part of their culture, of the way they see and understand their world of forest and river.

Dennison Berwick

Paris, France

✉ We have an American friend who has opted for the quiet life. He sold up almost everything he owned, bought a pretty stone house in the French Pyrenees and lives there extremely simply and almost always alone.

We visited our friend recently, and were intrigued to notice a TV set in his house, a small, almost minimal affair, but still – a TV set? We asked our friend what had happened to his ideal of escaping all that.

"Oh, no, it's not TV," he said. "It's my Minitel. It's part of the telephone." He had gotten it free with his telephone. Anyone with a phone can have one in France.

The Minitel is a computer, and you tap the buttons to gain access to vast stores of information. All French phone directories are available, and masses of information about current films, music and theatre performances, together with times and prices, which are playing anywhere in France. You can book any theatre tickets through your machine, paying by credit cards. You can also book train seats, couchettes and airplane flights; find out about church services and order the latest books to be delivered to your house. Statistics, dates, lists of officials for thousands of societies, pornographic messages, the weather at any given place, your daily horoscope – technology provides all this on your telephone screen, at a cost of less than a franc a minute.

France has taken to computer technology as no other European country has done, and has begun to use it for social ends with total Gallic concentration. It's never been pleasanter or more convenient to become a hermit in France.

But even hermitic existences are invaded, these days, by the sound of guns firing. It is the hunting season, and absolutely everything that moves, in field or mountain, lives in peril. People keep their cats indoors, because hunters are said to vent their frustration by killing them – rats, cats, squirrels, sparrows, anything.

We ourselves witnessed the terrible *chasse aux palombes*, the shooting of the wild pigeons in the high Pyrenees. Hundreds of tiny wooden box-like cabins dot every peak. Heads belonging to carefully dressed and heavily equipped hunters peer over the top of each box, and hunting dogs by the thousand wait for the arrival of the *palombes*, migrating in this season to North Africa.

There are not many *palombes*. About twenty or so occasionally appear, and at once the guns start popping. The hunters are so numerous that they seriously hinder each other's efforts, and there is much cursing when a wily group of pigeons veers away at the first blast that comes too quick off the mark. Presumably the few birds that have survived so long are the cleverest of the lot. When a pigeon is downed, the dogs bound off after it. One wonders how many dead birds get back to the people who actually shot them.

We spoke to the wife of our hotel's proprietor about hunting. Her husband is an avid hunter, she says, and he is furious because there are so few *palombes* left nowadays. (There used to be huge flocks, thousands at a time, and people were allowed to capture them in nets.)

She is convinced – everyone is convinced, she says – that the British are killing the *palombes* before they get to France. The British are said to drug the birds somehow, making them go to sleep; then they kill them, pluck them, freeze them and export them to France!

She went to her freezer and brought back a box of frozen birds to show us. "There, you see?" she said triumphantly. Sure enough, British wood-pigeons. They are clearly farm-raised, obviously for the French market. We tried to explain that the pigeons in the box would never have had an opportunity to fly over the Pyrenees in the first place. But she was adamant.

"We have to shoot down as many pigeons as we can get," she said. "They are all the British leave for us. And soon," she added sorrowfully, "there will be no *palombes* left." I felt guilt and discomfort in several different forms. I had eaten pigeon the previous night – frozen, I now knew, and imported from a farm in England. It was done in the *béarnaise* manner, and was absolutely delicious. My last pigeon.

Margaret Visser

Phnom Penh, People's Republic of Kampuchea

✉ Today we said goodbye to a friend.

Neak Samral is twenty-two years old. He is one of Kampuchea's thousands of orphans; all of his family were killed or died during the Khmer Rouge reign of terror. Since Kampuchea's "liberation" in 1979, when he was only twelve, Samral has lived in one of the country's many orphanages.

We first met him at the Boeng Kak restaurant, where he has been working as a waiter, his first job. The Boeng Kak, one of several state-run restaurants in Phnom Penh, is our favourite, partly because of its proximity to our hotel, but more because it is built on the shores of a large water reservoir and provides a quiet and cool place to enjoy an evening's meal.

Samral is a slight, somewhat nervous young man, and his eager attentiveness and cheerful smile makes him a favourite, too. Like so many young people in Kampuchea, he is intent upon learning English and took every opportunity to practise his limited vocabulary with us. Many nights he'd hover over us as we ate, struggling with a question or wanting us to teach him a new English word or phrase. (We'd ask him the Khmer equivalent, but to our linguistic shame, we've managed to learn little Khmer.) Sometimes the impromptu English lessons were a success; other times we'd have to resort to pantomime as we tried to bridge the gulf of language.

Over the past several months, and with little credit to us, Samral's English has improved greatly. Each morning, before beginning his work at the restaurant, he has been attending private English classes. English is not part of the Khmer school curriculum, and while the Kampuchean authorities have not approved the instruction of foreign languages, a blind eye is turned to the proliferation of private language classes – mostly English – throughout the city. Such courses are taught by off-duty teachers and government workers who learned a foreign language before 1975. During the Pol Pot years anyone who was caught speaking a language other than Khmer often was singled out for death, as English and French were considered reactionary or corrupting influences.

Our orphan friend diligently pursued his English-language studies; his progress from week to week has been noticeable, and his increased mastery of English has seemed to give him more self-confidence. We seemed to be going to the Boeng Kak more and more often, if only to talk with Samral and to find out more about him, his experiences and his hopes for the future.

Before we left Kampuchea for a month's home-leave, Samral presented us with a souvenir, a small brass plaque of a Khmer Apsaras dancer. He shyly asked if we could bring him an English dictionary from Canada. Several weeks later, we presented him with an English dictionary designed for use in Canadian elementary schools. Samral couldn't have been more pleased.

A few weeks ago Samral told us he soon would be leaving the restaurant. He had been drafted into the volunteer Kampuchean armed forces. Five years of military service is required of every Kampuchean male, except those few selected for higher education either in Kampuchea's limited technical training schools or in institutions abroad, in the few "fraternal" countries that recognize the People's Republic of Kampuchea.

On Samral's last night at the restaurant, we went to say goodbye. The next day he would start a few months of military training before being sent to the border to fight against the opposition forces, notably the Khmer Rouge, which still receive both Western and Chinese assistance. With no negotiated political settlement yet in sight, it is sure that Samral will see active service in the bloody war that continues to ravage this tiny country.

We may never see Samral again.

It is hard to escape the realities of Kampuchea's ongoing "half peace, half war." Armed troops are very much in evidence, including those being trained in the centre of the city at the very foot of Wat Phnom, the man-made hill that gives the city its name. We hear of the shifting security situation, with access to some provinces still restricted. As members of the Western aid community of some one hundred and thirty persons, we trade rumours of isolated guerrilla attacks on civilian targets. Kampuchea's hospitals are filled with the victims of land mines and military skirmishes, or with those dying of drug-resistant malaria from having served in the forest areas along the border with Thailand. And everywhere, we see young veterans – Samral's age and younger – their poor, thin bodies shattered by war. Amputees, they hobble down Phnom Penh's streets, bereft of any future.

Excited by his departure the next morning, as well as by the send-off dinner planned by his friends at the restaurant, Samral showed no fear or reluctance. He thanked us again for the English dictionary, and said that he would take it with him everywhere. And as if to reassure us, he repeated what must be official propaganda, carefully translated into English: he was joining the army not to fight, but to "help end the bloodshed between Khmer and Khmer."

Grant Curtis

Opononi, Hokianga County, New Zealand

✉ In the bush, your neighbours are your main source of amuse, ment and irritation. Opononi's beauty and amicable anarchy appeal to Mormons and motor bikers, earnest young families and transsexuals, poets and survivalists. Depending on your tolerance for idiosyncracy, you can form your own blend of independence and interdependence.

When I first lived here, I found my frontier on the floor of the steep Waiotemarama Gorge, about two hours from town. My neighbours, a religious recluse and a couple from San Diego, lived a mile in either direction. I had a phone, so I was only cut off when the phone was cut off two or three days a week. I found that twenty-six years of politicized city living were poor preparation: no one forms *ad hoc* committees in the bush. They know how to fix things themselves.

I'd been referred to Rob Lawrence, to rent his house while he travelled. The dramatic landscape, bushy gardens surrounding the hand-built house and the pastoral cows grazing nearby grabbed my imagination. On his way out the door, Rob mentioned the compost.

"Of course, where's that?" I asked brightly, looking for a trash compactor. Rob pointed to the garden. "Exactly how does that . . . work?"

"Burn what you can't bury."

"Burn?" I repeated. His kids explained while Rob tried to look unconcerned. They piled into their car and I said through the win, dow, "What about rent? References?"

"Feed the cat," Rob shrugged, and they left. I found the cat, found some cat food and wondered whether to burn or bury the empty cans. Briefly, I considered burning or burying the cat.

Once I was informed that the hissing under my window at night was that of possums and not psychos, I settled in happily. I took to wearing lacy sundresses and floppy hats and carried my groceries in a straw basket. I quite liked the image.

The day before Christmas, while hiking home with my groceries, I found that all the pastoral cows had grazed their way through the electric fence and into my garden. I dropped the groceries and backed away: I'd never touched a cow. I slipped in through the side-door to call a neighbour. I'd never used the gorge's party line, so I had to call an operator first. She didn't know much about cows, either. Finally, I got through to Candy, who typifies bush practicality.

"Merry Christmas, Candy," I said cheerfully. "Say, I'm curious. Do cows bite?"

"Bite? No."

"Well, that's good to know."

"But they sure can kick."

"Oh."

"Marilyn, would you like me to come over there?"

"No, no, everything's under control. But tell me, how do you fix an electric fence?"

"Turn the power off."

A cow poked its head through the door as I hung up. "Baah!" I shouted, waving my arms, and it retreated. Encouraged, I ran after it, screaming wildly. All the cows in sight plodded around the corner of the house. "Not that way!" I hollered, and they went a little faster in the wrong direction. I chased them twice around the house and sat down to think.

Rob had been building an addition. Gathering all the construction materials I could find, I made a complicated road-block, stretching from one corner of the house to the break in the fence. It took half an hour. Sneaking up behind the cows, I drove them at high volume once more around the house, along the barrier and into the paddock. I moved the wood to build a mound at the gap in the fence, and drew a skull and crossbones on top. I added "pioneer" to my résumé.

That was two years ago. Now I live in Pakenai, a settlement of about seventy on the coastal road. I live with Geoff in a pleasantly dilapidated fisherman's cottage. Our neighbours are close enough to live in each other's kitchens, close enough to be deeply entangled in each other's lives. It takes tolerance.

Joanne and Howard moved next door on the same Saturday I moved in here. Joanne is a close friend, six feet tall and slinky. Howard is Maori, with dreadlocks and a most ingratiating smile. They'd lived for two years in a shed on the Tasman seashore, without power, hot water or indoor plumbing. The rough access road guaranteed their privacy; their Alsatian, Halen, was thus used to roaming freely. When their son, Michael, was born last January, they opted for a few more amenities and bought the newly renovated house for $60,000, including a coop full of hens.

That first weekend, Joanne and I unpacked kitchen crates. Michael explored his new house while Howard hunted for a cheap fridge. Late Sunday night, the dog went hunting in the henhouse.

Monday morning, after Howard left for a construction job, most of Pakenai awoke to Joanne's screams. The yard was littered with dead hens. One wounded survivor fled to the hills, and the dog, Halen, prudently followed. Our next-door neighbour on the other side jumped two fences to get to Joanne. (Wayne has four hens and an all-terrain cycle that he revs outside my bedroom window at dawn.) "I'll shoot Halen," he offered breathlessly. "Want me to shoot Halen?" Joanne screamed louder.

Geoff only had to jump one fence to establish that Joanne simply wanted to *find* Halen. They went to the beach, thinking he might have gone there for some quiet. They picked up Bruce, our neighbour over the road, to drive him into town. Bruce is an animated refugee from the Auckland cult-poetry circuit. He's got lots of hens, and a dog who chases nothing more attainable than cars. Bruce responded to the news with his usual energy. "If Halen ever comes near our hens, my wife'll shoot him!" (If you knew Bruce's wife, you'd agree that she probably would.)

Halen slunk home late that afternoon. His life expectancy seemed poor. The story had spread across kitchen tables, through the check-out line at the general store, over pool tables in the pub. Everyone agreed, "Once a hen dog, always a hen dog. Shoot him."

But it would be unfair to say that we were taking the law into our own hands with Halen. The nearest cop lives about twenty-five kilometres away, so the law is effectively ours already. Normally, we just make better use of it. This incident became one of those flash fires that ignites when you rub seventy personalities together. That was clear at a barbecue the next night, when Halen was accused of every animal death in the county. Ian MacDonald, known as McBoing Boing for his ricocheting creativity, accused Halen of killing his pet sheep, Baa Baa BaRam.

"Aw, that's only because you don't like Howard," someone pointed out.

"Not entirely," Ian said defensively. "Anyway, I told Howard that if Halen ever came down to my beach, I'd shoot him on sight."

"And what did Howard say?"

"He said that if I ever shot Halen, he'd shoot me."

It is axiomatic that someone does something noteworthy every few days, so the county has a short attention span. John Fysh, the former resident wild man standing six feet ten inches tall, came home to announce his marriage to a nurse he'd met in the hospital following a car accident. The county was distracted. Two Swiss immigrants then declared theirs an open marriage, and the county was positively hypnotized. By the time Darryl set the woods on fire at a party, Halen had been forgotten. Howard fenced off his yard, and I haven't told anyone that Halen jumps the fence at will. Joanne began buying eggs from her erstwhile foe, Bruce Over The Road, and Pakenai settled in for a neighbourly round of Christmas parties.

✉ I was prepared to make changes when I moved from downtown Toronto to the New Zealand bush. But the language barrier was unexpected.

228

It began with the names. Sprog and Frog and Plankton, Quail and Snail and Jonathan Livingston Peanut, Hucky and Pucky and Titch. These men, with their wild Father Time hair and rambling beards, introduced themselves with the one bit of slang I most detest. "Hello," they'd say. "You must be Geoff's new cook."

"No," I'd bristle. "Geoff is my new gardener."

Most of the argot isn't objectionable, it's just confusing. If you take your anger out on someone, you "deal to" them. John Fysh wrapped his truck around a signpost, and everyone said he'd dealt to the signpost. I thought the post had dealt rather convincingly to John. At his wedding to the nurse he met in the hospital, no one wore gumboots.

There are many Maori (it rhymes with dowry) words in use. A meeting is a *hui* (hooey), a barbecue is a *hangi* (hung ee) and a funeral is a *tungi* (tongue ee). When four of our neighbours had a terrible three-way fight, I remarked brightly that if someone didn't call for a *hui* or a *hangi*, we'd surely be attending a *tungi*. From that still-simmering dispute, I learned a wealth of vivid local insults, and found that men's chest-shoving rituals do not vary across the hemispheres.

My living room is the lounge, and cleaning it involves some novel routines, like the twice-weekly spider hunt and shooing possums from the door. None of my city apartments came equipped with a smokehouse. The bathroom is a room with a bathtub (or else it's the nearest creek), while the toilet is a separate room with a toilet. I've asked directions to many a bathtub at parties, when that wasn't at all what I wanted. Dinner is *kai* (kie), and a big meal is *kai mungus*. The usual procedure is one I call *mungus* for the masses, who have a way of dropping in at six each afternoon.

"Privacy" is not a term in common use. Now, I love the freedom with which people float through each other's houses; and each home, converted cow shed or bus has a pot of something bubbling on the stove (if there is a stove). But just try planning a quiet dinner party. I tried it with my city-bred neighbour, Joanne, when we waxed nostalgic for restaurants and good wine. We would have a relaxed meal for ourselves and our boyfriends, during which no one would eat with their fingers or discuss their fishing prowess. We would not race to make last call at the pub.

It was a major undertaking. I was negotiating the purchase of a snappy 1971 Isuzu Bellet that still had its four doors intact. Joanne's truck could no longer make the trip to the nearest supermarket, about fifty-two kilometres away. And Joanne kept forgetting to get a driver's licence. But everyone shops on Thursday, when the unemployment benefit is paid, so we hitched a ride to Kaikohe (kie kow hee). Broadway, the shopping street, was bursting at the seams. Thursday is also court day, which always brings in crowds, invited or otherwise.

I went first to Pete's Meats, Deli and Home Kills. Pete sells sides of mutton, beef and pigs' trotters. The deli consists of a shelf of sauces and a bowl of coleslaw. I've never asked about the home-kills department. I've seen enough buckets of blood under people's front stairs. I asked for a pound of hamburger, which got me a blank look. "Sorry," I said. "Half a kilo of mince."

I take pride in bypassing the green grocer, because I have a garden. To be honest, the first time I jumped on a spade, I nearly broke my instep. Since then, I've assumed a distant managerial role befitting Ronald Reagan; so I'm not sure what's in this garden. During a back-yard chat with Wayne one day, I watched him dive into my jungle and pull out a watermelon. He told me I had lovely, ripe *kumikumi*.

I sighed. Wayne built his own house. He didn't know that my concept of self-sufficiency was fulfilled the day I dyed a dress purple. "Wayne," I said in a small voice, "what does a *kumikumi* look like, where is it growing and how do you know that it's ripe?"

He waded intrepidly into a tangle of thorny vines and hauled out a zucchini, longer than my forearm and as thick as my thigh. In that first lesson, we harvested pumpkins that took two hands to carry and discerned that the corn was nearly ready.

With vegetables in perpetual supply, I headed straight for the New World Supermarket. They play rock and roll, and the aisles are full of unfamiliar packages. I usually trundle along behind Joanne and ask questions. Last on my list was laundry detergent.

I'd ordered some from a direct distribution company for my old washing machine that I'd bought for ten dollars. It took two months to arrive, so I needed an interim supply. I asked a clerk, who said nothing.

"Laundry detergent," I repeated slowly. I offered half a dozen brand names, raising my voice in case she was hard of hearing.

Joanne popped around a corner and whispered, "Washing powder."

The clerk led me to it, saying sympathetically, "Just up on holidays, are you?"

"No," I said pointedly. "I live here."

I spent two hours making lasagne. I was ready to check the pub's assortment of red wines when people began arriving at both our houses. Over the garden gate, Joanne and I wondered how to stretch dinner for four into *mungus* for eight. Her boyfriend came to lift the baby's high chair over the fence, and he brought a crate of home-brewed beer and a large pot. I opened the lid: pigs' trotters. I didn't bother with the wine. Everyone grabbed a handful of *kai* and adjourned immediately to the veranda to discuss the New Zealand-Pakistan five-day cricket test match. Joanne and I closed the door, fed the baby, ate the lasagne and agreed loudly that *we* couldn't possibly find the time to play the same game for five straight days.

✉ The Maori principle of extended family dominates Hokianga life. Elders are addressed by people of both races with the honorific of Auntie or Pappa. There's a deep sense of belonging, and every celebration takes place within a warm cocoon. My wedding cemented that feeling for me. It was a typical community production, planned in a week. If we'd had any longer to worry about it, Geoff said, we might have screwed it up.

We were formally engaged late Thursday night. On Friday, Geoff told one friend and I told one friend and by nightfall, everyone knew.

"Of course," said Auntie Bunty. "It's the first thing I heard in the pub."

"Yes, I know," smiled Christian, a German traveller who can't seem to leave. "But I heard it was a secret."

Marcel announced that we were the talk of the Rawene (rah weh nee) pub, twenty-five kilometres up the harbour. "They're not sure who you are, but they're all coming to the party."

"You're what? When?" my mother gasped over the phone. "But, dear, these things take six months."

Not around here. We planned it Friday night, sitting on the veranda and waving at each passing car. We would sail an historic boat, the *Sierra*, up the harbour and be married by the postmistress at Rawene. The pub rocked and rolled with the news Saturday night. My family couldn't make it on such short notice, so I asked old Pappa Squirt to give me away. He danced about organizing the offers that began to pour in. Margaret baked the cake and found maple leaves to decorate it. Geoff was outfitted, his hair cut for the first time in three years. Freshly killed wild pigs, sides of lamb and beef, gardens-full of vegetables came at us from all sides. Ian would hold the *hangi*, and a crew was formed with a tractor to clear the necessary beachfront land. When Cyclone Harry arrived late Tuesday, the workers thoughtfully began to enlarge Ian's boat shed.

Whipped with rain, Wednesday brought disaster. It began with a dog fight, which had prompted a people fight. For the past ten days, Howard, my bridesmaid's boyfriend, had been itching for a punch-up with Ian. Now Ian insisted that he'd need a full apology before Howard stepped onto his land. Howard wanted no apologies, he just wanted one clear shot. Despairing, we jumped Ian's fence and plodded fifty yards to Terry's caravan.

Terry's the biggest man I know, heavily muscled with a braid that hangs to his waist. We call him Buddha, for the look of serenity that comes over his massive face when he picks up a fishing rod. "Stupid!" he snorted, stamping one foot and shaking the caravan. "Have the *hangi* here, and I'll keep the peace."

Terry lives on tribal land, so we got the approval of the elders and the caretaker, who tossed in a sheep for the barbecue. To secure a treaty of non-aggression, I added to Terry's three hundred pounds of insurance the promise that I'd be carrying a crowbar. At the first harsh word, I'd let loose across the bridge of the appropriate nose. That did it.

The water line failed the day before the wedding, and Geoff woke up sick. I put the word out in town, and crews fanned out to gather firewood, peel fifty kilos of vegetables, prepare the pit. That night, with the boys threatening to put Geoff on a boat for Australia, I found myself defensively hosting a stag party. I had in mind a quiet night with guitars, but the guitar player was carried out early, to be replaced by a mob in cars, motor cycles and mutant vehicles with other ideas. We threw them all out to retire at 1:00 A.M. Surveying the wreckage of our house, I retired from stag parties entirely.

At 3:00 A.M., a strange face stared into mine. "I'm a very old friend of Geoff's," the man said. "I just heard the news, and I drove right over."

"Geoff's asleep," I said unnecessarily. "Have we met?"

"I'm Nigel," he said, "and I'm going to wake him up."

He did. We went back to bed at dawn. At 7:00 A.M., Kevin burst in. "I just heard that you had to move the *hangi*, and I think you should have it at my place."

Kevin lives on tribal land. "Okay," I mumbled, "it's at your place."

Purdy brought more food in at 8:00 A.M. Euen dropped Geoff's shirt off at 9:00, and John hurried in at 10:00 to ask what time the boat sailed. At 11:00, I peeked into the kitchen, opened one curtain, and said with no trace of sentiment, "Geoff, the house is ruined and it's still cloudy. I think it's all over for us."

I trudged into town to phone my mother. No, I snapped at a dozen people, we had no rain plans. We were taking the damn boat. But some unknown work crew had assembled to shovel away the clouds, and we set sail at 3:00 P.M., with a barrel of iced champagne and a few dozen friends. There were people of every age and six nationalities, some who were feuding and others who hardly spoke, and a few who didn't know each other. The mix was magical. We were married at mid-harbour, with our friends lining the deck around us. Rice flew, ships' horns blew and the fire department threw in a timely siren. An operatic singer tossed in an aria; his wife offered a Hebrew folk-song. Pappa sang a Maori prayer. Someone has since mentioned that the open-water arrangement is entirely illegal, but we haven't troubled the authorities with that.

We returned to cut the cake in Opononi. A phone call from the beach announced that the *hangi* was ready, but first I had to say how lovingly I'd been accepted into my new community (and no one thought for a moment that I'd keep quiet at my own wedding). I said how sorry I was that my family wasn't there to share it all.

"But, Marilyn," a voice said from the crowd. "We're right here. Your family's all around you."

Marilyn Garson

REMEMBERING STAN

The folk-singer Stan Rogers was killed in a plane crash at the end of my first season as host of *Morningside*, but we still cherish the songs he left us, and nearly every time we play one on the air people write to us in gratitude. Even six years after his death, he holds a special place in Canadian music.

I remember him once at the Winnipeg Folk Festival, where he'd been a pioneer. Rain, as it often does, had cast a pall over the opening concert (I've often thought that in years of drought the Winnipeg festival could go on the road and guarantee downpours wherever it went); people were feeling pretty gloomy. But when Stan stepped up to the microphone and strummed out the opening chords to "The Mary Ellen Carter," the rain suddenly stopped, as if even nature couldn't resist the power of Stan's big, true voice, and by the time he was into the chorus – "Rise again," as it goes – the sun was reflecting off his bald dome ("I grew right through my hair," he used to say), and everyone's spirits lifted.

In person, as you'll see from some of these letters, Stan could be abrupt and prickly, and, when we gathered a few people one morning in 1988 to celebrate his music – Connie Kaldor, James Keelaghan and Stan's brother Garnet, who's just coming into his own as a singer now – we didn't shy away from that part of his personality. But there was another Stan Rogers, too, the one that came through in those unforgettable songs. Mendelson Joe, whose letter I've included here, has a point. But I know even Joe would agree it would be nice if we'd all got to know Stan a little better.

✉ I am one of the many who knows Stan only through his music, and that music speaks very clearly to me of what it means to be Canadian. My own profession as a designer and technician for theatre has taken me to many parts of this beautiful country and the songs of Stan Rogers have always seemed to add to that beauty.

I've driven across the prairies and seen the farmers watching "The Field Behind the Plow." I've travelled north of Superior humming "White Squall" to myself and whistled "Barrett's Privateers" while sitting on a pier in Halifax.

It is indeed a loss that this talented troubadour is no longer with us.

Mark Stevens
Toronto

✉ I first saw Stan Rogers at the Folk on the Rocks Folk Festival in Yellowknife in 1982. It was a rainy summer solstice, so the festival had been moved from the graceful shores of Long Lake to a humid and noisy high school gym.

I'd never heard of Stan Rogers, so when this tall, balding man came up to the microphone, I was prepared to be unimpressed. And then he sang "Northwest Passage" with that voice. I was stunned. Thunderstruck. I'm sure my mouth hung open. The noisy chair-shuffling, the coughing and the murmur of the crowd that had persisted throughout the evening stopped dead. And for the next year, whenever anyone in town talked about Folk on the Rocks, they talked about Stan.

In March 1985, I took the ferry from Kangaroo Island to Adelaide, South Australia. It was pouring rain, so I hitched a ride with a big Irish-Aussie who said his name was Dennis O'Neill. We drove through the pounding rain, getting to know one another, sipping from the many bottles of beer stashed away on the floor of his station wagon. He said he was a folk singer, and sang one of my favourite tunes to prove it: "And the Band Played Waltzing Matilda," the Australian anti-war song.

His deep, rich, a cappella rendition, combined with the rain, put me in mind of "Northwest Passage," so I asked Dennis if he'd ever heard of Stan. He took one look at me and sang, "Ah, for just one time, I would take a Northwest Passage . . ."

When he finished, I thrust my hand into my backpack and produced a cassette of *From Fresh Water*, the last album Stan made before his death. From Dennis's reaction, you'd think I had produced a rare treasure, and I suppose I had. I had thought there was something quintessentially Canadian about Stan Rogers that spoke to me through his music. I now realize there was something quintessentially human about him that speaks to people around the world.

Doug Earl
Yellowknife, Northwest Territories

✉ I first discovered Stan Rogers on an album brought home from the library. It was not only that "bigger-than-life" voice that caused me to sit still on the couch and listen to every word. It was the pictures he painted with words. Like Norman Rockwell, he used everyday experiences and made observations about them to which anyone could nod in agreement.

From Stan's songs, I had concluded that he must have been a sensitive, caring man rather than the somewhat abrupt, obnoxious individual some people say he was. Now that I think of it, I know several people who protect a painfully sensitive soul with a prickly exterior. Perhaps Stan was the same. Whatever he was as a person will not affect my enjoyment of his music and poetry. He was one of a kind.

Nancy Bateman
Craven, Saskatchewan

✉ Connie Caldor is correct when she refers to Rogers as *the* Canadian folk writer. His songs speak to us with a simplicity and sophistication that goes to our very core. My husband and I have every one of his albums, and many of his songs seem to speak to us personally. We listened to *Second Effort* a great deal at the conclusion of an unsuccessful, emotionally draining business failure. The words to "The Mary Ellen Carter" lifted our spirits and helped move us forward. "Turn to, and put out all your strength in arm and heart and main" had special meaning at our house, and "The Mary Ellen Carter" will always be the definitive song of optimism for us.

The beauty of tone and great expressions of Stan's singing leave the rest of us singers in his wake. He sang with every fibre of his being, and I can only imagine the sense of joy and power he must have felt to be able to produce that sound. Writing this letter is my way of thanking Stan Rogers for the music that has become so much a part of our lives.

Marie Anderson
Cobourg, Ontario

✉ I have always found that Stan's music brings a lump to my throat and a swelling of my heart.

One thing that has struck me is that Stan is alive every time one of his songs is sung. It's the strength of his personality that shines through, "the strength of his genius." I put that in quotes because it's a phrase the French filmmaker Bruno Mont St. Jean used to describe that quality of greatness that made Glenn Gould so special.

You talked about Stan's gruff, rude, abrupt manner. But in his songs he is a gentleman – a gentle man – in the most noble and forgotten meaning of the word.

Michael Poulton
Victoria Road, Ontario

✉ Listening to your belated post-mortem tribute to Stan Rogers (whose voice was rich) makes me very sad. What's sad is that we celebrate almost anyone who croaks while we ignore those who are still producing.

Mendelson Joe
Toronto

✉ For Christmas 1984, I gave my husband Stan's *From Fresh Water* album – the one that was released shortly after his death. Our first son, Jimmy, was five months old at the time, and when we played the album he sat very still and listened intently. We soon found that if Jimmy was fussy all we had to do was put on the record and at the first chords of "White Squall" he'd quiet down and frequently would fall asleep before the end of the third song.

As Jimmy grew older, he began to dance to the fast songs, particularly "The Nancy" and "The Idiot" (which he calls "Dee-dee-dee" because when my husband sings it he can never remember the words). He had no idea what the words meant, he only knew what they sounded like.

Jimmy is almost four years old now. Every night after he's tucked into bed I sing him two songs, and the one he falls asleep to is "Dee-dee-dee" – "The Idiot."

I've started many letters to you over the years that I've listened to *Morningside*. Some have been completed but not sent. This one will go because it is a possible way of telling Stan's family how much his music means to a little boy who wasn't even born at the time of Stan's death.

Barbara Irvine
Winnipeg

✉ I'm listening to James Kellaghan singing "45 Years From Now" and every hair on my body is standing straight up. Stan's music has done this to me ever since I first heard him on the CBC radio program *Touch the Earth*. I met Stan once, very briefly, after a concert at the University of Calgary and was surprised at how much smaller he seemed standing on the floor than on the stage. Stan's voice and music are so powerful and direct that the very faintest radio or stereo hint of one of Stan's recordings would stop me cold until it's finished.

Time stood still when Stan sang. I think this is Stan's gift to us in this busy world – to hold our attention, make us listen and feel his caring. And to know for those moments that is all that matters.

Marnie McCall
Calgary

AND THEN
THERE WAS THE
TIME . . .

S tan Rogers, who like all folkies enjoyed an evening's gabfest, would have liked this chapter, I think. It's just a collection of letters that have nothing in common except that each of its authors has a story to tell, and found *Morningside* a good place to tell it – a kind of epistolary festival of spinning yarns.

✉ I was born in 1940, the oldest of nine children, eight boys and a girl. In those days, when women had babies, they stayed in the hospital much longer than they do now. My mother would often be away for two weeks at a time when she had a child. Once Mom and Dad hired a housekeeper to stay with us all at home, but we drove the poor woman insane. So the kids were farmed out to various friends and relatives until Mom got back.

I was lucky enough to get sent to Mrs. Riddle. She was a lumpy lady from England who wore polka-dot dresses and sturdy shoes. She was about sixty years old, and her long grey hair kept coming loose from the combs that held it back. She had a tiny moustache and a few funny long hairs that stuck out from the very bottom of her chin. But she had the most beautiful eyes I have ever known.

What are the usual things to say about eyes? That they sparkle or twinkle? Well, Mrs. Riddle's eyes certainly did those things, but they did something far more: they loved. From the first moment she looked at me, I felt warm and trusted, and all wrapped around with kindness.

Mrs. Riddle had no children of her own. She was married to a tall, scholarly Englishman named Edward. Coming from the chaos of a large, noisy family, I was enchanted by life at the Riddles. Everything was orderly, burnished and calm. The Riddles spoke French at the dinner table, and I learned to say "Passez-moi le sel et le poivre, s'il vous plaît," and that the butter was "le beurre."

For a nine-year-old, I was made to feel quite grown-up in other ways. Mr. Riddle always called me "Barringer" in the gruff British public-school manner and, before bedtime, he would play me records of Saint-Saën's "Carnival of the Animals" or "Danse Macabre," giving me a delicious fright with images of skeletons cavorting about in graveyards. I had never heard classical music before. And, while everyone in my family called me Billy, Mrs. Riddle always addressed me as William. I found out that her first name was Virginia.

But the most important thing was that Mrs. Riddle got me interested in bird-watching.

She would get me up at five o'clock in the morning, bundle me up in warm clothes and we would go down to Lawrence Park before the sun came up. There, we would meet a tweedy little group of people – never more than eight or ten – and sneak silently through the woods, sharing binoculars, and spying on the birds as they hunted for their breakfasts. On those mornings I came to see and identify many birds I had never even known existed.

These outings gave me so much pleasure that, even when Mom came back from the hospital, I arranged with my parents for Mrs. Riddle to pick me up in the mornings. It was wonderful to be up before anybody else, going on this adventure with a woman I loved. This went on for about a year.

One morning, Mrs. Riddle announced that our guide that day

was to be Stuart Thompson, one of the most famous ornithologists in Ontario; he was a nephew or great-nephew of Ernest Thompson Seton and I had read all of Seton's books.

I couldn't believe my good luck and I wasn't disappointed. Thompson's skills were far above the level of our little band. He could hear the faintest cry and see the smallest motion in the tree leaves and spot the bird. We went beyond our usual sightings of blue jays and towhees and chickadees—this time, we saw kinglets and vireos and mysterious thrush and downy woodpeckers. In that one morning we saw sixty-six different kinds of birds!

At that time, I had a little printed card called a "life list," which was a list of all the main North American birds, and you checked off every one you had seen. I have since lost that list, but on that morning I made up my mind: I would become an ornithologist, a naturalist as great as Thompson.

The next week, Mrs. Riddle did not come to get me. I waited on the cold sidewalk for an hour and then went back upstairs. I was not allowed to go to the park by myself. Mom said she would phone Mrs. Riddle later in the day.

"Mr. Riddle has died," Mom told me when I came home from school. "Mrs. Riddle won't be able to take you for quite awhile, Billy. She's very, very sad."

This was the first death of my life. I had never known anyone who had died before. I had no idea what to do. I was afraid to see Mrs. Riddle, I was too young. Shortly after that, my family moved.

Five years later I met Mrs. Riddle on Yonge Street. She looked much older, but her eyes were the same, her kindness was the same.

"Do you remember me?" I asked.

"Of course I do," she said. "You're William. Well, you've certainly grown up."

"Do you remember that day we saw sixty-six different kinds of birds?" I said.

Those beautiful eyes. They went suddenly wet.

"I'll never forget that day," she said.

That was the last time I saw Mrs. Riddle; but I see her still whenever I look at a bird.

Bill Barringer
Vancouver

✉ I live in a small village in Ontario. Beside the old general store, where I have my home and studio, is a stream called Grass Creek. When I moved here seventeen years ago, I built a small stone dam across the creek so we could hear the sound of the water from our bedroom window.

Every spring the dam needs repair work, and over the years I have found that by a "just so" placing of the stones I could orchestrate it with burbles and blips, from a deep base to a high treble. The look of the water going over can be moulded, too. It's like sculpting with glass.

I play with it all summer, and when friends come to visit they find it very difficult to resist helping me. Once they have moved a stone or two or helped clean up the river bottom, they are hooked. It's occupational therapy for burnt-out city friends, and a wonderful way to spend a hot afternoon.

I have had the good fortune to have travelled a great deal; and I always bring home a stone or a few pebbles for the river. Of course, once in the river they get mixed up with the indigenous stones, but it's the thought that counts. My friends, intrigued by the idea, bring pebbles, too, and toss them in. Out there, somewhere, there is even an infinitesimal piece of the Himalayas and a fossil shell from the top of the Andes.

A couple of years ago I began adding to the overall effect by arranging a random pattern of standing stones in the mill pond above the little dam. I wanted the stones to appear as if they were floating on the surface. As the water is about four feet deep, this entailed the building up of piles of stones beneath the surface for the top stone to perch on. As a painter, this is artwork as valid or invalid as anything else I do. I'm pleased to say that it is a success, and cars frequently stop on the bridge for a look. Complete strangers take photographs. I think *they* think that it is some sort of natural phenomenon, but I can't be sure.

Last summer I found that my stones were not remaining on their perches. I discovered that three boys were using them for target practice. I talked to them about it, then waded out into the snapping-turtle-infested water to set them up again. The next chance they had the boys knocked them down again. I explained how much work I had done to get them there, and they told me I didn't own the river. I set up some other stones for them to throw at, but these proved to be no fun. I realized I had a war on my hands.

It finally culminated one hot August night when the boys were caught in the act by their parents. Joined by sleepless neighbours, they stood under the street light in the village and talked for an hour. I had no trouble after that.

My stones are still out there, although winter has taken its toll. But then, summer isn't far away. These cold evenings I like to take a cup of tea down to the bridge and watch the two beavers that swim amongst my stones. Where a stone has toppled they will perch themselves to gnaw on a twig, perfectly camouflaged among the silhouettes of the stones that still stand. When one dark silhouette slips into the water and glides across the still surface, it is truly beautiful. It takes one damn builder to understand another.

Michael Poulton
Victoria Road, Ontario

✉ I recently returned from a trip to The Gambia, West Africa. I was there for six weeks as a volunteer, repairing grinding mills in the villages of that tiny, unnoticed country. The work was slow and frustrating. Transportation was hard to get, spare parts were unavailable and the government bureau that I was working with was irritatingly untroubled by the lugubrious pace of our work.

I had a small apartment in a suburb of the capital city, two concrete block rooms where I fretted away many afternoons, perspiring, worrying about my work and listening to the lizards scamper over the corrugated iron roof. From this hot apartment I occasionally burst forth with an excess of useless energy for long aimless walks through the city's haphazard network of sandy rutted roads and paths that seemed to come about by default rather than excavation.

There weren't many whites in that part of town, so I was a novelty where entertainment was scarce. The Mandinka word for white is *Toubob*. Every time I passed a group of children playing in the dust they called out: "*Toubob! Toubob!* Give me twenty-five *Bututs!*" (about four cents). It is a heady but disconcerting thing to be exotic in one's skin colour.

I remember one kid who asked me what my religion was. Agnostic was clearly not an acceptable answer in this devoutly Moslem country. I thought my stock alternate answer, Unitarian, would be inadequate as well. I hemmed and hawed for a bit. "Ah," he said knowingly, "you are a pagan." This struck me as a good answer. I was a pagan–ignorant, untutored, a stranger in a strange land.

This was my first trip to Africa. I like to think that I went with fewer misconceptions than most North Americans, but I still went with plenty of trepidation. What I found was a land disconcertingly devoid of menace. I never saw any poisonous snakes, nor lions nor crocodiles. The mosquitoes may have been carrying malaria, but they were the smallest, most lackadaisical mosquitoes I have ever seen. They had not one-tenth of the gumption of Vermont mosquitoes. It was hot, but at least on the coast there was always a pleasant sea breeze. Parched as the land was in the dry season, it seemed impossible that any hothouse tropical diseases could survive there. Through blind luck, or a cast-iron stomach, I never had any intestinal trouble. The dark continent proved remarkably innocuous.

It was not hardship that made me think so much of home, nor fear. It was only the unmitigated strangeness. My eyes ached for the sight of a wooden house, or a spruce tree, or snow. I wondered what it would be like to be a Peace Corps volunteer, to not see home for two years. And then I thought of the slaves who were taken from Africa, many from The Gambia. They all knew for a certainty that they would die without ever seeing home again.

I was thinking such thoughts one day, on one of my aimless walks, when I stumbled across a small, neatly tended cemetery. The grass was green; it was watered and well tended. The hedges were clipped, and the gate opened on oiled hinges. The little plot was deserted. It was a cemetery for Second World War dead containing perhaps a hundred graves. About half were Africans; the rest were from Britain or the Commonwealth. There were twelve Canadian graves, all belonging to men who had served in the Royal Canadian Air Force.

I returned many times, but I was always the only visitor. I saw only the implied presence of the gardeners who watered and raked and clipped. There was one wreath of faded artificial flowers hanging on a British grave. Tacked to the back of the wreath was a card with a return address in Chester, England, printed in ballpoint pen. All the other graves were bare. I felt admiration for the widow or child who, forty-five years later, was still sending flowers to a grave that she may well never have seen.

I am a baby boomer. I grew up during the Vietnam war. The dead had body bags and jet planes–everybody that was recovered in Vietnam was quickly flown back to the United States. In fact, flag-draped coffins smoothly gliding out of airplane luggage compartments on conveyor belts are one of the familiar images of that war. So it is hard for me to understand the necessity of overseas graves. I was to return home in a few weeks; these soldiers never returned. And yet this little plot is nothing compared to the enormous graveyards of Normandy.

The soldiers had been buried outside the city of Bathurst in one of the two British colonies in West Africa. In 1965, The Gambia gained independence. In 1976, that most English-sounding of names, Bathurst, was changed to Banjul. The city spread, and now the cemetery is in a suburb, halfway between the American embassy and the open market of Sera Kunda. It is a pretty spot.

I went there quite often to read or write letters, or just to sit on the grass. Perhaps it was easier for me to reflect on this wonderous, boggling African world I was in when sitting among the graves of fellow North Americans. The cemetery was very peaceful; it was quite lovely, really. Only it did seem so sad that these Canadian graves were never to be touched by snow.

Could it be a tiny consolation to the relatives of those soldiers that although their graves are not in Canada to console them, they did at least console a lonely traveller in another continent?

Here is a list of the twelve Canadians buried in the Fajara War cemetery:

J.R. Rozon. Age 29. Wireless/Air Gunner
J.F. Lawless. Age 32. Air Observer
S.J. McCammon. Age 28. Navigator
C.C. Blamey. Wireless Operator/Air Gunner
J. Shulman. Wireless Operator/Air Gunner
K.M. Miller. Pilot
T.B.T. Moor. Age 29. Wireless Operator/Air Gunner
C.S.G. Crombie. Age 23. Wireless Operator/Air Gunner
B.R. Yorke. Age 26. Warrant Officer
S.F. Santy. Age 26. Pilot.

Jonathan Herz
Plainfield, Vermont

✉ My father was a devout Presbyterian cleric. From him I inherited a deep love for the haggis. We often argued over fine points in theology, but a savoury haggis healed all the wounds.

After the Selkirk grace and a brief address to the haggis, my father, with a flourish of his carving knife, would cut the cross of St. Andrew on the quivering paunch, turn back the flaps and scoop out the steaming delicacy.

"A good man loves his haggis," my father said. "And nowhere can you get better ballast for the storms of life. The haggis is honoured in castle, farm and croft. It bonds the heart, soul and intestines. But treat it wisely, eat it with your eyes closed. Shut out all distraction!"

Haggis comes in all sizes. Some haggis are as big as a soccer ball. For the novice it is best to choose one of modest circumference. A haggis is concocted from humble ingredients: heart, lights, liver, beef suet, onions, black pepper, stock and pin-head oatmeal. Everything is fried lightly, then stuffed into the stomach bag or paunch of a sheep. The haggis must be brought slowly to the boil and allowed to simmer until the whole mass is piping hot. Occasionally one may have to prick it with a needle to control the swelling. It should be served with mashed potatoes and turnips.

In later years when I was far from home I always received a parcel for my birthday. Inside was a mealy pudding, shortbread and a haggis. Sometimes my father would also enclose a few words from one of his latest sermons.

One year when I was in exile in snow-bound Saskatchewan, I received my usual parcel from home. At the time I was courting a charming lass from Glasgow, and I chose the occasion to invite her to my one-room basement apartment for supper.

It was to be a kind of candle-light and wine ceremony. But since I was a rather timid soul, and my father a founding member of the Temperance Union, I decided to serve a small glass of ginger beer instead of the wine. For background music I had "Roaming in the Gloaming" with Harry Lauder doing the honours on my new Victrola.

So that we both might anticipate the meal to the full, I slipped the haggis into my glass coffee percolator where we could watch its progress to a swelling fruition.

My friend (I will call her Jeannie, although that was not her real name) was entranced with my digs – the painting of Robbie Burns on the wall, the tea cosy, my bold tartan bedspread. I, in turn, was equally enthralled with the lovely silver locket Jeannie wore suspended above her bosom. Inside the locket was a picture of her great-grandmother, born near Stornoway on the Outer Hebrides.

Life is full of odd twists and turns we never foresee. There is always the unexpected. The best laid schemes of mice and men gang aft a-gley. And so it was that when an ominous trill drowned out Harry Lauder, I was shocked to discover my haggis swelling and bulging from the neck of the percolator.

For a moment I was overwhelmed with disbelief. Then I began a frantic search for a needle to bring down the swelling. But Jeannie, full of resourcefulness, bounced from the sofa with a bobby pin she had at the ready, and with one valiant stab into its quivering paunch the haggis slowly subsided to the bottom of the percolator.

Jeannie and I met several times after this calamity. But things were not quite the same. Obviously the haggis had come between us, and I felt strangely deflated in her presence, something of a bungler. But despite the blow to my self-esteem, I never lost my love for the haggis and consoled myself with selected passages from my father's sermons sent along with his parcel: "Keep to the straight and narrow. Count your blessings. Remember the lost sheep who had gone astray."

Sam Roddan
Vancouver

✉ I love Sundays. I especially love Sundays in winter. There is an intimacy, a distinctive rhythm to winter Sundays. It's possible that the same rituals take place at the same time in summer, but the closed windows and trapped sensations bring things into sharper focus in winter.

Essential to my feelings of peace and well-being on winter Sundays are my two neighbours. In my apartment building are four apartments above a store, two up and two down. I'm up. Below me live two women who, because I do not want to hurt or embarrass them, I'll just call Mrs. Mac and Mrs. R. They are eighty-four and eighty-two respectively. The tenants in my apartment before me used to refer to them as Mrs. Downstairs and Mrs. Downstairs Sideways.

I have to believe that the architect or builder who constructed this place, around 1918, must have been European – French possibly – because all four apartments open onto two wells, which drop from the skylighted roof to the lower apartment floors. These wells, and the large interior windows that open onto them, ensure that you are never really alone at any given time.

As I write I can hear Mrs. Mac's robust rendition of "All of me, why not take all of me" wafting up the well.

These two women have lived across the hall from each other for about twenty years. They are both childless, CNR widows. In the six or so years I've been here, I have never known either one of them to step more than one or two feet inside the other's apartment.

For their age, they are in relatively good health, although Mrs. R. has lung and circulation problems and Mrs. Mac has bad arthritis in her knees, hips and back. Mrs. R. is the one who braves the forty steps – twenty up, twenty down – each morning to collect the mail. And Mrs. Mac is the one who has a code she uses for knocking on Mrs. R.'s door so she will know who it is and not be nervous.

As well as these two have managed to get along over the years, given their backgrounds, small-town conventions and the normal course of events, they probably would never have met, let alone become friends, if they had not by circumstance ended up living across from each other.

Mrs. Mac is of Irish Catholic descent and Mrs. R. is of English Protestant heritage. Temperamentally they are also opposite.

Plagued by various health problems from her early twenties, Mrs. R. is actually the more cheerful of the two. Long ago she learned to listen to her doctors and curb her life to fit her health. From a family of ten children – most of whom are now in their nineties and still living in Stratford, their home town – Mrs. R. spends a great deal of time on the telephone consoling and encouraging various members of this clan. She lives by a rigid schedule of household chores, meal preparation, exercise (she loves to walk), televised hockey games in winter, and, in summer, baseball games.

Mrs. Mac has not adjusted as easily to being alone as Mrs. R. has, so she travels. Every month or so, she gets the bug and off she trots, suitcase and CNR pass in hand, to visit relatives from Thunder Bay to Flint, Michigan. She likes a party, does Mrs. Mac, and she likes company. When she's home and feeling a little blue, I hear the secret coded knock on Mrs. R.'s door, and I know comfort is at hand.

On Sundays, I hear them up at 7:30 A.M. Mrs. R. tunes into the local radio station's big-band sound, while Mrs. Mac keeps in touch with her home town, Toronto, by listening to a Toronto station, while she faithfully does the painful exercises that keep her mobile.

If the snow is not too bad and the snow-removal people have done their job by 10:45, Mrs. Mac, dressed and made-up to the nines, can be seen, cane in hand, striding across the bridge on her way to mass at St. Joseph's, while downstairs Mrs. R. tunes in to the United Church broadcast. The best part of Sunday morning is listening to Mrs. R. sing along with the hymns. Sometimes there is a little teary-eyed snuffle to accompany the singing. I don't think they are unhappy tears, just nostalgic and comforting.

When Mrs. Mac comes home from church, there is the secret knock, then a good twenty minutes of the best kind of gossip exchanged in the hallway. Then it's time for their noon meals and the most delicious smells wafting from Mrs. Mac's kitchen. She loves cooking.

Mrs. Mac always has a nap in the afternoon and Mrs. R. reads. Actually, Mrs. Mac lies down to read but most often it turns into a nap. They regularly exchange romance novels.

About five they each have their supper, and at nine Mrs. R. makes her cup of tea while Mrs. Mac can be heard hammering away at the ice cubes she breaks up to pack against her aching knees.

This past Sunday, a new element was introduced to the lives of the people of Stratford and other small communities across the province. The two large grocery chains opened their doors. I went, I admit it. I was curious. And we were out of milk. But I didn't like it.

It occurred to me that this resistance to change, this wish to keep everything snug and warm and comfortable, is actually a sign of aging. I worry about the aging, and I worry about the worry of aging.

Then I take a good look at Mrs. Mac and Mrs. R. and I wonder, if this is aging, what am I worrying about?

Lynda Weston
Stratford, Ontario

✉ When I was a little girl, I used to "play the piano" most magnificently on the lacy table-cloth that covered our Arborite dining-room table. In my mind I was a concert pianist. To my mother, I was a child elaborately stalling over my supper. My mother, however, finally relented, thinking that perhaps there could be some talent in this child. She bought a beautiful 1904 Weber player piano for six hundred dollars and placed it in the basement. The choice of the player piano was probably wise in the long run. However, it was the demise of this concert pianist.

I remember my first few lessons and the shock of not being able to play as I had imagined that I could on the lacy table-cloth on the dining-room table. As I had no special talent, it was indeed work.

To protect her investment, my mother persevered. At her insistence, I descended each afternoon to the red and white linoleum "music room," as our basement was re-christened after the piano's arrival. There, for my half-hour practice, I did my best to think of a way in which I could gracefully get out of my ill-chosen career.

My chance came when my parents departed for a two-week vacation to Hawaii, and my six fellow siblings and I were left in the care of a housekeeper. The dear lady was faithful to my mother's instructions and insisted on the daily afternoon ritual.

But to this lady, I was a true prodigy. For two weeks, I practised for hours playing the many classical rolls of our player piano. There was Bach, Mozart and Berlioz. She was enchanted. So encouraging. So innocent of what I was really doing down there in that linoleum cellar.

Of course, the sour note was struck upon my mother's return. The housekeeper's glowing reports of my exquisite playing, combined with my complete inability to remember anything I had actually learned, ultimately meant the termination of my concert career. I was disgraced, but relieved.

A final note. Perhaps as a punishment, reminder or in faint hope of success in my later life, my mother gave me the old player piano last year–twenty years after my career ended. It now sits–where else?–in my basement. I plunk away at it, straining to now remember what I had learned; but most of all, I sit with my young son and play the many old rolls that fed my imagination when I was ten.

Kathy Butler
Kelowna, British Columbia

✉ I was born and raised in Australia, and my father never owned a car in his life. As I think of it now, this is strange, because he was a circuit magistrate in the country towns of New South Wales. He always travelled around by bus or train. Every couple of years our family, which grew to five children, moved on to another town. I remember travelling by taxi at night on one of these moves. Each one of us took turns being carsick, and Dad would walk along the road with the ailing kid, both of them lit by the taxi's headlights. He must have walked most of the three hundred miles between those towns!

By the time I was in college, we were settled in Sydney, and I decided that I needed a car. I know this will be hard to believe, but since I had rarely been in one, I'm staggered now when I recall my utter ignorance of their workings. I took a book out of the local library, *Learning to Drive*, and got myself ready for my first lesson. For weeks I drove my bed around the city–sitting on the edge and using three upturned shoes for the accelerator, clutch and brake

254

pedals, a broomstick for the gearshift, and my father's hat for the steering-wheel. When I felt I was driving pretty well (no accidents, anyway), I made arrangements for my official lesson.

Now, the book I'd studied must have been an old one even then, for it used illustrations of a snub-nosed Morris 8's instrument panel and interior – a little English car that was no longer being imported into Australia. (I don't know what the "8" stood for, but it sure wasn't for eight cylinders.) So I had to telephone dozens of driving schools until I found one with an instructor whose wife happened to own a Morris 8. He wasn't too keen on teaching me on it since it didn't have dual controls, of course, but I insisted. I wasn't about to waste those many hours of weaving my bed through peak-hour traffic.

When he turned up to collect me, I said, "Could I take over right from the start?" I then drove that little car all over the city, pressing on the shoes, moving the broomstick and turning the hat. The instructor thought I'd driven for years and was just taking a refresher course. I got my licence after two lessons.

I bought a car the following week – a Morris 8, of course, what else! It was the only car I knew the faintest thing about!

I'd love to be able to say I'm driving some kind of Morris still, but I'm not. My car talks to me coldly if I forget to belt up, and its metal gear-lever lacks the warmth of a broom handle.

Paul Zann
Truro, Nova Scotia

✉ One glorious summer, for reasons I can't remember, I was deposited with two brothers, a sister, a weekend father and a full-time mother, by a lake so large we couldn't see to the other side.

"Is this the ocean?" the youngest asked when we arrived. The rest of us, tugging off shoes and socks, didn't stop to answer; we were in a race to enter the lake. Within seconds, we were stumbling over the stony beach, hesitating briefly at the water's edge, then squealing with joy and fright as we plunged into the foaming water . . . up to our ankles. The bravest went up to his knees. We stumbled back almost as rapidly, repelled by high waves, cold water and decomposing fish. After scores of similar forays in and out of Lake Ontario, we soon grew strong and brown.

And we discovered, to our delight, that with a flick of the wrist, we could "skip" the flat stones we had been tripping on; for hours we practised the art of skipping stones over the crests of incoming waves. Whose stone would dance the longest before sinking without a sound? Small circles formed where stone kissed water; we watched these circles spread wider and wider, linking up with one another, as they began their long journey across the lake.

"Will the circles reach the other side?" the youngest asked. And all night, the waves answered, "Yes, yes."

The artist among us noticed a coloured stone among the mass of grey rocks, spit on it and pronounced it red. Then we all were spitting and dipping stones in water to bring out their true colours. We put the prettiest in our pockets. For days, we stooped and squatted at the water's edge, picking and rejecting stones, like women selecting the best fruit at market. We developed a critical eye for the shape, colour and texture of stone – and a decided slouch from walking the ragged beach, heads bent to the ground.

Our pockets sagged with rocks that rattled and grated with each step we took. Scores of stones rolled indoors with us in long, slow waves, scattering themselves through the rooms of our small cottage. Oh, we gathered the occasional shell, or feather or piece of water-softened glass, but it was stone treasure we were after.

Sacred stone heaps formed on bedside tables. Stone birds and animals sat in silence on window sills. In the kitchen, red, white and yellow pebbles glowed like jewels in glasses of water. The wealth of the ocean was moving in . . . and summer had scarcely begun.

Perhaps it was this creeping invasion of stone that prompted my mother to her inspired act, for one fine morning she presented us with four small hammers. We did the obvious thing with our gift: we hammered the nearest objects at hand – rocks.

With a crack, we broke open our first stone, and gazed in wonder on an ancient world of fragile ferns and crystal "pools," whorls of shells and spines of small animals. Winding "rivers" of silver and gold cascaded down jagged mountain ranges. "We need a magnifying glass," the middle sister said and ran to get it.

Someone cracked open another rock, crying, "Look!" and we gazed at a world of small islands set in a vast black sea. Soon four small bodies hunched over four stone slabs, taking a crack at every available rock. Some hard stones, like nuts, refused to be cracked; we set them aside for the strong arm of our father and continued in our relentless search for the beautiful, the unusual . . . the stone beyond compare.

With all this potential treasure underfoot, we could leave no stone uncracked and neither could any child who came within sound of our tapping. "Let me borrow your hammer – just for a minute," pleaded cousins. "Can I take home a few stones?" asked friends, their pockets already bulging with tell-tale booty. We said yes to all requests, for we knew if we sat and chopped forever, we would not run out of treasure.

The problem soon became: what to do with our growing heaps of chopped stone. Happily, the solution was close at hand: pop-bottle caps half-buried in the sand were just the right size to hold stone chips and crushed powders. We set out our wares on wooden planks, and the trading and bartering began. Stone chips of a single colour were worth twice the common, mottled type, and pure powders went to the highest bidder.

To the adults, it must have seemed as though the narrow strip of beach between the back door of our cottage and the high-water line had become a stone quarry. For us, it had the unmistakable aura of an archaeological site. And we, surrounded by shards of broken and discarded stone, were workers in an ancient tradition.

Day after day, we sat and chopped under the hot summer sun; the tap, tap of our hammers mingling with the slap, slap of the waves. We were in harmony with the universe. Waves spoke to us, sun blessed us and stones revealed their secrets.

No one ever told us the names of the stones we chopped and we never asked. What could granite, quartz and limestone mean to us who had discovered something far greater? We had seen gold and silver. We had uncovered pearls and jade. That summer, coral and amber were washed up daily by the waves.

Nancy Prasad
Toronto

THE HOME
FRONT

One of the most common misconceptions about *Morningside* – and though it's fading now it drives me as crazy to hear it as telling a woman who runs her family's life that she is "just a housewife" drives her – is that we are a program for and about "women at home."

For one thing, we're not. In a world of shift work, long retirement, travelling salespeople, Walkmen on tractors (and on "kangaroos," as I learned to my pleasure when we visited Kelowna in 1989 and found that's what apple farmers call the machines they ride – and listen to radio on) . . . of students skipping lectures, people listening in offices, artists and craftspeople keeping themselves company while they create, lawyers on their way to court, truck drivers, cabbies, trappers, sailors and, sadly but realistically, one out of ten Canadians of working age with unwanted time on their hands, *Morningside* – or any other serious radio program – would be quickly off the air if it set its sights on only that part of the audience. (Why the phone company, among other service industries that think every home of the 1980s contains a little homemaker in her gingham dress, waiting around till it's convenient for the installer to call, isn't out of business is . . . well, that's another story.)

For another thing, though, what if we were? Many of the smartest and best-informed people I've met are "women at home," and if *Morningside* were designed solely for their use, I don't know if it would be any different than it is now. A lot of mothers of two-year-olds, I know from my travels as well as my mail, are grateful to us precisely *because* we assume their interests are wider than figuring out what kind of detergent gets the cleanest dishes or what kind of diaper stays most dry.

That said, the *issues* that staying at home engenders are real ones, and, when they raise them, as we do, we receive some of our most eloquent mail. To wit:

✉ I was just getting over my latest identity crisis when it happened. It was five o'clock in the afternoon, the "arsenic hour," when low blood sugar and "all that togetherness" have the kids and me feeling blah.

My two-year-old wanted to nurse so I plunked down in the rocker and stared absent-mindedly at the tube. Jack Webster, that blustering teddy-bear mascot of British Columbia, had just started interviewing the first guests on his daily talk show. They were two members of the U.N. High Commission for Refugees, but of more consequence to me was that one of them was a former schoolmate. Susan had been two years ahead of me in a school in a small town in Saskatchewan. She was the same age as my sister Donna; her younger sister and I were classmates; and our youngest sisters were in the same grade.

There she was facing off with Webster (who knows, the Prime Minister may have sat in the same chair at one time) while there I was, still in my pyjamas and housecoat in the late afternoon – a bird in a littered cage. I felt as if Susan had suddenly marched unannounced into my living room and caught me unprepared. In fact, she had.

Her looks hadn't changed in twenty-one years (is there no justice?) but now there was a softness to her that wasn't evident in her younger days. Her family had moved from the "big city" of Regina. It wasn't until I was in my twenties that I heard a term (bitch goddess) that adequately described girls from big cities who moved to small towns.

In fairness to her, it must have been a let-down having to live in a place with two grocery stores, two general stores, one pool hall and a bank after having Simpsons, Kresge's, and Woolworth's at her disposal. That, as well as the usual teenage turmoil and the fact that her barber father had wanted sons and would occasionally give his three daughters boys' haircuts, would affect any kid's disposition.

Instead of feeling pleased that she'd obviously grown as a human being, I was even more disturbed at the thought that she was involved in a humanitarian cause. Any full-time mother can handle a young female economist discussing the latest dips of the Canadian dollar, but helping homeless refugees is a different matter entirely. Not only was Susan in the "big time"–being interviewed by Webster (probably dining out in some chic restaurant, then catching a play and, later, retiring to the Pan Pacific for the night) –but she was furthering the cause of humankind at the same time!

After spending almost thirteen years staying home to feed and water and nurture three children, I feel that I have also furthered the cause of humankind; unfortunately, the monetary benefits and society's recognition of my efforts aren't nearly as great. There are no pension plans, no medical benefits and no annual "Full-time Mother of the Year" awards nights. At one time, that didn't matter to me; we were a young, struggling family like all the other young, struggling families we knew, and I felt a noble sense of purpose in choosing, like most of my friends, to stay home with my children. Now, however, most of my friends' children are in school, and their mothers are either working or back in school themselves.

Deciding to have another child has effectively put me back at square one as far as having some measure of control in my life. My daughter has added a new and important dimension to my life, and I love her dearly. I know I wouldn't be happy leaving her in the care of others. Still, I am not at peace. There is a voice inside me that says, "You have done this already. What else can you do? You should be contributing financially to this family. You could help pay for the extras that mean the difference between savouring life and merely surviving it."

Over the years I have acquired skills that I am yet unable to use. I know how to plan a wardrobe that is well co-ordinated and put on make-up, but I have neither the money nor the reason to do so. I can construct some pretty fancy desserts and have a well-thought-out plan to remodel my boring bi-level house, and I have a design for a doll that I really should do something about. I have also acquired some skills in human relations after starting and organizing two local self-help groups.

Is all this just talk? Can I convince others that I am capable of more than wiping finger-marks off walls? Can I convince myself? When I do decide to break out of the cocoon, will I really turn into a butterfly? A few times I've mentioned to people that I feel that I'm not even qualified to work at McDonald's any more. They invariably point out that I'm too old to work at McDonald's anyway.

Getting back to Susan. I thought of phoning in to say, "Hey, remember me?" However, not only did it seem inappropriate to discuss personal matters on the program; I also knew that the minute I got on the phone, my two-year-old would come screaming down the hall looking for me, and my nine- and twelve-year-olds would suddenly become Iraq and Iran.

When they heard the clamour in the background, Webster and Susan and the entire viewing audience would look at each other knowingly. "Ah, yes, a full-time mother, probably still in her pyjamas, her noisy brood going wild in an unkempt house."

As she tucks herself in to bed at the Pan Pacific or the Royal York or the Waldorf Astoria, Susan will still occasionally think of me and wonder where I am and what I'm doing now. She will probably never know.

Nadine Erickson
Salmon Arm, British Columbia

✉ I think it is time I come out of the broom closet and tell all. You see, I am a housewife.

That's not the same as a homemaker, for I am terrible at making flower arrangements, and the only redecorating ideas I have I get out of a wallpaper book. It's not the same as a stay-at-home mother, either, because all my kids are in school. The only time I'm called a stay-at-home mom is when the kids don't seem to appreciate that I pick up after them and I threaten that I'm going to go out to work. Then they all yell, "Please, stay at home, Mom!"

No, I am just a plain old ordinary housewife. The dictionary tells me that that means I manage a household. Yes, I manage to vacuum, dust, scrub and polish the house and all it holds. I manage to wash the clothes, hang them out to dry and put them all away again, with some ironing and mending thrown in once in a while. I manage to buy the groceries and the clothes, which is quite a feat when you consider the amount of money I have at my disposal to feed and clothe a family of six.

But managing a household is much more than managing a house and the things in it. As any true housewife will tell you, it also means managing the kitchen garden. That means digging, planting, weeding and picking outside, which translates into canning, freezing, pickling and jamming inside. It also means managing the compost box and cleaning out the manure from under the rabbit cages, as well as starting the gardening process inside under lights in the early spring.

Yes, I'm one of those relics from the past – a true housewife. I look after the freezer and the cold cellar, the mending and the baking. I make sauerkraut out of cabbages and pillowcases from old sheets. I get bread from flour and meat from rabbits. I use compost to feed the garden and a big pot of soup to feed the family. My dishes are made out of china and are recycled by washing them in the sink. My clothes-line is almost worn out after years of use, but my ten-year-old dryer is as good as new.

All old-fashioned things like me should go the way of the Model T Ford. Yet somehow, I haven't found a cheaper way of keeping house. The vegetables and fruit that I grow and the food that I make are all more expensive in the store. The wind and the sun that dry the clothes are free. I only had to buy my diapers once, and even saved on garbage bags. Fertilizers for the garden are as cheap as grass clippings and fallen leaves. Even the old furniture pieces that I pick up at garage sales or auction sales, and then refinish, are cheaper than anything I can buy in the store.

Besides, no one has yet found a way of bottling the smell of freshly baked bread, clothes off the line or a pot of soup simmering on the stove. No one has yet been able to give plasticized furniture the deep, warm glow of polished wood. No one has yet been able to grow and transport for thousands of miles a tomato that tastes as good as the ones I grow in my back yard. No one has yet been able to make a meal more delectable than a rabbit meat pie served with gooseberry sauce and a fresh tossed salad, topped off with peach cobbler, all made from home-grown ingredients.

Why should I give up a job that offers such a variety of interesting and challenging work? No two days are exactly the same, and each season offers its own variety of activities. The rain beckons me to spend a day curled up in my favourite chair with a book, while a sunny day takes me outside to work in the garden. I am free to pace my days, spend my time and arrange my duties as I like. What other job offers such a benevolent taskmaster and such delicious rewards? Then again, when someone is needed to care for a sick child, volunteer at the school or help out an elderly parent, I'm there.

Being a housewife fulfils a deep need in me, because I feel that what I am doing is best for everything that I hold dear. It's best for my husband that he comes home to a clean, pleasant home, where he can relax from the strains of the workaday world. It's best for my children to come home to a mother who is glad to see them and greets them with a kiss and freshly baked whole-wheat bread spread with home-made jam. It's best for the environment, for the air and the water, that I don't contribute to the pollution by wasteful and consumptive household practices.

I'm aware, of course, that I am not very popular with anyone outside my immediate family. Restaurants hate me because any meal that they can serve, I can make better. The fashion industry hates me because all I need for my job is a pair of old jeans. The drug industry hates me because my kids are hardly ever sick. The auto industry and gas stations hate me because I don't need transportation to get to work. The large food companies and chain stores hate me because I buy only the basic ingredients of food, which are much cheaper than their processed products.

I guess it's no wonder that I'm one of a dying breed. Soon housewives, the old-time and true variety, will be extinct, just like the dodo bird.

Femmie VanderBoom
Burlington, Ontario

✉ I am a single mother. I have been a single mother from the day my son (now six years old) was conceived. He owes his presence in this world to a doctor who incorrectly inserted an interuterine device into my body after trying, for two years, to convince me to stop using The Pill on the grounds that it would lead to heart problems. Well, I don't have any heart problems.

I was thirty years old when the doctor told me I was pregnant. I had wanted a child since I was sixteen, but I had never married and unmarried women just don't have children. I did.

I wanted to spend as much time as I could with my child after he was born, so I worked right up to the moment I went into labour and then we had four and a half wonderful months together. Then I went back to work, not because I loved my job, or because I had embarked on a career that was important to me. I went back to work to support myself and my child. Responsible middle-class women do not go on welfare. Well, eventually I did.

When my son was three years old I looked at him and realized that I knew very little about him. I didn't know what he liked or disliked; how to play with him or how to talk to him. How could I? I dropped him off at day care at 7:15 A.M. and picked him up at 6:00 P.M. We went home, I cooked him dinner, he ate it and then went to bed. On the weekends we shopped (it takes most of the day since we do not have a car), cleaned and napped. Then it was Monday morning and at 5:30 A.M. we started all over again. I hated it. I had guilt that would amaze a Jewish mother and I just about went round the twist. One day in a last-minute rush at work, with one eye on the clock (I lived in terror of being late for work and late in picking Matthew up from the day care) I lost my cool, slammed the photocopier lid down and broke the machine. Then I broke into tears. The next day my supervisor suggested that I leave the company. Finally, someone had given me permission to give up and I took it.

I stopped working for a year. I admit it, I used the system. I managed as long as I could on unemployment assistance and then, when they finally caught on to the idea that I really wasn't looking for a full-time job and cut me off, I went onto the dreaded welfare.

I'm grateful that I had the courage to put my son ahead of my pride. Being on welfare is not fun. The money barely covers the rent and the utilities. If you insist on eating fresh fruit and vegetables, you eat well but not a lot. New clothing is a dream, and a meal out or a movie are so beyond the realms of possibility that you learn to keep such fantasies packed away. For a year my world consisted of my home, my son and his school. Transportation was too expensive to contemplate very often so we rarely went anywhere.

By the time the year was up I was totally depressed and very lazy. I would spend the time when my son was in school reading or day-dreaming. Many of the things I had dreamed I would do with my son if only I could stay home were beyond my reach since I didn't have any extra money. Even simple crafts require money for glue, tape and paper. But in spite of all this I did alleviate the initial problem – I got to know my son better, and we are a much better team now than we were three years ago. We developed a bond during that period that will never be broken and I finally began to feel that I was the mother of this child, not some night-time baby-sitter who left the actual work of raising and caring for the boy to someone else.

I returned to the work-force one year and two months after I left it because I hate being poor. But I gained more from that time out than I had planned. I gained a new respect for the women who insist on the right to raise their children themselves – even if it means suffering from a daily battle for survival in the system to do so.

Kate Pemberton
Toronto

✉ One of my sisters has begun to call me Yvonne Junior, and wonders if I am clicking around the kitchen with high heels on and my gold bracelets clinking.

Yvonne was born in 1913. One of ten, she then had six children of her own. We are all over thirty by now, but she continues to nurture us through our life crises and bad colds. She keeps a black journal of all the people she has entertained and what she has served them to eat!

In my revolting teenage years this log really irked me. It was the epitome of superficiality. My mother was an airhead who never did anything of importance or interest. Tiny shortcomings on my father's part were her fault. She was not athletic, nor was she a scholar. As far as I was concerned there was no talent, no merit. She spent far too much time in prayer, and I certainly had no intention of resembling her on any level.

Against all urgings to become a secretary or bank clerk I chose university and ultimately agriculture. Although embarrassed by my choice and uncertain that this was the route to independence, my parents did support me financially and finally emotionally as I obtained my M.Sc. During summers I farmed, worked with bees and surveyed Quebec barley fields. I was unlike anyone in my family.

Last week, at nine o'clock on Monday morning, I was frying onions and peeling apples – in short I was thinking food and menus. My two-year-old was "helping" me coax the rather crumbly pastry off the somewhat sticky counter when I had a flash of watching my mother do the very same thing. I saw myself as a young child, standing on the very same stool my daughter was now on, watching her fold and transfer the pastry for my favourite dessert, cherry pie. The memory brought back a warm rush of happy, uncomplicated times alone with my mother.

Yes, I have become my mother, and I can see my daughter as I once was. She is under the ironing board, or sitting at my feet in the kitchen. I hum and sing; she follows me around. The more my children grow, the more I remember of my childhood and the warm secure feeling of knowing that Mom would be home when I got there. There would be warm vanilla pudding, hot chocolate-chip cookies and a pile of damp clothes to be ironed.

I don't wear heels or blue eye shadow, and I'm certainly not five feet three inches. I never say novenas, but then I don't need to as Yvonne is always ready to pray on my behalf.

I am beginning to look more and more like my older siblings, and they in turn are looking more and more alike. It will happen, and I'm no longer fighting it. In fact I am much calmer these days. I wonder if I could find myself a black journal?

Julia Casey Common
Lennoxville, Quebec

✉ After eighteen years of being at home in the traditional domestic roles of wife and mother, I'm now at the point so many women are: I feel redundant in the only job I've had since I stopped teaching to have a family. I'm alone at home most of the time.

With so many women all around me going back to work, to fill the void in their lives, I have of course thought of doing likewise. But always I've been stopped by what I see happening to friends' lives once they take on full-time jobs outside the home. They seem never to stop "running," except when they collapse. They "run" from work, to grocery store, to home, and after a thrown-together or name-brand meal, they go to their choir practice or Japanese lessons or school meetings. Week after week they sprint from job to recreation to home, until a weekend comes when they simply shut down, too weary even for conversation. They look perpetually drained, haggard and stressed. They have little time for visits and no time for heart-to-hearts.

Maybe they no longer need friendships in their lives. Maybe when a person is that busy, friendship is just an extra demand on the scarce free time in life.

During this week, I've had a taste of my friends' working lives, and I learned once and for all – I don't want to live like that!

I've just spent four days at an Ontario Municipal Board hearing, supporting the Kitchener-Waterloo Field Naturalists in their confrontation with the Region of Waterloo over a road widening that would mean cutting down or degrading more than four hundred mature trees. It's all over now and this morning I was once again "free." In the past four days, I've learned what it is to rush home for lunch so that I could let the dog out; to go for a "power-walk" with the dog in the same lunch hour – it had to be a power-walk because there wasn't time for all the stopping and sniffings that dogs love to do.

I've learned what it is to stop and buy the evening meal's groceries on the way home from work; to resent the time that shopping takes; to be outraged at line-ups; to arrive home two hours after my kids are home from school and find them overwhelmed by chores – a dog that desperately needs exercise and attention, homework, piano practice and often dinner preparation (that is, if I'd managed to have something organized ahead, with instructions left for them). I also learned what it felt like to be too tired to care what my kids were saying to me, and to resent their intrusion on my mind and consciousness because I was simply too full of my own thoughts. Somehow their prattle about their day didn't seem important compared to the weighty issues I'd been considering.

I learned what it was to have my husband get home after I'd fallen asleep from sheer exhaustion, and to miss him in the morning because he'd left for work before I got up. (He also was working on the Field Naturalists' case, and was preparing evidence for the hearing.)

Most of all, however, I learned about guilt, and feeling inadequate. All the things I've described to you are completely foreign to the life this family has led so far.

Some people might say I'm lucky, and I'd agree whole-heartedly. I'm lucky that I have a choice – I don't *have* to work. But has it really become a luxury, a privilege, to have time for friends and family and pets? Time became a luxury for me this past week.

I understand now why my working friends neglect me, why friendship is so low on their list of priorities: they simply don't have time. But it's still hard for me to understand how a job – any job and the money that goes with it – can be a substitute for friends, for family time, for leisurely walks in autumn leaves with a bounding dog, for sharing your children's and your husband's lives.

So many women who don't have financial hardship, who don't have to work, are choosing the life-style that I experienced this week. It baffles me. And I'm afraid this forced neglect of family and friends will have a long-term destructive effect on the very fabric of society. Even as I write this to you, I'd like nothing better than to be wrong about it.

Samm MacKay
Waterloo, Ontario

✉ My ears pricked up when I heard the letter from Samm MacKay from Waterloo with her thoughts and reservations about returning to the work-force after eighteen years out of it.

Samm MacKay and I are a very rare breed. Just as we graduated from college, a change was underway although I for one didn't realize it at the time. Most women were deciding to stay in the work-force and attend to their careers, rather than have children and stay home with them, as we did. As a result, our contemporaries now tend to have small children and are either still working or have recently left the work-force to raise children. Although I'm told they exist, I almost never meet women in their early forties who have teenage children and are contemplating going back to work.

So I was interested in the experience of someone else who had tried it and I listened closely to see if Samm's experience matched mine.

She is right when she says people have no time for friendships any more. My contemporaries are too busy with their small children and/or their jobs to contemplate returning my invitations to coffee, dinner parties or get-togethers.

A job with work to do and people to talk to begins to look good to me. But I worry. What about the loss of freedom and the loss of time? The exhaustion that might make me too tired for anything but the job? Will my family suffer? Will I?

Very tentatively I drop my résumé here and there. And to my surprise, I'm given a try-out for two weeks in a job I'd like to do. I almost say I'm sick–I am sick! It's like flirting with a married man and suddenly having him interested in me! I'm chicken! But I go. Surely, I think, I can last two weeks.

The world of work holds many surprises. I am surprised at how out of it I am. I haven't been exactly hibernating at home: I read two newspapers, a newsmagazine and about seventy books a year besides running a small calligraphy business and raising three teenagers. But I still realize I've approached the world as something done to me rather than something I do. As well, rightly or wrongly, I perceive it's not cool to have "older" children, nor to be, as I am, married to the same man for twenty years. In the world "out there" if you do these things, you don't admit to it.

I'm surprised at how low my self-esteem has fallen from being at home.

I'm surprised at how many new degrees and diplomas there are to get and how important it is to get them. Where before a degree in philosophy or English might have marked you as being educated and therefore useable, now a diploma that certifies a very particular knowledge and training is a prerequisite for employment.

Finally I'm surprised at how terrific it is. I had expected to be tired at the end of a day of outside employment. I had arranged things so that I had to do virtually nothing but work – eating out of the freezer, not going to night classes. But to my great surprise, I'm not tired at the end of a day, I'm energized! It's all so clarifying. You go out of the house and you work and you actually see something accomplished and then you come home and do something completely different and the change is as good as a rest! I feel like I woke up after being asleep or broke the surface after swimming underwater. I'm exhilarated! All my cylinders are firing; my brain is in gear. I talk to my children and my husband with zest; I'm less tired; I accomplish twice as much as in a normal day at home. I have people to talk to; I feel useful, used. I do not "rust unburnished," I "shine in use." The kids pitch in and help at home; they even cook – they surprise themselves as much as me. I'm even going to be paid for all this!

The two weeks were just a taste of what I need. The world has changed. There's no one left at home – friends are working and when the children aren't at school, they look after themselves. Cooking supper can't be the be-all and end-all of my days. I don't want walks in the woods with the dog; I need challenges, changes, the courage to be less safe, the abrasion of ideas discussed to sharpen my mind. I regret the time I've wasted worrying about going back. I'm sorry I wasn't overwhelmed with the positive aspects of working sooner so I could have started the long road back sooner.

If I have to walk on water, I'm not going under again. The job market is tight and it's tough to keep up the optimism alone, but I'm going back. I'm dying here at home.

Gail Stevens
Calgary

CALLING IT QUITS - OR TRYING TO

Ah, yes, smoking. No subject – or so it seemed to the shrinking number of us still stupid enough not to have kicked the habit – so dominated social conversations of the late 1980s, and *Morningside*'s mail reflected the trend.

Our correspondents, though – or so it seemed to this member of the shrinking number of . . . etc. – were remarkably free of the kind of (I have to say this) self-righteous rant that characterized so much of the discussion.

If I do finally quit, in fact, here are some of the reasons, even though, as you'll note, I've sneaked in one quiet plea from the other (and losing) side.

✉ I started smoking a long time ago, but I remember the difficulties I had in learning to do it. My smoking friends taught me how to inhale and told me that after awhile, I'd get used to it. I'd no longer cough, my eyes would stop watering and, if I was really serious about learning to smoke, I'd even get used to the ugly taste.

Well, I persevered, and sure enough, soon my taste-buds didn't care anymore. I'd also successfully mastered the technique of holding the cigarette so that I looked like I had indeed "come a long way."

At first smoking gave me a feeling of belonging, and I only smoked after lunch or when I was out with people. My life was fairly uncomplicated then, and smoking was something I did only to look "cool."

Then I joined the Royal Canadian Air Force and left behind my simple life. Smoking began to serve another purpose, although it took me a long time and a lot of cigarettes before I realized it.

In basic training our lives were definitely not our own, and smoking often filled periods of waiting or soothed frustrations over delays.

Later, long after I'd left the RCAF behind, I smoked because my husband drank, because appointments were broken, because I had to sit through meetings or attend parties I didn't want to attend, because I had to associate with people I neither liked nor respected, because I had to work under policies I didn't agree with and because I couldn't express my thoughts or opinions without risking my job or my image.

I smoked because it had become a crutch, and deep down inside, I no longer liked myself very much. Finally, despite "playing the game," I lost my job. After that announcement, I spent a lot of time examining my life. Among other things, I discovered that I smoked to keep myself from doing what I really wanted to do. I smoked so I could continue to do what I thought I had to do. So I quit smoking, and began to do what I really wanted to do. Sound simple? It wasn't.

Quitting smoking was the easy part. Learning about the parts of myself I'd ignored was the hardest. In the process, I have lost what I thought were friendships and have endured disapproval from relatives and acquaintances. But I've also found strengths and abilities I'd succeeded in hiding.

So I have no patience with those people who say they can't quit smoking. They can but they won't. And they won't because, somewhere deep inside, hidden where they can't see it, is the knowledge that to do so means a change in life-style – a taking on of responsibility for themselves.

It is, indeed, frightening to stand alone, but the fact is, we stand alone anyway, and we fool ourselves if we believe anything different.

Marion Patrick
Prince Albert, Saskatchewan

✉ I don't smoke. I have smoked very little during my lifetime. Oh, once, when I worked a summer digging cable ditches for the CNR I smoked. It was the only way you could get a break from the shovel. It was all right to stop every hour or so for a smoke, but you could not just stand there and lean on your shovel. It just didn't look right to the bosses and foremen. Somebody passed cigarettes around and I, of course, accepted them. After awhile I felt guilty using "OPS" and I bought some. Another time I spent a summer as a deckhand on a Great Lakes freighter. We smoked for the same reason.

When I got back to school in the fall we had to take a patch test for TB. Mine was positive – it scared the hell out of me! I never smoked again . . . well, maybe the odd cigar or cigarette at a party just fooling around. Not inhaling or anything like that. But that isn't the only reason I don't smoke.

When I was a kid in the dirty thirties during the Depression, we lived near some railway sidings. The Algoma Central and Hudson Bay used to marshall their freight trains for the northward connection with the trans-Canada CPR and CNR lines. Where there were freight trains, there were hoboes. They were just kids, really – teenagers chasing rumours from east to west and back again. The Westerners heard about the tobacco crop in Ontario, and Easterners headed west for the harvest. Just rumours, that's all. It did keep a lot of people busy, though, travelling.

Not far from our house and across the tracks was a bush, as we

275

called it. There was a shack that one of our neighbours had built to keep his garden tools for the garden he had cultivated nearby. The hoboes had taken over the shack and had fashioned a wooden bed. A stove appeared and then some blankets. In the summertime we used to spend a lot of time playing in the area and picking berries. We got to know the hoboes who had to wait a few days for the next freight train.

At the end of the day the hoboes would show up at the little shack and empty their pockets of whatever they were able to scrounge – some potatoes, some beans, some bread, maybe a little tea. We were on relief ourselves then and didn't have much of anything in our home. Just the same, whenever I told my mother that the hoboes didn't have anything to eat, she would scrounge around the house for some vegetables and stuff and send me over with them.

One particular day, three hoboes who were there for a couple of days or so had nothing in their pockets for supper. They looked hungry to me. Hunger was more visual then, not like you see in a fast-food advertisement. It was of the belly kind and recognizable. I went home and told my mother about it. She looked around the house and couldn't find anything to send to the mothers' sons across the tracks. Finally, the saint of a woman took a quarter that she had been saving for an emergency and told me to give it to the boys for bread and bologna. In those days you could buy a loaf of bread for ten cents and get about four or five inches of bologna for fifteen cents.

I ran across the tracks as fast as I could and told the guys the good news. I asked them if they wanted me to run over to the store for the bread and bologna. They said no, they would go themselves. Since I had a pecuniary interest in the affair I followed them to the store. Besides, I had nothing better to do. To my surprise, they stopped at a little candy store on the way to the grocery store. I looked through the glass door to see what was going on inside. The three beneficiaries of the quarter bought a package of cigarettes. I couldn't believe my eyes. How could they rather smoke than eat?

I didn't tell my mother what had happened. I thought it would break her heart. (It probably wouldn't because she was an amazingly strong woman.)

I have thought about that day many times. I have even discussed it with psychologists. There are stages of hunger. In the early stages a smoker would rather smoke than eat. Another day or so, food would have predominated. It makes sense to me now as an adult. It didn't make sense to a little boy trying to learn the true meaning of charity from the most unselfish person he has ever met. That's why I don't smoke.

Ray Stortini
Sault Ste. Marie, Ontario

✉ I was just sixteen, a month before school would begin in the fall. I was asked to spend the time helping look after a man at his cottage in the North. His wife explained that he was seriously ill and she needed my help to make him feel comfortable. I noticed that her eyes were often red and damp, but I never saw her cry. She said very little and obviously tended to be shy and unobtrusive in the presence of company. Five times a day she rubbed her husband's back and left shoulder for periods of time, and the relief was obvious.

The husband was a chain-smoker. One Sunday afternoon his supply of cigarettes ran out. He became very agitated and frustrated because the water taxi that brought us to the cottage could not be contacted. The weather had changed: it had become cool and very windy, with white-caps forming across the lake. The most violent movement was on the other side two kilometres away near the only general store in the area.

When we'd first arrived at the cottage I noticed a small twelve-foot home-made boat with an old outboard. When I asked if I could use it, I was refused; they suggested I was inexperienced and would not likely be able to start the ancient motor.

On that windy afternoon the husband told his wife to bring in the washing. As the screen door slapped shut, he quickly led me out the front door to the dock. He was constantly looking back, and at the same time pressed a dollar bill into my pocket. "Now's your chance," he said. "Take the boat across to the store and get me a package of cigarettes. I'll start the motor for you – watch closely."

I was ecstatic. I almost overturned the boat in the quiet bay before heading off into the white-caps. It was one of the great thrills of my life – way beyond skiing or driving a car at seventy-five miles an hour. The first wave covered the flat floor of the boat. I got smart and learned how to lean into the waves. I lost track of time until the last wave on the other side almost launched me right on top of the dock below the store.

Soaking wet, I ran up to the store with great leaps of exultation. The only person in the store was the proprietor, who at first refused to sell me the cigarettes until I gave an explanation. His face became almost purple with rage, and the invective might have redirected the storm the other way. "Who sent you in this storm?" I was having too much fun and pulled away from him as I ran back to the dock.

I will never know how I got the motor started with a short length of knotted rope. When I got back, the husband was stand-ing on the dock, his hand outstretched – not to help me out of the boat – but to grab the package of cigarettes. Once in the cottage the wife asked me to go out back for an armful of wood. For the first time I heard her other voice, now uncharacteristically shrill, muffled by the thickness of the cottage wall. She was stamping so that the floor sounded like a drum.

Once I returned with the wood, concerned about what was happening, I could see him looking out the window, his back to us both.

She was not crying.

He died of lung cancer in Christie Street Hospital six months later.

Robert C. Agnew
Brantford, Ontario

✉ I forgot to smoke in the fall of 1953, after I went on a fishing trip in the Cascade Mountains in north central Washington and ran out of smokes on the first day. Three days later after I got home, I forgot to buy some more and didn't think about it for several days. I have never smoked since.

Prior to that I'd been burning up three packs a day and had been doing so for over ten years. I'd tried to quit dozens of times with no luck. The only way to explain my secession – I won't call it quitting – is that I simply forgot to smoke.

However, the iniquitous weed cost me my wife.

Since I wouldn't let her smoke in the house, she went out to smoke in the pumphouse for several years. She made many trips a day and some at night. A little over a year ago I came home from work and found the house empty and my wife gone. She even took the bed so that I had to sleep on the floor. All she left was a crumpled empty Marlboro pack on the kitchen floor. I've given up crusading against smoking.

Warren C. Brown
Coeur d'Alene, Idaho

✉ I am sixty-three years young and quit smoking ten years ago. In 1936 I started smoking Cameo cigarettes, which were then in a salmon-coloured pack with the illustration of the cameo lady on the side. I smoked all kinds of cigarettes.

The worst day of my life happened when my parents drove from Hamilton to Welland, Ontario, to visit relatives, and I had hidden a pack of cigarettes for the occasion. After they left, I lit up and continued to smoke until after lunch. Then I heard a knock at the door, which I had locked. I ran downstairs and tossed the rest of the cigarettes into the furnace, then rushed upstairs, thinking my folks had come home early, and discovered the mailman. My parents got home after 7:00 P.M. I almost died the rest of the day, wanting a smoke. I really suffered.

Then I started smoking a pipe at the age of sixteen. My first tobacco was Picobac, and with all due respect, it felt like a blow-torch going off in my throat. I tried Edgeworth, Three Nuns, Pres-byterian Mixture (said to have been smoked by Stanley Baldwin, prime minister of Britain); I even tried Irish Twist, a curled hard black piece of tobacco that looked like a dog's leavings, and smelled like old rubber tires. For this I almost got tossed out of a car pool. I ended up smoking Field and Stream, and later some Dutch tobacco called Amphora Plain, which was my favourite until the day I quit.

For twenty-four years I worked in research for Saskatchewan's largest trade union, consisting of government employees. If there is a place where you feel like smoking it is a union job. You fight all day and fight all night and you fight on weekends, too. Once another chap and I were on the road, I smoking my pipe and he, his cigarettes. On the way to Prince Albert, he stopped the car. "Smoking is crazy," he said, and we threw our smokes into the ditch, including my pipe. It was an Irish Peterson pipe, a dandy, and a bit costly, too. Ten miles down the highway, we turned around and spent hours looking for the spot where we had tossed out the smokes. And so help me, we found the spot, too, even though it cost us our suppers as we had to go straight to the meet-ing we were scheduled for.

While returning from yet another union trip I had a bad cold, lit up my pipe and darned near choked to death. That did it for me in 1979. I kept my pipes (I still have them), and in fact, bought a new pouch of Amphora and carried it with me plus matches. I kept them in case I ever wanted to start smoking again. Maybe that's a tip: I know I can start up any time – but I don't want to.

Reg Shawcross
Regina

✉ I started smoking as a young adult at the age of twenty-one, I think. It had something to do with establishing my maturity and independence. I figured I could stop whenever I wanted to. (It really took some determination to get started!) When I told my dad that he said, "Uh-huh, I smoked for fourteen years and for thirteen of them I was trying to stop."

I discovered soon what he meant. After trying for about the same number of years to stop, I finally made it about eight years ago. I tried all sorts of things but the result was always the same. I would buy yet another pack, hide them under the car seat and race around with the windows down puffing away when the urge overcame me. Or I would get my hit in some equally surreptitious way until I had the face to admit yet another failure to those around me. And then I would set myself up again by promising my secretary, or my wife, or God, "This is the last one!" I hated being an addict. I knew the health risks and I feared an early death, but it was all that sneaking around that finally clinched it. I just couldn't stand the private humiliation of admitting failure to myself any more.

Murray McFarlane
Holtville, New Brunswick

✉ My non-smoking friends gasp when I say that I started smoking at about age thirteen. I was the last on my block to begin, though I'd spent at least a couple of years thinking about it. Like most smokers, I spent several years thinking of quitting, and, contrary to the draconian Protestant ethic that declares only quitting cold turkey will work, I spent some three years taking tobacco out of my life.

During the first year or so, I gradually reduced the number of places where I smoked. Eventually, I did not take cigarettes out of the house. I was then a freelance writer and musician and part-time teacher, and so I was lucky enough not to be constantly stuck in the presence of convivial smokers. My worst habit then was smoking while I read on the toilet, and I had to bribe myself to break this: I bought myself any suitable reading matter, no matter how expensive. Since this was when high-quality paperbacks started hitting twenty to thirty bucks in some cases, reading such fare *was* a treasured indulgence!

I began to count the cigarettes I smoked. I didn't quite ration them, but I informally aimed at some number, ten or twenty per day. I made a point then of *enjoying* them – something habitual smoking interferes with (as I'm sure you know). The point of all of this is that I gradually, almost willingly, took control of this pastime. (Pastime – that's what smoking is called in the pipe section of the Métis display at the Glenbow Museum. I was shocked when I saw the term; it made me think!) It was easier to quit doing something that no longer ruled my life.

I smoked for some twenty-five years, primarily cigarettes, sometimes pipes, rarely cigars. I developed one very naughty habit towards the end of my addiction when I discovered that I could enjoyably inhale pipe smoke. I certainly do not recommend this to anyone, but it did, ironically, assist me in quitting in the long run. Then came the day I'd promised myself that I'd smoked my last cigarette – by nightfall I had a pipe in my mouth and smoke in my lungs. It was, of course, harsh smoke, and I could not smoke a pipe as constantly as I had cigarettes. However, because the pipe tobacco was so much more flavourful than cigarette tobacco, I did feel satisfied, and I still had some degree of control. A good pipe is worth waiting for! Within a year, I'd packed my pipes away in the cold storage, where they remain.

For the first few weeks, I gave myself a cigar every few days, then every week, then every month. I never did (and still don't) really enjoy the taste of cigars, but they did satisfy my need for nicotine. Eventually, as my lungs cleared out, it became debatable whether or not I enjoyed the act of smoking at all. It began to burn my throat. Once I turned green and upchucked – second childhood!

It's been nearly four years since I smoked a cigarette, and two and a half since I packed my pipes away. I haven't consumed tobacco for three or four months. I figure I'm entitled to a cigar every now and then, but I just tend to forget about it.

Meanwhile, have you got a sure formula for losing fifty pounds –twenty-five of them put on during tobacco withdrawal?

George W. Lyon
Calgary

✉ Three packs a day for several years after years of one or two packs–that was 1968. One afternoon in October I got home about five o'clock. The house had been shut up all day; it would be shut up all day all winter. Suddenly I was appalled! The house stank! I said to myself, "You don't have to live in a house that smells like this," and I haven't had a cigarette since. Everything in the house that was washable was washed – clothes, bedding, walls, floors – everything. I was too busy to get withdrawal symptoms. But food began to taste better; in fact, food began to have some flavour.

Quitting is easy. But one must have a reason that makes sense to oneself.

Barbara Whyte
Medicine Hat, Alberta

✉ I feel a rising sense of panic in regard to the smoking ban that will be implemented on September 3, 1988, on all North American flights. The airlines' position is that this ban is for the comfort of passengers; however, no mention is made of the number of passengers for whom this ban will result in considerable discomfort.

I am, of course, a smoker, but I think I am as polite a smoker as is possible to be in this day and age. I don't blow smoke at elderly ladies, small children or babies or anyone using oxygen or an inhaler. I never kiss or hug anyone who objects to my smoky odour. I don't smoke in peoples' offices or homes who object to smoking – if humanly possible, I don't even go to such places.

I can make a one-hour flight with minimal discomfort, cigarette-free. Unfortunately, by the end of a two-hour flight, I get very antsy. The idea of flying from, say, Toronto to Vancouver without a cigarette has me almost in tears. I haven't even tried it yet!

It appears smokers are becoming a guilt-ridden minority, but I can't honestly think of a single person I know who smokes who doesn't attempt to minimize the potential discomfort to non-smokers. I have never heard of anyone trying to minimize the discomfort of a smoker in a non-smoking environment. We hear so much about the rights of non-smokers but as a smoker, I'm beginning to feel I have no rights and that disturbs me. Even though smokers may be a minority, there still are a great many of us, and I don't understand why apparently no effort is being made to fight this latest legislation concerning cigarette smoking on aircraft. Perhaps you have some insight in this regard?

I was going to do some research to accompany this letter; however, since you can't smoke in the library, I'll make the following points off the cuff knowing that the research has been done and can be retrieved by a non-smoker.

First, the great push to ban smoking on aircraft followed the fire on an Air Canada aircraft in Cincinnati, where there was considerable loss of life. It was reported by the American media – with absolutely no confirmation and before any kind of investigation – that the fire was started by a cigarette thrown into a garbage receptacle. The subsequent investigation proved this irresponsibly reported theory to be incorrect and that the fire was the result of an electrical problem; however, the non-smoking ball was rolling.

Second, I have heard it said that when people smoke on an aircraft, the cabin can become so congested with smoke that no one can breathe. I was almost ready to accept that theory until a pilot friend assured me that the ventilation system on any aircraft flown in North America could suck the smoke out of the cabin about as quickly as I can dig into my purse and light up a Viscount! This apparently only means increasing the air flow.

My third point is the most important. In the event of an emergency, the cabin crew has only about ninety seconds to evacuate an aircraft. This means passengers have to be alert to the instructions of the flight attendants and be able to move quickly when directed to do so. Please, God, if I am ever in that situation, put fifteen smokers in front of me instead of one drunk! Don't let me have to try to fight my way around someone who has popped a Valium and then had a little drink or two to relax on the flight.

The most difficult individuals flight attendants have to deal with are those who have had too much to drink, and a lot of people have learned the hard way that one drink in the air is like two on the ground. It isn't the smokers who are loud and obnoxious or vomit all over the lavatories; it's the gentlemen and ladies who have sipped one too many! (I'll ignore for the moment that it is conceivable that they may be smokers also.) At present drinkers are the biggest threat to life and limb on an aircraft and not the much-maligned smokers. If we are committed to making all our aircraft nice, clean, healthy places, then the booze has got to go along with the cigarettes. That would most certainly save the airline industry millions of dollars!

Please don't get the notion that I am a chain-smoking teetotaller; however, if you are a smoker, I know you will recognize that a drink really isn't much good without a cigarette anyhow. It has really burned me to watch at least one of our elected, political proponents of the no-smoking ban cavorting in the aisle, drink in hand, while I sit fuming, smokeless. I believe they should be sitting quietly in their seats, sipping tea, so we can all be miserable together. Fair is, after all, fair.

Perhaps meal service should be eliminated also. For many of us, the best part of a meal is the cigarette and cup of coffee afterwards. The money saved by the airlines on food and drink could be put towards building faster aircraft that would get us to our destinations more quickly.

Heather E. Cooke
Dartmouth, Nova Scotia

✉ It all began when my husband decided to give up smoking – again. He's been giving it up periodically for years. Once he actually quit for two years. Then our first son was born, and he had a cigar to celebrate. When our boys (now plural) started to "play smoking like Daddy," he once again resolved to quit.

Out came the weird greenish gum, followed by the small round tins of "Bandits." (The latter led to running arguments as to whether they caused mouth cancer.)

And the howling began. At first it was a joke, or so we thought. One night, when the urge to smoke became particularly over-powering, he opened his mouth and howled. The kids rolled on the floor with laughter. I grinned. He howled again.

A few days later he did it again. And again. The first time he howled at a family gathering the relatives took it in stride. After all, everyone was a bit tipsy. The fact that he doesn't drink didn't sink in until later.

He took to driving around town, occasionally leaning out the window of his jeep and howling at passers-by. He howled at work, the sound drifting through the building, causing customers' heads to turn in bewilderment.

In a bigger, more impersonal city, he might have been quietly taken away one day for treatment. In our small-town atmosphere, however, his strange behaviour was tolerated and largely ignored. Some people even howled back.

The howling was insidious. It began to spread, cropping up in unexpected places. The sound became a familiar one in our town. It came faintly from the back offices of a dozen businesses, resounded off the rafters at hockey games and was even known to echo across the hallowed greens of the local golf course.

We realized how prevalent it had become when my husband missed going to the Big Valley Jamboree for the first time. We heard from a dozen different sources that "the crazy man in the white trailer who always stuck his head out the window and howled didn't show up this year." My husband just smiled and gave a small howl as he walked away.

Sad to report, the howling hasn't cured his smoking habit. Nor has it alleviated his ulcer. But he obviously gains some degree of satisfaction from his unique form of self-expression.

One is tempted to speculate that in the dim shadows of time, other men have gained similar comfort from howling. Could that be the real origin of the wolfman tales?

Judi Herrem
Melfort, Saskatchewan

THE GREAT
CHILI SAUCE
COOK-IN

One bright morning in the autumn of
1988, *Morningside* did its best to unite
the country by linking together cooks
from various regions to prepare, simultaneously, their
own versions of a classic relish. If nothing else, we
thought, the aroma that would waft from kitchens across
the land would bring us all together.

Did it work? Maybe not, though the note from Gail
Irvine I've included here was one of a number of heartening responses. At one point, in fact, when Richard Hatfield, the former premier who was our New Brunswick
cook, offered the opinion that chili sauce was unknown
in his corner of the world, we feared we were driving
people *apart*. Elizabeth Ireland, however – as you'll see –
was one of, again, a number of listeners who leaped to heal
the breach.

Here, in any case, are some of the recipes we helped to
spread around, beginning with the one the restaurateur
Hugh Garber and I worked from in the Toronto studio.
If the program itself couldn't unite us, maybe printing this
material here will do the trick.

✉ Chili Sauce I

24 large tomatoes
6 medium onions, diced
6 sweet green peppers, diced
2 red peppers, diced
2 cups brown sugar
2 cups cider vinegar
1 tablespoon celery seed
1 tablespoon mustard seed
1 tablespoon salt
1 clove garlic, minced
¼ teaspoon ground cloves
1 teaspoon allspice
1 teaspoon mace
1 teaspoon cinnamon
1 tablespoon chopped fresh ginger, or 1 teaspoon ground ginger
12 half-pint bottling jars, or 6 pint jars

Cut tomatoes in quarters. Place all ingredients in a large stainless steel kettle. Bring to a boil, stirring occasionally to prevent sticking. Cover and let cook on low heat for 2 hours. Remove lid and cook for 1 more hour, or until mixture is quite thick and no longer watery. Ladle into sterile jars and seal while very hot.

Hugh Garber
Toronto

✉ Chili Sauce II

12 ripe tomatoes, skinned and cut up
2 large red peppers, seeded and cut up
1 large onion, chopped fine
2 cups vinegar
1 cup brown sugar
1 tablespoon salt

1 teaspoon allspice
1 teaspoon cinnamon
1 teaspoon cloves
1 teaspoon ginger

Bring all the ingredients to a boil in a large pot, then cook slowly until the onions are soft. This will make approximately 5 pints.

This recipe was one my mother always used, and I think her mother before that, who was from a small town, Lenore, in Manitoba. The flavour and quality of the tomatoes are very important, and I find sometimes I have to pep it up with a small amount of chili powder. I do add peaches to mine simply because I did it one autumn just to use them up and we really enjoyed it. You must be careful, though, because you tread a fine line between chutney and chili if you add too much fruit.

Chili sauce is a truly versatile relish or pickle. I add it to beans, and it is good on raw vegetables. When I want to make a nice sauce for meatballs or meat loaf I add a glug of red wine – good!

Eleanor Bailey
Calgary

✉ As your panel talked and cooked, I packed my car for a trip from my home in Ladner to Comox, to visit my lifelong girlfriend, Lois Warner, and her children.

When my kids and I entered her house at eight-thirty that night, guess what was simmering on her stove? Yup, your chili sauce!

The following week, after returning home with a copy of the recipe, I made my own batch. Your panel was right about the aroma – neighbours came out sniffing from two directions, and even the paperboy on his bike called out, "Whatever you're cooking, it sure smells good!"

Imagine, something as small as chili sauce uniting Canada!

Gail Irvine
Delta, British Columbia

✉ My kitchen, too, is filled with the wonderful smell of chili sauce simmering on the stove. My recipe is very simple, with no spices or seasonings except salt. The flavour of the vegetables, including our own tomatoes and onions, shines through.

The recipe has an interesting history. It appears in my old school cookbook entitled *Theory and Practice in Household Science* (Winnipeg Public School, 1937). My mother, Florence, was one of thirteen graduates of the Faculty of Home Economics at the University of Manitoba in 1923. She and her classmates tested and developed these recipes, which were used by students in Winnipeg schools for many years.

Chili Sauce III

18 large ripe tomatoes (6 pounds)
6 onions (2 pounds)
2 green peppers
1 small head of celery
2 tablespoons salt
1 cup brown sugar
1½ cups vinegar

Chop tomatoes, onions, peppers and celery, and put into a large pot. Add remaining ingredients. Cook slowly about 1 hour. Seal in bottles.

Cathy Fry
Saskatoon

✉ I can't stand it: even Mr. Hatfield – a New Brunswicker – says that chili sauce was never made in the Maritimes.

As a former Nova Scotian I have been making chili sauce for years. This recipe comes from the well-known Marshlands Inn in Sackville, New Brunswick. It is the best chili sauce I have ever made.

Marshlands Chili Sauce

3 cups celery
9 pounds ripe tomatoes
3 green peppers
3 sticks of root ginger
6 cups white sugar
3 cups cider vinegar
4½ tablespoons mixed pickling spice
2 tablespoons salt

Wash and chop celery. Scald, peel and chop tomatoes. Remove veins and seeds from peppers and cut in thin strips. Combine all three vegetables in a heavy preserving kettle, then add the remaining ingredients and simmer until thick. Remove ginger and fill sterilized jars to overflowing with chili sauce. The yield is about 8 pints.

Elizabeth Ireland
Owen Sound, Ontario

✉ I survived your Great Chili Sauce Caper with mixed emotions. I, too, grew up with a cellar full of jars of the stuff. My mother's philosophy was simple: if it grew in the ground, put it in a jar for the winter.

Everything from elderberries to watermelon rind was canned. Chili sauce took up a great amount of shelf space and provided us with the spice of life through many a meagre Depression supper.

However, after many years of making chili sauce for my own family, a friend introduced me to hot sauce. Never again was chili sauce a vital part of my kids' winter culinary delights. Henceforth and to this very day, hot sauce is September. In late August I had a brief stay in hospital, and although my kids were most anxious and caring, I really believe the burning question in their minds was, "Did she get the hot sauce made before she went to hospital?"

I did, and I made the second and third batches after I got home. There is never enough. Only the faint of heart and stomach shy away.

Hot Sauce

20 large tomatoes
12 hot red peppers
6 onions
5½ cups granulated sugar
4 cups white wine vinegar
3 tablespoons salt

Peel and chop tomatoes and place in a large kettle. Add chopped peppers, including seeds; chop and add onions. Stir in sugar, vinegar and salt. Bring to a boil then cook until thickened, about 3 hours. Stir as it thickens (it does stick). Pour and seal.

June Robinson
Owen Sound, Ontario

✉ Chili sauce is dandy! But you need to try tomatoes as a fruit, not a vegetable. Try my mother's tomato marmalade. Given unexpected company and no pie, rush baking powder biscuits into a hot oven. Serve hot buttered biscuits with the ultra-deluxe tomato marmalade!

This makes a tea party fit for even expected guests. Try to keep some jars hidden away for guests.

Tomato Marmalade

1. Scald and peel 4 pounds ripe tomatoes. Chop roughly and place in a very large pot.
2. Grate the peel coarsely off two lemons; cut up lemons and add fruit and peel to tomatoes.
3. Add 4 cups sugar and stir well. Add several large pieces of stick cinnamon. Boil up until the mixture is as dense as jam. (A

day without rain gives faster evaporation.) Place into small sterilized jars.

Clare McAllister
Victoria

✉ I particularly enjoyed your chili sauce program, but I have the best recipe with the least amount of work.

No endless chopping of pears, apples, onions, peppers, peaches and so on. It looks like chili sauce, tastes like chili sauce, but has few ingredients and little work.

Tomato Jam

12 good-sized tomatoes
2½ cups white sugar
2 cups white vinegar
1 teaspoon ground cloves
1 teaspoon cinnamon
1 teaspoon salt

Boil together chopped peeled tomatoes and sugar for at least 1 hour, stirring frequently.

Add vinegar and spices and continue boiling till thickened, stirring frequently.

Bottle in sterilized jars, then enjoy!

June Morrison Smith
Lakefield, Ontario

✉ I got home from a busy day a bit after ten o'clock to deal with four quarts of green tomatoes – busily turning red before their time even in the fridge – and turned on the radio to the chili sauce debate. It was most appropriate for a person who was slicing green tomatoes late into the night.

Now I'm not about to cast aspersions on the undoubtedly fine recipe from the Marshlands Inn, but I will speak from the perspective of a born and bred New Brunswicker. Moreover, I am currently working through my grandmother's cookbook with a view to eventual publication. These hand-written old recipes, which were shared and swapped, probably date from when Granny Jarvis was setting up her household. I'm not sure just when she married, but her first three daughters were born in the 1890s. There are no recipes for chili sauce; *no* chili sauce. However, a large number of recipes for green tomatoes: Mrs. Hall's Tomato Pickle, which simmers (for the first time) as I write; Mother's (my great-grandmother's) Mustard Pickle; Nell's Mustard Pickle; Nell's Sweet Pickles; Mrs. Fisher's Kracklejack and Mrs. Dibblee's India Relish. That's among twenty-one pickles and relishes. Only two call for ripe tomatoes – Lucy Digby's chutney and Mrs. Hawkin's tomato pickle.

This seems to back up the idea that native thrift combined with a short growing season militated against chili sauce down East, and none of Granny's recipes are the chow chow I remember growing up with. That one may well be in my mother's cookbook (circa the 1930s I expect), which I intend to tackle next.

It's been interesting. I expect old recipes to be delightfully vague on quantities – "enough to make a good batter," or "a bag of raisins," or "a package of pickling spices." But the spiced crab-apple jelly was equally vague on ingredients – "Add the whole spices." Which ones? I tried cloves, allspice and cinnamon, and it's good. But often I'd love to be able to reach the old dears whose recipes I'm trying, recipes which may well not have been prepared by anyone for fifty years. I can almost feel their ghosts in my kitchen, murmuring, "No, no, dear. You have to use a silver spoon for that," or "You shouldn't chop those peppers so finely." And I wish I could ask them – *Please*, what do you really mean by thick enough?

As I say, working through the old cookbook is fun. This is my twentieth batch of pickles, jams or jellies – it *is* the season – and my apartment reeks wonderfully of spices and vinegar and sugar and fruit smells even on the days I'm taking it easy.

Katie FitzRandolph
Toronto

ON MAKING THE
BEST OF THINGS

Krista Munroe, whose letters end this chapter, has been a part, and – at least to me – an important one, of all the *Morningside Papers*. She first wrote, as readers familiar with the earlier editions will recall, in September, 1983. We had had a panel on suicide, and the right of the terminally ill to seek euthanasia. Krista, who was twenty-six then, had been through a terrible battle with Hodgkin's disease, and had thought about the issues we'd raised. Her letter, written in the wry, chatty style that characterizes all her communications, was as moving an affirmation of life as I'd ever encountered–my favourite, as I later admitted, of all the letters in that first collection.

Since then, Krista and I have become friends, though we see each other perhaps once a year. A picture of the son she bore after her disease went into remission – the redoubtable Ben Longshot Munroe McFee, whose latest adventures enliven her most recent communiqué–adorns my office wall, alongside one of my own granddaughter. She has been among the winners of a contest, conducted by CBC Calgary, to imitate my rambling, stammering radio prose (as the judge, I should admit to a little prejudice in that decision, since the prize was a trip to Calgary to have breakfast with the imitatee), and I have carried messages to her from across the country: In Fredericton, on my book-promotion tour of 1988, I asked both Krista's mother and Vivienne Anderson (of Weaver's Hill, as Krista notes here), whose letters I matched with Krista's in the *New Papers*, to sign a two-dollar bill; later, her brother-in-law, resplendent in naval uniform, showed up at a store in Victoria, and added his name to the same bill, which I presented to Krista – and Ben – during the victory breakfast in Calgary. And so on. We keep in touch.

Those details, I hope, will explain both Krista's inclusion in the dedication of this edition and the unusually personal tone of the letter I've included here. Before we get to it, here are some other letters from remarkable people, and some other thoughts on dealing with a mixture of frailties.

✉ My name is Dennis Kaye. I'm just over five foot ten, with brown hair and blue eyes. I like to think I'm an okay guy, but unfortunately, at thirty-four years old, I'm dying. Although I'm reasonably tolerant, I find this whole dying thing an imposition. The fact is, a terminal diagnosis can ruin your whole day.

The vast majority of people with my condition last three to five years, so you could say that, in my fourth year, I'm on the home stretch.

Does the name muscular dystrophy ring a bell? How about multiple sclerosis? Of course they do. These names and others, like cerebral palsy, cystic fibrosis, Alzheimer's, Parkinson's – the list could go on – all have something in common. The mere mention of any of these names usually conjures up a variety of clear images. I have ALS, and after four years of facing ignorance and indifference, I believe that both public awareness and the financial support that awareness brings are long overdue. When I mention ALS there are no bells. If I say instead that I have Lou Gehrig's disease I often still draw a blank. To physicians ALS means amyotrophic lateral sclerosis, but to thousands of others it means slow death. I read recently that ALS is as common as MS. After careful study I have come to a conclusion: due to the high turnover of those afflicted, statistics only reflect the number of patients alive at any one time. Put more simply: they aren't counting the dead ones!

I find it hard to believe that people would not respond if they were made aware of the scope and effects of this disease. Four years ago I enjoyed good health and performed well at a physically demanding job, but now I need assistance at even the simplest of tasks. This disease attacks the motor centre at the base of the brain, and in turn slowly robs you of voluntary muscle control. The doctors say the end will come when the muscles controlling my lungs are affected. With a keen mind, a healthy heart and open eyes, I will suffocate.

Many people, like me, have grown tired of chasing magic cures and paying quacks; we have had a belly full of denial. I'd like to pass on the single most effective treatment I've turned up so far. It is, quite simply, a healthy sense of humour. I know it sounds corny but, like *Reader's Digest* says, laughter really is the best medicine.

The other night, while getting ready for bed, I was going through my usual contortionist throes of disrobing when the funniest thing happened. I was down to the second-to-last garment when suddenly, with one eye straining for the light at the end of the turtleneck and one arm almost free, my body stiffened. With a final desperate surge of strength I entered a horizontal spin, coming to rest in a panting heap of arms, legs and shorts. Any other time I would have slipped into an all-consuming pit of manic self-pity and frustration, but instead I was seized by the sweet slapstick of the situation. Laughter came grudgingly at first but soon built to manic proportion. My wife, Ruth, who had by this time awakened, looked over the edge of our bed. She joined the chorus. Together we shrieked and howled. When Ruth finally regained enough composure to pull the sweater off and saw the look on my face, the whole foolery started anew. Laugh – I thought I'd die! I had discovered the true meaning of comic relief.

Had I expended that much energy on any other activity, I would have been sapped of all strength. Instead I felt rejuvenated. It may not be a cure, but it's better than anything the specialists have come up with.

I've indulged many times since that night, and the result is always the same – a genuine boost of energy. To promote my treatment I even considered a career in stand-up comedy, but it's getting too hard to stand up, and I'm sure the world is not ready for fall down comedy. I'll remain a household humorist.

So my message is simple: lighten up. Humour is fail-safe and free, and you may already possess it. It can make a seemingly unbearable situation bearable, and in the process it will make life far more bearable for those around you. You still may not outlive your dog, but you'll have fun trying.

The coffee's always on.

The Incredible Shrinking Man
Dennis Kaye
Quathiaski Cove, British Columbia

✉ Last week CBC televised a documentary about runaway children. I waited anxiously as the program was advertised the week before. I was scared to watch, yet drawn to it. My husband, twelve-year-old son and I watched together, my emotions churning as I sat, stone-faced. I taped the program on our VCR and have since watched it twice in private, in tears and thanking God. I survived. I was lucky.

I remember the first time I ran away from home. It was a beautiful autumn morning when I packed my school books into a suitcase, careful not to wake my sister, and sneaked out of the house. My mom caught up to me at the railroad tracks, the short cut to my grandmother's house. I didn't have to go to school that day. I was six years old. No one asked me why I ran away.

After that I ran away often, always locally. I was never asked the big question: why? I was labelled a "bad kid" in our small town. I always had boyfriends but rarely any girls to chum around with. People didn't seem to want their children to be friendly with me.

When I was fifteen I began to date a guy who was a year older than I. He had just moved from England and hated Canada. Just weeks before my fifteenth birthday, I became pregnant. He was scared to face his family. The solution seemed obvious to us. We wanted to be together, so we ran away. We lived on the streets of New Glasgow, Nova Scotia, often sleeping at the YMCA. In August he found a job on a garbage truck for eighty dollars a week. We found a cheap, one-room apartment above a store in an old run-down building. There were some good times, but the pressure seemed too great. By October we had contacted our families and returned home. His family sent him back to England. I have not heard from him since.

I went on welfare and lived at home, returning to school the next fall. A month before my eighteenth birthday I was pregnant again. I attended some prenatal classes at school with five other girls, all younger than I. The health nurse kept trying to persuade me to consider adoption. I faltered, and my mom decided to keep the baby. My second son was born in January, and in May I ran away from home again, taking my first-born son with me. I went to Ontario with a man who left behind a wife and three small children. We stayed in a small apartment with five others. I endured many beatings and was finally abandoned. In desperation I contacted my parish priest, who made arrangements for me to meet with another priest to get money to come home.

I returned with my life in shambles. There were people who could have helped me – social workers, teachers, the parish priest and health nurse. None asked me why I acted as I did. They dealt with me as their jobs dictated, handed out my cheques, listed my options and followed the rules.

By February I was pregnant again. This time I was devastated. I could not understand how this could happen to me. I considered suicide. The father of my unborn child stuck with me, insisted on marrying me (causing a great many problems in his own family). Our beautiful daughter was born when he was nineteen, I was twenty.

We celebrated our ninth anniversary this year. My husband has a good, steady job; we have three happy children and live in a house that is perfect for us. I'm able to be at home with the children.

So, why do I sit in the stillness of the autumn afternoon nursing a pot of coffee, watching the traffic go by? Why do I cringe when the topic of runaways or "bad kids" is brought up? My second son is still with my parents. He went back after the school year ended this year, after spending three years with us. He is a very troubled child. We tried everything; we even consulted a child psychologist. Our three other children began to resent him and we had many family fights. *Will he end up on the streets as I did? Will he be as lucky as me and survive?*

I just don't understand. I would have embraced the chance to share my secret, had anyone asked. I asked. I am still shut out.

Karen McNamara
Queen's County, New Brunswick

✉ I am the mother of two girls; my youngest, Nicole, has Down's syndrome. When Nicole was born, I was in shock and grieved the loss of my perfect baby, uncertain of the future for this not-so-perfect baby and our family. I loved her but often wished she would just go away.

Thank goodness, she did not. Today she is a bright, curious, active four-year-old child who goes to a regular play school and Sunday school. She had her first piano recital last spring and loves life. Sometimes she is happy, sometimes she is sad and sometimes she is angry. It often takes her longer to learn things but she can and does learn.

Nicole is just a regular little girl who needs some extra help. She is not an exceptional child who has Down's syndrome. Like in the "normal" population, some children learn faster and better than others. Nicole is average.

When should a child be allowed to live and who should decide? I don't believe we should have to ask these questions. If any child needs an operation to keep him or her alive or improve his or her quality of life, and you would operate on any other child, then the child who has Down's syndrome has the same right to that operation. Would you allow your child to die when a standard operation could save his or her life? Our children have the right to life. They are valuable human beings.

We parents carry this fear long after the child is born. One mother, for example, is afraid to take a family vacation next summer in case they have an accident, and she or her husband are unable to sign the consent forms. Could someone choose not to treat their youngest son because he has Down's syndrome? In the past I would not have thought this possible, but now I believe this could happen in rare cases.

When I apply for a Medic Alert bracelet for Nicole's sister, which will inform people of her allergy to penicillin, should I also request a bracelet for Nicole? Perhaps the inscription should read: "This child is a valuable human being. Please treat her if necessary. She has the right to life."

Today parents of children who have extra needs are showing society that these children are valuable and do belong in the community. People must allow them their right to live not just a simple life but a quality life – a life in the community where they are integrated into regular preschools, schools and recreation programs and where they can hold regular jobs that offer extra help if necessary. This alternative is cheaper than institutions and a lot more fun for everyone.

Barb Doucette
Dartmouth, Nova Scotia

✉ My brother Arthur was a talented musician, a delightful human being and a schizophrenic. Like so many of the mentally ill, he drifted into life on the street and ended up as a vagrant, shabbily dressed, often disoriented and undernourished. His social worker could never keep track of him for long, and when the family tried to help by sending him money, he would give it away to someone he felt was less fortunate.

There is no reward in our society for such misguided saintliness. Seven years ago Arthur died in a fire in a run-down old rooming-house where he was temporarily taking shelter. I am convinced that if the fire hadn't got him, exposure, street violence, drugs or suicide would have.

When I see a long-haired, gaunt young man on the streets of Toronto or Vancouver, I sometimes still think for a split second that it's Arthur. My logical mind knows that it can't be true. But my heart tells me that all these dispossessed souls are somebody's brother, somebody's mother or sister or child – somebody's someone.

Our society looks upon the homeless as a kind of expendable sub-species. This is not too different from the way the Nazis regarded the Jews. Seeing them as less than fully human is easier for us, because then we can look the other way. Those of us who don't ignore them completely tend to pass judgement. Surely their misfortune stems from some moral weakness, some lack of will. Perhaps they just didn't *try* hard enough.

But I know how hard my brother tried. Mental illness, addiction and disastrous turns of fate have little or nothing to do with human will. These events just happen, sometimes causing decent people's lives to spin out of control.

I have no neat solution for this complex and painfully visible social problem. But I do know that compassion and empathy must come first. These people all have names and faces and families. They are human. If we see them as anything less, we perpetuate a small, quiet holocaust in all the cities of this affluent and supposedly enlightened country of ours.

Margaret Gunning
Kinron, Alberta

303

✉ Every winter when I pass a certain spot near Portage Avenue, my memory goes back to one bitterly cold day in February seven years ago. Mother and I missed the bus and decided to walk home – it was a way to keep warm. After walking a few steps my mother suddenly stopped, looking very agitated, and pointed to a dark shape in the snowbank. "Look, there's a man lying in the snow. He'll freeze to death . . . he needs help," she said with concern.

Together we tried to stand him up but he was a dead weight. I bent over the grey, whiskered face and reeled back from strong, sickening whiffs of whisky breath. I felt his wrist – the pulse was weak, but it was still beating. "He's hardly breathing," I said.

Mother's lips tightened. She squared her shoulders, tightened her scarf and stood in front of the oncoming crowd.

"Please!" she appealed. "That man over there. He'll freeze. Help him!"

The flickering lights showed muffled faces, red from the cold, bright-eyed and eager to get home to a hot supper. Politely they walked around Mother, deaf to her pleas.

One young man stopped to listen for a moment. His eyes flickered over the man's body with contempt. "Darn drunk!" he muttered. He turned to his girlfriend, who was stamping her feet in her high boots, her mitts over her ears. She giggled, tossed back her blond hair and grabbed his arm. Laughing, they walked quickly out of sight.

"Disgusting!" my mother said. "He could freeze to death and no one cares. Let's try again to lift him up."

I knew that it was useless to reason with her when she was in a determined mood. We lifted the man under the armpits and dragged him over to the brick wall of the drugstore. He was heavy! Miraculously, without opening his eyes he stayed propped up.

But we could not just leave him there in the below-zero weather. I ran out to Portage Avenue to see who I could flag down. A police car stopped. When I pointed out the man slumped against the wall, the cop said, "Yeah, we get lots of them. Every winter we pick up six or seven frozen drunks on Main Street. We'll take him to emergency, or to the Sally Ann. At least he'll be warm. Thanks!" he said with a smile.

"It's my mother that deserves the thanks," I said.

I looked at her. Her nose was red. Her grey curls had strayed from her hat, and there was frost in her hair. But her eyes were shining. We ran the mile and a half home.

Elinor Pitchford
Winnipeg

✉ My father has had Parkinson's disease for many years. It has been very hard on my parents, since they have been robbed of their retirement years and companionship as my father lives in the hospital.

There is, however, a humorous side. A number of years ago, my father and I went to a Blue Jays game. He was in great shape for the entire game. Towards the end of the eighth inning he started to stiffen. The game was over before we could reach the tunnels to the covered area, about a ten-second walk for a healthy person.

People were kind and very helpful. Before long, a wheelchair arrived and a short trip on the VIP elevator took us to the ground floor. The cab driver was reluctant to take us because my father, at this point, was locked into a semi-foetal position and speechless. I carried him to the cab and wrestled him into the front seat.

Thirty minutes and fourteen dollars later we arrived home. His medication suddenly kicked in, and, much to the shock of the cab driver, who thought he had witnessed Lazarus rising from the dead, my father let himself out of the cab and stuck me with the fare.

John P. Clancy
Scarborough, Ontario

✉ The handicap from which I suffer will not likely shorten my life, but it has taken from each day the spice and zest life once had. I have multiple sclerosis. Trying to come to terms with it has taken the biggest part of my spiritual energy since I learned the diagnosis more than a year ago. The thought that I will probably never again be able to enjoy long walks, late nights, hot baths or many other physical pleasures leaves me in an existence lacking most of what once made it a life. I am reduced to getting through one day at a time: the thought of the remainder of my existence is unbearable.

But I must not give in to depression. My family and friends have shown wonderful kindness. I can still walk, though not far. My hands have been very little affected, so I can still play the piano and type. My vision is still functioning, so I can drive normally and watch television, games and concerts. I have very little pain, so my physical sufferings are small compared to what most cancer victims face. But that sometimes is extremely cold comfort.

Multiple sclerosis is in some ways the bastard child of the important diseases. It does not usually shorten life dramatically or cause severe pain. It thus seems (and is, I suppose) less serious than cancer, heart disease and cystic fibrosis. It is also almost completely unpredictable. As of now, there is no known cause or cure and no foreseeable development of the disease in the individual. It is difficult to pin down, as spontaneous remissions occur in the vast majority of victims. Yet it places a huge burden on tens of thousands of Canadians, most of them in the most productive years of their lives, between the ages of twenty and forty-five. We wait, hope and pray, doing what we can to promote research and consciousness in the general public and doing our best not to impose our long faces on those around us.

It does us good to hear about triumphs of the human spirit.

Ron Carleton
Cremona, Alberta

✉ We arrived a little past eight in the evening. The back door to the church kept swinging open as more people arrived. Some were alone; some couples arrived together. Coats were hung up, and everyone dissolved into a collection of folk that spelled safety and friendship. Hands were thrust out in greeting and names like

Doris, Paul, Mac and Earl were spoken in warm recognition. A group had gathered by one of the coffee urns and someone was pulling sleeves of Styrofoam cups from a large cardboard box that stood on the floor. A woman with yellow-white hair was pouring cream into glass pitchers and stuffing sugar bags into used margarine tubs. They were all strangers to me, and I felt dwarfed by their ease with one another and by hands and faces not bound or gagged.

The chairman called the meeting to order. He noted the occasion of Al's five years of sobriety. He also noted Al's many friends and family members in the audience, and said this would surely produce a hefty "silent" collection when the plate was passed later on. The audience laughed easily and a lot. We remained seated to say the serenity prayer. Someone was called forward to say the twelve steps; someone else went through the slogans: easy does it, remember when. He remembered when he and Al had taken a trip to Las Vegas last fall. The story didn't really bear on the slogan, but everybody laughed again. Both speakers began and ended with congratulations to Al. Several other people spoke, some haltingly, others more fluently.

The chairman told a story about his waking up in the middle of the night and having to pee. This was forty years ago, and it meant walking fifty yards from the house to an out-building. He had fallen off the wagon that night and wasn't sure what would turn him around. He discovered upon waking that he couldn't see. He asked his wife to turn on the light, and she told him it was on already. He lay back on the pillow and breathed a sigh of relief thinking, "By God, I'm a fortunate man. I've gone blind. My drinking days are over, my problem is solved. Unless someone puts a glass into my hand, I'll never see to take another drink. God damn it, I'm lucky!" He groped his way along the wall and eventually found his way out of doors. Back in bed he marvelled once again at his good fortune.

In the morning he still couldn't see, and he repeated once again the phrases he had spoken in the night – like a litany that would protect and sanctify his new-found freedom. His euphoria continued throughout the morning. By two in the afternoon his sight had returned. He remembered feeling disappointed and let down. It appeared that getting sober wasn't going to be as easy as out-of-sight out-of-mind. But that was forty years ago, and tonight he has forty years' sobriety under his belt.

It was my turn to go to the front of the room to present Al with his five-year medallion. I wasn't prepared for the features of the room to be suddenly obliterated. The moulded metal ceiling, the green walls, the Sunday-school felt-board figures, the rows of wooden chairs holding a roomful of people all receded into a myopic blur. But Al was clear enough. He was sitting astride his chair, halfway back on the aisle. It reminded me of years ago when he used to sit that way at the kitchen table after we had finished a meal. He would always turn ninety degrees in his seat and rub the palms of his hands together – rubbing away the crumbs, I guessed. Now I think it must have been a sign of deep contentment, perhaps with how ritual becomes life. There were two or three things I wanted to say: how special it was to be his daughter, how he had a capacity to live one day at a time (I couldn't); how I was honoured to share this moment with people who I expect now knew him better than I did.

Apparently I figure in my dad's story. I was the one who forced him to go to his first meeting, the one who found him one January night in an underground parking garage. His testimonial is full of gratitude – the engraved words on the gold medallion read "Forever Grateful." Sitting in a church basement on a Thursday night in January, I am struck by his sense of purpose in life, by the fact that he is consumed by the present, that he is resilient and forgiving. For a moment I have ceased to be self-preoccupied and have turned off the narcissistic pulses of my life.

Gayle Johannesen
Waterloo, Ontario

✉ My father died eight years ago, leaving my mother, then seventy, alone in her house. It had been a difficult and stressful marriage in the latter years, and I had hoped that my mother would find some happiness and be able to live without being verbally abused, able to pursue her interests in peace. However, her agoraphobic tendencies, coupled with the grief and adjustments of losing her partner of forty-three years, sent her into a severe depression. In spite of my very frequent visits and ongoing requests from friends, relatives and neighbours to take her places, the agoraphobia became invasive and the loneliness acute. After two years she was hospitalized with physical as well as emotional problems. She received some tremendous help, but I knew if she ever had to live alone again the recovery would be short-lived. She moved from the hospital to my home.

We had very little room, and one of the most difficult things I have ever had to do as a parent was to move my son, then eight, to a cement basement so his Nana could have his room. I rationalized that children had slept in barn lofts before and he would survive. He did, and we were okay, but it was still hard for me. Then, shortly after my mother moved in, I became pregnant with my third baby. I was thirty-six. My mom was still not totally well: she was very anxious, depressed and still struggling with agoraphobia. She hated it when I had to be away from the house, but she hated even more requesting me to stay. It was the only time in our lives that my mother and I argued frequently. This was likely a result of my worry at the prospect of having a nursery and a nursing home at the same time, coupled with my mother's concern that she was a source of my stress. She wanted to be independent, but she was unable to live alone.

She chose to apply for accommodation in a senior citizens' lodge and moved there after living with me for almost a year. In the lodge she has her own bed-sitting room and bathroom, and a small fridge of her own, but she has her meals in a communal dining room. Of course there have been some adjustments, but she moved with an incredibly positive attitude that this was going to be the best possible alternative to meet all our needs – and it has come to be just that.

My mother is once again one of my greatest sources of support – the person that I remember before my father's death. She has a beautiful close relationship with my little daughter, born a few months after she moved from my house. She is at our house frequently, but loves to return to her little room that she has fixed up so cutely with plants, pictures, her own TV and stereo, and books, books, books. When she is not in her room she is likely to be out walking around in her Reeboks listening to Neil Diamond, Beethoven, or Sharon, Lois and Bram on her Walkman – quite eclectic at seventy-eight! She doesn't miss shopping for groceries or cooking meals one little bit.

For some independent, reasonably healthy people, being able to remain in their own home in their senior years is extremely important and possible. For some families, three generations can co-habit, and it works well. But for others, like my mother, living alone is a death sentence; and living with married children whose energies are directed so heavily towards their own young families presents a different set of problems. For these seniors, the semi-independence of seniors' residences are a boon, not an evil. I have never seen my mother happier and worried less about her well-being – a blessing for us both.

Marilyn Coull
Edmonton

✉ How's your year going? I haven't been able to listen as often as I'd like this year: Ben loves the "Peter Gzowski music" but has no time for "all that talking," so he usually competes by increasing his volume. From what I *have* heard, though, it sounds like things are going very well. It also sounds like your grandfather job hasn't lost any of its initial charm. I hope you share your toys! (Kids love computers, don't they?)

Ben and I enjoyed seeing you last fall. I didn't realize what a big impression you made on him until we got home. He was having a bubble bath, and I thought I heard him say "Peter Gzowski" so I said "Pardon me?" Honestly, this is what he did: he picked up two handfuls of bubbles and put them on his chin. Then he looked at me and said, "Hello. This is *Morningside* and my name is Peter Gzowski." No fooling! He told me that the bubbles were his beard. (I knew he thought your beard was bonzer but I had no idea he was that tuned in!) He's done this ever since – every time he has a bubble bath. We even have him on tape. (Ben has been Bruce Springsteen, Murray McLauchlan, Eric Bogle, Jennifer Warnes and, of course, Stanley the pig, Coal Dust the calf, a Lipizzaner stallion and the lawn mower – you're in treasured company.)

Some interesting things have happened to me because people heard you read my letter or they read it themselves. One guy called to sell me a herbal cure for cancer. Another man, who was passing through Medicine Hat, offered to take me for a ride in his plane. (I passed on the cure, but, I confess, I accepted the plane ride.) And I received a warm letter from Vivienne Anderson of Weaver's Hill, who contributed to *The New Morningside Papers*. I hope to get the chance to meet her eventually.

I've also met some remarkable people. A woman whose daughter was dying from cancer called just to talk. And a man whose son was in the same position also called to talk. Both of these people were gracefully handling what must be a terrible pain.

Because of that letter people seem to have some very odd expectations of me. It's as if they expect me to be heroic or saintly or know the answer to some mystery like the secret of life, the universe and everything. I almost feel like I should live up to these expectations, too. But knowing that I would have to give up swearing, sneaking the occasional cigarette and drinking; that I would have to remember to (cheerfully) clean the cat boxes and mow the lawn; and that I would even have to refrain from drinking too much coffee or playing too much computer golf . . . I manage to talk myself out of it. Trouble is, they also seem to be waiting to hear about some miracle of "coping" (or whatever the proper jargon is these days) that I've figured out. Since I haven't got any answers, I sometimes get the feeling that I'm only as good as my last recurrence. It is probably unnecessary to mention that I don't spend lots of time pampering those particular expectations.

Things are moving on in our lives. This year Ben memorized all of "The Cremation of Sam McGee," licked half a roll of "the red stickers" (they were thirty-six-cent stamps); learned to boot up the computer and access "Golf," "Jet" and "Battlezone," found out what "Control/Alt/Delete" will do; went to French-immersion play school and started to feel sorry for his parents who, he informed me, "don't have much French" unlike Monsieur and Ben who both have "quite a lot of French"; and found out what neutering a cat means. In Ben's words: you take him to the vet and then they *yank* out his testicles! My husband paled at Ben's enthusiastic hand motions. I'm beginning to feel left behind, and the kid is only three and a half!

This year I have listened to endless repetitions of "The Cremation of Sam McGee," steamed about a half a roll of stamps off the grocery list; spent lots of time trying to explain things like neutering a cat somehow, not exactly getting it right; and got a job as a part-time copywriter for a local radio station. I tried to learn enough French to tell a little kid to sit down and eat your peas. (I didn't and he wouldn't, but I don't think it was a language issue.) I discovered that my few grey hairs have been acting like bunnies when I wasn't looking, and now I have many grey hairs. (I told myself to relax – at least I had lived long enough to be able to dye them if I wanted to. So I did.) And I enjoyed myself immeasurably during the 1988 playoffs. This year Gretzky amazed and entertained as only he can and, like everyone else, I blinked in disbelief and impatiently waited for the replay so I could see what had happened.

Ben and I were considering coming up to the Big City to practise our sycophancy on you. Hope we can get it in gear and that it's all right with you. Don't worry. We won't bring anything we've written that we – be honest now – just *knew* you'd love.

In actual fact, I can't bring Longshot as "Longshot," since he's been Chris de Burgh for the past month. He's been speaking with what he imagines is an Irish accent so he's really hard to understand. I liked it better when he was Inigo Montoya from *The Princess Bride* or even Mont Vésuve, *le géant endormi* (although all that stabbing and blowing up and dropping lava on people did get a little depressing after a while). All attempts to encourage him to be someone else have failed. He was Marvin Gaye for a few hours, and he was Smokey Robinson and the Miracles for two afternoons. He even tried Aretha Franklin, not because he entertains fantasies about being female (I think), but because he really likes to sing "Natural Woman."

Something has changed in the last few months. I'm not sure what it is but I think this has something to do with it: a friend of mine died. Her name was Emily Stonhouse. We weren't the kind of friends that had tea together or even shared very much of our daily lives. But she was important to me. She was the first person I talked to after I was diagnosed the first time. She had breast cancer and had had radiation and chemotherapy. She decided to start a CanSurmount group in Medicine Hat so that she could help other people with cancer.

She did quite a job! Whenever I talked to her, I always got the impression that she was sure that we were going to live through it. But I think I had that wrong. For Emily, there was never an end to her "dealing" with cancer. She dealt with cancer and its treatment for eleven years, more often "on" than "off," yet she was always very much alive. She was busy, committed, interested and interesting. She never seemed to spend much of her time just putting in hours. It takes courage to enjoy living when so much of your time is spent being so very uncomfortable. I think that was what she had in mind when she said that we'd live through it. Her emphasis was always on "live." And she lived every second she had.

She was a rock for me. You see, Emily was always certain that I would be fine – far more certain than I've ever been. And, selfishly, I always expected her to be there when I needed reassurance or needed someone to talk to during the next recurrence. (We would commiserate about losing our hair or the terrible conditions in Emergency where chemotherapy was given, or even about throwing up. Sometimes you just feel like talking about nausea with someone who knows exactly what you mean!)

She also understood the nightmares that often precede a check-up. We'd both heard the "I'm sorry but you have it again" speeches, and we would both have restless nights before appointments. *She* never told me not to worry–she knew that was idiotic. Heck, *she* worried! Besides, she also knew that there were plenty of doctors just dying to tell worried people not to worry. That kind of help was easy to come by. She just understood. Emily was sixty-four years old when she died of metastatic breast cancer. I miss her. I'm glad I knew her.

It's nearly suppertime here. Ben's had a full day so he'll be starving. We went down to watch the trains in the yard this morning. Then we walked all over the place. He heard pigeons cooing (do pigeons coo? Anyway, he heard that noise that pigeons make that is as comforting as cats' purring) and he was impressed. He also threw rocks in the river and saw a church. This church stuff really intrigues him. Too bad he lives with a couple of heathens.

Right now he's swimming with his dad. They're probably playing "What time is it, Mr. Shark?" since Ben is the original, blood-thirsty four-year-old. He also explained to me that since people kiss with people lips, then cats kiss with cat lips. Then he decided to show me the lips on our cats. The cats remain unimpressed. I was interested to see that Ben had no qualms about kissing lips that are thin and black – like our tabby's. That particular cat is being unimpressed under the bed.

Krista Munroe
Medicine Hat, Alberta

314

A GIRL CALLED BRUCE, AND OTHER MISADVENTURES OF NAMES

Remember Bruce Blakemore, who wrote about breakfasts in Chapter Ten? Well, Bruce is a . . . I guess the title of this chapter gives it away, eh? – though Bruce is a woman now. Her story is one of several we collected that revolved around what their authors, or their authors' friends and family, were called.

✉ Before I met Peter, he attended a small college in upstate New York in the late sixties and early seventies. During that time there was a writer for the *New York Times* Sunday Magazine, also named Peter Wood, who wrote about such subjects as wildlife, canoeing, kayaking, and other outdoor activities – topics my husband Peter is also passionate about. My Peter enthusiastically looked forward to reading these articles by the "other" Peter Wood. While my husband was also in college, one of his classmates spotted an advertisement in the classified ads of the *New York Times* that read something to the effect of: "The perfume the woman was wearing who was with Peter Wood last night was such-and-such a perfume; was she wearing anything else?"

Although Peter knew nothing about the woman or the perfume, he enjoyed the teasing from his classmates the ad provoked.

Several years later, after Peter and I met and lived together for a few years, we moved to a small British Columbia interior town where I worked and Peter went to school. Soon after we settled there, we read a report in the local paper about a Peter Wood who had won a prize in a kayaking competition. After seeing an article about yet *another* Peter Wood who shared his interests and life-style, my Peter related to me the stories about the Peter Wood who had worked for the *New York Times*. My husband is a sensible, practical person, but he seemed to take these series of coincidences with Peter Woods and outdoor activities a little more seriously than I did – I found them amusing, but nothing more. Peter has a bit of a superstitious streak in him and was quite intrigued by the synchronization of names and events, and marvelled that there must be a reason or message behind the pattern that was evolving.

At this point, we had been living together for a few years and I was getting impatient with the status or rather lack of status of our relationship. I had begun to hint about getting married, and Peter had pretty much ignored the issue. My approach became more direct – I suggested we get married; Peter maintained his distance by avoiding the issue. Frustrated by my lack of progress on the subject, I came up with an idea, another approach that might speak to him more potently. I reasoned that if I converged on him through the media, speaking to him as another one of these coincidences of Peter Woods, that he would at least take notice and consider the concept of marriage. (And a tactical change might also give us both a bit of a break from my nagging about tying the knot.)

I took out a four-inch ad in the same paper that had reported about the other Peter Wood's kayaking achievements, an ad that was an expensive fifteen dollars for our tight budget, with Peter at school. The ad read: "PETER WOOD: A good woman is hard to find. Hold on to her." I considered simply proposing to him in print, but decided that a vaguer message, warning of the consequences if he didn't marry me, might speak to him on a more subconscious level than an out-and-out proposal. Remember, Peter is the sort of man who would never put his hat on the table for fear of some terrible thing happening to him or his family.

Peter saw the ad, and although his immediate reaction did not seem epiphanic or anything, he did seem embarrassed by the lengths to which I had gone to make him take note. If it was that important to me to get married, he said, sure, why not, let's get married. I considered the fifteen dollars I'd paid for the ad a sound investment in our future.

Two days later, when the wedding plans were in full swing, a friend told me he had just returned from the newspaper office where he had taken care of some personal business. While he was there, a call had come in from a Mrs. Peter Wood, wanting to know who had put that ad in the paper. She said that she was getting several sympathetic calls from friends and neighbours who hadn't realized that her marriage was in trouble. After hearing this, I was terribly embarrassed by my thoughtlessness about the consequences of my act to the kayaking champion and his wife. I called her right away and sheepishly explained the scenario. She did not seem amused by my scheme, but was, however, relieved that the ad concerned yet another Peter Wood, and not her own.

Brita Wood
The *real* Mrs. Peter Wood
Nelson, British Columbia

✉ After learning of the story of the Peter Woods of this world, I thought I just had to bring your attention to the plight of those few of us blessed with the Christian name of Cherry.

Now tell me honestly, how many women called Cherry do *you* know? I would be thrilled to hear that you know just one.

No one I have ever come across in my thirty-odd years has ever heard the name before. There is almost always a reaction, ranging from polite incredulity ("Is that short for something?") to outright hoots. Ever since I began mingling with the world at large at the age of three or so, when my nursery-school career started, I have endured the jeers and sneers of those ordinary mortals with plain old names like Peter.

For example, I once placed a collect call to my parents. When the operator asked for my name and I told her, she said caustically, "I said, your *name!*" "That *is* my name!" I bleated plaintively.

There is a great deal said these days about the influence a name has on a person's success rate in school and elsewhere. I hold my name responsible, in part, for the fact that I have never been able to take myself seriously enough to pursue a real, high-powered career. That theory has been deflated recently, though, when I saw in our local paper one of those little career announcements, complete with a small photo, of a very successful Halifax lawyer named Cherry Ferguson. Well, I wondered, how *did* she do it?

I don't want to cast any aspersions on her obviously considerable abilities, but it might have helped that she had been spared the added handicap of my surname. I was born Cherry Heard, so not only did people feel inspired to exercise their wit on my first name, they also had to of course make the standard joke, "Cherry Heard what?" Ho, ho, ho.

I grew up with high hopes of marrying someone with a sensible surname such as Ferguson, to name just one, and I had a terrible fear of marrying someone with the last name of Stone, Pye or maybe even Cherry!

As it was, my husband's name is Jean-Yves Lamarre. (Try living with the name Jean-Yves in Anglo-Canada!) If I had hoped for some respect with my new surname – and yes, you bet I was going to change Heard – I was sorely disappointed. When I proudly announced my engagement to this Lamarre person, my friends shrieked and hooted louder than ever, and then promptly nicknamed me Boom-Boom. So I am stuck with the label Cherry Lamarre, which sounds like what one might politely call a stage name.

I worked for a while as a secretary in a radar station in Alberta. My boss endeared himself to me forever by introducing me to a visiting bigwig and quipping, "This is Cherry Lamarre. No, she's not a candy bar, and she can type, too!"

So, Peter Brown, count your blessings! No one even cares if you can type.

Cherry Lamarre
Greenwood, Nova Scotia

✉ My name is Bruce Lyman Blakemore, which is a nice, unremarkable name except that I am a female. Bruce is not a nickname; it is my given name. I am named after my Aunt Bruce. She was what they then called a "blue baby," who was not expected to live. She was hastily baptized and named after my grandfather. Sixty-five years later Aunt Bruce is still alive and kicking.

When I was growing up my name never seemed to be an issue. It was just accepted by other kids, and I never gave it much thought. Only when I entered the "adult, working" world did the fun begin; the reaction ranged from suspicious bank tellers to boyfriends who were thought to be gay because they were going out with a "Bruce."

I find it amusing now to find new reactions to my name and am at the point of judging someone unimaginative if they say, "Your parents must have wanted a boy." One of my favourite reactions happened when I was introduced to a giant bear of a man, who broke into a broad grin and said, "Far out. My name is Claire."

I guess I have further complicated my life by retaining my own name after marriage. You see, I married a wonderful Mr. Jones but Bruce Jones didn't quite have the nice ring of Bruce Blakemore. The final clinker was when the minister pronounced us man and wife and turned to me and said, "Congratulations, Mrs. Smith." I realized then that I was entering a whole new ball game of mixed identities.

There is the question of title. I am no longer Miss, and Mrs. Bruce Blakemore makes my husband Bruce Blakemore. The supposed universal solvent "Ms." invariably gets the "s" slashed and changed to "r" by some well-meaning clerk. Lots of mail comes to "Mr." My husband has gotten very used to people calling him Bruce. He just grins and says, "Call me anything but late for supper."

Bruce Blakemore
Cape Negro, Nova Scotia

✉ I have lived under a great disability because persons called Parker are always menials. In *New Yorker* cartoons, the butlers and other flunkies are always called Parker. You may remember that in *Dr. Kildare*, Dr. Gillespie's nurse was Parker and he treated her so badly.

Many years ago, I had a phone call from a gentleman with an accent rather like mine, who said, "I wish you would tell your students your phone number because I am tired of giving them extensions on their essays." I discovered that his name was the same as mine – Graham Parker. We became friends. We also discovered that we were about the same age. We were born about twelve thousand miles apart (he in England and I in Australia) but we had much in common. We both had fathers named Eric. He had a wife named Nella, and my wife was known as Nette. We both had mothers-in-law named Marjorie. Our first-born were both named Simon. We talked about our second-born; I told the other Graham that we had two names chosen if the baby should happen to be a boy. Those names were Dominic or Duncan. Actually, we chose Duncan and the other Graham chose Dominic.

Over the years we have had great fun inviting each other to parties and anticipating the incredulity of the guests when both of us claimed to be Graham Parker. We have also shared each other's glory. He is an accomplished film director, while I used to publish articles on legal subjects, and we were always being credited with each other's accomplishments. Not all the confusions were happy ones. We were divorced from Nette and Nella at approximately the same time. Unfortunately, the income-tax people filed my court order in the other Graham's file. I had great difficulty in persuading the Department of National Revenue that there were two of us. At one stage, we both lived in the same house. The daily sorting of mail was a little hair-raising.

Suddenly, we discovered there was a more famous Graham Parker on the scene. Graham Parker and the Rumour was a well-known rock group for a few years. We concocted the idea of renting Maple Leaf Gardens with the announcement that "Graham Parker Plays His Greatest Hits." We would take a turntable down to the arena and play our Mantovani and Barry Manilow records. We thought we could really clean up but we chickened out because we thought we might be lynched. Actually the idea might have tickled Mr. Ballard's fancy, particularly if we had convinced him that Graham Parker and the Rumour were actually Russians.

Graham Parker
Toronto

✉ You should have asked me. I have the answer – and it is simple and obvious. Everyone should do what I did – marry someone with the same last name.

Not only does my son, Matthew, have two Snell parents, he also has four Snell grandparents and numerous Snell aunts, uncles and cousins on *both* sides of the family.

Now, I realize this won't be easy, especially for the Gzowskis and Feherengahazis of this world. I took the precaution of marrying the first eligible Snell I could track down. Luckily, I found him lovable for other reasons. Your listeners may have the same experience since I expect we are all well-disposed to our namesakes.

Because I expect that many will opt for my solution, I have a few pre-nuptial pointers to offer:

1. When having those questionable wedding invitations prepared, write a special note of reassurance to the printer.

2. When receiving the reply cards to your invitations, make very sure to distinguish between, for example, the groom's cousin and

the bride's brother with identical names. Keep those envelopes. This is why Canada Post gave us the postmark. Use it.

3. When dealing with officials at City Hall, be patient. Assure them repeatedly that, yes, you *do* understand the difference between birth and married names. This will take time. You may decide to forget the whole thing.

As more of us choose this straightforward solution to the name game, it will become less remarkable. Until that time, however, be prepared to give the following answers constantly: "No, we're not related," and "Yes, it's spelled the same way."

Carol Snell
Thomasburg, Ontario

✉ May I call you Peter? Gee! What a *nice* name. You could be ten years old, twenty, forty, fifty or seventy. But what about my name – Dorothy? Who names their babies Dorothy? I don't even have to see a person named Dorothy to know she will always be at least fifty. I have not been wrong yet.

My advice to all you expectant parents – don't give them a trendy name. Would you believe that Dorothy was a trendy name in the thirties?

One more thing: I never knew a Kevin in all my years in school in the thirties and forties.

Dorothy Vincent
Toronto

✉ A name like Peter isn't so bad. Think of the many times someone was called Patsy. Why did they pick that name, which was pinned on me? It has the connotation of flunky; it is even in my dictionary: "a person easily imposed upon." I wince every time I hear my name used in such a fashion. Maybe that is why I have the inability to say no to people. In any case, I would like to see a

Patsy club, one I could use to bop people on the head every time the name is used in such a way. All of us should unite – and urge the world to find another name. What about Peter?

Patsy MacMullin
Sydney, Nova Scotia

✉ I am not going to send you a list of ten of anything but, if I were to do so, the list would be titled Ten Things on *Morningside* That Make Me Cringe. Number one would be the expression you use so often – "Holy Nellie."

But may I suggest you resolve to not use it anymore? Use "Holy Peter" if you have to; "Holy" anyone – Peter was holy, wasn't he?

Thank you.

Nellie

RICHARD'S DAY

When I asked Richard Osler, the longest-surviving member of *Morningside*'s longest-surviving panel – our Wednesday column on business – to write up a day in his life, I didn't know (1) that he'd be going through the process of job change when I called or (2) that he'd include my call in his memoir.

But, as I ought to have remembered, Richard is Richard. The only thing missing from his account, I guess, is the distinctive cackle he often inserts into the otherwise most solemn of financial discussions.

The Business Column – A Life in a Day,
Wednesday, March 8, 1989

5:20 A.M. Finally, the alarm. I've been chasing it most of this sleepless night. My wife describes sleepless nights as "struggling with night vapours." Last night our eleven-month-old daughter, Tella, punctuated the night with ear-splitting screams; and I couldn't shake the refrain from Cyndi Lauper's hit tune "Time after Time." It echoes as I scramble into my suit. I know it's time to leave Pemberton Securities, my employer for almost nine years; time to find a new challenge. Coincidently, I have had two unsolicited job offers. Both look good.

5:40 A.M. What kind of day is this going to be? I am sitting in Susan's 1980 yellow Austin Mini, foot on the floor, going nowhere, wheels spinning uselessly. I am trapped in large ruts in the alley behind our house. Damn. I push the Mini up against a neighbour's garage door (I hope they don't need to get their car out) and take the big car.

5:59 A.M. Made it. I'm at the CBC studio, headphones on, files out. I scan clippings on today's topics. The Time-Warner Brothers merger (mega-marriage of conned-venience?) would create the second-largest media conglomerate in the world. Takeovers just keep happening, time after time.

Then there is the grounding of Three Buoys Houseboat Builders Ltd., another broken entrepreneurial dream. We've had our share: Northland Bank, the Principal Group, Dome Pete, Suipetro and Turbo. And there is the strange state of our stock markets – maybe they'll go up, maybe they'll go down.

As the news comes on in my headphones, Peter breaks in. I can hardly hear him over the news. "The International Monetary Fund (IMF) says Canada needs to cut $9 billion off our annual deficit," he says. "We're going to cover that off the top," I think I hear him say. What's the rest? I think I hear him talk about another edition of *Morningside Papers* and a chapter on the business column. Will I write it? He'll call me to talk about it. This day is getting curiouser and curiouser.

6:06 A.M. The news is over. Now the thirty seconds of dead airtime before the *Morningside* theme song hits my ears. How many times is it now? Forty times a year for six and a half years, minus about four months in 1987. That makes about two hundred and forty times or sixty hours – hard to believe.

When Sandy Ross called me seven years ago to see if I would be part of a weekly column to discuss business, I never thought I would be making the *Morningside* theme song a once-a-week fix-

ture in my life. Sandy, one of Canada's first and best full-time
magazine business writers, had been in Calgary to start up the ill-
fated *Energy Magazine*. When it went down the drain along with
oil prices in the early 1980s, Sandy went back to Toronto and
initiated a number of new ventures. The *Morningside* column was
one of those.

"Good morning all."

"Good morning, Peter." We are on air, live in Halifax and Newfoundland. (Dead everywhere else?) It's nine o'clock in those
places and much earlier everywhere else. Our words begin a cross-
country journey that will take four hours.

Dianne Francis and Barbara Kinnear hate the deficit. But this
morning they are attacking it with uncustomary gusto. How many
times have we discussed this topic? It's probably Canada's most
disturbing problem. If Richard Six-pack Canadian was making
$40,000 a year, spending $52,000 a year and was in hock for
$120,000, he would be a financial goner. Yet this is exactly where
Canada stands today.

"Canada is the next Brazil," Dianne Francis exclaims. She is
entertainment – incisive, outspoken and irrepressibly well-
informed. She *is* business reporting in Canada. Not everyone is
happy with her astringent remarks, but Dianne doesn't seem to
be afraid of anything or anyone. Last year she was slapped with
two or three lawsuits, and she didn't miss a beat.

I can't think of the business column without Dianne, but she
didn't become a regular until the winter of 1984. In the first year,
after Sandy left, I was joined by Seymour Freidland, a business
columnist at the *Financial Times* of Canada and a university professor. In those days business was not the popular media subject
it is now. We wanted to make it exciting – because it *is*.

Business is not just about interest rates, the dollar and earnings
reports. It's about daring winners, and about the sons who sue
them (Robert Campeau). It's about wealthy families that break
apart in anger and bitterness (the Billes family of Canadian Tire;

the Bingham family of Louisville, Kentucky). It's about devastating defeats (the collapse of the Principal Group; the destruction of Osler Inc. – no relation). There is egomania (all the big oil takeovers in the early 1980s). There's folly (Conrad Black selling Norcan to the Bronfmans when oil prices were low) and finesse (Conrad Black buying the near-bankrupt *Daily Telegraph* and making it a big money winner). There's Maxwell and Murdoch, Trump and Ted Turner, Pickens and Perot, Belzberg and Bronfman, Rogers and Reisman. There are partners who make it (Cohen and Rueben of Central Trust) and those who don't (Kaye and Posluns of Dylex).

Chris Waddell, who was a *Financial Post* writer, joined me in the second year. His attention to facts and details combined with a low-key but approachable manner were a great foil for my periodic spontaneous outbursts. Then Dianne joined us, and Chris kept us on track.

6:18 A.M. The demise of Three Buoys Houseboats, our last topic of today's show. Two kids barely out of school dreamt up a scheme to build houseboats and rent them on Shuswap Lake, about five hundred miles west of Calgary in British Columbia. Five boats quickly turned into five hundred and fifty. Soon Three Buoys had marinas and rental boats scattered across North America. It was a good idea, and it needed good management. It didn't get it. Everyone was having too much fun – parties and fast cars. Then bankruptcy, and banks that want their money back after they gave it away so easily.

Whether it's Three Buoys Houseboats, Apple Computer or Dome Petroleum, the result is often the same – the entrepreneur who made the company great can't keep it going.

6:24 A.M. Sign off. One part of my day is finished and another begins. In six minutes the Toronto Stock Exchange opens. For six and a half hours we'll match wits with people we can't see. Some call it investing, others gambling. I call it my livelihood.

There's nothing like it. For almost nine years I have made a living through the market. Not by trading, but through analysis and deal-making. For six years I was an oil and gas analyst; I monitored companies and industry trends. It was my job to advise clients when to buy or sell oil stocks in general, and which to buy or sell in particular. In this business, the highs are high, but, boy, the lows are low. Your stocks move up or down every day – and so do you.

What's the thrill? It's being able to match yourself against the "market" – that funny amalgam of hopes and fears – and win. The key is to match your hope against someone else's fear, and their fear against your hope. It's like this: when I buy a stock I think it's going to go up in price. The people selling don't think so, or they wouldn't sell. Similarly, when I sell I think the stock is going for a tumble, unlike the folks who are buying.

The market teaches you how to be an independent thinker. If you don't learn to think, the market will make you humble – and broke. Once in a while, gurus appear who seem to have figured the market out. Through the modern-day equivalent of reading the entrails of chickens, they perform mathematical wizardry on the market's chaos of numbers. Trends, chart lines, regression analysis, fundamental analysis, technical analysis. The gurus come . . . then they go. Remember Joe Granville, the seer of seers? He is credited with kicking off the 1982 market crash. (He's now Joe Who.)

The tricky part of investing is how to dodge accepted truths. Usually when you buy (or sell) based on one of those truths it is goodbye money time. One accepted truth in Calgary was that oil prices would never collapse, just drop slowly for a short time. My journal helps me remember:

February 3, 1986   The Dow Jones average has climbed above 1,600 but oil – the grease of my livelihood – has collapsed; it is now less than $15 per barrel. The Toronto Stock Exchange oil index has fallen to less than 2,800 for the first time in three years. Some other dreams exploded this week. The space shuttle Challenger has gone, transformed from a soaring symbol of American know-how into a shocking fireball of failure, raining debris on the ocean near the cape, and despair and grief around the world.

February 12, 1986 Life is difficult. (What an understate-
ment!) Just finished the radio show with Peter. Last week the
dollar plunged to 69¢ U.S., and I said it could fall farther. But
Canadian government intervention and buying power have
snapped it back to 71.5¢. The oils are down again, 2,750 and
dropping. Meanwhile the Dow Jones average keeps defying
gravity and has reached 1,660. It's been tough sledding these
past few days. Being an analyst specializing in oil, a crazy com-
modity controlled by people half a world away, has always been
hard, but this is the hardest. I did not get people to sell enough
before the crash. We recommended only three stocks – Poco,
Renaissance and Canadian Roxy – but we didn't say sell everything else. We should have.

February 19, 1986 The oil price hits $14.30 and the TSE oil
composite dives below 2,600. My morale sinks, too, and I struggle with a sense of helplessness as the oil world collapses about
me. Just three months ago oil was $31.70 a barrel.

February 22, 1986 Oil prices have hit $13.50 a barrel. I feel
more positive – what the hell.

These journal entries tell a story. Although prices were at disas-
trously low levels, this was the midnight when noon is born. Anyone who bought Poco and Renaissance, for example, would have
made a small fortune. By May 1986, both were at more than $8
per share; a year later, Poco was $20 per share and Renaissance
reached $34 per share. Investing is no game for the weak of heart.

The shock of the oil-price massacre of 1986 seemed like kid's
stuff compared to the pyrotechnics of the stock market meltdown
in October 1987. I wasn't on the business column that fall – the
rampant bull market of 1987, when we seemed to be doing a deal
a day, kept me too busy – but I talked to Peter the day after Black
Monday. That's also when Barbara Kinnear first came on air. She
was so articulate and expressive that she seemed a natural to join
the column. And she did, in early 1988.

On Black Monday, panic was the order of the day. Business

commentators world-wide were predicting an economic crash that would make the crash of 1929 look like a picnic. Mike Ryan, Pemberton's market strategist, had a different view: he claimed that the market had been over-valued, and was overdue for a correction. The economy of the United States and Canada looked robust, he said, and he wouldn't buy the argument that the market was always an accurate predictor of a market slow-down. He pointed out that the market had predicted eight of the past two recessions. (Mike may have been right, but a year later he fell victim to management politics and was unceremoniously fired. Business is never dull.) I gave Mike's view to Peter that morning, and I had my fingers crossed. Here is what I wrote in my journal:

Friday, October 16, 1987 Wow! Shaky turns to shock. The market indices have been mugged, manhandled and pistol-whipped in a two-week beating. Is the worst over, or has it just begun? The market (the Dow Jones) strutted to a high of 2,722.4 in August and closed yesterday at 2,355.1, down a stomach-turning 13.5%. Rough stuff, but kid's play compared to the 12.8% collapse on October 28, 1929.

Monday, October 19, 1987 Massacre Monday, Malevolent Monday, Black Monday. Shocked. Pummelled. Devastated. Stock markets, those barometers of human emotions, got socked by a low-pressure system unparalleled in modern financial history. The Dow Jones lost 197 points on Friday, and today there was a 508-point plunge. Close to $700 billion of value was wiped out across the globe. The truth was that prices were too high – about forty per cent too high. My wife reminded me that I had been predicting a correction for a long time. I hadn't done much about it because I was surrounded by people who thought everything was fine. Now everyone will be trying to figure out how bad it really is. Out of this cocoon the next soaring butterfly of optimism will be born.

Friday, October 23, 1987 The week is over. Violent swings of mood and money madness. By Monday night expectations were shattered and fear reigned. I had no cash. That's all I could think about. We joked about lost jobs, no bonuses. We talked of digging in. On Wednesday, in a momentary upturn of the market, I was able to sell some Pemberton shares. Thursday was quiet. A sense of resignation took over. The initial shock had worn off.

Well, the market did not collapse further, but the volume of trading did. The Dow Jones average stands at about 2,300 now, but my business has seen a staggering drop in revenues. Before the crash, I often saw sixty million shares trade on the Toronto Stock Exchange. After the crash, trading on some days was less than fifteen million shares. Our staff has been cut by one-quarter, and the Stock Exchange is not a fun place to be. [Note: two weeks after this article was written, Pemberton Securities was taken over by RBC Dominion Securities – which is controlled by the Royal Bank.]

The big banks have bought the biggest firms in our business, and the days of easy money are probably over. As the conservative thinking of the banks seeps into the brokerage houses, many of us will no longer feel at home in the business. That's why, after nine years, I want out. Even if Pemberton Securities survives in the new competitive world, it won't be the same.

10:20 A.M. We got the order! After months of negotiations, we have been hired to sell a small oil company worth about $25 million. This kind of "fee" business is keeping us alive during these difficult times. In the past year and a half, more than $14 billion of oil and gas assets have changed hands. It's unprecedented. In most cases, these deals have investment bankers on both sides. The fees can be juicy.

10:45 A.M. This is turning out to be a good day. Martin Fortier, president of Finex Capital Corporation, just called. He wants me to meet with him and his partner, Weiland Wettstein, later in the day. These guys are deal doers. Their partner is the Belzberg family, from Vancouver. In just two years Finex has used its deal-making ability to gain control of about $150 million of assets. They want to expand their activities. I think this is the opportunity I have been waiting for.

2:05 P.M. Another turn-around story. Ken Lambert, president of Coho Resources, called to tell me about a $20 million deal with an Australian company. The money will be used to drill in Mississippi. Coho Resources, now worth more than $150 million, was on the financial ropes three years ago. The company had no money to drill on its properties in Mississippi – but only by drilling those properties could it hope to survive. Even if it got some money, the odds were long – in the late 1970s and early 1980s, more than $4 billion was lost by Canadian companies exploring in the United States.

Lambert did raise some money, more than $6 million, and immediately started to drill. The first well cost about $300,000 U.S., and initial indications looked good. When a well looks as if it will be successful, high-quality pipe, called casing, is put into the hole as a lining. Halfway down the ten-thousand-foot well, the casing parted and fell one mile to the bottom of the well. The well was destroyed, and another one had to be drilled from scratch. Not a good way to start a company-saving program.

Through the new well, Coho discovered an oil field that now produces about two thousand barrels a day. Another major field was discovered under the town of Laurel, Mississippi, and is now producing close to four thousand barrels a day. Coho now has a yearly cash flow of more than $10 million, and a share price in excess of $5 per share. That's a turn-around story. That's business.

Business is "hot" news today. The trouble is that the flashiest or hastiest business types are the ones we most often hear about. We read about Boesky, the man who said, "Greed is all right, by the way," and paid a record-breaking $100-million fine for inside trading. We read about junk-bond king Mike Miliken, fingered by Boesky. Miliken's firm pays a fine of more than $700 million for illegal activities, and Miliken is charged by regulators who hope to recover more than $1.8 billion U.S. if they prove his guilt. These are the bad guys.

We read about Robert Campeau, Garth Drabinsky, the Bronfmans, the Reichmanns, and how they turn millions into billions. These guys may not always be nice guys, but in their own ways they are good guys. Most important, they are not just businessmen. They have dreams and visions and ambitions, like most of us. The difference is that they take risks. They bet fearlessly on their own ideas. We don't always like them or their goals or their rewards. But they are not invincible. What fascinates me is how they climb and how they fall and sometimes how they climb again.

Money is the score-card that shows how they make it and how they lose it. Making it is sometimes the easy part. Learning how to keep it and make it grow is the tricky part. Ask a lot of the fancy oil men who were worth millions ten years ago. Money is a hard taskmaster. It tends to get those who treat it lightly.

We can take a front-row seat and watch these guys. The referees are the regulators. They keep the game honest for the most part. But remember, except for the millions they make or lose, those guys in the business ring battling it out are remarkably like you and me.

That's where the *Morningside* business column comes in – it brings the financial giants into our living rooms. I think of business as a book of great stories. The stories differ, but they all have the good guys and the bad guys fighting it out for high stakes. We get to see all the drama, colour and tension. I hope the column has brought business alive for many listeners. Hate it or love it, the business of business is a great story.

Richard Osler
Calgary

CHRIS'S YEAR

Chris Czajkowski (it's pronounced "Tchaikovsky") is, like Krista Munroe, a pillar of the *Morningside Papers*. But, unlike Krista and a lot of other correspondents whose personal acquaintance I've made over the years, she remains only a literary presence in my life – or, occasionally, when she returns a message, a faintly accented (from England, where she was born) voice on the phone.

No wonder. Chris lives most of the time, as she said in the first letter she wrote in 1985, "seventy-five miles from a store, and twenty-five miles from a road," in the wilds of the Bella Coola Valley of British Columbia. There, when she has time, she writes about her extraordinary life, and her letters have become a regular feature of *Morningside* – as they have of these *Papers*.

To my delight, I can also tell you that we won't be able to keep her gifts to ourselves much longer. Next year, Camden House will publish a more complete account of Chris's discovery of the Canadian wilderness, and even before that – this Christmas, in fact – Aquarelle Press of Louisiana is bringing out a collection of her letters and drawings from a trip through the Arctic. Here, as she wrote them for us, are some events in a year in her life.

March 13

I am writing this by a camp fire on the edge of a large, snow-covered lake. The sun has set behind me and the last of its orange light is fading. Five miles across the lake the horizon is low, and the north sky is green and endless. A moon rides high among the lodge-pole pines above my head. It is utterly quiet. No drip, no stir of wind, no movement anywhere.

I am about halfway along the lake. For a couple of hours, the line of my tracks has stretched unbroken behind me, but ahead are dark patches of open water. I will tackle that area in the morning when I am no longer tired and less likely to be careless.

The fire has sunk deep into the snow, and it is getting hard to see what I am writing. The temperature has dropped, and it is beginning to freeze.

March 14

Tonight, I dwell in luxury. I write by candle-light in a cabin belonging to a trapper. I sit on a wooden box close to the warped and rusty tin stove made from a five-gallon gas can. The rest of the furniture consists of a few log rounds for seats, and a shelf holding plates, books, a bit of food and a jar full of boxes of matches. My dog is flopped out on the wood-chip floor. Split firewood, gas cans and snowmobile parts litter the porch, and beyond is the hitch rail for the horses, almost buried in snow. There must be three or four feet out there.

There was a freezing fog at first light, and a film of tiny crystals whitened my sleeping bag. I stuffed it, damp as it was, into my pack while the porridge boiled. Real stick-to-the-ribs stuff it was, and it stuck to the pot, too, but I scraped off what I could with a numbing handful of coarse snow before making the tea. Then back onto the ice, which the fog had turned into a formless world of white. I donned the snowshoes for extra safety and gave all the suspicious areas a very wide berth.

Once off the lake, I picked up the trapper's snowmobile trail through the forest. Trapping was finished four weeks ago, but the faint depression in the snow was firm enough so I could discard my snowshoes. The sun, which rises early in this high country, had banished the fog and striped the trail with tree shadows. How clean and fresh this snow was, so different from the patchy, dirty ice I had left at home.

The snowmobile track ended all too soon. The only signs of the way were blazes on the pines. A slash of the axe creates a wound that fills with sap and hardens into a golden mass and stands out like a flag on the dark trunk. But some of the blaze trees had fallen over or been buried in snow, and in places they were hard to find. The trees also hid the mountains. I have no sense of direction whatsoever, but I could not go far wrong, for the river ran constantly on my right, and its chatter was my guide. It was a beautiful river. Slabs of clearest water mirrored the dark trees and wound among shelves of ice loaded with whorls of snow like whipped cream. Sometimes the water rushed through ice-choked falls and hid behind a veil of icicles, or slipped silently beneath an unbroken blanket of white. The mountains were beginning to surround me, and they reared into the sunlight above the forest. Some day I would climb them.

The travelling was heavy and slow. The dog and I were packing two extra days of food in case of emergencies, and I was carrying far too many clothes for this mild, spring-like weather. But at least the dog didn't sink, or I would have had to add her ten-pound load to mine.

It was a relief to hit snowmobile marks again. I could travel three times as fast. I came to the foot of a lake shaped like a four-mile-long question mark. Near the outlet, under a couple of densely branched spruces, was a small patch of bare ground, and I built a fire for tea. Under the other spruce was a fox trap in a little tunnel of twigs that led to the base of the trunk. I was glad that the season was finished and there were no trapped animals to look at. It is not a way of life I could contemplate.

But the trapper who operates here is like a king in this vast stretch of country. He has been doing it all his life, and he has long ago learned to manage his species so they continue to multiply. He knows no other way to make a living in the bush, for he has no patience with the kind of businessmen who spend a couple of weeks a year blasting at big game. He could not be an outfitter, and how could you put a man like that into a grocery store? I had reason to be grateful to him, for without the information about the trails and cabins, I could not have attempted this trip. No one else knew much about this area.

Query Lake had a mushy snow cover, and I plodded onto it in snowshoes. I assumed the ice would be safe, but after a while I chopped a hole. To my horror, I broke through the weak white snow-ice in a couple of inches, and water started to well through. I got off that lake as if I were walking on newly laid eggs. Afterwards I realized the water must have been overflow on top of a firm base, but at the time I took no chances, and round the edge I went.

The cabin was not far from the head of the lake. I filled it full of smoke before I remembered to climb on the roof and remove the can from the stove-pipe. It has become too hot in here, and I have opened the door to see the moon shining on the snow. Owls are calling, and my sleeping bag is warm and dry. The wood-chip floor looks very inviting.

March 15: noon

It froze hard during the night, and the snow was a winter traveller's dream, firm and crisp and sparkling in the hazy morning sun. The open water in the river had a new skin of opaque ice, and the trees were a soft goldy green. We had only seven miles to go, and I took a day pack and left the dog unladen. She was in seventh heaven as she sped over the pristine surface, scooping up mouthfuls of snow and reading messages that were invisible to me. We were climbing steadily, and quite suddenly the surface grew powdery and much looser. Precipitation, which would fall as rain lower down, would produce snow at this altitude of five thousand feet. I stepped onto another lake, three miles long and one wide, and tested the ice immediately. There was a foot of white snow on top, four inches of slush, then firm ice. I couldn't see it, for water ran onto it faster than I could shovel it off. But it sounded good, and I launched myself towards the rocky point that was my destination.

My time at Lonesome Lake is coming to an end. The property is to be sold, and rather than wait for the uncertainty of negotiating with new owners, I have staked a claim on Crown land. It is outside Tweedsmuir Park, but close to the boundary and only two days' walk from my present house. But the direct route involves a series of steep bluffs, easy enough in the summer but very difficult at this time of the year, and I have approached the point from the opposite direction.

The lake, which has no name, is surrounded by mountains, the highest being Monarch at twelve thousand feet. Today, they are half-hidden by a light snow that blurs the ink as I write. A keen wind whips the little fire, which is melting snow for tea, and I am glad, after all, that I have packed my down coat so many miles.

The point is no stranger to the wind, for the snow has been scalloped into great drifts, and the stunted trees have bowed to the relentless pressure. It is not a very practical place to build, for materials are scarce, and it is too rocky to use a horse, but aesthetically it is fabulous. Life would be dull if we stuck to practicalities.

I must not dream too vividly: the land office may refuse to let me have the place. I applied last fall, but bureaucracy works slowly. Wish me luck.

I have fished the pine needles out of the tea and drunk it, and the fire has died down to ashes. The snow has quit, and soft blue patches are appearing in the sky. Even Mount Monarch and his henchmen are beginning to thrust rocky spurs out of the cloud. I must start back, or I will not make the cabin before dark.

March 16

Coming out was much easier. I no longer had to search for the route, and knowing what to expect took away some of the fatigue. Also, I was going down.

It was a dull morning but not too cold, and by mid-afternoon the fresh skiff of snow began to grow sticky and clog onto the bottom of my snowshoes. A wolf had used my incoming tracks, placing each of his paws in the depressions I had made. I tried to do the same, but found the unevenness of my stride so tiring that it was easier to stumble on afresh. The trees were bare of snow and they soughed in the wind. The dark trunks hung from the mass of foliage like a paper collage. One or two deformed tops retained a piled dollop of snow, and they reminded me of ice-cream cones. After days of trail rations, I was beginning to fantasize about food.

I made such good progress that I decided to go out in one day. How strange to emerge from the womb of the mountains onto this enormous sea of white with a dark slash for a horizon. The sky was a muddy yellow, and ghostly fingers of snowshowers began to march across the ice. The wind drove the frozen pellets into my face, and the surface of the snow began to move in hissing skeins.

The final half of the lake was demoralizing. For six miles I could see the ranch at the end of the road every step of the way. On the flat, unyielding ice, my back and legs were slowly cramping up, and I never seemed to be getting any closer. In the end I had to play silly games, like forcing myself not to look up for a thousand steps, and that way I could see I had made progress.

It was almost dark as I stumbled through the looser snow onto the shore. In three or so days I had travelled seventy miles, and I had one more to go before finding friends and supper. Did I really want to live so far from a neighbour, with this long and lonely trek to reach a friend? Then I thought of the cleanness of that silent winter wilderness, and I knew I would not be satisfied till I had tried.

Regards,
Chris

April

There can be few places more beautiful than the Bella Coola Valley in spring. The leaves open early, but slowly. For weeks the trees are misted with spring green, and the scent of balsam pours from the cottonwood buds. The steep valley walls are rich and dark and patched with cloud shadow. The freshly painted peaks soar blinding white among towering columns of vapour, while roaring avalanches crash down their sheer northern faces.

Like most of the West, we have had an easy winter. Not that it has been much warmer than usual, but there have been no cold spells. The temperature hovered around freezing, and where the river splashed over rocks and logjams, the spray froze onto overhanging branches and created a fantasy world. Each swollen icicle was adorned with a chandelier-like fringe of frills and knobs. But the river did not freeze over: there were no broken ice slabs along its edge, and parts of the lake remained unsafe. Only once was I able to walk its full length.

I saw the wolves again in the new year, on a lake three miles upstream. I was counting birds and had left the trail to follow the braided channels of the river, looking for dippers. The wolves saw me the moment I stepped from the trees. They were lying on the ice about a mile away. Seven jumped up and ran up the nearby mountain. The other three crossed the lake, stopping every few yards to bark and howl – not the kind of singing that travels so far on a moonlit night but a disgruntled sound, like a chained dog.

I heard them for a while, and later found their tracks leading out of the valley. They were gone for about three weeks, and then they were back, yipping and barking in the forest. Although I found the remains of several kills, I never saw them again.

The mother moose and her two yearling calves, whom I'd seen frequently through the winter, disappeared from the lagoon for a while. I feared they had succumbed to predators. But just before the snow melted, when the wolf pack had split into small groups and pairs, no doubt to have their young, the moose were back again, feeding unconcernedly in the willows as I watched them from the canoe hardly more than a paddle length away. And when the snow had gone, and the deer had come down from the sunny ridges in groups to feed on the new growth, as they always do, there seemed to be just as many as ever, staring bat-eared from the forest.

The ice went out of the lake three weeks early, and I began the long business of packing all my possessions down to the lagoon so that they could be flown out to Nimpo. What a terrible amount of stuff I have accumulated these last four years. The walls of my house are bare and lonely, and I look at these logs that I raised myself and remember the problems of each of them, and the place where once they grew. And as I sit on my porch in the sunshine, while the blue grouse boom on the mountain and the river rolls at my feet, I know it will be hard to say goodbye.

For the next couple of months I will be tree planting and living in a camp with thirty others, a prospect that I, who love my isolation, find somewhat daunting. But I need the money to go to the Arctic to visit friends who are working in Cambridge Bay. For the summer I will camp on the tundra and paint the flowers and the sea ice and the wonderful northern light until the weather drives me south. It is only then that I will know if I will have title to the Crown land I staked last fall. I don't know where I will spend the winter, for even if my claim is accepted, I will not be able to build a shelter in time. But something will turn up – it always does.

Tomorrow I will start at daybreak and slip down the lake in the early dawn to a future that has no shape – a good situation to be in as I approach middle age. But whatever happens in my second life, the one that begins at forty, I know that the wilderness will be a part of it, for I cannot live without it.

Yours,
Chris

October

There was a quarter of an inch of ice over the silty shallows at the end of Miner Lake. We smashed it with our boots, tensing our muscles for the resistance and the sudden, slithery crash into the uncertain ooze below, until we had a channel wide enough for the canoe to reach open water. It was my canoe, which had been strapped to the floats of a Beaver and flown out of Lonesome Lake with the last of my possessions the day before. Now it was piled full of freight. The dog got in the middle, and Sam got in the back. As we slid away from the embrace of the trees into the calm bowl of water, the mountains swung into view: Perkin's Peak with its sharply conical summit and its rash of hematite mines long disused, an unnamed plateau with impressive bulbous bluffs, and between them, the deep, U-shaped cut of the river valley with the jumble of the Pantheon Range beyond.

The lake was long and thin, but the sides were little more than hills, for we were already at four thousand feet and on the very fringe of the mountains. Dense green spruce flowed to the water's edge to the south. To the north, on the sunny side of the lake, lodge-pole pine straggled brokenly over the curve of land. There was enough space between the trees so that the light could penetrate and the grass could grow. A wave of pine-bark beetle had killed many of the mature trees a couple of years before, and they stood in clumps like venerable ghosts, their tangles of naked twigs clutched densely about them. Among them grew stunted, spidery, white-barked aspens; gold-green, feathery young pines; and the bluer spires of spruce. They were still attractive, these dead trees, but when they rot and the wind blows them over, they will tumble like ninepins. It will be difficult to travel through the country for a while.

We paddled for three miles, shedding layers of clothes as the climbing sun burned off the frost and Sam turned the canoe around a little point among the pines. "It's just past that rock," he said, but I could not spot it although I did see the weathered poles nailed to trees where he had once corralled his horses. Then the canoe squeaked against a dead stick that leaned into the water, and the cabin was before us. I wondered how I could have missed it, but the pale gold logs in the pale gold grass, screened by trees and dappled by their shadows, were invisible until you knew they were there.

Sam is a log-house builder. He manufactures massive, smooth, clean-jointed edifices on his ranch near Kleena Kleene, then ships them to the buyer's site and reconstructs them like giant Lego sets. This cabin was his first, built when he and his wife were fresh out of the city fourteen years ago. I was surprised, then relieved in a shamefaced sort of way, to see that his initial joinery had been just as crude as mine at Lonesome Lake. The logs were small, and had been felled and peeled green when the sap was running. They had a silky texture free of axe marks and huge, badly chinked gaps through which the sun winked in little gleams. The floor was made of axe-hewn poles, uneven and rough, worn and comfortable-looking, but I could see daylight there, too, and I hoped the snow would come before the cold so that I would be able to bank the walls and seal the drafts. The door was perhaps the most solid thing about the place: hewn trees placed upright and braced with heavy horizontals and diagonals. "It must have weighed two hundred pounds when I built it," said Sam a little self-consciously. "It was as green as I was, then."

Sam checked the stove-pipes and replaced a couple of sections, then showed me the areas where the roof needed patching. He felled several dead pines that might have blown onto the cabin. After I have bucked those up and cut down a few more, there will be an unlimited supply of stove wood for the winter, cured on the hoof, as it were.

There is a different quality to the air on this high, dry plateau in the interior of British Columbia. It is as sharp and clear as glass, and there is a tactile brittleness to the vegetation. The dark pine bark is scratchy and painful to touch; the grass stiff and sere, white-gold and burnished by the sun and frost. The autumn leaves are sugar-crisp, and little puffs of silky dust float up at the fall of a foot. When we launched the canoe into the lake again and paddled back to the vehicles, the sun was close to the mountains, and so clear in the taut drum of the sky that the molten-steel shaft of its reflection in the water burned red through our eyelids, and was impossible to look at. So we steered by the hills to the right and the left of us, until we hit the blue, frost-nipped mountain shadow and glided through the shallow silt to the shore. Sam climbed into his truck and drove over the bumpy logging road to Kleena Kleene. I loaded the canoe and pushed it once more into the lake.

I would have to get everything up to the cabin before the lake froze and snow blocked the road. And I would have to fix the roof, cut and haul the firewood and chink the walls before the weather turned bad, which it sometimes does before the end of October in this part of the world. But as I paddled slowly down the lake, the canoe sluggish with its overload of freight and my head full of logistics, the silence and peace and aloneness of the wilderness crept into my soul. The soft, rhythmic plop and bubble of the paddle seemed loud in the stillness, and a troop of ducks bobbed gently on the silver shimmer of my shadowy wake. And as the first star shone like a lamp in the clear, frost-green sky, I thought of the little cabin that was to be my home for the winter, blending like a deer into the grey-gold forest, and I was well content.

Regards,
Chris

8 December

I have been nibbling at the edges of your life for two and a half years now since I started writing about Lonesome Lake. But it was not until recently that you erupted, with a bang, into mine.

In one of the Lonesome Lake letters I mentioned the poor radio reception, and the fact that I could not pick up CBC during the day; so I never heard your program. It was only when I went out for mail at the end of the month that I would hear from friends that my letter had been read.

It was hard for me, who had had no experience as a writer, to communicate with a faceless name belonging to an institution that was, as far as I was concerned, as remote as the moon. Once you mentioned Stuart McLean in a letter, referring to him as if he were a household word. Who in the world, I wondered, was Stuart McLean?

A piece of copper wire, twenty feet long, has changed all that.

At Miner Lake, radio reception seemed, at first, even worse. But my neighbours showed me a marvellous device that everyone up here is familiar with. An aerial by itself does not work. But take a piece of thin, insulated copper wire twenty feet long, attach one end to the aerial and the other to the ground, feed the rest through a hole in the wall, wind it into a tight coil about six inches across, then tape the coil to the back of the radio. You have to move the coil about until you hit the right spot. Now I can receive CBC all day. It's not good reception, for it sometimes fades away, and there are always a couple of other stations nudging in. One manifests itself as a monotonous series of croaks, no doubt the bass beat of some rock music program, and the other is in the rhythm of a speaking voice, but so distorted that the words are indistinguishable, and it sounds like a message from a little green man on Mars. There is also a whistle that rises and falls in intensity with the volume of the CBC signal. Occasionally the aliens win, but most of the time I can hear *Morningside*. It has changed my life. I will now sit inside when the sun is shining. I have no clock, but suddenly I am in danger of succumbing to a nine-to-twelve, five-day week. Does this mean I may be a candidate for such suburban afflictions as "the Monday morning feeling"?

Yours,
Chris

21 December

The snow has come quietly to Miner Lake. There was a sprinkling, a thaw, an inch, another thaw, then every second day or so the small white flakes would spin dreamily from a soft, grey sky, until gradually they began to accumulate. This snow has a completely different texture to the flat, wet flakes of the coast. Instead of packing so readily to ice as it usually did at Lonesome Lake, it remains fluffy and fragile, even when the temperature is above freezing.

On the steep, south-facing slopes behind the cabin, where some of it melts, the brittle grass pokes through like the bristles on an old broom, each stalk a separate being, an exclamation mark, attached to the delicate, purple brush stroke of its shadow.

Round the cabin there are eight inches, but it is deeper on top of the hill over which I must travel before I can go down to the highway. I broke trail up there today, for I am going out tomorrow, and I wanted to make the start of my journey easier. I could not see the lake from the top – it was hidden in a forested fold of land – but the view of the mountains was spectacular. All around, blue-shadowed peaks, haloed by the writhing, golden flames of sunlit, wind-blown snow, stood stark against the cold, winter-green sky. I was surprised to find a snow-machine track on the logging road, drifted in by the wind. I had heard no one and had assumed I was the only human being for miles.

The lake froze in November, then broke up in a wild storm, but it froze again as soon as the wind dropped, although it was not very cold. That was the end of canoeing, and I must now chop ice every day to fill the water bucket.

I have never had much opportunity to ski. At Lonesome Lake, the snow was always too wet, too thin or too icy, and the country was steep and rugged, and full of boulders and windfalls. Up here, I anticipated ideal conditions, and I imagined myself shushing with long, crystal-glittering glides over the smooth white sheet of the lake or floating effortlessly down the logging roads. But things never quite work out as one expects. On land, my feet, skis and all, sank in above the ankles. The skis snarled on hidden rocks and branches, causing me to slither and lurch like a drunkard. Progress with skis was slower than without them. When the ice was a couple of inches thick on the lake, I ventured onto it, shuffling cautiously round the edge (yes, I know it's supposed to be safer in the middle, but if I went through close to land, I would not sink far, and the proximity of solid ground was comforting). After a day or two, I was striding out with confidence. This was more like it: I would soon be skiing like a professional.

Suddenly, with a jerk, the skis stopped dead. I could not move them forwards or backwards. When I tried to lift them, it felt as though a ton weight was anchoring them to the ground. I had discovered overflow.

I grew up in England, and spent a decade in the Southern Hemisphere before coming to this country eight years ago. Canadian winters are still something of a novelty to me. The behaviour of water in sub-zero temperatures never ceases to fascinate me.

I had seen spring holes and suspicious dark patches in parts of the lake, and had given them a wide berth. But water had leaked insidiously from these cracks and punctures and had percolated around them for yards, hidden by the bland, white blanket on top. The moment the skis hit the soggy grey stuff lurking underneath, the stuff clogged onto them in great, sodden lumps, and every scrap had to be scraped off or the skis would be useless. I was delighted when the mild weather blew away and the sky cleared to a diamond blue. A hard freeze was just what was needed to get rid of this mess. Not a bit of it: it was worse. The cold had cracked the ice in many places, sometimes clear across the lake, and the overflow was everywhere. My journeys were reduced to careful slithers, frequent miscalculations and endless stops to clean the skis. Now, I can understand how the weight of the snow would push the ice down and cause the water to well through, but why on earth, at twenty degrees below zero, doesn't the blasted stuff freeze?

Oh, well, I go down to the Bella Coola Valley tomorrow for the winter solstice. There is probably no snow down there at all. It will probably be raining, and the valley will be dark and gloomy and choked with cloud. Christmas will be wonderful with my friends, but I'm glad I'll have the snow to come back to.

Yours,
Chris

February

When I arrived at Miner Lake after my last mail trip, there were snow-machine tracks in front of the cabin. It was the first human sign I'd seen there since before Christmas. The cabin hadn't been locked, and it was plain that someone had spent the night. Dishes had been moved around, and the radio had been tuned to the William's Lake station, which I never listen to. Although the woodpile by the stove was much the same size as when I'd left it, the chunks of wood had been split differently, and they were powdered with snow – as if they'd only recently been brought in. My visitor must have left only that morning, for there was barely half an inch of ice on my water-hole, and there's always at least an inch if left overnight.

A few days later, my visitor returned. Dave Lulua is a Chilcotin Indian from the Redstone reserve. He comes into this country every year to operate the trapline that has belonged to his family for three generations. His low-roofed, dirt-floored cabin lies about four miles down the valley past the end of the lake. The day he'd come in from the road, pulling his supplies behind him like a barge on a sled, the snow had been too soft and deep to break trail all the way to his place, so he'd spent the night at mine.

On this, his second visit, he'd brought some snares to set by a beaver house close by. The beaver had built on the shore of the lake, and, before the water had frozen properly, they'd climbed far up the steep hillside to groves of aspen trees, and their webbed paw prints and dragged stick marks had been plain in the early snow. After freeze-up, there'd been no sign of them. They would live their winter lives under the ice, in darkness.

Twigs from the woodpile poked through the thick blanket of snow that covered the lake, and Dave stepped cautiously towards them. The beavers' constant swimming underneath would have weakened the ice. (He *had* fallen in once, up to his chest in the frozen water – he laughed when he told me that.) He chopped two holes in the ice and inserted dead willow poles with the snares wired to them. If that didn't work, he'd flounder up the hillside to the aspen groves, and cut green limbs to tempt them. A bait trap almost always works, he said.

He came inside for lunch and tea, but first he reached into the canvas mail-bag lashed onto the back of his snow machine and pulled out a salmon that his people had caught in the Chilco River, then dried. Its flesh was a deep, dull red – rich and greasy – and we ripped off chunks and ate them with our fingers. He'd also brought me some fine, gold snare wire to set for rabbits. As there is no adequate root cellar in this place, I've been unable to keep fresh produce, because it would freeze and spoil when I spend time away, and because I can't carry much when I ski in from the road, I've been living off canned meat and dried vegetables. Fresh food would be a real treat.

So I set the snares as Dave had shown me, in a patch of spruce where rabbits' feet had made regular trails among the dwarf birch and red willow bushes. I marked them with flags of survey ribbon scattered by weekend hunters last fall. When I returned the next day – skiing through the forest, then wading knee-deep through the loose stuff to where I had strung the snares – I found a rabbit in one of them. It was surprisingly small. Its fur was white on the surface, but the soft down underneath was grey and tawny.

A death is always saddening, and yet there was almost a right-ness to the light and lifeless corpse I held in my hands. I've lived in the wilderness for years, but only as an observer. This is the first time I've deliberately planned a wild creature's death. I enjoy eating meat, particularly in the winter when vegetables are scarce. But I've always eaten beef killed on a farm, or deer or moose shot by someone else. By accepting responsibility for my own killing, I've become a part of the wilderness in a way I never was before. I begin to understand man's desire to hunt, although I will never condone hunting for sport, nor the attitudes of governments, and others, who kill to manipulate the wilderness solely for economic gain. I feel a small kinship with the Indian whose heritage this land is.

I've had some experience at skinning farm animals, but the rabbit was different; its body was tiny and its legs papery thin. I cut the back legs free, then eased the skin over the animal's head, like pulling off a sweater. Although I worked as carefully as I could, it was clumsily done, and I ripped it in two places. I stretched the skin, fur side in, then hung it on a nail under the porch to dry. It has little commercial value, but I would like to try to make something with it. If I get another skin, I'll have enough to line a pair of gloves.

That night, I dined off rabbit stew. It has a delicate flavour, but the lean, dark meat must be eaten with care, because the small, brittle bones snap like matchsticks. It's amazing that this harsh and unforgiving environment should create such a thin-skinned, easily broken creature.

When I went outside to toss the stripped bones to the eager dog, the night was very dark; the moon was past the full and had not yet risen. The sky was clear and full of billions of stars, glimmering and quivering in the spaces between the trees and over the frozen lake. I touched the rabbit skin where it hung against the cabin wall. It had stiffened and hardened in the cold, but the fur that sprang from the tears and around the edges was cool and sensual, with a life of its own. It was weightless beneath my fingers, slippery as silk and soft as snow, faintly pale and mysterious, and magical in the starlight.

Yours,
Chris

"I NEVER SAW ..."

"... a purple cow," goes the old rhyme, as Wink Biehl reminded us from West Vancouver.

But *Morningside* listeners had seen *blue* cows, and when, one morning, the same person (me) who had wondered about the intelligence of cattle dared to question the existence of a species coloured blue – Stuart McLean was the culprit here again, I think – they jumped to set the record straight.

That correspondence, in turn, opened a palette of other subjects, from eggs to cauliflower to radio itself. If it didn't run the risk of starting another series about colours, I'd say I blushed to learn how ignorant I'd been.

✉ When I was a child, our family lived in Manitoba, three hundred miles north-west of Winnipeg. We always had a milking cow to supply our daily needs. At one time we had a blue cow. Her hide was not a solid blue, but a slate blue that graduated to lesser tones of blue and grey, giving her a blue-grey patched look.

We were puzzled by this unique colour. Her milk was not bluish, but had the normal colour and texture.

My father eventually sold our blue cow to a farmer way up in the hills. One day, a year later, to our astonishment, our blue cow arrived at our house with a calf in tow. This calf was the same colour as her mother. The mother went directly to the trough and proceeded to drink the water, as she had always done when she had been with us. It was as though a friend had returned to show off her baby. It was a very touching moment!

How had she managed to find her way back to us? The next year, we had another visit, with another calf in tow. Shortly after that, we moved to Winnipeg. I do hope our beautiful blue cow had a comfortable old age.

Sally Allister
Montreal

✉ The blue cow is not indigenous to one county in Quebec. The blue cow is everywhere. Although declining in numbers, blue cows can still be seen in many Nova Scotian pastures, on both beef and dairy farms.

The blue cow is not a breed, but a cross-breed. In Nova Scotia it was commonly a cross between a roan (red-white) Dual Purpose Shorthorn cow and a Holstein bull. Occasionally it was the other way around. These crosses produced the blue Durham (the old name for Dual Purpose Shorthorn) or the blue Holstein, depending on the namer.

The blue cow is a combination of white, red-roan and black colours coupled with the "roaning" gene, so that black and white hairs are interspersed throughout the animal's hide. There are also blue ducks (blue Swedes) and many varieties of blue chickens. The animals cannot breed true, so offspring may be blue, white or black when two blues are mated.

I doubt that one can tell a blue cow by its moo. However, a good stockman can tell many of his cows by their own noises – as distinctive as your voice.

A. Dean Cole
Halifax County, Nova Scotia

✉ There *are* blue cows. When I was a boy, my favourite pastime, while riding in the back seat of my Uncle Bob's 1956 Dodge, was to gaze at the cows in New Brunswick and Quebec pastures along the way to the cottage. I looked at all the pure breeds and Heinz 57s and picked out my favourites. The blues were *always* my favourites. They were rare, and I had to look at a lot of cows before finding one.

They were not blue in the sense of bright sky-blue colours. They were more a denim-grey sort of blue, bluish grey colours that could only be described as a subtle blue wash over a cream or pearly white background. So there were, and still are, blue cows.

As I grew older, I discovered Nova Scotia and became an avid fan of ox-pulls at country fairs. In the Annapolis Valley, in the early 1970s, the winning teams were often blue oxen. Many of the other teams I saw in action also had the same delicate wash patterns on their backs and sides, but had kept the rusty brown colour of the Ayrshire. I loved the blues most of all. And they always seemed to win.

Peter Hicklin
Sackville, New Brunswick

✉ I take up my blue ink to write on the topic of animal colouration – blue in particular.

Blue pigment, such as may be found in ink, certainly also exists in the animal kingdom and can be found in mammals, the face and nether regions of the mandrill (a large forest-dwelling baboon) being the most spectacular case in point.

However, many of the "bluest" of blue animals, including the blue jay, *do not* possess blue pigment. They are blue for essentially the same reason that the sky is blue. That is, the microscopic structure of the feathers scatters the incident light, selectively reflecting back only the blue wavelengths. Thus, a blue jay is not a "blue" bird, but merely one that appears so. The same is true of the large, beautiful and intensely blue butterflies often seen in collections or framed as decorations, and of many other blue animals.

To deny that a blue jay is blue simply because it contains no blue pigment is patently absurd. The blueness of a blue jay is as blue as blue can be, despite its origin as what is technically known as a "structural" colour. Blueness, whatever its basis, is in the eye of the beholder, a perception rather than a physical fact.

Jerry Bloom
Campbellville, Ontario

✉ I was raised on a mixed farm in Alberta. Among the cattle herd, there was almost always something my father called a "blue roan." My sisters and I always thought they were the prettiest of the mixed lot.

When I finally was old enough to join the local 4-H club, I jumped at the chance of raising the blue steer Dad offered me. I am pleased to report that my calf placed third in my group on Achievement Day.

I know that doesn't seem too impressive, but it was: the next four years, my mongrel calves and I always had a view of a dozen or more pedigree rumps when we stood in the placing's line-up.

I still wonder why that blue calf placed so well. It could be that it genuinely deserved it. Or perhaps the judge was just tickled pink (or is that blue?) at the sight of a seventy-pound girl wrestling a half a ton of beef into show stance. All along, I have preferred to believe that there was at least one other person as partial to blue cattle as I.

Carol Jess
Rocky Mountain House, Alberta

✉ The old farmer on Allen's Alley had a blue cow. She gave blue milk. He sold the cow to a famous milk company. And he told Fred Allen, "Somewhere in them Carnation barns tonight, there's a cow that ain't contented."

Al Flemming
Tatamagouche, Nova Scotia

✉ What? Never heard of a brindled cow? What about a mackerel sky? It has the same sort of interesting beauty. I append the English Jesuit Gerard Manley Hopkins' appreciation of both in the first lines of his sonnet "Pied Beauty" (about 1880, possibly in Wales):

Glory be to God for dappled things –
For skies as couplecoloured as a brindled cow:
For rose-moles all in stipple on trout that swim.

Fred Reed
Port Huron, Michigan

✉ When I was a young teacher at Tofino on the west coast of Vancouver Island, I boarded with a family who served blue milk for the breakfast cereal. Curious about the colour, I queried the schoolchildren whose families supplied fresh milk to Tofino residents.

Tales of woe came tumbling out as the young cowherds related their misadventures when attempting to recapture cows that had made a bid for freedom beyond the limits of the town. Those cows knew where they were going and why. They were heading for the low-lying bogs around the lagoons beyond Long Beach, or Wikaninnish as it is correctly known.

When logging roads were cut through from Ucluelet to Tofino, this area was designated as open-range country and cattle were free to roam at will. The Tofino cows were searching out a low-growing plant of the gentian family, which they relished when it sent up its tender stalks topped with clusters of dark blue flowers (sometimes called forest forget-me-nots). A botanical reference book describes this particular blue gentian as "growing wild in rocky and sandy coastal habitats, requiring a cool moist atmosphere and appreciating a mulch of seaweed and rotting fish. In recent years grazing animals have made it a rare plant, now found only in inaccessible places out of reach."

Now that the west coast area has been declared a Pacific Rim park, procedures are no doubt in place to ensure the survival of this rare blue gentian.

It is not likely, however, that the park authorities have ensured the survival of the herds of wild cows that developed beyond the outskirts of Tofino. When I walked along these early roads, it was pleasant to hear the tinkling of bells from cows hidden among the underbrush.

Although I cannot call them truly "blue cows," I suspect that the thin skin of their underparts would have had a tinge of blue when the gentians were in flower. Certainly what I poured on my breakfast cereal was a vivid blue milk.

Thelma Reid Lower
Vancouver

✉ One time, many years ago in Quebec, my sister was having lunch with a boyfriend. He ordered milk. When it came, it was so blue he paraphrased this verse:

I never saw a purple cow
I hope I never see one
But from the colour of this milk
I'm sure that there must be one.

He didn't know about Charlevoix County cows!

Wink Biehl
West Vancouver

✉ A: Did you hear about the cow who drank India ink?
B: No, what happened to her?
A: She mooed indigo.

Jim Chaplin
Toronto

✉ I heard about the blue cows of Charlevoix County, but do you know about blue eggs? This is a subject I am familiar with. Eggs of varying shades of blue and green are laid by Araucana hens, a breed originating in South America. I have two lovely little Araucana hens that produce two minty-green eggs every morning. They are a tad smaller than the white eggs my leghorns lay but are just as tasty, and prompt thoughtful questions like "Where's the ham?"

Vicki Scobie
Saskatoon, Saskatchewan

✉ Last summer some friends from Michigan, who summer in Charlevoix, acquired some chickens, and lo and behold one of them laid decidedly turquoise-blue eggs. None of us had an explanation, but you may be sure it was discussed at some length. On

357

Good Friday I was watching TV, and there was a show about blue eggs! A man from Nova Scotia told about Araucana hens that lay blue, green and sometimes yellow and pink eggs. I must admit that the ones he held up to the camera wouldn't have proved it to me, but the Charlevoix eggs were definitely blue!

Now I'm not talented – I can't cackle like a hen or lay an egg for that matter, but my eyesight is still good, and I don't tell too many lies. You will just have to come to Charlevoix and see the colourful sights for yourself. The Laurentians are blue, too, you know!

Mary Jane Mackay
Halifax

✉ There are farmers in our district who have a few exotic hens just for the novelty; I was not one, nor did I intend to buy any. Then one year my husband brought in a blue egg from the hen-house. At first I thought it was a joke, but after only a little investigation I found out what had happened.

The girls wanted to hatch chicks the old-fashioned way so we purchased a rooster from the neighbours. He was an ordinary red rooster but his father (or grandfather) was related to the Easter Egg chickens, and it was this rooster's daughter – a sweet, little, *red* hen–that laid the blue egg. Inside, it was the same as any other egg.

By the way, did you know that only white hens lay white eggs? Hens with black, brown or mottled feathers lay *brown* eggs.

Wendy Caldwell
Ceylon, Saskatchewan

✉ One time we decided to raise chickens on our small farm. We found a catalogue from a chicken hatchery, filled out the forms and sent the money. We received our little chicks some months later. A long cold winter followed. We trudged through the snow every morning before work to feed our chicks and make sure they had water for the day. In time the little chicks grew and began to lay eggs. One hen laid a mysterious blue egg! We examined the egg in the sun to make sure our eyes were not playing tricks on us in the dim barn light. The egg was blue all right, the size of a medium grocery-store egg and the colour of a robin's egg, with a brilliant yellow yolk. It was quite tasty.

I brought an egg to church with me to share my discovery. The minister immediately borrowed the blue egg from me. He intended to show the children the egg on Sunday morning prior to the sermon. He would explain how we are all different but loved just the same by our God. A good moral story.

The story was well received by the children, but there was some disbelief as to its origins. The minister assured the children he was given the egg by the church secretary who collected it one morning and that a *rooster* did indeed lay the blue egg!

The minister was born and raised in Toronto – a city kid. It was pointed out to him later that the egg probably came from a hen, not a rooster.

Patricia Truesdale
Wilkesport, Ontario

✉ I was once watching my mother making the dinner: steamed fish, mashed potatoes and cauliflower with a white sauce. In a moment of inspiration I poured some drops of food colouring into the vegetable water. With our all-white dinner, we had *blue* cauliflower.

Frances Quetton
Toronto

✉ Unusual vegetables have a permanent place in my organic garden. They offer colour and variety to both the landscape and the dinner plate. More importantly, they lure my young children into the wonders of the growing world, the adventures of experimentation.

Orange cauliflower will be eagerly welcomed into my garden and given its place beside purple broccoli, golden beets, yellow tomatoes, purple beans, red lettuce, pink and white radishes, purple potatoes, white corn and red Brussels sprouts.

Variety is the spice of garden life! *Bon appétit!*

Margaret Norrie
Stouffville, Ontario

✉ There is green rain and orange snow, but I wonder if you know that *red* snow has fallen on Vancouver Island. More than fifty years ago, while holidaying in the Forbidden Plateau area west of Courtney, my chums and I climbed Mount Albert Edward, which is a little more than five thousand feet high. Near the summit we found a pinky red snow patch. I have a snapshot showing me holding a red snowball in one hand and the usual white one in the other. Even in the old black-and-white picture you can easily see the difference.

Ken Leeming
Victoria, British Columbia

✉ The story about red snow has a very simple answer: algae. While algae are very obvious in sea-shores and rivers, an alga (*chlamydomonas rivalis*) lives on the surface of permanent snow. Why are algae red and not green? They produce a large amount of astaxanthin (a carotene similar to the pigment that makes carrots orange) in addition to chlorophyll. Simple! No "blue cow" here.

Charles Trick
London, Ontario

✉ In 1905 the Dawson City Klondikers challenged the Ottawa Silver Seven for the Stanley Cup. They made their notorious way across Canada by train to Ottawa, to play on the natural ice inside the Cattle Castle. It got so heated inside that they had to open the huge doors to let the cold air *in* so the ice wouldn't melt!

The Klondikers lost by the most lopsided Stanley Cup score, twenty-three to two. I'm sure the air was blue! What do you think?

Frank Bradley
Ottawa

✉ I caught the (now presumably) famous "blue radio" flub on the *Morningside* program and, being a conscientious listener, I have three things to say in the form of a statement, a question and a suggestion.

The statement: Be advised, Mr. Gzowski, that there are large numbers of careful listeners out here as far as the airwaves reach who hear and never forget every word you speak, including those said in moments of tongue and brain failure likely caused by live-broadcast stress and/or hype (for which you are forgiven).

The question: Does "blue radio" mean that sometime in the future you're going to start talking dirty? If so, I approve, having had enough of all this Canadian purism–the kind of stuff Margaret Laurence raised her pen against. The suggestion: How about another list contest (based on the blue radio theme), where listeners are encouraged to send in their ten favourite nasty (naughty?) words or phrases, and the winning contributors get their lists read on national radio and eventually receive a hot-off-the-press copy of *The New-est and Blue-est Morningside Papers* (uncensored). What do you think?

Linda Laird
Salmon Arm, British Columbia

AND IF YOU THINK COLOURED CREATURES ARE FASCINATING...

What about *little* ones? Fleas, to be exact. This all started with a report we had from a museum in New Brunswick, whose exhibits included – or were said to include – a perfectly dressed pair of once-famous performing fleas, their tiny souls, thankfully, departed.

When (once again) I and (this time) some correspondents expressed some, shall we say, scepticism about the history of such show-biz phenomena, our listeners rose to the occasion again.

Appropriately (if you don't count David Fraser's pig poems), this is the smallest chapter in the book.

✉ My children, now adults, don't believe me when I tell them about the flea circus. But flea circuses, which at times had flea weddings with live fleas, were not uncommon in the north of England up to the 1950s. The flea circus was brought to the fair by gypsies in their colourful caravans. The flea-circus master used a pair of padded tweezers to put the performing fleas on the "stage" and also to control, direct and then remove them. He fed his fleas by letting them sit on his arm and bite him. They were kept in matchboxes.

I saw my last flea circus in about 1951. It was held on a covered table, under a magnifying glass. The fleas did ballet – they were dressed in little tutus and pirouetted around. Some fleas pulled miniature coaches with a flea coach driver. There was also a flea wedding.

Jean Feliksiak
Winnipeg

✉ In the early thirties, my father, a railway man, used to take my brother or myself on mystery tours. We would just get on a train and go somewhere.

This Saturday (my turn) he and I finished up at one of the great fairs at Hull, Yorkshire, in northern England. So one of the most vivid memories of my early childhood was of a one-ringed flea circus! There was a tightrope walker in a tutu, chariot races and gladiators. It was terrific! I enjoyed myself tremendously, especially when the owner showed where his "stars" had fed on his arm! My father said to the man standing next to us with his son, "I don't know who is the daftest – my daughter for enjoying this . . . or me for paying to come in!"

Wenda Kurany
Edmonton

✉ As the possessor of three groups of dressed fleas, I must share the wealth. I was born in 1915. At that time my engineer uncle was working in Mexico and lived there with his family. Mexican artisans were adept at fashioning miniatures of all kinds – tiny pottery vessels, glass pieces and little scenes of festive events peopled with figures fashioned from a variety of materials.

My mother's unmarried sister, who then lived in Columbus, Ohio, had begun a collection of miniature objects when she was a child. This was continually added to by her friends and relatives. Whenever we visited Columbus (we lived in Toronto), I made a beeline for the round glass case that held Aunt Jo's collection. It was soon noticed that I spent a great deal of time marvelling at these things, so it wasn't long before the toe of my Christmas stocking contained a few items and thus my collection was begun about 1920. And whenever Uncle Guy sent things from Mexico for my aunt's collection, there were often duplicates for mine. Eventually I inherited her collection.

In it, there's a little pot that dates back to about 1920. The pot contains a wee box containing fleas. There is a slightly larger pot, almost identical, holding a flea dressed as a peasant carrying a back burden. I cannot make out even with a magnifying glass whether there is a second flea on the right or whether it is meant to be something else. I am developing cataracts so even with a glass I have difficulty seeing any detail in the costume. When told it is a bride and groom, as I was, it is easy to see it. The bride seems to be wearing a pinkish veil, even though the "dressing" may be somewhat of an illusion.

More impressive is a hinged walnut shell, with little scenes constructed of paper and bits of dried vegetable material. The one in the right half appears to be a quite charming, angled adobe house with arched doorways and two flea men in rather lively stances in the courtyard in front. The left half has a roadway with a fence curving up to the façade of a small house nestled in some "trees" on a rise. In front of the door to this house is a flea, and down in an open space in the right front is another. Both fleas are dressed in white with touches of red. The illusion of perspective is quite remarkable on such a tiny scale.

Ruth W. McCuaig
Hamilton, Ontario

✉ When I was about ten years old, in Columbus, Ohio, I was given by someone a tiny box in which were housed two fleas in wedding costumes.

Truly, truly the bride was in a white dress and the groom in a black suit.

I can't remember if there was a magnifying glass over the box or whether I just used one of my own to view the happy couple.

Leslie Klenck
West Jeddore, Nova Scotia

CHILDHOOD HAUNTS

More of the response to my solicitation of sentimental journeys – in this case to places the writers knew as children. In fairness, too, I should say that the story that opens this chapter, which was written and read on the air by Stuart McLean when he sat in for me one week in the autumn, was probably responsible for at least as many entries in our contest as my own efforts. I heart Stuart's piece, as it happens, as I drove around Vancouver Island and, as other listeners have told me about other readings they've heard on *Morningside*, found myself unwilling to leave my car until he'd finished.

✉ It was summer and I was driving around Montreal unexpectedly with time on my hands. My family was at the lake, and I wasn't supposed to be home until after supper. The interview I had begun that morning hadn't panned out. It was hardly past lunch and I had nothing to do. An afternoon free. Unaccustomed to such liberty, I drove foggily around town trying to eke out some sort of plan. I made it almost all the way to Brock Avenue before I realized what I was doing.

I was fifteen when my mother and father sold their house on this street. I had driven by it once or twice in those twenty-five years. The last time was the summer I got married – I had wanted to show it to my wife. I used to have the bedroom on the top floor on the side, I'd told her, twisting my head and slowing the car down slightly. We were late for something and couldn't stop to look.

This time, however, I had the whole afternoon. I drove by slowly and then came back around the block for another look. On the third pass I parked and gazed at the house I had grown up in. There were workmen installing new windows on the second floor. There was nothing wrong with the old windows, I thought peevishly. I wondered what else had changed.

It took me about ten minutes to get up the nerve to get out of the car. I wanted desperately to ring the doorbell and go inside, but it seemed like an embarrassing and improper thing to do – an intrusion I had no right to impose. It wasn't my house any more.

I stood on the sidewalk for a few minutes and decided that there was probably no one home anyway – only the workmen replacing the perfectly good windows. Disturbing them wouldn't be such an imposition, would it? What would they care? So I walked up to the front door and rang the bell. As I waited I practised what I should say, wondering if the workmen would let me in. I also prayed that there was no one left in the neighbourhood who would recognize me should they happen to glance out the window. I felt self-conscious and didn't feel like explaining why I was there.

The workman who came to the door was a woman wearing a dress.

"Excuse me," I said tentatively.

This is silly, I thought. Maybe I should just ask for directions and go, or maybe I should say I was selling encyclopaedias and could arrange for a demonstration if she wished.

"My name is Stuart McLean," I heard myself stammer. "And I . . ."

The woman in the dress took a step forward, smiled and finished my sentence for me.

"And you used to live here," she said. "Come on in . . . the house is a mess."

The house *was* a mess. The workmen were changing every window they could get their hands on. But it didn't bother me and she didn't mention it again. She was called Mrs. Fulgiano and, together with her husband, she had bought the house from my parents twenty-five years ago.

Mrs. Fulgiano took me upstairs and let me look out the window in my old bedroom. And then we walked together through the entire house top to bottom, including the other room upstairs where my brother and I had played Davy Crockett. I'd been Davy; Al had been the Indian. As the Indian it was his job to attack me with the knife. We'd used a comb as a knife.

Downstairs, looking at my parents' old bedroom where I'd spent the days when I fell sick, I remembered the afternoon I'd picked the spy book out of their bookcase called *On Her Majesty's Secret Service*. A different decade, a different hero. I had never dreamed such adventure could lurk in a book.

I stood in the kitchen and wondered where the phone used to be.

"Your mother had it there," she said. "On the counter."

She was right.

When she asked if I liked the way she had changed the kitchen, I answered I did. "It looks nice," I said. But the breakfast nook and the pantry were gone. Why would anyone do that, I wondered.

In the basement I opened the cedar closet my grandfather had built and smelled the pungent wood – the smell was still as strong as it had been when I was a boy. I touched the table where my father had taught me to shine my shoes – in those days you shined your shoes every morning. I poked behind the furnace where one Christmas, to my horror, I had found a cache of Christmas presents.

She took me outside and pointed to the far corner of the yard.

"They had to cut down the maple tree you planted," she said. "It had grown into the telephone wires. I hope you don't mind."

368

I had planted it from one of those little helicopter seeds. The tree had been as thick as my arm the last time I had seen it. How did she know I had planted the tree?

Mrs. Townsend, the neighbour, had told her.

And so we said goodbye. She told me she was happy I had stopped by and that it was a good house and that they had been happy in it. They had brought up five children, she said, and she knew we had loved the house, too. Sometimes she had thought of us, and once she had met my mother at a party and had invited her to stop by.

"Tell your mother she would be welcome," she said as I turned to go. "Tell her to phone me if she would like to come by."

As I drove away, I realized I had been there less than an hour. It had felt much longer. I thought back to my anxious moment at the doorbell and suddenly realized that it had probably been the first time I'd ever gone in through the front door. We used to use the side-door off the driveway. Next time, I thought, I would go to the side-door.

Imagine that a tree I had planted could have reached the telephone lines! Next spring when the buds spin off the maple trees, I must remember to show my son how to peel the seed out of the middle, and how to soak it on a piece of wet cotton wool. Then we'll go out together and stuff it in the ground and see if we can reach the sky.

Stuart McLean
Toronto

✉ I am eight years old and I am on my way to Grandma's house. We are driving in my father's car. I am up front with Mom and Dad, and my brothers and sisters are in the back seat. We drive for miles over dusty dirt roads while Mom calls out place names as we pass – Boisdale, Shunacadie, Christmas Island – rich Cape Breton names. Finally we arrive at Grand Narrows (Mom calls it Gran Narris) and the ferry.

We watch the ferry come to our side. We can't wait to get on board. The husky, ruddy-faced ferryman grins and touches his hat as he lowers the ramp so we can drive on. He looks as ferrymen have always looked, a match for the elements.

My older brother and sister get out of the car and walk to the side to watch the water. Wind whips at their hair and spray splashes their faces. The motor groans loudly. I watch from inside the car, no less impressed. Before long we are on the other side, and the ferry bumps against rubber tires hung against the wharf. We drive up a steep road, across railroad tracks. Mom points to the narrow green train bridge and tells us how she walked those tracks each day to her first teaching job across the water. We've heard it before, but we like to hear it again.

Beyond the track we get a better view of Iona – that magical, mystical place on the shores of Barra Strait. It is a small farming community with one Co-op store, one gas pump and one beautiful brick church. We round a few curves and we're there. My grand-father's house sits high on a hill that is close to vertical. The drive up or down is frightening. Timid souls who choose to get out and walk find themselves puffing halfway up or clinging to branches to reduce their speed on the way down.

My dad shifts into low gear and the old car thunders up, up, up and around a sharp turn, then comes to a shuddering stop right beside the house. Dad grins like a Cheshire cat at his accomplish-ment. Grandpa comes to meet us. For years he's had complaints about the driveway; city visitors suggest that he really should grade it down a little. He won't consider it. The Scot in him likes to challenge and be challenged. It's a form of initiation to the MacDonald clan. To Grandpa, it was the grade of the driver, not the hill, that was the problem.

Grandpa is a tall, broad-shouldered man with snow-white hair, a thick white moustache and an even thicker Scottish accent. He wears heavy dark pants with suspenders and a flannel shirt. Close behind him is Grandma, a tiny pretty woman with fine features and lovely white hair piled high on her head in a loose bun. She wears a navy and white small-print dress with a full-length apron, the kind that slips on like a blouse and ties in the back. She has on dark stockings and high black-laced shoes. She takes us in and puts on the tea.

My aunt is taking fat molasses cookies from the oven. The house smells wonderful. My mother laughs with her brothers and sisters. At times they break into Gaelic. My uncle starts to sing, and Grandpa joins him. I love this strange world.

After a long talk and plenty to eat, we go off to explore the barns. Next to the house are three small sheds. Higher up is a huge barn for horses and farm machinery. We look in one shed, and Mom tells us how they sheared sheep and hung the wool on the clothes-line to dry. My aunt runs to get the album. She shows us Mom as a young girl surrounded by lines of sheep wool blowing in the breeze. She is the record keeper of the family and insists on a picture now.

We pose by a huge sundial my uncle has made from growing flowers. Twelve sections of different varieties mark the hours, and a pole in the centre casts a shadow as the day passes. My uncle teaches us how to tell time with this clock. Then he suggests a boat ride. Just below the house is a lake with an island in the middle. We row out to look for beaver dams.

After supper, Grandpa goes to pray. I watch him kneeling, whispering, passing prayer beads through aging hands. The rosary is fifteen decades long instead of the usual five. The large wooden beads, once painted black, are now worn to a warm wood from years of faithful fingering.

It is time to leave. I close my eyes as we head down the hill.

I remembered this sentimental journey recently when I read of a proposed permanent link between Grand Narrows and Iona. I imagine the residents will welcome the convenience, and I would not deny them that. I am not one who fears the loss of my Iona. Most of my relatives rest peacefully in the cemetery beside the lake just below my grandfather's house. That is not where I look for them. The people, the place and the time are carried securely in my heart – my private, personal, permanent link to my Iona.

Donna Doyle
Richmond County, Nova Scotia

✉ I journey back in time, to my childhood, through an old mirror that I call Grandad's mirror. It's a rectangle of flaking silvered glass measuring about a foot by two feet, framed in a filigree of wood, once painted, now worn, topped with a faded sepia-toned photograph of a mangy black bear. The bear is fifty years dead, at least, but it was a cub when my grandad was a young man.

It's Grandad's face I see yet when I look in the mirror; he is brushing the fine, thin strands of his hair into place as he did every morning. I see his leather-brown skin and his shy brown eyes ready to find a laugh. Behind him, through the mirror, I'm again sitting in the big, bright kitchen of Mount Edith Cavell Chalet in Jasper National Park. It's summer, of course, because the chalet was only accessible from late June till Labour Day. Snow might fall even in July; the big log building was covered with it all winter.

The kitchen where the mirror hangs is full of the smell of a dozen loaves of Grandma's orange bread baking in the ovens, to be served to tourists in the tea-room. Outside, where the air is nippy with the smell of glacial water chuckling down the creek to the lake, there's a marmot on the back porch eating up the leftovers Grandad set out for it. Golden-mantle ground-squirrels skitter by, looking for handouts too, although they'll get plenty of peanuts (raw, unsalted ones sold in the souvenir shop) from the tourists who feed them by the path that leads up to the alpine meadows. Clark's nutcrackers, cousins to the whiskey jack, circle the chalet and parking lot, skreeing into the chilly air as the sun rises on another day of successful begging and stealing for them.

Several times each summer, my brother and I got to stay overnight at the chalet and wake up to this most magical of childhood memories. And we drove there each Sunday afternoon for a big supper of Grandma's farm-style cooking. The first nine miles of the drive from Jasper were over the Banff-Jasper highway, which was paved and fairly straight. At Astoria Falls, however, we turned onto a winding, narrow, gravel road that switch-backed its way the next nine miles to the chalet. The most welcome curve for me was about half a mile from the chalet, when the skirt of Angel Glacier, which nestles between Mount Edith Cavell and Mount

Sorrow, came into view. The white hem of her tumbling gown was dirty in places, but where it was creased and folded from calving into thundering little avalanches, it was a thousand heavenly shades of aqua. From the youngest age I remember being thrilled anew each time I saw those fairyland colours.

The most welcome curve for my brother was the final one in which the chalet came into sight, for his face was always a hellish shade of green when we arrived. He was so carsick that he'd stumble out of the car and make his way tremblingly into the chalet for some of Grandma's all-time remedy: a bottle of 7-Up. I was seldom sick enough to be so lucky and had to be contented drinking water, but how sweet it was, straight from the meltwater creek of Angel Glacier.

The chalet was made from logs cut, skinned and skidded on site. Grandad had helped to build it in the summers of 1928 and 1929, when he'd been young and single. A year later, he met his bride at another log chalet he had helped build at Mount Robson. They homesteaded in the foothills, where my dad was born, moved to Jasper for the last few years of the dirty thirties, worked in the shipyards in Vancouver during the war, then bought Cavell Chalet following the war, when Jasper opened again for the tourist trade. We thought of it as Grandma's business, because she did most of the day-to-day running of it, but it was always Grandad's building, and he kept it in fine repair.

By the time I was about ten, the glacier had receded so much that its skirt was no longer visible from the road. A little magic was lost, but from the chalet, the Angel was complete, and from the alpine meadows, she was as splendid as ever. I suppose she still is, in her shrinking way, but I haven't seen her for nearly a decade. I haven't seen the chalet in fifteen years, and Grandad's been gone for more than twenty.

Last time I drove up to Mount Edith Cavell was in 1980, with my new husband, who'd never seen "my grandma's mountain," as I'd long called it, or the chalet. I pointed out to him the stretch of road where I used to anticipate seeing the skirt of my Angel. But another memory overshadowed that early, joyous one: I also pointed out to him the tree that Grandad accidentally slammed into in his new red pickup truck, which had burst into flames and half-cremated him. As we rounded the last curve, where the chalet used to come into view, we saw nothing, for the chalet had been torn down a few years after Grandma was forced to sell it. Well, *I* saw nothing; my husband saw tall, ragged evergreens and the bases of Mount Edith Cavell and Mount Sorrow. At the foot of Mount Sorrow, in a very private little glen created by moraines, I pointed to where we had scattered the rest of Grandad after he'd been fully cremated.

My husband and I parked in the spot where Grandma and Grandad used to pull in beside the chalet, and I wandered over the area where it stood. I could see where the huge stone fireplace had been, and in my mind, as I stood there in front of absolutely nothing, I was a child again, warming myself by another of Grandad's snapping hot blazes. When my husband pulled me away, I thought he hadn't understood the depth of my loss and the meaning of my tears, but he was simply preventing me from being run over by a Winnebago that wanted to park right on top of the chalet's fireplace! How could these tourists know? How could I tell anyone about the very real world that now only existed in my mind?

We walked up the crooked path my grandad had made to the alpine meadows, and when we reached the upper levels, which few tourists huff and puff their way to see, it was all exactly the same as it had been so many years ago. Tiny, fragile alpine flowers nodded in cool breezes under the hot July sun; pikas, or rock rabbits, popped up and squeaked here and there among the rocks; a fat marmot whistled, but didn't show itself; and a motley black and white crew of ptarmigans – Momma and half a dozen chicks – shared some of our lunch. Too soon came the time to make our way back to the car where we were forced to see from on high the empty place where the chalet should be and, across the parking lot and creek, the lonely little spot where Grandad's ashes took to the wind. I couldn't face it; I made us fight our way down through the forest and come out on the parking lot from behind, thus preserving what I could of my precious memories.

We moved to Nova Scotia a year ago, and of course, my grandad's mirror came with me. I've yet to find a place for it on the walls of our new home, but I will, in time. I'll drill a hole in the freshly painted plaster, put in a screw and lovingly hang that beat-up old thing. In the worn silver, I won't see my reflection at all. I'll see my handsome grandad and, in him, my handsome, recently deceased dad, who drove us to the chalet every week of the summer for Sunday dinner. And behind their reflections in the mirror, I'll see the big, bright kitchen of the chalet, the air thick with the scent of baking orange bread. A fire will crackle in the big fireplace in the tea-room, and outside, the marmot will be eating up his leftovers on the back porch, while the sun climbs high and bright over Angel Glacier, nestled in her long gown between "my grandma's mountain" and Mount Sorrow.

Brenda Gillespie
Dartmouth, Nova Scotia

✉ *The Monarchs of Merry England*, by Roland Carse, illustrated by Heath Robinson, is a large book that was given to my father when he was twelve. I thought about this book a lot while living in Australia for the past three years. I grew homesick and worried that Dad had sold it or given it away.

My dad was proud of *The Monarchs of Merry England*. I think he told us that his father, a newspaper editor in the north of England, had known Heath Robinson. Occasionally when we were growing up, Dad would gently take it off the bookshelf in the den, chuckle and then show us the droll colour plates of kings and conquerors making fools of themselves. One of his favourites was William the Conqueror landing headfirst in English waters. Dad didn't play with us often, so the book seemed very special.

Six months before my return from Australia, my dad had a stroke and was unable to speak. Physically he was all right. I thought my long-distance telephone calls would somehow jolt him out of it and that his garbled sounds would be transformed into chatter about his garden or the weather. It was a disappointment, even more so when I realized I couldn't remember all the important details of the stories he used to tell, the ones about his coming from England to a farm near Wainwright, Alberta, and how his mother had dressed him in a sailor's suit for his first day at school. The other children had teased him and pushed him in the dirt. He used to help his uncle harvest the grain using teams of horses. Then there were his wartime stories about putting in a telegraph line from Clinton to Bella Coola, getting bogged in thigh-deep mud and returning to civilization at William's Lake.

Though I had tried to prepare myself, when I came through customs at the Vancouver airport and hugged him, thin and frail, I was shocked. He pecked me on the cheek happily and uttered a flow of consonants, hands and arms accompanying, trying to make sure I understood. I did not understand, and I felt even worse that night. We spent over an hour passing notes and diagrams between us as I tried to figure out what he desperately wanted to say. I couldn't tell how much he comprehended of what I said or wrote.

My parents' frustration level was high. They had been coping for six months. I had only just arrived, but at this home-coming I felt loss – loss of my father's dry humour, of his stories, of the part of me that was still a child.

The next day, I remembered *The Monarchs of Merry England* and found it on the bookshelf in the den. It was much the same as I remembered it, only now I understood it much better.

I showed the book to my dad and he got really excited, laughing and gesticulating. He looked at the pictures and carried it around with him for quite awhile before putting it where I couldn't find it.

That night, as I was sorting through some things in the basement, he came to me with the book. He gave it to me and nodded. I asked him if he was sure he wanted me to keep it. Yes, he nodded definitely, he was. He went to bed early but appeared content.

The next morning, on Sunday, Dad had another stroke, this time physically debilitating.

I still want to hear Dad's stories again, and each time I visited him in the hospital I yearned for him to say something coherent.

I have left home again. This time I have Dad's best book to keep me company.

Joan Buchanan
Sherbrooke, Quebec

✉   This morning I thought about *the place*, and going back, which I do periodically when the longing for grain elevators strung out in a row and forty-five-mile wraparound sunsets becomes unbearable. But then I begin to get a twinge or two for the place where the St. Lawrence meets the Ottawa, where Thomas More wrote "The Canadian Boat Song" one night while he was sitting around Simon Fraser's house, and I realize I live with one foot firmly rooted in Saskatchewan and the other in Quebec, where the rest of God's finest people live.

The place is a big old farmhouse near Leslie, Saskatchewan, full of people, full of life, with a bedroom box in the upper hall under the window where I used to sit, my pockets full of B.C. Delicious apples, and read and dream. And here I am, in a big old French-Canadian house in Ste. Anne de Bellevue, full of people, full of life, with that self-same bedroom box waiting for me under the living-room window.

Vikings are wanderers. They root – fiercely and proudly and loyally – but their eyes constantly watch the far horizon, looking. My great-grandmother, a widow with five little kids, came from Iceland to Winnipeg, to a strange language and a strange culture. My grandparents decided that Gimli – in 1905 – was too crowded, so they homesteaded on the prairies. And what about me? A parent alone at the time, I brought three little kids to this French-Canadian town, to a strange language (as anyone who has taken French in Saskatchewan in the 1950s from a teacher who spoke English with an Icelandic accent can attest). In turn, my daughters have both found themselves wonderful young men who have taken them to big old houses, one in a tiny French town on the

Ontario border, on the Ottawa river; the other to a farm near Orangeville.

Great-Grandma didn't bring much but hope, courage and unquenchable faith. She did bring her talisman, a slip of a particularly fragrant, pungent Icelandic fern called Little Old Lady. I have my clump here along with my own second talisman – four Saskatoon bushes. My daughters each have their fern, for remembering, for roots, for faith.

Go back? I don't think I've ever gone away.

My desk is in the kitchen in our old house in Ste. Anne's. After trying out every possibility in our ten-room house, I announced to everybody – or to nobody – that I was moving my office into our kitchen, and I did. This is where I write, beside the one window in the house that offers a view that satisfies. It is a simple view: two sumacs, my neighbour's three pines, the corner of a weeping willow, a little curving rise to the train tracks and, beyond, the clouds and forever.

I can lean back in my chair. Looking past the sumac and through the pines, I can see over the hill to a straight-as-a-die road lined with glass insulator-capped telephone poles, the target for every stone-throwing child on the prairies. I can trudge home again down that dusty road, listening for the particular ping of stone on thick glass, down to the curve at Reynold's slough, past the stand of fragrant silver willow, around the next corner where the lady's slippers bloomed, past Ridley's, over the three smooth stones that had, in time long lost, worked their way through the hard clay road, past the haunted house, down the last stretch of road and across our fields, the alfalfa hazy mauve, a murmur of pollen-laden bees, the wheat heads bristling in my palm where I rub them to extract the golden-green chewy kernels while I skirt the last ruts and swing through the gate into the houseyard, up the two steps, through the entrance hall, past the cream separator and into the kitchen.

I am home.

Mom is cutting a loaf of hot bread, which she then feeds us, drowning it in fresh home-made butter. We eat the front-end crust and the back-end crust, the bottom crust and the top crust, leaving the pale, crustless remains to be dried for stuffing. It's a treat worth the two-and-a-half mile walk from school.

My kids share these trips, although they never really lived in the West even though Inga was born in Cold Lake, Alberta.

Some days, I think about going back, but while I am still as prairie as a wind-kissed golden wheat field, I am also as Quebec as the Big O and the place that sells *patates frites* at the corner. When I cross the border into Saskatchewan I am home, I sit up a little taller. But when I cross the border into Quebec, having sped through Manitoba and Ontario as quickly as I could go, holding my breath, I am home, and my eyes fill with tears.

I wonder what Great-Grandmother would say.

Joan Eyolfson Cadham
Ste. Anne de Bellevue, Quebec

✉ What a delight it was to hear Joan Cadham's sentimental journey. It made sorting laundry tolerable. Her second home is Ste. Anne de Bellevue, Quebec – but to me Ste. Anne's *is* home.

My mother's family settled there sixty years ago from England. My father's mother and four small sons returned there in the 1920s, after a brief foray to Ontario, where streets were *not* paved with gold as her husband had promised they would be. At that time Ste. Anne's was the Military Hospital and she worked there at night, in the mental hospital, because that paid extra money to support her boys alone.

I have lived in Ontario for almost thirteen years, but Ste. Anne's is still home. Where else could one walk "down the village" and never fail to have someone say, "Oh, Audrey, I didn't know you were home"? Where else would your mom's landlady take you aside to get your phone number and reassure you that she would call to tell you whenever Mother was doing poorly because she was too proud to call herself?

In some ways time stands still at home. I had the occasion to go to my old high school, which was also in my old elementary school, and my mom's school before that. Walking down the hall with my two children in tow, I passed the eternal chemistry teacher, Mr. Ross, head down, reading as usual, still in tweeds and a bow-tie. My respectful "Good morning, Mr. Ross" was acknowledged with a quick glance up. "Morning, Audrey," he said, as if I had never left school! He was halfway down the hall before a spark ignited and he spun around to talk.

Many changes have taken place in Ste. Anne's: the once-run-down waterfront is "yuppified" with back yards expropriated for a board walk and turn-of-the-century buildings now boast *croissanteries* and cafés for the yacht set. The once-forbidding convent now houses seniors' apartments where many townspeople have retired. But the *frites* stand is still across from Harpel Ball Park, and Ste. Anne's is still home.

Thanks for brightening a November day, Joan. Maybe we'll meet "down the village" some day.

Audrey Desjardins Dow
London, Ontario

✉ "Just a little farther . . . slow down . . . stop! There it is! The white house with the red roof. See it? That's where I lived. For fifteen years. That was my home."

The car comes to a full stop.

"But it's so small!" exclaims my younger daughter, never one to spare my feelings.

Small?

"Well, yes, I guess it is kind of small. But maybe that's part of what made it so special. Doesn't it look cosy?"

"I dunno. I can't see it very well. Those big trees are in the way."

Those "big trees," two magnificent Colorado blue spruce, had been planted by my father when they were hardly more than seedlings. Special occasions were nearly always documented by photographs of me standing beside one of those trees, marking both their growth and mine. Now the trees dwarfed the house they had been planted to grace, acting as sentinels to the front entrance with its red-tiled steps. These had been built to replace the old curved wooden ones, but somehow they failed. They also proved to be extremely slippery in wet or cold weather, prompting my father to warn our visitors to "watch yourself on those darned fool steps." Strong language for my conservative Baptist father.

I realize that the neat white picket fence it was my job to paint every summer has disappeared, as has the wooden swing that my father built in the narrow space between our house and its twin next door. I never thought to ask why he built it there rather than in the more open space of our back yard. It could have stood next to my playhouse with its white clapboard walls and black shingled roof and brass door knocker. I had the only skeleton key. Oh, the fantasies that were created, the lies that were told, the dreams that were dreamed inside those walls!

It is fall, so I can't tell if the crab-apple trees that scented our yard in spring and crowded our cold room in winter with jellies and spiced apples are still there; or if the lilac tree still blooms outside my parents' bedroom window. I can't see the Icelandic poppies or the sweet peas that sprung to life under my mother's green thumb and tender care; nor can I see if offspring of the weeds it was my tedious job to pull still flourish as bountifully as ever.

The front windows are no longer shielded by venetian blinds to keep out the hot prairie sun. I wonder what hides behind the now neatly draped eyes of "my" house, even as I know what does not. There is no longer the old maroon plush sofa and chair or the Duncan Phyffe table that was my mother's joy. The built-in china cabinet at the end of the minuscule living room (we had no dining room) no longer holds my great-grandmother's silver tea service. That was passed on to me on my twenty-fifth wedding anniversary.

Something tells me that the built-in breakfast nook is gone, and suddenly I once more hear my father say sternly, "Go to your room. Now. And close the door. Don't come out till I tell you to." And I smell again the acrid burning smell and hear my parents' muffled frantic voices and feel the pounding of my five- or six-year-old heart. Later, much later, I stare at the charred remains of the picture I had coloured that morning – a picture of elves, I remember. My mother gazes in sorrow at the scorched wall behind our tiny stove on which my father had chosen to display my childish art, heedless of the porridge pot on the back burner.

Once again I find myself straining from inside the cocoon of the Kenwood blankets on my bed to catch scattered fragments of the story on Lux Radio Theatre. Was it *Boston Blackie* or *The Shadow*? It matters not. They all came on well past the hour of my bedtime, and only the compactness of our house allowed me to enjoy bits and pieces of dialogue that filtered from our old Westinghouse radio to my well-trained, ever-alert ears. Thank goodness my parents weren't given to much conversation! Those heroes are long gone, and so is the radio.

"How would you like to have a little sister?" my father asked me one day when I was maybe eight.

"Yes! Oh yes, Daddy! When? When?"

"Soon, I think. Soon."

But it never happened and no one ever said why and I was afraid to ask. I never have, and I still feel the aloneness of being an only one.

"Red rover, red rover, who do you call over?"

I hear the shrieks and the laughter floating through the dusk of a prairie evening and Dorrie's voice saying, "Call *me*. I want you to call *me*."

Suddenly I am once more standing at our front door staring across the street at Dorrie's house when she was five and I was six, and willing her to get well, the quarantine card an obscenity on her front door.

"Will she die?" I ask my mother. "Will the scarlet fever make Dorrie die?"

"I don't know, dear. No one knows. The best thing you can do is pray that it won't."

So I prayed. But in case God wasn't listening just then, I spent what seemed like hours every day staring up at Dorrie's bedroom window, willing her with all the will that was in my small skinny self to get well. Either God or my will worked – that time. I never got the chance to see if I could make it work twice. Dorrie died suddenly when she was only fifteen. No one even knew she was sick.

But by that time we had both moved into different neighbourhoods and new and larger houses. Dorrie and I had drifted apart, despite our sworn allegiance that we would be best friends forever.

"Mom! *Mom!*" insists a voice from the back seat.

"Pardon?"

"I said can we go now? Please?"

"Go? Yes. We can go."

The car pulls away and the house disappears. Because for a few brief moments I have "gone home" to a place I can never wholly share with anyone else.

Then I realize that this is not the first time I have returned there, nor will it be the last. For when the night is deep and I am alone in my dreams, somehow, whenever I dream of home, it is always of the little white house with the red roof and the red-tiled steps and the two blue spruce trees standing guard. For me.

Alison French
Merrickville, Ontario

✉ My wife thought we should ask at the house. I said that there appeared to be no one at home and anyway they wouldn't believe me. I had not told her what I was up to and she was a trifle impatient. We were not exactly skulking but we certainly were behaving in a somewhat suspicious manner as we walked around to the back of the property. This was the house in which I had lived as a boy some twenty years ago; it was not the building itself I was interested in but a certain spot in the back garden.

My boyhood friend and I, fired by stories in *Chums Annual* with lurid titles like "To Sweep the Spanish Main" and "Rogues of the

Roaring Glory," acted out those seemingly romantic days in our vivid imagination with desperate sword fights on his garage roof. We repelled snarling pirates as they attempted to board our stout ship, cutlass between snaggled teeth, pistol in garish sash. Pirates had names like Red Castaban, Rat o' the Main and the Barracuda. Alas, boys' stories don't have marvellous names like that any more.

One of the best parts was the lair. My chum had his bedroom in the attic. At one point, in his room where the sloping roof reached the floor, there was a small door hidden behind a bureau. It led under the eaves to a dark wondrous place where we had covered the rafters with some wood to provide a floor – a secret place that only *we* knew. Pictures had been hung up, and there were suitable artefacts of various kinds and a document embellished with our own crude illustrations, which we had copied from our favourite reading material, and which pledged our undying allegiance, properly signed in blood.

There was also a map depicting in graphic detail the spot where our treasure was buried. The treasure chest was a tin cash box purchased from Woolworth's, that wonderful store where in those days one could buy almost anything one's heart desired for fifteen cents. In the chest were some foreign coins given to me by a wandering uncle, tarnished jewellery discarded by our parents (whom, we admitted, did occasionally have their uses) and pounded-up bits of glass, as good as diamonds to our eyes. Of course we had endless arguments about where the treasure should be hidden – the merits of this place and the drawback of that one.

In the end, a site was chosen at my place at the bottom of the back yard, near the corner of the garage in the wall. An opening had been cut there to allow our dog access to his sleeping place on a pile of burlap bags. We dug the hole about a foot deep, put in the chest, covered it with earth and, then, to cunningly foil any intruders, we placed a large flat rock over the spot before filling in the rest of the hole. Afterwards, we would occasionally inspect this hiding place to make sure it had not been disturbed. Inevitably, over the course of time it became neglected. The pirate fights were replaced by other interests, a war intervened and we went our separate ways, got married. The buried treasure with its secret map became a childhood memory.

Many years later my wife and I found ourselves back in Toronto for a visit, and I decided it would be fun to see if anything remained of our cache. The neighbourhood had of course changed: the vacant lots across the street where we used to play football and baseball or knock out flies (kids don't seem to do that any more) was now a row of houses, and the trees were bigger. Curiously, the little grocery store had survived, the store where my mother used to send me occasionally to buy ten cents' worth of "round steak, minced" for supper. The house hadn't changed very much, though, and the back yard seemed much as I remembered it; even the dog's hole in the garage was still there. I didn't need the map. My memory was clear and I went unerringly to the spot, but I must admit that my heart was beating more heavily than usual. My wife was astonished and more than a little bewildered when I began to dig. First came the rock and then, miraculously, the box. It was badly rusted as befits a treasure chest, but still intact. Gleefully and with shaking hands I opened the box. There it all was – treasure beyond one's wildest dreams! Forget about stout Cortés and his wild surmise; here was the *real* stuff of dreams. After letting memories flood over me for a few minutes, I carefully replaced the little chest in its hiding place and covered it again with the stone and dirt.

This happened over forty years ago, and I now live on the West Coast and have not been back. My boyhood friend and I, although we live at opposite ends of this big country of ours, still see each other at regular intervals, and the years roll back as if we had never been apart. We are as much a pair of romantics as ever.

Sometimes I wonder if the treasure is still there, but I don't really want to know. Instead, in my mind's eye I like to picture the scene as someone turns it up with a spade. Hopefully the discovery will be made by small boys who have the same imagination as we did so long ago.

Reid Townsley
Ganges, British Columbia

✉ I sit in my house in Prague, Czechoslovakia, a lovely city, already old and stately when Canada was unknown and home was only waving prairie grass. I have just come from attending mass in a baroque seventeenth-century church. Wandering back to the car through narrow cobble-stoned streets, surrounded by history, I congratulated myself on how fortunate I was to be living in such an ancient, cultured civilization. Yet now, only a few minutes later, I find myself dreaming of a place these Europeans seldom hear of: Saskatchewan.

The source of my ruminations is prosaic – a CAA atlas called *Drive North America*, which was lying open on the kitchen table when I returned. It's full of maps – lines and dots and blue blotches, yet those tiny circles with the strange names can conjure up sights and sounds and smells I thought I had long forgotten.

There's Gravelbourg, where I was born and of which I am so proud, as it gives me a biculturalism by association that my strongly WASP roots deny me. There, a dot just below Old Wives' Lake, is Mossbank where I grew up, and straight down from it is Assiniboia, the big town where all the "cool" kids lived. There's Wood Mountain where Sitting Bull found refuge and I went to summer camp, and Coronach that led to the border and the States and all the bounteous wonders the Americans had to offer. On Victoria Day and Thanksgiving weekends, rain or shine, we headed to the States and took advantage of our $1.03 dollar. We bought towels and sheets and work pants and, once, a brand-new bicycle.

I find Moose Jaw easily. It was *the* city of my childhood, offering wonders for a country child to gape at: Eaton's for the good stuff and Woolworth's where even a kid could afford Pond's lipsticks in the brightest shades of red. Then there was Joyner's where the funny little boxes zipped around tracks hung from the ceiling, taking your money to some mysterious place and bringing back the change.

I can still hear my footsteps echoing in the grand hall of the CPR station with its picture-taking booth and the white-tiled bathrooms and a water fountain. There was a special smell to the station: I am sure I would recognize it instantly if it were ever to waft its way back to me.

Going to a restaurant was a very special treat. We children were allowed fish and chips: *real* fish and chips with the fish flaky and the batter puffy and light. We had vinegar with it, never ketchup. Daddy always ordered breaded veal cutlets – the same "Wiener schnitzel" my children love now. It was only later, as I was leaving high school, that the chains arrived and eating out became more commonplace. A & W was first but my dad held out until McDonald's and the grandchildren came.

Moose Jaw was special too because of the Natatorium where we could have a swim (really a splash as none of us could swim) before going home. Except for the two weeks we spent at camp each year, it was our only chance to swim in a pool. There were two movie theatres and a dance hall called Temple Gardens, which to a whimsical child of ten was the most romantic place on earth. I knew that when I was old enough to go there, Gene Kelly or Fred Astaire would ask me to dance.

Temple Gardens was near Crescent Park with its swans and a little bridge and lush green grass and tall trees and beds of flowers. That was in the days before Mossbank had water, and the park was paradise for someone who had never walked on soft grass.

My eyes wander back to my map to Regina. Regina was reserved for special occasions – the Shrine Circus, a visit to the Natural History Museum and the Legislative Buildings – because it was so far away: one hundred miles! Moose Jaw was a trip but Regina was an expedition. All of Mossbank was in awe of Leslie who went to Regina every Saturday for voice lessons at Darke Hall. Many of us admired her as much for her stamina in enduring the five hours of travel on STC buses as for her voice whose quality we had all recognized at an early age.

I glance at Regina again and realize that nowadays it is just another airport to me, a point of arrival and departure. We never did become acquainted.

I can trace my journey into a greater world on this road map: from Mossbank to Assiniboia to Moose Jaw and finally, to Saskatoon and the university. How awkward and hayseedish we freshmen must have appeared to those suave, sophisticated upper-classmen from Fox Valley and Neidpath and Mikado. (Mikado? Where did it get its name? From a Gilbert and Sullivan aficionado? A Japanese restaurant? Curiouser and curiouser.)

I may have had no impact on the U of S but the U of S certainly had an impact on me. If it were ever possible to represent learning and scholarship in a physical manner, it would, to my mind, be well represented by the limestone Gothic buildings of the Saska-toon campus in 1959. Picture it: a child of the prairies whose only association with structures other than those of wood was the post office and CPR station in Moose Jaw and the Legislative Buildings in Regina, buildings that were meant to be impressive and mem-orable. This child is set down in a small city of venerable stone buildings with carvings and gargoyles everywhere. Even the worn stone steps leading into Saskatchewan Hall, the girls' residence, gave me a thrill because they represented generations who had passed that way. Throw in serene green lawns, contemplative human beings . . . and the College of Engineering! What more could a young girl ask for?

It was in that girls' residence that I got to know more of this map. One room-mate came from Yorkton. I went there to her wed-ding. Another came from Indian Head. She lived in one of those old brick houses I now take for granted. There were girls from Watrous and Naicam and Kinistino, boys from Kamsack and Whitewood and Kindersley. So many names. So many tiny dots that ring bells, stir memories, bring back a face, a class, a party, a love affair, a friendship. Raymore: a special friend I met on my eighteenth birthday. Unity: a friend of a friend. Carlyle: an idyllic summer.

I'm taking my daughter "home" this summer. I hope her feet, accustomed to the cobble-stones and winding narrow streets of Prague, will not stumble on the hard earth of the prairies and the streets that go on forever. It's time to make these names on a map come alive for her; to have her smell that indescribable smell of

dust and clover and heat; to see a grain elevator against the canopy
of that enormous blue, blue sky. It's time, too, for me to go home.

Gail Kirkpatrick Devlin
Ottawa

✉ "It's only a building," my friend said. "It's not as though it's
a person or an animal or something."

To *you*, I thought, it's only a building–the old cottage, not much
more than a shack with its sagging roof, its musty smell of damp
wood and coal oil and fly tox, its colony of bats and generations
of mice, and now it's no longer fit for human habitation. To me,
however, it is a place of magic, of endless childhood summers, a
reminder of the only time in my life when I knew the meaning of
the word "happy." How can I tear it down?

Then I thought: I don't need the actual building. As long as I
am alive, it will remain, every detail vivid in my mind, every memory treasured in my heart.

And so I had the old cottage torn down and replaced with a new
one. The tall hemlocks with the bar for my swing are cut down,
the hole in the ground where we kept our food cool is filled in, and
the home-made mast and sail that reposed on the rafters for years
have gone to the dump along with the little wood stove with
"Favourite Box" embossed on the side. But the memories remain.

It is fifty-two years ago, and I am seven years old. I am wearing
faded blue shorts and a jersey, and a farmer's straw hat with elastic
under the chin. I have taken off my shoes and my sweater because,
although it is cold in the woods by the lake in the early morning,
up here in the fields it is hot, and I like to feel the soft, warm dust
of the road under my bare feet. I am carrying the green and gold
straw basket with the two milk bottles to fetch the milk from the
farm for breakfast. I am not really afraid, but a little in awe of the
great trees that stand so tall and silent at the edge of the field. I
hope I will not encounter the cows, and I listen for the tinkle of
cowbells in the bush.

My mother always boils the milk on the coal-oil stove to sterilize it before we use it. Sometimes it boils over, and flames shoot up from the burner. She tries to make me drink the milk using cocoa to disguise the taste, but I hate it and gag at the skin that forms on the top.

I pause on the log bridge over Fairy Glen Falls and watch the coffee-coloured water splash down over the rocks and tree roots. Sometimes we climb down the falls to play in the shadows; the water is ice-cold on bare feet, and the moss-covered rocks are slippery and treacherous. I don't have to open the big gate because there is a little log gate and foot-bridge beside it. I unhook the ring on the chain that fastens the little gate and go through.

I go to the kitchen door at the back of the farmhouse and hand in my milk bottles to be filled. The door is open, and chickens wander in and out. The kitchen smells of sour milk and poverty. If I am with my friends, we may stop near the sawmill to play on the lumber piles with their sweet smell of freshly cut wood. Or we may linger in the field picking blackberries or wild strawberries, and be scolded for delaying the breakfast.

When I return to the cottage, I see smoke rising from the chimney, and I can smell wood smoke and bacon frying. When the fire burns down, we make toast, crouching in front of the open door of the little box stove and holding the long-handled toaster over the coals. The toast is crisp and brittle and tastes faintly of smoke.

I am sitting on the sagging couch beside the open window. The leaves hang limply on the maple saplings; an oven-bird hidden somewhere in the brush calls, "Teacher, teacher, teacher," and an unknown bird chirps lazily from the tree-tops. I smell the hot smell of clean cotton from the pink quilt as the noonday sun falls across it, and the whole bush waits breathless in the July heat.

I spend hours lying in the hammock slung between two birch trees, pushing myself gently to and fro with a stick, gazing up at the tops of the ancient maple trees towering against the sky. I also like to sit on my rope swing under the hemlocks, feeling the rush of air on my face as I go as high as I dare, and singing all the songs

390

I know. One of my favourites is "Listen to the Mocking Bird," which I learned from the scratchy seventy-eight record we play on the wind-up Victrola.

Every evening, we meet our neighbours and walk over to the landing to wait for the sunset. This is the big event of the day. We climb up through the long grass and weeds and sit on the rocks at the top of the hill beside the stunted white birch and watch the colours blaze and fade in the sky.

As the light fades from the sky, a coolness rises from the land, the tall dark hemlocks press close around the cottage, and the thrushes begin to sing. We sit on the screened veranda in the gathering darkness, watching the leaves of the silver birch move like black lace against the sky and listening to the hum of millions of mosquitoes. It is so still that we can hear the little rustling sounds made by the dew worms in the dead leaves outside. Sometimes the loons' haunting laughter echoes around the lake, a distant whippoorwill calls to the night, or a rhythmic bullfrog chorus breaks the silence. Sometimes faint violin music comes stealing through the trees – it is old Dad Williams playing his violin alone in his house in the bush.

Later I lie in bed behind the curtain and watch the shadows made on the roof by the yellow light of the coal-oil lamp. I can see pictures in the various stains on the rough boards over my head – there is one that looks like a paintbrush with a bent handle. The tank on the coal-oil stove gives a soft little gurgle and the fire murmurs in the stove. A firefly drifts across the square of black velvet that is my window. The darkness is not an enemy to be kept at bay, but a gentle friend that comes partway into the cottage.

Now I look in vain for the children who used to run over these paths and play among the trees. Sometimes when a high wind is blowing through the leaves I think I can hear their laughter, distant and faint. So many memories, so many ghosts.

Now the thrushes sing no more. The peace is shattered by the roar of motor boats, and the loons have fled. But it is still quiet in the spring and fall, the stars still glitter in the cold night sky, and the clamour of the wild geese still stirs the heart.

Nancy Goldring
Scarborough, Ontario

✉ Being at the tail-end of our family, I was often alone at the summer cottage, but I was never unhappy about not having a special playmate or groups of children to take sides with. I learned that if I sat quietly in a room with my parents and their friends, I could hear incredible secrets, most of which I did not quite understand, but I sensed the excitement of the news.

There were, however, great memories of my brother and his friends, before he found summer jobs to take him away. Forts we made in dense sapling groves, cutting down small trees to form paths and rooms, even one for the dog, which he would dutifully go to on order and sit and stare balefully at us through the saplings, waiting for a smile or a snap of the fingers to come bounding to our rooms. We would raid Mother's pantry of crackers and jelly powders for our fort. We also buried our special treasures; I buried a bit of money I had in a lovely wooden inlaid box given to me by my grandmother before she died. I was quite dismayed when I dug it up after a time and discovered it had become completely unglued and turned into a bunch of little pieces of wood.

Of course, the cut saplings were carefully honed to make dreadfully sharp spears to protect us from enemies, who never came. We were the only children around. Then, when I was twelve, a new family moved in, who had a fourteen-year-old boy with a bicycle! One day at the post office he bought me a chocolate bar. (To this day the smell of Crispy Crunch brings back his memory.) He then asked if he could come swim with me the next day. I was pretty pleased about my first date, but was horrified that night to discover Nature had decided my childhood was at an end and menstruation had begun. Back then, young ladies did not go swimming at such times. How I explained this to my new-found friend

I cannot recall – I blanked that embarrassing situation out of my mind. However, our friendship survived and I wore the seat out of many pairs of shorts riding a rough board attached to the back carrier of his bicycle as we explored back roads, killing snakes, eating wild strawberries and smelling empty liquor bottles.

June Jennings
Toronto

✉ I've never wanted to go back to the farm – too many regrets, too much grief tangled in my memories.

My return, in the end, was unplanned. My brother owns the land adjoining the farm, a piece of Muskoka that contains all the best features of the Canadian Shield: glacier-scarred granite, Christmas-tree spruces and meandering creek waters gurgling under shelves of ice attached to the shore.

I'd been invited to go for a day of cross-country skiing, skating on the pond and a snow-picnic lunch. Fun! It had taken me forty years to discover the gourmet pleasure of hot dogs toasted over an open fire on a bed of snow.

After lunch, we skied around my brother's property, crossing the creek at a place where the ice looked "safe"; nevertheless, I couldn't help holding my breath till I was on the other side.

We came out of the bush at the edge of the old farm. Two over-grown fields separated us from the family homestead on the hilltop. Even from that distance I could see that it was no longer the home I'd known.

New owners had marked (I want to say "marred") it with their territorial signs. Modern casement windows replaced the multi-paned ones that, as a child, I had loathed cleaning. A green vinyl-clad porch had been added at the kitchen door – an insult to the natural red-brick exterior. (Our windows and our porch may have been just as ugly as these new ones, but they'd been *ours*.) And most offensive of all, a grotesque, white, TV satellite dish shouted its presence from the top of whippoorwill rock.

This was an enormous bare rock face that had accumulated so much heat in the hot days of summer that it stayed warm till morning. A whippoorwill would come to that warm rock every night and sit there, repeating his rhythmical cry over and over, "WHIP-poor-will, WHIP-poor-will, WHIP-poor-will . . . "

I find myself recalling this bird song nostalgically now, but at the time it was anything but heart-warming. I was never able to sleep through those persistent calls close to my window, and in desperation I'd go screaming and flapping out to the rock to scare the bird away. It would go, but only for about five minutes, long enough for me to get back inside and settle into bed, then it would begin again.

Now, gazing resentfully at that invasive satellite dish, I wondered if the whippoorwill still found a place to call there on a summer's night.

I've always been sad that Mom sold the farm. But after my dad died, she had no choice. Summers were fine—we could manage the house and the roads then. Winters were the problem. As I stood looking at this house of my childhood, memories trickled in.

The house was half a mile from the township road, and in storms we were often snowbound till someone could plough us out. When Mom became the only wage-earner, she had to be able to get out to teach.

When my dad was alive, he was a one-man roads department. We had two roads into the house, one for summer and one for winter. The idea was that, if we didn't harden the snow on the summer road, the ground under it wouldn't freeze. And when spring came, the lane wouldn't then thaw into pot-holes and muddy bogs, becoming completely impassable.

The winter road was just a bed of hard-packed snow. Instead of ploughing it during the first snowfalls of the season, Dad would drive over it repeatedly, packing it into a driveable surface, ploughing it only after several snowfalls had dumped enough snow for his road.

It was a system that worked pretty well. But it was this winter road that, in some measure, killed him.

The road was really just a swath cut through the bush, so forest maintenance was a necessary part of the road works. Dad had noticed a tree leaning dangerously towards the road. Always concerned for our safety, he decided to fell the tree himself before it harmed one of us.

He was such a careful man, so skilled in the bush, that it's still hard for me to believe that he didn't see the dead branch lodged above him. I can only guess that its position must have been deceptively natural, that its point of contact with the leaning tree must have been sheathed in snow. Whatever the reason, he didn't see it and as the leaning tree fell exactly where he'd planned, the dead branch dislodged and plummeted.

He lived for two days, but never regained consciousness. We found out later that such limbs are known among foresters as "widow-makers."

The grieving returned in those moments that I stood contemplating the house, the farm. The pain, dulled for almost twenty years, sharpened, and tears for my father and my lost home flowed again.

Samm MacKay
Waterloo, Ontario

✉ Three weeks ago a young man took me back in time fifty-five years.

I was revisiting Montreal after many years, and attempting to walk up the side of Mount Royal from Pine Avenue West with a tall, robust young man who lived nearby. I had forgotten how steep the path would be to the top, and quite soon I became an early drop-out. With polite regard for my age, he agreed it would be better if I walked sideways around the mountain rather than straight up. So he very kindly directed me past Montreal General Hospital along an avenue with brilliant autumn leaves in the trees above me. Spread out below me was the vast panorama of Montreal.

Several steps and a few photographs later, I came to an inter-section with traffic swooshing up and down a long hill. I stopped and looked up to my right. There, on the opposite side, almost on the crest of the hill above me, stood the mass of a huge old complex of apartments. After all these years, the name "Gleneagles" sud-denly flashed into my mind. I had not yet read the street sign, but before I looked, I knew it would say Côte des Neiges.

In a moment I was once more a small child.

My mother and father, our bulldog and I had moved from what was then Port Arthur to Montreal in October 1933. We had taken a small, rather dingy apartment on Côte St. Luc Road. The second Sunday there, we went for a long exploratory walk and found ourselves somewhere along the side of Mount Royal.

Suddenly that walk of fifty-five years ago has come back to me. Here is the crescent where I first learned the meaning of "cul-de-sac." Here are the great stately grey stone mansions. My mother looks at them with great longing, while my father seems to per-ceive them with some bitterness I do not understand.

Over there a little girl is playing on her front lawn among the fallen leaves. Almost bursting with joy, I run to her because I *know* her. How, in all this vast, teeming city, could we ever have found her? We had met a few months before near Minneapolis. As bosom pals we had shared our holidays and little-girl secrets and pledged to be friends forever. Then, at the end of the summer, our parents led us away. We had known that her family lived in Mon-treal, but not that they were rich and lived in a mansion. And, now, my parents greet her coolly and decline her invitation to go in to see her mother. They do not encourage me to stay and play. Having found the only kindred spirit I know in Montreal, I feel devastated to be hurried away and surprised by my parents' behaviour – they are usually so friendly.

Over the years I forgot the walk, the cul-de-sac and the girl, and never thought of them again.

As I walked along that afternoon three weeks ago, tears began to fill my eyes. The whole of that long-ago walk was still present deep within me, and the question still begged an answer. But as I walked I began to understand something that I had been too young to understand fifty-five years ago.

Those were the Depression years. My father was a struggling civil servant with several salary cuts behind him. My mother sat up late every night making or mending all our clothes and preparing bundles of clothes and food parcels that she would then send to family on the prairies.

There would be no grey stone mansions or apartments in the Gleneagles for us. During that walk my parents were wondering whether we would be able to survive a winter in this expensive city. There would be no dinners or afternoon teas in a grey stone mansion, because there could be no return invitation to our drab little apartment where the hallways always reeked of stale garlic and the hot-water radiators hissed or leaked on very cold days. There would be no risk of rejection by snobbery, for there would be no hob- nobbing with the rich. I know now that my parents were protecting me from some of the hard knocks that children cannot understand.

If you were walking down Côte des Neiges and Pine Avenue West one afternoon three weeks ago and saw an elderly woman walking with tears in her eyes, now you understand. Have compassion for her parents, please. I do.

Dorothy Deakin
Kelowna, British Columbia

✉ I float home – not in the nautical sense, but on a sea of memories, usually launched by something insignificant in the everyday of life, like a song on the radio, the smell of sauce simmering on the stove or catching the best parts of an Italian argument falling out of a window in the suburbs.

Home was the north end of Hamilton, the very north end; if you went any more north, you'd walk into the steel mills. We lived in the upper part of a brick house on Beta Street, one of three identical dead-end streets surrounded by Stelco, train tracks and busy Burlington Avenue.

There were only eight houses on each of the three streets (Alpha, Beta and Keele), but in my mind of thirty years ago, this was the whole wide world. My Italian grandparents lived across the street and my best friend – she was Hungarian – lived next door. This was where the chicken man came every week with his horse and wagon loaded with Sunday's dinner ready to be slaughtered. The clanging of bells signalled the return of the man to sharpen knives and scissors. Neighbours on the corner near the tracks kept a cage of rabbits for special meals. At wine-making time we built great forts out of grape crates that were delivered by the dozen with much ceremony. The constant hum of life on the street was defined by mealtime and the whistle that signalled the shift changes at Stelco. Ever present was the clanging of train bells as the trains chugged by not more than thirty feet away.

I couldn't really go home to visit the street even though I live close by in Burlington, because the neighbourhood is no more. It was bulldozed to the ground years ago, silencing forever the arguments and the laughter and all that life that was held fast in a very small area. In its place is more of the heavy industry that once surrounded it.

It's nice to float home for a visit now and again because I'm reminded of where I came from, of why I am the way I am. It's important for me to keep in touch with the old place.

Andrea Bishop
Burlington, Ontario

✉ I grew up in a small farming community in southern British Columbia, ten miles from the tiny town of Creston. When my parents received a cheque for the milk they sold to Purity Dairy, they would go to town to pay bills and to shop. Going to town was a special event for me. It meant a visit to the Co-op Drygoods

Store to finger the fresh-smelling new clothes on the shiny racks. (The town girls on the street always seemed to be better dressed than me.) I would cross the street to Webster's Five and Dime store, to gawk at all the brightly coloured treasures on the shelves. The wood floors would creak as I moved down one aisle and up another. The trip would be capped with an exotic meal of fish and chips or chicken chow mein and red Jell-O with whipped cream on it at the local Chinese diner. Then we would go home to milk our cows.

When I was fifteen, my father died. A year later my mother sold the farm and we moved to Edmonton. My images of Creston crystallized and remained frozen until I returned nine years later, with my boyfriend. Our trip was unplanned, a lark. We strolled down the main street past all the haunts I had frequented as a young teenager. Some of the buildings looked smaller and shabbier. The clothes at the Co-op Drygoods store looked rather plain. Webster's Five and Dime had been transformed into a shiny new drugstore.

Then I met Elaine Miller on the street. She was a town girl, the prettiest girl in my class. Her blonde hair was always perfectly curled. She always seemed to have boyfriends. Now she was pregnant, with two little children clinging to her dress, her hair in large pink curlers. She didn't look as pretty as I remembered. She told me about being married and about the new avocado-coloured fridge and stove she had just bought.

I told her about my life, about going to college for two years, about working as an audio technician. Then I stopped. Elaine was fidgeting. She said she had to go home to prepare her husband's meal. I realized she was no longer the princess I had made her into. I was glad I had been a farm girl and hadn't been popular with the boys. In fact, I quite liked my life; it took going home to realize that.

Carol Siebert
Vancouver

✉ It was to be a truly memorable trip: the first visit in thirty years to the city where I spent four years of my childhood. I had only three clear memories of the city: my grandfather's dark, musty, cluttered shop (the word "pawn" meant nothing to me then), the snowbanks towering high above my head and an address – 411 Avenue C South.

I was born in Kinistino, Saskatchewan, a tiny prairie town seventy-five miles north-east of Saskatoon (we had no kilometres in 1937). The Depression brought us to the "city" in 1939. We lived one block from my grandparents, and much of my time was spent in Baba's warm kitchen. They had escaped from Russia and, like many other immigrants, had made their way to the prairies. To ensure continuing employment for sociologists, we left Saskatoon for Vancouver in 1943.

My excitement grew block by block as I approached Avenue C. The neighbourhood was totally unfamiliar, but as I parked the rented car down the street from 411, I began to get glimmerings. The house was run-down but the porch – I recognized the porch. I ran into the yard, ignoring the calls from my family.

"How can you just go up to a strange house like that?" my two teenage kids asked. I could. I knocked at the rickety screen door and explained to the old woman who answered that I had once lived in this house. Could I look inside? She peered at me curiously, as if I had found a new way to sell encyclopaedias, but she let me in.

The house was both familiar and unfamiliar. A few rooms I remembered, particularly the living room where I had first listened to jazz records with my father. Others – a corner, the shape of a window, a doorway – some things I recognized but much was strange. It was sobering to think that a house in which I had spent four of my most formative years had left so little impression. Did time erase so much? After fifteen minutes of prowling, and increasing complaints from my children, who did not appreciate nostalgia, we left.

The last phase of my trip was to describe to my mother our

experiences in Kinistino and, particularly, the odd mixture of strangeness and intimacy in 411 Avenue C South.

"That's not surprising," she said. "That was your grandparents' house. We lived on Avenue D."

Leon Sharzer
London, Ontario

THE
ELDERBERRY
SOLUTION(S)

T he elderberry *problem* was posed by a listener who'd had troubles trying to make jelly. When I read her letter on the air, we uncovered a wealth of lore – and some recipes – about a much-neglected Canadian delicacy.

✉ Just heard the sad tale of the elderberry jelly that wouldn't – gel, that is. Your respondent related her experience with puzzlement, as she had followed a recipe that she thought would work, even though it was for berries other than elderberries. She's quite right that it should be possible to interchange recipes – that there is a basic principle involved in the making of jelly. Her problem was in trying to make her jelly using Certo, a commercial pectin.

Now, I'm not saying that you can't make jelly with Certo, but I *am* saying that when you do so, a totally different set of culinary criteria come into play, in my opinion, complicating a simple process. Certo fans would argue that it speeds up the making of jelly, an "advantage" I would not deny; but its use requires more sugar and also creates an instability in the cooking (witness your writer's failure).

Did it never occur to your writer to wonder what people did before Certo? They cooked up berry juice and sugar until it reached the set point – the point at which the mixture will gel when cool. Different mixtures may take different lengths of time, although they are usually about the same; the important part is that the correct temperature (about 222° F) must be reached. Enough water must be cooked off to elevate the mixture sufficiently above 212° F (the boiling point for water), ensuring a dense mixture that will form a gel.

All old cookbooks assumed that their readers understood this principle as it applied to jam, jelly and candy. May I suggest that your writer do some reading about the basic process of jelly-making, which she can then apply to her elderberries.

Heather Graham
Montreal

✉ I just heard the letter from the lady with the elderberry syrup. It took me back fifteen years, to the time we came across an elderberry patch in a neighbouring swamp. Our two oldest children were in school, and I was pregnant with our youngest daughter. Every day I went to the swamp. Every day I came home with my treasure and processed bowls and bowls of berries into elderberry jelly – two hundred jars in all. I never made elderberry jelly again. The next fall I had a six-month-old to look after, and a few years later the swamp had no more elderberries.

Elderberry Jelly

4 pounds ripe elderberries (5 quarts)
Juice of 4 lemons (about ½ cup)
7½ cups sugar (3¼ pounds)
1 bottle Certo fruit pectin

Remove stems from berries. Place berries in a saucepan and crush. Heat gently until juice starts to flow, then simmer, covered, for 15 minutes. Pour into jelly cloth or bag and squeeze out juice. Place 3 cups of juice in very large saucepan. Add lemon juice and sugar and mix well.

Place over high heat and bring to a boil, stirring constantly. Add Certo, bring to a boil again and boil hard for one minute, stirring constantly. Remove from heat, skim off foam with a metal spoon, then pour quickly into sterilized jars. Seal with paraffin.

Yield: about 5 cups

Elsie Herrle
St. Agatha, Ontario

✉ I had never heard of or eaten elderberries until I met and married a man who was born in Fenwick, Ontario. My in-laws would make a family outing of collecting elderberries in brown paper bags while my father-in-law, a monument salesman, would take tombstone rubbings in the many small county cemeteries. Elderberries used to grow wild all along the county roadsides, but weed-control sprays have almost done away with this wonderful free fruit. Cleaning the tiny stems from the berries is best done immediately after picking them, and they freeze well for winter enjoyment.

Waiting until the tiny fruit changes from bright green to almost black for the harvest means conducting a race with the birds, particularly the robins, which try to get more than we do. Every family reunion there is another race–to see if there is an elderberry pie. Every little seedy bit is consumed.

Elderberry Pie

Pastry for 2 crusts
2½ to 3 cups elderberries
½ cup white sugar
2 tablespoons flour
3 tablespoons lemon juice or white vinegar
1 tablespoon butter

Line pie pan with pastry. Fill with elderberries. Mix sugar and flour and sprinkle over berries. Add lemon juice and dot with butter. Cover with top crust. Make several holes in the crust with a fork.

Bake in a hot oven, 450°, for 15 minutes, then reduce heat to 350° and bake for 30 minutes more.

Linda Johnston
St. Catharines, Ontario

✉ It's pig-butchering time here on the homestead, but I have been side-tracked from my morning's work (making fifty pounds of country sausage on a hand-crank grinder!) to leap to the aid of your friend with the elderberry problem.

I am beguiled every fall by the cascades of smoky-blue berries along the roadsides, and this year we had a bumper harvest. I make elderberry and apple jelly, and if you use the greenest and tartest apples you can find, there is enough pectin in them to "jell" the jelly.

I also make elderberry wine. A word of caution, though – most recipes call for far too much fruit. I have had some elderberry wine (not my own!) which, if it couldn't peel paint, at least felt as if it was taking the skin off the roof of my mouth. I use only two pounds of elderberries per gallon and obtain a light red, palatable dry wine.

Elderberry Wine

2 pounds elderberries
3 pounds sugar
1½ teaspoons acid blend*
½ teaspoon pectic enzyme*
1 teaspoon yeast food*
1 crushed campden tablet*
1 gallon water
General all-purpose red-wine yeast*

Remove stems from berries, then mash berries in a crock (not one made of metal). Add all the ingredients except the yeast. Stir well. After 24 hours, add the yeast and cover the container with a plastic sheet.

Let the mixture ferment in a warm place for 5 days, stirring daily. After 5 days strain out the pulp. Siphon wine into a one-gallon glass jug, top up to within 3 inches from top and attach the fermentation lock. Let it ferment in a warm place. Siphon the wine into a clean jar and leave it until the wine is clear. When it is clear and has stopped fermenting, siphon it into sterile bottles and cork.

*All these products are available in a wine-making store.

Christine Wilson
Denman Island, British Columbia

✉ In Newfoundland we have many and varied wine and beer recipes, and my father-in-law's is probably a classic. We don't much care to disclose or make public the fact that we make wines and home brews because of these cussed laws about that sort of thing. Probably they're right, though, in the case of Rufus's dogberry wine – there probably should be a law against it.

Anyway, here goes. You take two gallons of fresh-picked dogberries (I imagine it will work just as well with elderberries) and crush them in a clean five-gallon salt-pork tub, with a loose cover of cloth tied with a string. Cover the crushed berries with lukewarm water to about three-quarters full. Throw in a couple of handfuls of raisins and a pack of prunes – and possibly two or three cut-up apples or anything else you have handy or an excess of. Toss in a five-pound bag of sugar and stir vigorously with a wooden spoon or a large split, if you're not fortunate enough to have a wooden spoon. Carefully place a slice of good home-made bread on the top of the mixture and sprinkle the bread with two packs of brewer's yeast, if you're lucky enough to have any. If not, Fleischmann's fast-rising yeast will do. Cover with the cloth and place behind your kitchen stove (this should be a wood-burning stove).

Keep the mixture lukewarm for about three weeks. Then siphon and bottle – carefully. There is really no need to bottle this mixture after the three weeks. You can just dip your soup ladle into it, and spoon it out to your distinguished visitors as they arrive.

This recipe is gospel according to Rufus and it works if you can tolerate the taste.

John Randell
Deer Lake, Newfoundland

✉ Elderberry Chutney

3 pounds elderberries
1 pint (20 ounces) vinegar
½ pound onions
½ pound sultanas
½ pound sugar
1 teaspoon ground ginger
1 teaspoon cinnamon
1 teaspoon allspice
1 teaspoon cayenne pepper
¼ pound salt

Pick the berries before they are fully ripe. Remove their stalks. Add the berries to the vinegar and start to heat. Meanwhile chop onions and when the berry mixture boils, add them together with all the other ingredients. Continue to simmer until the berries break and the mixture thickens. Bottle the hot mixture in sterilized jars and seal.

This recipe was taken from *Home Cooking* by Henry Sarson published in 1940. Sarson also writes: "Elder shoots were used a good deal during the eighteenth century for bamboo shoots, as the latter are a striking constituent of Indian chutneys and Chinese chow-chow. They need no brining but can be packed into jars and covered with spiced vinegar and used later in mixed pickles."

Joan Streets Godfrey
Hudson, Quebec

✉ Elderberry Cleansing Cream

In a double boiler heat 1 cup home-made buttermilk and ¼ cup elderberry flowers for ½ hour. Remove from heat and let rest a few hours. Heat again. Strain out the flowers. Add 2 table-spoons honey. Store in a really cool place.

This recipe was taken from the *Old-Fashioned Recipie Book* by Carla Emery. You can also dry the berries to have year-round. Drop a few in your bath water. These flowers have been long famous for being good for the skin.

Dawn Oman
Lasqueti Island, British Columbia

THE POWER OF
SEASONS

Politics, the economy, the issues of the day. Whatever divides Canadians, it seems to me – and in the late 1980s there was much to be troubled about – we are held together by our closeness to the land. Herewith an almanac of some of *Morningside*'s most eloquent and often lyrical mail – a record of the changing weathers, from west to east, from the bonds of winter to the joyful release (well, sometimes) of spring.

✉ I am a poor country pastor serving three rural churches in southern Saskatchewan. I arrived four years ago in August amid a heat wave, at the end of a dry year. The waving wheat fields of my memory, in which a small child could hide herself, were nowhere to be seen. Scraggly brown sticks of wheat stood everywhere in the fields, desperately trying to touch the top of my socks.

Driving was a panic. With no air-conditioning in my car, and heat that melted and twisted my Pete Seeger cassette tape into a bow-tie, I had to travel with my windows open. It was a no-win situation. With the windows open, the hordes of grasshoppers that missed splattering themselves on my windshield tumbled dizzily into my car, where they clung to my arm, to the side of my face, and crawled up my accelerator foot.

When you travel at one hundred kilometres an hour, those things hit like rock-salt from a shotgun, smarting the skin, and then tumbling into the folds of clothing. From there, they find their way to the nearest spot of bare skin and bite, spit and deposit other grasshopper remembrances until their exact location can be found. At this point, the driver brakes suddenly, leaps from the car and shakes clothing while yelling loudly. (Grasshoppers are hard of hearing – yelling is essential.)

The only way to avoid hoppers in your duds is to roll the windows up, and put up with the suffocating heat, the yellowing windshield and the warm aroma the vents emit because of locusts frying on the front grill of the car.

I am writing about this memory now, because for the first time in four years of *my* life here, things have changed. We have snow – not the layer of white stuff on the ground that will soon melt to ice, but real snow. Children up to the age of ten haven't seen snow like this in their lives. They are learning how to play in it and how to eat it off their mittens without getting wool in their teeth. They are making forts and tunnels and living in the deep silence of snow.

The adults are shovelling driveways, sliding into ditches and getting stranded in drifts. But as they dig themselves out, as they tell their stories in the coffee shops and the hotel bars, they smile – genuine smiles of relief, of nostalgia, of gratitude.

Last Sunday I drove fifteen miles to church for the first service. The sun was just rising, pushing soft purple clouds higher into the sky. The highway was deep in snow, the ditches being too full to hold any more. I made the first path on the road, silently crushing the wide stuff beneath my tires. Grouse stood ahead of me, wading in the fallen snow, and then disappearing behind the purple-blue shadowy drifts on the hills.

The few trees along the road shimmered with frost, and ice-mist hung heavy in the air. Ice-mist – billions of tiny dancing diamonds, prisms of ice showing off the rainbow colours of the sun.

The silence of snow, the beauty of ice, the gift of winter – real winter at last. We gathered that morning in church to praise God. To give God thanks for the beauty of this creation and this life. And to give God thanks for the promise, and the hope for the prairies contained in the snow.

Deborah Laing
Radville, Saskatchewan

✉ It is quiet, now, out here. Winter has arrived, and all the powerboats and summer guests have fled. Night, and a fat full moon rides balefully above. It has been a tiring, yet rewarding day. There was wood to chop; wood to stack; and finally, wood to restack, after it all fell over. I stir the stove's slumbering embers, and then I yawn and stumble away to bed. But sleep eludes me, for I am troubled by our reluctance to learn to live, to coexist, with nature.

As in counterpoint to my thoughts, there filters from without a mournful cry, a lament. The voice echoes again, again: haunting, piercing. Roused, I toss aside the blankets and struggle into my clothes. The crisp inky air is like a tonic; an icy crust crunches under my boots.

Where is the sly caroller? Ah, there he is, roosting in that leaf-stripped poplar! His imperious golden eye studies me coolly; no words do we exchange, but still we seem to understand each other. Man and owl; owl and man. Again his lusty screech – and suddenly the forest explodes into a fine snowy glitter, as I attempt to knock the stupid branch-hopping pest into orbit with the five-iron I keep for this purpose, long ago having realized I was just no damn good at golf.

Pierre LeClair
Edmonton or thereabouts

✉ The blowing snow of this week's blizzard has got me thinking. Reports on the radio have been advising people to stay indoors.

411

In this province, people who were once accustomed to winter are forgetting how to manage in what used to be normal January weather. Last year at this time, the grass in the pasture out back was green. There wasn't even any frost – the weather was better than the last couple of Julys.

As I listened to the morning show out in the barn while doing chores, it struck me that people were having fun, despite the surprise of the storm. As one newscaster put it, everyone is "into" the blizzard.

Yesterday at six in the morning, it was above freezing and felt and smelled more like January on Salt Spring Island than in the Medicine Lake hills of central Alberta. With a roar that could be heard for two miles in the calm air, all that changed – and fast. That cold front came through the woods north of us and hit like the back of a big cold hand. Rain turned to snow, water froze almost instantly on my coveralls and I watched the mercury drop from plus two to minus five in less than a minute.

This morning at six, it's minus thirty-two with a strong north wind. All the animals are in the sheds, looking distinctly cold – they've gone soft, too, I guess. The radio advises me not to go outside, but I've already been out for an hour and will be out for another one yet. It took awhile to find my felt-lined boots, heavy coveralls and favourite toque. But now that I've got them, I'm not that cold. I know that every other rancher, dairy farmer and stockman is out there, too, worrying about his livestock. No one has passed by on the country road for two days. Everyone is dug in and held firmly in the grip of nature, with time to reflect as normal routines come to a halt. And I know that everyone here is profoundly thankful for the promise of real moisture this spring, for the first time in several years.

John Gorham
Winfield, Alberta

✉ Twenty years ago, we were newly-weds of two weeks. A recent immigrant from England, Martin was enjoying his second winter in Canada. It was a beautiful warm Sunday in January. In the middle of the afternoon, he was called out to work. A farmer was having trouble with a piece of machinery. Would Martin please go have a look?

Wanting to spend as much time as possible with my new husband, I volunteered to go for the drive in the country. I started to get boots and parkas together only to be met by Martin's comment, "Don't take the time to bring all that stuff. It's so warm the water's running in the streets." What followed was our first serious disagreement – with me making comments that I, at least, wasn't going to be caught out. I managed to put a shovel in the trunk, but Martin absolutely balked at a jug of water or emergency chocolate bars. He also refused boots and mitts. We both vividly remember my parting shot: "Don't you know that we can get our worst storms right after a beautiful warm spell?"

I haven't been subtle enough to surprise you with the fact that a terrible blizzard engulfed us about one hour out of the city. A white nothingness descended upon the car. I have no sense of direction, and Martin's normally good one was soon confused. We became stuck in the soft deep snow on a Saskatchewan back road. Martin gratefully accepted the loan of my mitts and was overjoyed to find the shovel in the trunk. Together we dug the car out, only to become stuck again. Neither of us remembers how many times we dug out our little Vauxhall.

By now lights were coming on in the farmhouses around us. They looked deceptively close, and I had to talk fast to convince Martin that our chances were better if we stayed with the car. We didn't know that the closest light was in fact the farm that we were looking for. The observant farmer, a widow who operated her farm with her two sons, aged thirteen and fifteen, had been watching our meanderings and numerous unscheduled stops in the snow.

The fifteen-year-old dug a path to the machine shed, shovelled the snow away from the door so he could open it and drove the tractor to our stranded car. He towed us into the farmyard, and he and Martin shovelled out the door again to return the tractor to its place in the shed. The space he had cleared had completely blown in while he was rescuing us.

I can't describe the feeling when everyone was finally warm and safe.

We were, of course, put up in the farmer's own bedroom; I wore the nightgown she loaned to me. We were lulled to sleep by the monotonous whine of the blizzard and then awakened by the smell of coffee brewing and bacon frying. The wind was still howling, but it didn't seem quite so angry. The phone lines were still work-ing, and later that day a dark blue Bombardier rumbled across the fields and picked us up. I was used to riding in one of these snow vehicles because I had lived up north, but it was a first for Martin. Our car remained snow-bound for another week. It was only then that Martin confessed that he no longer thought the danger of a prairie snowstorm was exaggerated.

I called out to one of my teenage sons as he was leaving this morning, "Are you dressed properly?" They don't argue with me, because if they do, they'll be subjected to Dad telling them about the day the water was running in the streets.

Margaret Dodson
Regina, Saskatchewan

✉ Cadomin just became an official hamlet with a population of ninety-six. That is, if we counted the recent babies accurately. It sits on a flat, former riverbed (the Macleod River is a small stream in Cadomin), with the Rockies one block west and a kilometre or so south, and the foothills north and east. Its elevation of five thousand feet is close to the tree-line. Cadomin is the nearest thing to the joy of Eden, except when it's as ugly as that nether region when clouds cover the mountains and mud and wetness rule. Most people who live here are ex or present coal miners, quarry workers or CN track workers. We have lots of quarrels and hurt feelings. But we close ranks and pitch in when there is the need.

As for our weather, in spring and fall we can leave Cadomin in snow and cold winds, and take our coats off when we reach Hinton and warm sunshine. Of course, in summer we can leave sweltering Hinton and put on our coats upon reaching Cadomin. Our major affliction, however, is the wind! Many chinooks and mountain configurations often channel violent winds into Cadomin. During the storm of November 1988, the wind that tore off a large part of the roof of my new home registered 214 km an hour at a nearby mine. Lots of fun!

Walter Mast
Cadomin, Alberta

✉ In Bahamian Canada (or British California, as we who live on the West Coast are fond of calling it) we have a real problem with snow. From the moment the first snowflake splats on the windshield, Vancouverites go into a type of snow hysteria.

First, we *point out* the snow to each other. "Hey, look, it's snowing!" This is guaranteed to assemble your whole office at the window, watching in silent reverence, like tribal people seeing their first Big Mac.

Snow day is a sort of Festival Day. Vancouverites set aside this day of the year to have all their fender benders. This is convenient for the Insurance Corporation, because they *know* this only happens one day a year. They just call in all their redundant and auxiliary adjustors and put the coffee on.

We acknowledge the severity of the storm by what is *running*, as in, "It can't be all that bad, the busses are still running," or, "You should see it out here, even the busses aren't running!"

Vancouver hotels offer discount room rates when there is a snow warning. Don't you love this? Who would have thought that in Canada you had to *warn* anyone about the snow? In Edmonton, if you asked for a reduced rate because of the snow, you'd be laughed right out of your long johns.

We have to close our schools, of course, so that the children can go home and make their token snowman for the year. In spite of our isolation, we are very much aware that Canada's world image is at stake here, and we are happy to do our part.

Vancouverites do not feel it is mandatory to shovel snow, and only one family in twenty owns a flat-bladed shovel. Those people came here from Kenora. I must admit, though, that when I picked up my son in the Shaughnessy area during the last Snow Festival Day, I saw a man using a *snow blower*. He was just showing off because he lives in John Turner's riding.

In spite of our hysteria, we *love* the snow. It gives us all an excuse to have one more holiday than the rest of the country. You see, you have to leave the office early on the *day* it snows, and you know there will be a power outage *that night*. This resets your digital alarm to 12:01 A.M., and fails to wake you up for work the next morning. That's okay, though: the kids are home from school anyway, and the busses aren't running.

Gail Mackay
North Vancouver

✉ I was just feeding my horses this morning while on my way to work when I realized what I was wearing. Tights, leather moc-casins, a shirt, and a fake leopard-skin coat, and – I almost forgot – a miniskirt. This wouldn't be so weird if you hadn't read the first line – I was feeding horses in the middle of winter! I thought you might get a kick out of this thought: I balanced a large forkful of hay trying to avoid stepping on cats, dogs chasing cats, and frozen horse poops (pardon the expression but there is no other way to put that phrase). My car radio is blasting, and the cats have fol-lowed me out of the barn to sit on the hood of the car to listen. I make this trip with the hay and the miniskirt about five times, until the horses have enough food. Then I climb into my car and go to work. I get home at noon and it's about -5° C. My brother asks me to climb into the tractor and operate the hydraulics – in a

miniskirt, ha, I just had it hiked up to my waist to tackle the problem when he said he didn't need me. You know it's a darn good
thing that I live on a farm or I might just get embarrassed.

Two days later: It's -35° C, -35° F. The air is so cold that when I
breathe I can feel all my little tracheal branches getting covered
with hoar-frost and snapping off. My fashions for this fine morning
are boots, two coats, a scarf, a respirator mask, two pairs of gloves,
jeans, a shirt and tights. I am so cold – picture this – me budging in
with the cats to get my hands under the heat lamp. I usually keep
them there until my gloves are smoking, and I've only been in the
barn five minutes. In retrospect (while I sit in my car, tears forming
in my eyes as my hands and feet get warm), I reconsider: the best
form of winter protection I own is my tights. They are rarely off
my body in the winter. (Just for the record I own about four or
five pairs.)

Maureen Epp
Rosetown, Saskatchewan

✉ Today my thermometer reads -27° C so my response to the
outside ice world is to stay inside all day, reading under a mountain
of blankets. (I'm a student so this is possible.)

While sitting on my cosy couch reading about the dynamic inter-
actions of an ecosystem, I saw something I had not seen since I
was small and able to stay inside often. Against the dark background of the six huge evergreen trees that fill my front yard, I
watched the mid-morning sun twinkle upon the quickly evapora-
ting early morning ice-fog. Our bright Alberta sunshine made the
miniature crystals dance with an energy that turned them into
little elf sparklers that jumped in a jungle of evergreen fur.

As I finish this letter it appears the dance has ended: the sun
has won the magical battle over the morning fog, and so I must
begin my battle with my biology text. I suppose this letter is a

note to remind myself that there are dreams to be had even here in our cold, icy home.

Sue Melnychuk
Edmonton

✉ How to cope with the winter blahs? Here is a real remedy, and cheap.

From a herbalist beg a few ounces of the stinging nettle. Put one teaspoon into a mug of boiling water. Stir and leave it to steep and cool. Drink. (It does not sting!) In a few hours you are ready to conquer the world.

Anna C. Childers
Thornhill, Ontario

✉ I've really got the blahs this morning. I feel lower than an eel's belly, and as jumpy as a grasshopper escaping a kid. My body is boneless, and my skin is filled with mashed potatoes. My brain is as functional as that of a rusted robot. My sense of hearing has not deserted me, though, as my ever-twitching antennae have picked up that incessant wail of the wind. It is not only viciously vibrating my ear-drums; it is also driving right into my mashed potatoes, sucking serenity from my very soul. In its wake my spongy, spuddy body wants to flee from its tormentor.

What remains of my memory flashes back to a lecture at the public library. How I wish I had never listened to that University of Lethbridge professor's dull diatribe on the effects of the chinook and mistral. This windy speaker expounded his stuff sufficiently shrewdly that he convinced me, and I suspect a smattering of others attending this forum of higher learning, that one can become downright depressed during a chinook.

He stated that the normal air pressure on our body, which presumably holds us together so we are recognizable, goes beserk during the ups and downs of pressures conveying a chinook.

With hands clasped behind back, Prince Philip-like, and with a slight stoop forward, this profound researcher peered floor-ward, and with the demeanour of a serious statesman said, "Just look in your toilet bowl. If the water is moving up and down instead of lolling in its usual tranquil state, then the same thing is happening in your body – even in your veins that lead to your brain." This pronouncement was made with a pinch of pomposity.

"The only escape from depression that you have," he sighed sadly, "is to go into your nearest closet and stay there until the chinook blows itself out. You will only experience slight pressure changes in that haven."

Back to reality. Filled with despair I meander my mashed-potato body as quickly as possible into the bathroom. I peer into the toilet bowl praying for still waters. No such luck. There it is heaving up and down. I head for the nearest closet to bury myself in garb long overdue at Sally Ann's. I hope I don't get caught here and have to explain why I inhabited this cluttered cell for hours. Horrors, what if I have to explain why I came out of the closet!

In my haste to recover my sanity within the confines of my windproof cubby-hole, I trip over my running shoes that I purchased for the seniors' fitness class. That's what we called them when I was very young. When they had holes in their soles, cardboard odour makers were placed inside. The average number of makeshift insoles was three. When our feet grew too large to be forced into them – all the family participated in this torturous plan – a new pair was purchased. I was a bit bigger by then and so was my vocabulary: we called them sneakers. Our feet had miraculously stopped lengthening themselves by then, and we graduated to fashionable corrugated cardboard inserts. They were great: air-cushioned inside and air-conditioned outside. When I grew up a lot we named them brothel creepers. Wasn't that naughty!

At the sight of my sneakers my soul soars. I kick off my slippers, slip into my sneakers and fairly fly out of the closet. Away I go, skipping rope, playing Kick the Can, Andy-I-Over and Red Light.

I am climbing trees and winning races at the Sunday-school picnic. I am released, unfettered and happy, happy, happy.

I sit in my rocking chair now peering down at my fifty-dollar joggers and think that is a small price to pay to blast away my blahs.

If you ever get the blues on a windy day in Lethbridge, Alberta, try slipping into your sneakers.

Dorothy Tewksbury
Lethbridge, Alberta

✉ You hear the ground thawing. It is a curious thing – nothing pronounced about it, no groans or creaks, just whispers and mutterings of earthy reluctance, as if in yielding its armour of frost it will again be vulnerable to harm. The rain is strongly acidic here.

Patches of snow, small, embarrassed drifts from a particularly no-show winter, linger within view. But not on the hillside. Even with sub-zero days, last week's layer of snow has given up, a string of sunny days inexorably compelling myriad crystals to undo themselves, refracting, reflecting, redirecting radiant energy, multiplying its effect. So the bed of long grasses is dry now, supine, layered, springy – an inviting sloped cot here in the late-morning rays.

At the foot of the hill is a pond; leading up from the pond, indeed passing under the small of my back, is a groundhog pathway. I amuse myself imagining one of the creatures, stupefied by sun, groggy with long sleep, trundling across my stomach on its way down for a drink. Maybe they know about the still-thick ice. At any rate, none puts in an appearance. Perhaps in April.

I marvel at a small birds' nest visible from where I lie, scarcely a metre off the ground in a short slender bush, secure within palings of three-inch thorns. With the bush in leaf, how do the birds find their way in and out, I wonder. Very carefully, I suppose. . . .

With my ear to the ground (nearly), and senses more closely

linked to the waxing and waning of things, I have the insistent feeling that there is more to all this than meets the eye. With a measure of annoyance, I recall that this is a scientific world and supposedly science has no categories for metaphysical speculation. Here, though, in the warmth of a private sun, I indulge myself in the luxury of meaning and purpose.

The sky. I forgot to mention the sky. It is blue—not a special kind of blue, just blue. In late winter, that is enough.

Steve Males
Delaware, Ontario

✉ I'm having a "Canadian moment!"

We are supposed to be counting flowers in Victoria this week. I have done so with fingers frozen proud after I've just walked in drifts, minutes after our second snowstorm of the year, in crispy, sparkling, delightful *snow*. It is a shocking phenomenon for Victoria but one I found giggly as I uncovered my one crocus, poor soul.

A local radio station decided to count centimetres of drifts instead of flowers. The count was 2,000,180 centimetres! I heard people were getting desperate three days ago and counting heather blossoms for heaven's sakes.

Well, I just waited long enough for winds to abate and in that gentle instant I ran out in the darkness to the sea. I ran circles around the lamp standards, weaving crunchy footsteps to the ocean edge—black on white. My virgin steps all around the bay, polka-dot pebbles through the sparkly white. Magic time . . . and I should be counting blooms? I bloomin' counted pebbles and drifts, not the frozen buds. Smile, Easterners! Wonder if I'm too old to toboggan?

Vicky Meacham
Victoria

✉ During spring thaw, when I was invited to Inuvik to give a workshop series, I arranged to take our eight-year-old daughter, Mischa, with me. Learning fast from her new-found friends, she introduced me quickly to the concept of "soakers."

When Inuvik finally warms up, six months of accumulated snow all simultaneously melts, making giant thirteen-inch-deep puddles more common than dry land in Inuvik. A "soaker" is what happens when a child's foot goes to the bottom of a thirteen-inch puddle, wearing only a ten-inch high boot. Mischa showed me her first soaker within an hour of our arrival for a four-day visit in Inuvik. It quickly became obvious to me why our hosts, Penny and Bernie, with their three children, did a minimum of three loads of laundry each day.

Pat Gallaher
North Vancouver

✉ All I can say is phooey! I'm glad spring comes around only once a year.

I know it's spring when my fifteen-pound Scottie brings in eight and a half pounds of sand and gravel off the streets after her walk and deposits it bit by bit throughout the house with complete impartiality.

I know it's spring when my teenage daughter refuses to wear her winter boots, then tiptoes carefully down the back lane skirting puddles and inching through gooey spring mud in her brand-new sneakers.

I know it's spring when my husband announces in a sonorous voice (as he takes off the storm windows), that "every one of these damn windows is peeling again and they must be done immediately or they will rot right out of the damn frames come next fall." It's usually about this time that he remembers that we forgot to paint the screens *last* fall.

I know it's spring when I see patches of dead grass where said Scottie did her business all winter. Once again I promise myself to start a fund . . . to pave the entire back yard, dead spots, green grass, the lot.

I know it's spring when I see last year's perennials lying in soggy grey lumps along my border. I'd fully intended to cut them back, just as I'd fully intended to rake away the layers of padded, moulding leaves around them. I'll add a few dollars to the paving fund.

Spring. Ah, yes, spring. A time of smelly rubber boots, dirty cars and splashed coats. A time when all my winter clothes have woolly little balls all over their exhausted exteriors and last year's summer clothes don't *quite* fit.

Spring? Phooey!

Margaret Buffie
Winnipeg

✉ This is not exactly the first day of spring or an annual ritual, but today I set out to clean the yard. "Big deal," you say. Well, our "yard" is six acres of unsheltered ten-year-old farm. The north and west winds blow here constantly, and I think our little trees feel that it's just too much work to grow. Anyway, our yard is large, and inhabited by two dogs, two horses and eight cats, each having special fuel requirements, thus each leaving garbage.

Horses eat hay, which is wrapped with orange or black plastic baler twine. No matter how hard I try to put the string in one place, I always end up tripping myself ungracefully on strings strategically placed all over the yard by the wind. These I gathered in the hundreds.

Cats are barn creatures, with the exception of two privileged go-betweens. They eat leftover food (sometimes very leftover), which is stored in old two-litre milk cartons. Even though there is a refuse can for them in the barn, I find them scattered by the four winds to all four corners of our yard. (I also think certain canine factors are involved.) Of these I found a few hundred.

Dogs. Now these dogs are of Labrador retriever type heritage and eat normal dog food. "No problem," you say, well, not now, we have ceramic dog dishes now. But there was a time when the dogs were fed out of your friendly neighbourhood reusables – ice-cream pails, cottage-cheese tubs and margarine containers. These in combination with wind and one-way retrievers led me to the ditch, where I found ten ice-cream pails and at least fifty other unrecognizable plastic objects. I left the countless numbers of bones and other biodegradable things dropped by dogs. (Our dogs would probably go on strike if I touched their bones.)

There is some good that comes from cleaning the yard. I found our old Crazy Carpet from about 1979 – it crumbled at my touch. Oh, well, we don't have any hills to slide down anyway.

This is the most exciting part. About five or seven years ago, we built an indoor pool. As I walked around outside, I picked up a few scraps of wood, which were probably about five or seven years old. Then I found an asphalt shingle. You know the phrase, "Let sleeping dogs lie"? I never pay any attention to those old sayings. I found an entire cache of building supplies under five or seven years of soil. (This is where I will plant my mini-meadow in a can.) I found a shovel, big sticks, little sticks, bits of metal stripping, soffiting, siding and, best of all, a whole carton of expensive asphalt shingles, which broke as I dug with my hoe. Barbie could have had a great house.

As I enter the house with dirt in my eyes and my Tina Turner wind-blown hair, I know I still have to take all this garbage to the rural municipal dump. And that was spring for me.

Maureen Epp
Rosetown, Saskatchewan

✉ It occurred to me that spring is a state of mind. I'm just like everyone else, searching for that snowdrop or crocus, braving the cruel air, listening for a robin (I *have* seen and heard a rose-breasted sparrow). No, spring is within us, because spring is hope and promise. It is the hope of rebirth and the promise of new growth;

it is the hope of change and renewal. If those things are in us, spring is forever present – whether it is June or December.

Mary Eleanor Hill
Glen Williams, Ontario

✉ All winter I feel half-dead. When frost touches the leaves on the trees, it touches me in my house and I start shrinking. I feel like a dark tree that all the birds have left. I buy seeds and save breadcrumbs to feed the birds that stay on with us. I take in stray cats I've seen lurking in garages and back yards all summer and fall. Sometimes I have a mother cat who gives birth to kittens, and that gives me joy. But these are only temporary measures. In my heart I have a kind of sickness – and the medicine is *sun*.

During these short, dim days and long, dark nights, I stay mostly indoors to better endure the siege of snow. When I must venture out into the cold, it is with layers of clothes between my skin and the sky. I might as well be on another planet for all the nourishment I receive from this place. So I become an in-dweller and try to live by the light the mystics speak of – the light of the inner sun.

I do a lot of work on the house in this crisis of darkness and cold. I organize closets and cupboards and drawers. I persuade myself to throw out the accumulation of the past year, and a lot of that is paper. I thank God for the fireplace that works so well in this old house, for my piles of outdated papers are an excuse to make a fire, to burn up the clutter in my life. As I hold my hands out to the blazing fire, I feel both warmed and relieved of a great burden. I burn papers in winter, to make room for new growth in the spring.

And I work on myself as well; I become self-critical and more self-aware. I remember the links of love, work and common interests that connect me to all the other beings who share this planet and reach out in long letters to friends and relatives. I write poems and stories for my son. I try to recall and record my dreams. I read

425

a lot in winter. But there is a growing uneasiness, a musty, closed-in, airless smell.

Then spring comes and saves us from ourselves. Spring comes and pulls us out of doors. And I emerge with the rest of the world like a mole from his underground burrow, blinking in the unaccustomed brightness, glad that I've survived the winter. The first days and weeks are intoxicating, like the beginning of a love affair. And it *is* a love affair – with the sun. Every morning I walk out while the grass is still wet and turn my face to the sky, rejoicing that the cold has gone, rejoicing that the sun has returned.

I dig in the earth with my hands, but it's still damp and heavy with sleep. I crumble the lumps between my fingers into small fragments while I listen to the robins sing. My cats roll in ecstasy in the warming topsoil. It is a momentous time.

The first few springs in this place, I'd shudder at every worm, at every squirming bug or beetle my shovel uncovered. It's better now. Affection and respect have grown strong over the years between me and these tiny beings, and I speak to them as gently as I do to my plants. We all live here. We all need each other. Of all the creatures who inhabit my back yard, I'm only the most visible. So every spring I set out to renew acquaintance with these small, forgotten ones.

There's a toad who has made his home with us – or is it we who have made our home with him? At some time in early spring, I come across him, sunning in a remote corner, half-hidden by a branch or stone. I gaze into his golden eyes and he gazes back into mine. I murmur a greeting to him, and in the silence something mysterious passes between us.

Before long I'm covered with earth and feel like earth; it settles in my hair and grits between my teeth, and for days it refuses to come out from under my finger-nails. I can't remain standing above the plants for long. I lean over, then squat and finally get down on my hands and knees to hill up young peppers and tomatoes, to weed out carrots, cucumber and corn. I become a handmaiden to earth and imagine that my head bobbing in and out among the green plants must seem like a strange and wondrous fruit, for it, too, receives the sun.

426

In bending down like this to earth, we pay homage to earth. We acknowledge our ancient origins, often forgotten by too much "civilized" living. We must cast off our usual ways of thinking and feeling before we can commune with earth. Then no words are needed. By following the simple routines of planting, weeding and watering we become our true selves. When we live by the cycles of sun and moon, life flows through us like a river. We become peaceful and simple like the processes of nature. And the growing process makes us whole.

Nancy Prasad
Toronto

SHARON
O'CONNOR'S
ALBUM

S haron whose what? I used to wonder myself, at least about who she was. Sharon started writing to *Morningside* in April, 1988, handwritten notes on lined loose-leaf pages, not always as neatly calligraphic as the lines we've reproduced here. At first, she just signed "Sharon," and once, when we wanted to ask her about some details, Shelley had to track her down from the return address. Later, I heard from her regularly, sometimes, as you'll see, on subjects other people were addressing, but sometimes – I can't imagine why she chose to tell us about her nose–just about something that occurred to her.

When we first started to assemble this book, I thought she'd crop up in a lot of chapters. But before we finished, I knew she deserved one all her own.

This is it. When you finish it, you'll know as much about Sharon as I do, although, you'll have to admit, you had an easier time discovering her last name.

In 1987 I was thirty-one years old, a mother of two delightful children. I had been a homemaker for seven years. Before that I was a procedures analyst; before that I was a student, sister, daughter.

I was a happy, friendly, average person, and quite content.

I was a good mother, a good friend with lots of hobbies and interests.

So what? Yes . . . well . . . hum . . .

As Christmas began to loom in my future and I slipped into overdrive – knitting, baking, shopping, buying, returning, wrapping, decorating – I began to recognize that something was amiss with me.

I was tired of trying to do it all. I was tired of day after day, week after week, the same tasks, demands, problems. I was burned out in my job, which demanded such time, effort and dedication.

Well, I took the geographic cure and went to England with a girlfriend.

I left my partner, my kids, the Brownies, the pre-school, the laundry, the mending, and I took my overcrowded little brain across the big pond.

So what? Yes . . . well . . . hum.

I was ripe, I was so ripe.

Being thirty-something was part of it.

Being a homemaker was part of it.

Being a mother was part of it.

Walking alone with my camera through the cloisters in Canterbury Cathedral gave me chills.

My life, my problems, were infinitesimal in space and time as I wandered. And it was delicious!

I walked along the pebbled beach in Dover, and the wind and rain cleared my mind, healed my heart and soothed my soul.

I met interesting people everywhere I went.

I ate trifle at tea, sole in Dover, squid in Chinatown – all firsts.

I'm home again. The laundry is done, the pantry stocked. I'm planning a craft for the Brownies. I've visited my daughter's school, repaired my son's favourite chair, sewed a stuffed animal that was leaking. All is well.

But different.

I'm different – forever changed.

So far the kids and I have not locked horns over anything major. For example, Sara was really upset because I said she couldn't wear a cotton dress I had brought home from London to a school concert. She stood crying while I refused. Then I stopped, as I have often done since I got back, and said, "Why not? Wear your new dress." It wasn't important.

I hear what my kids are saying to me and laugh at their freshness and wonder.

It's nice to come home.

So what? Yes . . . well . . . hum.

Just a little letter, from a little person whose life has changed, just a little. . . .

Family vacations were very important to my father. Alas, at the time we five children didn't always share his enthusiasm.

Through my childhood and early teens we rented cottages, drove to Prince Edward Island trailing a tent trailer, drove to Florida in March trailing a twenty-one-foot sailboat. One summer we rented a farm for three weeks. (We wound up staying July and August.)

When my family gathers to share a meal and enjoy the grandchildren, some of our fondest (and most hysterical) memories are of these vacations.

There were the toads that took over the kitchen while we slept upstairs in one cottage we rented. We awoke each morning to the dog barking at the top of the stairs while he watched toads hop in and out of his water dish.

There was the time the tide came in before we could float the sailboat onto the trailer, and we sat waist-deep in sea water in the back seat of our car. We spent the night at an all-night laundromat (our clothes had been in the trunk) while my dad was at a do-it-yourself car wash hosing down the car.

We remember driving to our destination, late at night, in darkness on a lonely highway, seven voices quietly singing the family favourites, folk-songs and show tunes by Cole Porter.

Invariably one of us would ask Dad to sing the "Kickerman Song." We had been bounced on his knee to this song, and now I sing it to my children.

History repeats itself – and ain't it grand.

The year of my nineteenth birthday my brother Mark, the eldest of five children, died.

My parents had been separated for a couple of years, and there was no communication between them. My older sister, twenty-one, had a two-month-old baby. My younger brothers were fourteen and seventeen and were still living in my father's house.

Mark had had a heart problem from birth and a kidney condition from infancy. He'd come to Toronto in 1960 for heart surgery and had many stays in the hospital throughout his childhood and teen years.

Mark died alone in his apartment. He had been dead about five days on the morning I slipped my SIN card between the door and door frame and gained entry to his single room.

I phoned my dad from Mark's landlord's apartment. After the coroner left we went to pick up my sister and her infant. Then I sat with my niece while my father and sister went to pick up my mother and my brothers. By the evening, when the minister came to discuss the arrangements, all six of us were united, holding hands, holding each other for the first time in two years.

After years of sibling rivalry, Mark and I had recently become friends, and he had spent a lot of time at my apartment. The last evening I saw him I had bought him a second-hand set of dishes, a complete service for four. He had been planning a dinner for a new girlfriend and was very pleased with my gift.

I've drawn a lot of comfort from our last encounter, and some wisdom.

Family is very, very important to me. Sometimes my family laughs at my sentimentality, but I know they know what's in my heart, and after all is said and done, isn't that what family is all about? Being in each other's hearts?

In the end that's all there is. My brother Mark taught me that.

A Page of Magic Words by Mark Richard O'Connor
(1953–1975)

cloud	taste
kiss	give
yes	you
believe	flower
body	love
sense	am
float	laugh
us	mind
feel	two
sing	share
learn	free

I'm a stay-at-home mother of two children, so my free time is very precious to me. In the wee small hours, I can enjoy the peace and solitude. I can indulge my passions – curl up with a favourite book, play a favourite album, play my flute or pursue my latest pastime – creating pictures out of wood bits.

One of my favourite creations is a fourteen-inch by eighteen-inch playroom with books on a bookshelf and toys on a toyshelf. Each toy measures less than one inch. There are wall decorations, a rug, paints and an easel, an electric train, building blocks and other things, too.

The background and all the wooden pieces have been painted,

then the toys are glued together and glued onto the background. When it's finished I apply three coats of clear varnish. In the end the picture may have taken twenty to thirty hours. I'm very proud of my work.

People who come into my home always comment on the pictures. Their enthusiasm is appreciated. My heart always sinks a little, though, when I am paid the highest compliment known to humans – "These are good – *you could sell these!*"

It took me five years of staying home with my children to resolve the issue of working without a paycheque; to realize and appreciate pride, enthusiasm and effort as the rewards of my labour. The children helped teach me this.

The first time my son printed his name is art. It is framed and hangs on my wall. But no one wants to buy it.

When my daughter sings herself to sleep, I hear a symphony – but I wouldn't sell tickets to it.

Cookies we bake together on a rainy afternoon are for sharing and enjoying, not for selling.

Children know that enthusiasm, effort and pride are the rewards of their labour. Sad to think they will unlearn this truth. I can only hope they will relearn it, as their mom has.

Before me I have "The Women's Book of Christmas," an insert in my daily paper, compliments of the Bay.

The first sixteen pages offer "Sensual Novelty Inner Fashions." (No longer need we worry about how to pronounce "lingerie.")

As I read the descriptions of these garments, I notice the advertisers are talking *about* me, not to me.

"A wonderful sensual gift idea she'll adore receiving."

"More sensational inner fashions to give her this Christmas."

"Fie!" I say. "Pshaw, not I!"

Rayon, nylon, polyester, spandex – the mere thought makes my skin itch.

Then there's the hardware on these garments, located often in places unmentionable.

Methinks this is a plot dreamed up by the boys: "Okay, give 'em clothes but make them impractical and uncomfortable out of synthetic fibres. Give 'em shoes, pointy with high heels. Pad those shoulders, cinch that waist."

Me, I'm a cotton-undershirt-sensible-shoes-kind-of-woman.

Santa, if you're listening, what I really want for Christmas is a variable-speed jigsaw.

"No time to read." These are words I cannot comprehend.

I confess I am a hoarder, and books are my most serious vice.

I was raised in a home where a child's question at the dinner table often resulted in encyclopaedias lying beside the mashed potatoes as we explored for the answer. Indeed, a great joke amongst my friends is, "Ask Sharon – she'll have a book about it."

The last quarter of a good book will be my downfall. For it I'll ignore my family, unplug the phone, hide in the bathroom, forfeit sleep. I've guiltily watched the clock change from 2:00 A.M. to 3:00 A.M. while I bargained another chapter from my conscience.

My daughter Sara has the passion, and it's hard to discipline her when I see the familiar glow of a flashlight an hour after I've sent her to bed.

"Just to the end of this chapter?" she'll plead.

How can I say no?

Benjamin has recently begun to print, and now a favourite game is "what is that word?" We play it at the breakfast table, walking down the street and in the grocery store, anywhere there are words. It gives me shivers to watch the world of words unfold for him.

Last winter I bought *The Call of the Wild* for him. It sits on the shelf with dozens of other treasures, waiting to take him away.

In fact, you'll have to excuse me. I haven't read that in years.

April 29, 1989.

Dear Peter,

I'm a south-paw I get by pretty well in this right handed world. Thanks to my early schooling I can manage with my right hand in most things. (much to the chagrin of my eight-ball partner)

My ambidextrous ability is also due to the predominance of right handed tools and utensils in our society.

Consider for a moment, tuning the average guitar, using a manual can opener, pouring from the spout of a sauce pan or tearing a cheque from a cheque book. All of these tasks favour right-handedness

When you sit down to dinner - notice the place-setting. I don't know how many times at a dinner I've had to do the south-paw shuffle to sit in an end chair so as not to be knocking elbows with a right-hander all through dinner

From the first day of school, where my knuckles were wrapped with a ruler (a gentle reminder to switch to my right hand) I have been painfully aware of my handedness.

Today I've taken pen in hand (left hand) to share something with you.

This is a virgin attempt at calligraphy with a left-handed fountain pen. yes left-handed, it has to do with the angle of the nib.

I have a passion for writing (as in the shape of the letters the form of the word) probably because it was such a hard won skill and until now I had met only with frustration and defeat in my attempts to master the fountain pen.

With a little patience and a lot more practice their is hope

From an inspired south-paw

sharon p. o'connor

435

My thoughts about my nose may have ranged from annoyance at its inability to hold up my glasses to an occasional adolescent concern about its size. That was before my first child's birth.

At twenty-four, when I was pregnant, my nose became a constant sense of wonder. I remember bolting awake at 2:00 A.M. and shouting, "Something's burning. Something's burning!"

Something *was* burning. Three bachelors at the opposite end of the hall in our apartment building had burned some french fries and found me and my nose headed their way sniffing when they opened the apartment door to air things out.

I worked for the Bank of Canada and found myself one day in the cash vault surrounded by mountains of new money. I fled, nauseated by the smell of formaldehyde, which is used as a preservative. I chuckle now when I hear references to "the smell of money."

On my first day of maternity leave, the father-to-be arrived home with a dozen long-stemmed roses. I can close my eyes and remember being surrounded by a fragrance I had never experienced.

On a trip to the market, I smelled green peppers, chives, leeks and strawberries fresh from the farm. Later I sat on my balcony cutting the strawberries, popping an occasional one in my mouth. Eventually overcome by their sweet fragrance, I devoured the entire quart.

Peeling an orange would set my nose to twitching–my nose was having a party.

Alas, once the baby was here I slowly became my old self, nose included. I suppose, knee-deep in diapers, this was a blessing.

Late at night I like to consider why this phenomenon occurred. I speculate on how noses enabled our pregnant ancestors to find the sweetest berries and the ripest nuts, to nourish themselves and their babes to be, and to smell danger quickly from a greater distance.

I have a soft spot for my nose, because I know its secret abilities. It's a blue-ribbon nose.

Sharon O'Connor
Scarborough, Ontario

A VERY ABLE
WOMAN

The rest of the world might apply a different label, since Angela Madsgaard, who, with her husband, Karl, is the author of this chapter, spends her life in a wheelchair.

She and Karl live in Havelock, Ontario. They both wrote, as you'll see, after I'd had a conversation with Jocelyn Lovell, the great bicycle racer who, after a terrible accident, was forced to live as a quadriplegic. That interview was, understandably, full of bitterness and despair, and both Angela and Karl – whose life is also strongly affected by Angela's condition – felt it needed an answer.

It was only later, when Angela sent me her painting of a rooster – Evelyn Hart's now hangs on a wall in Winnipeg – that I realized how able she really was.

✉ It is impossible for average healthy people to imagine themselves disabled. You "know" that you would not handle it well. You "know" that you would never be a Rick Hansen. He is an exceptional person – an exceptional disabled person. Therefore, whatever his accomplishments, you "could not" measure up. All this serves to emphasize the hopelessness that healthy people impose on disabled people. Hearing Jocelyn Lovell speak reinforces this average person's view. The truth lies somewhere in between. Most people who become disabled don't handle it as well as Rick, nor as poorly as Jocelyn seems to.

It is possible to live and enjoy life with a disability in the crystal-clear knowledge that there is no hope for a cure.

I am disabled by a rare type of muscular dystrophy. Even though millions are being spent on research, when a breakthrough comes, I don't believe it will apply to me. Yet I manage to enjoy my life and at times feel blessed.

I love to garden, which means I garden vicariously through my husband. I plan, he seeds; I supervise, he weeds; I watch, he fertilizes. Although he hates gardening, he realizes I get great satisfaction from it. I love to paint – colourfully and joyfully – as much as I'm able. I love old movies, watching the birds, the changes of the seasons.

My husband and I spend time together. We spend a lot of time together! Sometimes we get bored, but not with each other. When I get depressed (don't we all?) he teases me or comforts me as need be, and it doesn't last long. I do the same for him.

I wish we had more friends. The ones we do have live far away, and it's difficult to make new ones out in the country. We don't go to social gatherings in the evening and we just don't *see* people.

But our life is wonderful. I feel hampered by my disability only when it affects my husband, too – for instance an inaccessible building that he won't go into if I can't. But most of the time life goes on. There are a few highs and lows but mainly a level of above-average contentment, which many would envy us for.

I know that I'm a privileged disabled person because I have a devoted spouse and a great marriage, but my happiness doesn't depend on anyone but myself. It's my attitude that enables me to face the future and my increasing disability with grace and serenity. Unfortunately it's not a lesson one can teach.

Angela

✉ This is my third attempt to get this on paper. After hearing your interview with Jocelyn Lovell I felt compelled to write. I disagree with a lot of what Jocelyn said.

I believe that some of Jocelyn's attitudes are due to the short time since his accident. Two and a half years is too brief a time for someone who was as involved with athletics as he was to come to terms with his disability.

People should be aware that average disabled adults don't have the resources to have a house in Toronto that has been made fully accessible; don't have the resources to own a van that has been specially fixed for them to drive at a cost well in excess of forty thousand dollars; don't have the resources to have their own attendant to look after their physical needs and do the things around the house that they cannot do. If they are fortunate, they might be living in an apartment of their own where they share an attendant with other people. To be sure, to get an attendant whenever you want, you have to reserve one days in advance. To use Wheel Trans, you also have to book days in advance to get a ride, if available.

I believe that research is essential. A cure must be found to end all disabilities. However, until a cure comes along money must also go to help people live and function and enjoy life to the best of their abilities. In Ontario I believe that adults must buy their own wheelchairs and other aids. A manual wheelchair can cost a thousand dollars or more, and an electrically powered chair can be five times that much. The Muscular Dystrophy Association spends money on research. It also helps people by paying most or all the cost of physical aids such as wheelchairs.

My wife has muscular dystrophy. If we had to pay for the items that the Muscular Dystrophy Association has provided us, I don't know how we would be able to get by. Not everyone with a disability is fortunate enough to get such help as the purchase of wheelchairs and such aids.

The disability affects not only the disabled but also the family. Because of my wife's needs my life is almost as severely restricted as hers. We have a private joke. We say that I have a three-hour leash. When my wife is feeling well, I can go anywhere and do anything I want as long as I am definitely home within three hours. As the years go by, my leash is getting shorter. Seven years ago I could occasionally go away for up to eight hours.

Socially we are also disabled. Due to my wife's health we are not able to make social commitments. We never know until the last minute if she will feel strong enough to attend. Because we are seldom out after 4:00 P.M., it limits the number of people we encounter. Usually we do not go out on weekends, as the crowds make movement in the wheelchair difficult and my wife finds crowds tiring.

We are also disabled as to employment. If I went to work we would have to hire someone to look after my wife. Most of my salary would be used to pay that person. Why work for no gain? We are not on welfare. We have a modest income and by careful spending and leading a simple life-style we manage to get by.

Even with all the problems life is good. My wife was disabled when I met her. What attracted me to her was her joy in living and her good nature. She can put up with me and she makes me laugh. I have given up a lot but I have gained as much or more.

She enjoys life and has many interests. What most struck me about Jocelyn Lovell was that it sounds as if he has no joy in life. I don't mean to be trite, but life goes on: you must make the best of it and find joy where and how you can.

A final point. We are not a typical disabled couple, nor are Jocelyn Lovell, Steve Fonyo or Rick Hansen typical disabled adults. No single disabled person is typical of the rest, just as no single able adult can be typical of all adults. All disabled are individuals as far as needs, abilities, hopes and dreams are concerned.

By emphasizing the greatness of a few, our society makes the everyday courage and achievements of people, able and disabled alike, seem trivial.

Karl

440

✉ Nearly a year ago, my husband and I wrote separate letters to *Morningside*, and you were kind enough to read them on air. At the time we were managing to make ends meet but not much more. There were no job prospects, and we were living a very isolated existence. Now we look back on the "good old days" when life was boring. No longer is life boring. Several things have changed. Karl is now working at two part-time jobs. We had envisioned the possibility of his working if he could come home every two hours, and two jobs that might fit in. Both of these jobs became available within a month of each other! Karl goes to work at 9:00 A.M., comes home at 11:30 for lunch, goes back to work at 1:30, comes home at 3:30; he then leaves for his second job at 5:00, comes home at 7:00 and goes off for one more hour. It makes for a long, long day, but we manage. I have a jack-in-the-box husband who pops in every couple of hours, and I can page him if I need him at any other time. As if that weren't enough, we enclosed our porch over the winter and turned it into a studio from which to sell my paintings. The studio will bring the outside world to us instead of vice versa. Karl is going to run the studio on weekends. His fourth job is looking after me and running the household. Whew!

And what am I doing while my husband runs himself ragged? Well, I paint.

Ever since I "retired" from work, I've been looking for ways to occupy my time. At first I created traditional Easter eggs. Later when that became too physically demanding, I took a course in folk art – painting on wood (also called tole painting). When the wood preparation and finishing became too difficult, I switched to painting on paper and matboard. That was the moment when everything started turning out as a rooster. In my case, the egg definitely came before the chicken. I was initially inspired by the Polish paper cut-outs but now I'm trying to create a unique style. Because of my rather isolated existence, my ideas have to build upon each other and I have to gather inspiration from diverse areas.

The isolation affects me most in winter when I don't go anywhere but to the chiropractor. By February I have full-blown cabin fever and wish someone would drop in just to break the monotony. I joined Able/Disabled Artists – partly to help market my work, but also to have contact with other artists. I'm trying to find some artists locally who might want to get together. Who knows, I may also find some friends!

Angela

✉ If there can be blue cows and flea weddings, then why not ballerina roosters and Peter roosters? I am enclosing a Peter Gzowski rooster and an Evelyn Hart rooster. One is for you and I hope you will forward Evelyn's to her after looking at it.

I saw you dance together on Gzowski and Co. and the image hasn't left my mind. You've probably never thought of yourself as a rooster, but it seems appropriate for your *Morningside* role.

Roosters are nearly all I paint – male roosters are differentiated from female roosters by eyelashes.

As you may or may not know, the rooster is a favourite motif of Polish folk-art. Since my parents are Polish I grew up surrounded by many pieces of folk-art, especially the paper cut-outs *wycinanki*. Here is how to say *wycinanki*: WI is vi as in Victor, CIN is CHEEN, AN, and KI as in KEY. *Wycinanki* are complex symmetrical designs that are cut out of different coloured papers, then glued one on top of another to form intricate patterns.

When I got married I wanted similar things for my own nest but the only way to obtain them was to make them myself. When the cutting-out process proved to be too strenuous, I decided to paint the designs instead. The Peter and Evelyn roosters are a result of three years of evolution. I've tried to combine the aspects of layer-on-layer of paper (to maintain the characteristics of *wycinanki*) with the possibilities that paint presents.

I believe that these will be my only "personality roosters." I hope you enjoy my humble gift and the humour and appreciation that it attempts to convey.

Angela

AND, FINALLY, A
FOND SALUTE
TO THE TRAIN

Although, by coincidence, the last program of the two *Morningside* seasons this book represents carried a special hour on trains – a documentary, some poems and stories and the music of Murray McLauchlan, among other elements – only the story that begins this chapter, which was written for the occasion by the unsinkable Shelagh Rogers, comes from there. The rest of these letters just came in over the course of the two seasons: evidence, I would argue, of the part trains and train travel have played in all our lives.

A last chapter in this book, perhaps.

But offered with the hope that it is not the last chapter on that most Canadian of institutions.

✉ It was the end of July, and the countryside was swollen with growth. I settled down by a window, where the sun poured in like Lyle's Golden Syrup. Ottawa Valley farm fields passed by, and poplar and birch trees shimmered in the wind. Shiny plum-coloured horses stood under the trees, and a gangly boy in bathing trunks ran down to the tracks to wave at the train. I felt as though I were watching a silent movie – scene after scene, town after town.

The conductor, Orville Robinson, came for the tickets. He was about fifty-five, maybe older, a little Gleason-esque; he talked out of the corner of his mouth.

"How'd ya vote in the last election?" he asked. "Private matter," I answered. He proceeded to recite a little poem of his own making – "I'm proud to be Canadian, I'm happy to be free. I wish I were a puppy and Mulroney was a tree." He slapped his leg and wiped his eyes. "I call that my shocker," he said. "If you laugh, you get to stay on the train!"

My seat-mate wasn't bowled over by Orville's verse, but she had just returned from Vienna and didn't know who Brian Mulroney was. Orville filled her in.

We were in Shield Country by then, and the rolling drumlins had given way to jutting rock and arrow-straight evergreens.

I headed to the dining car for the first sitting. The tables were dressed in heavy linen with fresh flowers and silver-plate cutlery. The sunset was glorious, baking the view to a golden crisp. After dinner, back in my car, a party began – loud jokes and fish stories. One man got particularly loaded. He said he was going to Thunder Bay to marry a woman he didn't love. He told us all about it, as if he'd known us for years.

Knowing I'd never get to sleep, and because I hadn't reserved a berth, I wandered into the dome car – so named because of its spectacular rounded glass roof – and, in the quiet, I curled up in two seats and slept.

I jumped awake when the train lurched to a halt. I realized I was no longer alone. Six young men had taken over the dome car. They were railway workers. One of them explained that the train had hit a moose. Another member of the crew pulled out a giant soft-drink bottle. "Want some Seven and Seven?" (That's 7-Up and Seagram's Seven Crown whiskey!) Why not, I figured, and took a good long draw on the bottle.

Orville the conductor let me stay with the crew because, he

said, I'd laughed at his jokes. He was retiring, so he waxed nostalgic: "And ya know Diefenbaker, he *loved* to take the train, just to visit the folks."

We talked about everything. Gilles said the best time to hunt moose is mating season, when they're dazed and you can sneak up on them. He imitated the cry of a cow in heat. "The bull comes to you just like that," he insisted, snapping his fingers. We talked baseball, we talked bilingualism, something the crew–all bilingual –wanted for all of Canada. All the while we were surrounded on all sides–top, too–by inky black. Shooting stars went off across the sky like fireworks, and I wished on as many as I could follow. The crew got quieter and quieter as the Seven and Seven was drained, and I dozed off.

We woke to the sun-splintered water of Lake Superior–not a cloud in the sky. Orville brought coffee and muffins–and stories of what we'd all said the night before. Seems I told my life story to that crew in the dome car.

It could only have happened with strangers on a train.

Shelagh Rogers
Toronto

✉ When I was young, I taught in a small one-roomed school in Glencoe, in Restigouche County, New Brunswick. I spent weekends with my family in Campbellton and returned to Glencoe early Monday mornings on the local train, which ran from Campbellton to Edmundston. One winter morning, about six o'clock, I struggled to the station, about a mile from my parents' house, through unploughed streets, lugging my skis, to catch the local. As soon as I got on the train I fell asleep. I awoke sometime later to hear the conductor calling out "Rocky Gulch, Rocky Gulch." "Rocky Gulch," I screamed, "I've missed Glencoe!" "By several miles," said the conductor. I broke into violent tears. Would they

446

put me off at Rocky Gulch? There was some consultation, and then the train *backed up* all the way to Glencoe.

Frances Gammon
Fredericton

✉ Trains of dreams carry me on sentimental journeys home, and then away again, trains I waited for and almost caught and almost missed.

To be at the station when the passenger train came in was a thrill when I was a child. The great steam locomotive was deliciously terrifying; its bell clanged, its whistle screamed, and its mighty piston wheels drove with the power of a thousand horses. When it stopped beside the platform, panting and hissing steam, I was in the presence of a magic dragon.

I trotted along the platform, craning my neck to see inside the passenger cars. Gentleman, the kind that shaved every day, sat at the windows. Ladies in store-bought dresses leaned coiffed heads on smooth hands. Oh, to be part of that world!

I was – once – for a journey of thirty miles. The magnificence of dusty green plush was in no way spoiled by the stench of coal smoke and the odd cinder in the eye.

The other business I had with the CPR at that early age was less romantic. As the crow flies the school was three and a half miles from our farm. The village, with its railway crossings at either end, lay in between. If I rode old Venus the proper way around, by one of the railway crossings, it added a half-mile to our journey, a long way when it's twenty below and there's a south-easter blowing. The railway station stood exactly halfway between the two crossings.

Venus and I consulted. She reluctantly agreed to walk across the heavy planks of the station platform, step across the rails, go through a gate in the CPR fence, and come out at the school.

Great! But we hadn't consulted Mr. Mackie, the station agent.

Venus was not a lady's palfrey; she had the conformation of a knight's jousting charger. The first time I urged her onto the planking of the platform the thunder of her own hoofs terrified her. She pounded across the planks, cleared the tracks, and bolted through the gate.

Over my shoulder I saw Mackie on the edge of the platform shaking both fists above his head. He was yelling, but there was a ripping chinook blowing and I couldn't hear what he said. That night Venus and I crossed the platform again.

Mackie complained to Dad. Dad bawled me out half-heartedly. Venus and I continued to cross the tracks at the station platform. But Mackie got his revenge. It was only a matter of time.

The village school went only to Grade 10. To finish high school I had to go into town. This meant catching the west-bound passenger train on Sunday nights and returning for the week-end on the east-bound on Friday nights. The eventless east-bound journeys have faded from my mind. But the west-bound!

The train was due at our whistle-stop station at precisely 7:37 P.M. *Due*, perhaps. But there was a war on, as the dour old brakey reminded me when the train chuffed into the station in the middle of the night. I dared not depend on its being late; on four occasions it had been on time. I had to be at the station before 7:37 to get the flares lit to stop the train.

I allowed myself an hour for the walk from the farm to the railway station. The autumn walks were beautiful, with the flaming desert sunsets and the wild geese passing. Spring nights I waited on the platform with the pulsing stars and the great, singing silence of the plains. If the train didn't come till dawn, I didn't care.

But winter! Oh, Mackie got his revenge, all right. He supplied no lamp for the station waiting room. Nor did he supply heat.

Many Sunday nights I arrived in the frigid waiting room, cutting it as close to train time as I dared, ransacking my pockets with cold, clumsy hands, panicky lest I had forgotten the matches. What if the train should scream past before I got the flares set out? I would stumble into the cold to set the lanterns, one red and one green, on the edge of the platform.

Then I waited, hunched on the slatted wooden benches, or stamping my feet and swinging my arms to warm myself.

It wasn't all Mackie's fault. He'd have collapsed like a wet paper tiger if I'd threatened to go to the CPR authorities demanding that he supply heat and light in the waiting room, but it never occurred to me. I considered Mackie's meanness just retribution for sin.

Mackie's gone, long ago. And Venus. The trains that snorted like smoke-breathing dragons are no longer. Their whistles sound only in my dreams.

Betty Wilson
Nanaimo, British Columbia

✉ I was brought up in a little town named Gladstone, just south of Portland, Oregon. Every kid from Grade 1 on called it Happy Rock or Giggling Pebble. The nearest train track was at least two miles away, but I went to sleep at night to the sound of the steam trains blowing their whistles as they crossed the bridge over the Clackamas River.

When I grew older, I swam in that glacier-cold, fast-flowing river, right under the railroad bridge. The river was squeezed together at this point by rock cliffs of varying heights aptly named High Rocks. The tallest peak was called High Dormick by all the older, wiser swimmers. I have no idea where the name came from, but I well remember the heart-stopping thrill of my first dive off this landmark. I offered up silent prayers on the way down that I wouldn't belly-flop.

Swimming at High Rocks was forbidden by my parents. Some-one drowned every summer in those tricky waters. Always the someone was from out of town. I can still feel the heavy silence as we waited for the firemen to bring boats. We huddled in tight groups, then slipped quietly away to the safety of home. Secretly, we all believed that we were immune from death. It was, after all, our swimming hole.

The long metal train bridge, with its cross beams reaching sky-wards, brought out all the daring in the boys. They would dive from the bridge into the icy water. The rest of us stood watching them open-mouthed.

There was one real daredevil who would do anything to gain our admiration. His name was Jimmy. He would climb clear to the top of the bridge supports and swan-dive from the very highest point of the structure. His dives were always flawless, and we shouted and cheered when his head popped out of the water far downstream.

When the trains rumbled over the bridge, the engineer would blow the whistle and wave from the cab to the swimmers below. The noise was deafening, and to the last person, we all waved in return.

My best friend and I spent wonderful summers swimming with the boys. Her big brother was always nearby, but he had a girl-friend, so we were allowed to do as we pleased, as long as we stayed out of his territory.

One summer we "borrowed" a boat and dragged it far up the river, through several sets of rapids, then floated down to where we had found it. The owner was never the wiser.

The following summer was the saddest of my young life. It was the last year I ever went to High Rocks. It was the summer of *change*. Nobody wanted to race across the river anymore. No one wanted to brave the rapids. Everyone just sat around, and flirted, and sun-tanned. We had grown up. I was crushed.

Martha A. Scheel
Halfmoon Bay, British Columbia

✉ My sisters and I spent many long summer days exploring every inch of our local train trestle, trotting across the top (and it was a huge bridge) and clambering down the deep banks to the creek far below.

This was in the Peace River country of British Columbia and Alberta. We lived on the British Columbia side, in the little town of Pouce Coupé.

The train that so affected our lives was the Northern Alberta Railway, a four-hundred-mile-long branch of the CNR out of Edmonton. The NAR made its way north and west, following the pioneer settlers before the First World War. Construction was halted by the war and again by the Depression; the line was finally completed as far as Dawson Creek in 1931. There it halted, financially exhausted; and from there, ten years later, it launched soldiers and machinery for the building of the Alaska Highway. But that's another story.

We became adept at walking the heavy beams that stretched from bank to bank of the deep gully. The first and lowest beam would be a good fifteen feet above the creek, and the length of it, one side to the other, would be perhaps forty feet. In the middle there was a huge safety piling to cling to. With no fear and the agility of circus tight-rope walkers we stepped firmly across.

The next adventure was to scramble over bushes and up the steep bank to the beam above, which would be, of course, twice as high and twice as long. The trick was to keep your eye firmly on the beam ahead of you and never, never glance to the creek below.

We also liked to dangle our arms in the water barrels spaced along the top of the trestle, and we carved initials into the beams.

But we never got too close to the trains. On Tuesdays and Fridays, train days, we stayed away from the trestle. But we listened for the whistle.

When we heard it, the race was on. We triumphed if we arrived, panting, at the station before the train did.

The train never failed to steam in noisily, snorting, smoking, puffing outrageously like a winded dragon.

We would slip into the waiting room and hide on the slatted seats while the beast snorted in. Only the boldest of adults and a few foolhardy boys would stay outside. When the noise of the train subsided to a throb, we'd run outside to see who had come to town from Swan Lake, who had returned from Grande Prairie in their best hats, and what dignitary had arrived from Edmonton, dressed in a suit and bound for the Hart Hotel.

"Board!" shouted the conductor, and off chugged the train. We watched it as far as the elevators, then we leapt with the other kids to the back of the dray. What fun to clatter down to the post office perched high on the mailbags!

Did we ever get to ride on the train? Very seldom. But there were special occasions. For instance, I got a train ride one year for my birthday. It cost fifteen cents to ride from Pouce Coupé to Dawson Creek, looking down at the town from dusty, frayed velvet seats and hovering precariously in space above the creek as the train crept across the bridge.

But the thrill was a rare one, because the trouble was, how could you get home again?

Barbara Dalby
Lantzville, British Columbia

✉ We came from Britain in 1958, speaking something akin to the language here. In Britain, train travel was the regular way to go, so the Transcontinental seemed the obvious way to cross Canada. In Montreal we walked down the longest platform we had ever seen to the sixteenth coach (sorry – car. Didn't I say the language was only akin?) with our two-and-a-half year-old striding manfully along. It was seven o'clock, an hour past his usual bedtime, and he was holding firmly to Mummy's raincoat. Mummy hadn't as much as a finger to spare for him, burdened as she was with hand-bag, toy bag, nappy bag (sorry – diaper bag), small suitcase, and the baby. Daddy, with suitcase, briefcase, portable typewriter, umbrella, and the tickets, had his attention firmly focused on matching the tickets with the berths.

What a ride! Two and a half days, past more fir trees than we had ever thought existed, past the glorious north shore of Superior. (Yes, dear, that's a lake, not the sea.) Past Winnipeg – only a romantic name until then – the prairies, another romantic name, then Regina. We had an hour in Regina on a grey, cold April Sunday afternoon, when the prairie wind carried its usual complement of dust, which sandpapered our faces. We spent the rest of the journey hoping that Edmonton wouldn't be like *that*. It wasn't.

Long before this adventure, when I was a child, I used to lie awake listening to the trains in the shunting yard about two miles from my home in Liverpool. They would lull a child to sleep with dreams of distant places.

Joy Phillips
Hamilton, Ontario

INDEX